D1261724

MARITAL INTERACTION

Experimental Investigations

MCP HAHNEMANN UNIVERSITY
HAHNEMANN LIBRARY

MARITAL INTERACTION
Experimental Investigations

John Mordechai Gottman

Department of Psychology
University of Illinois
Champaign, Illinois

ACADEMIC PRESS   New York   San Francisco   London   1979

A Subsidiary of Harcourt Brace Jovanovich, Publishers

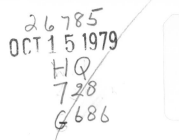

HQ
728
G685m
1979

COPYRIGHT © 1979, BY ACADEMIC PRESS, INC.
ALL RIGHTS RESERVED.
NO PART OF THIS PUBLICATION MAY BE REPRODUCED OR
TRANSMITTED IN ANY FORM OR BY ANY MEANS, ELECTRONIC
OR MECHANICAL, INCLUDING PHOTOCOPY, RECORDING, OR ANY
INFORMATION STORAGE AND RETRIEVAL SYSTEM, WITHOUT
PERMISSION IN WRITING FROM THE PUBLISHER.

ACADEMIC PRESS, INC.
111 Fifth Avenue, New York, New York 10003

United Kingdom Edition published by
ACADEMIC PRESS, INC. (LONDON) LTD.
24/28 Oval Road, London NW1 7DX

Library of Congress Cataloging in Publication Data

Gottman, John Mordechai.
    Marital interaction.

    Bibliography: p.
    1. Marriage––Psychological aspects. 2. Social
interaction. I. Title.
HQ728.G63   301.42   78–22527
ISBN 0–12–293150–5

PRINTED IN THE UNITED STATES OF AMERICA

79 80 81 82   9 8 7 6 5 4 3 2 1

To my wife Heidi

Contents

Chapter 15   **Epilogue: Structure Is Constraint**

Appendix

References

Preface

The study of marriage has traditionally been the province of sociologists, who have relied primarily on large-sample questionnaire or interview data rather than on direct observation. The investigation of marriage as carried out by psychologists, on the other hand, has been based on relatively small samples and has employed a variety of coding systems, many of which lack sufficient descriptive detail. The intended contribution of this book is twofold: to establish the importance of the role of *description* in the study of social interaction and to make *methodological* advances.

The book begins with a historical review of several research traditions that have concerned themselves with families and marriages, work from the sociological tradition, the family therapy or systems tradition, the social learning tradition, and the developmental tradition. It is important that people who do research in marital and family interaction become familiar with all four traditions. Research that points to the potential importance of the observation of consensual decision-making processes is also reviewed.

This book also intends to make methodological contributions. Perhaps the most important of these is the presentation of methods for the analysis of *pattern* and *sequence*. The dimension of time and the quantitative assessment of dyadic patterning have yet to be explored. Data in this book are analyzed by the use of new sequential techniques that are introduced in Chapter 2, and new methods of cross-spectral time-series analysis are presented (Chapter 10) for use in the study of dominance.

Chapter 3 is a review of research that derives four hypotheses and a model of marital interaction called the *Structural Model*. This model involves a reconceptualization of three dimensions—negative affect, negative affect reciprocity, and dominance. Most of the remainder of this book is devoted to research designed to test and to understand this model.

Chapter 4 presents the Couples Interaction Scoring System (CISS), my observational system for categorizing marital interaction. The system has several features. First, in an analysis of communicative meaning, the content of a message is coded separately from its mode of nonverbal delivery. This makes it possible to investigate separately the role of nonverbal behavior. Second, the nonverbal behavior of the listener as well as that of the speaker is coded. This led to an operational definition of the *context* of message reception. Methods for using sequential analysis for lumping coding subcategories in terms of their similar interactive consequences are discussed in this chapter.

Chapter 5 discusses modern concepts of the assessment of reliability, particularly the stringent assessment that is necessary for sequential analysis.

Chapter 6 presents the results of the initial study designed to assess differences between well-functioning and poorly functioning marriages. In Chapter 7, data from the newlywed phase of Raush, Barry, Hertel, and Swain's (1974) study, recoded in my laboratory with the CISS, are presented. Dimensions derived from the Structural Model consistently differentiate couples on a dimension of marital satisfaction. In Chapter 8, the Structural Model's ability to generalize across marital issues discussed by the couples, and to a non-decision-making discussion is tested.

Chapter 9 presents a taxonomy for classifying clinic couples' interactional styles in terms of communication skill deficits. The taxonomy is shown to be internally consistent. Its ability to predict differential change in treatment is tested in Chapter 14. Chapter 9 also introduces a univariate scaling of the CISS codes that produces the time-series data necessary for operationalizing the reconceptualized concept of dominance, introduced in Chapter 3.

Chapter 10 presents a mathematical model necessary for assessing the dominance dimension of the Structural Model.

Chapter 11 explores the issues of the usefulness, when discussing dyadic interaction, of the concept of an individual's social competence.

Chapter 12 presents results on couples coding their own interaction using a device called the "talk table," and demonstrates that the dimensions of the Structural Model applied to the couples' cognitions about their own behavior follow the same patterns with these kinds of data as with the CISS data. This work raises an issue that arises whenever strangers code messages intended for a particular receiver; namely, what are the differences in the coding of behavior between strangers and spouses? There may be a private nonverbal signal system that develops in close relationships that is ignored in neglecting the perception of interpersonal messages of the couple. This chapter also presents the initial results of a $2\frac{1}{2}$-year longitudinal study of couples planning to marry (Markman, 1977) that demonstrates that talk-table variables are excellent predictors of relationship satisfaction $2\frac{1}{2}$ years later.

Chapter 13 presents results on the generalizability of the Structural Model from the laboratory to the home. Chapter 14 presents the results of a series of intervention studies designed to test the ability of the Structural Model to predict changes in marital satisfaction, to evaluate the effectiveness of an empirically derived intervention program, to test the predictive validity of the classification system proposed in Chapter 9, and to assess the limitations of the intervention program as a function of the type of couple.

To summarize, there were two objectives in writing this book. One objective was to report results obtained in the pursuit of adequate description and model building, a phase of investigation that must precede theorizing. The second objective was methodological, that is, to draw together the diverse research traditions in this field—work on observational methodology, on non-verbal behavior, on behavior exchange theory, on reliability as conceptualized by the Generalizability Theory, and on the sequential analysis of observational data in dyads—and to make some of the methods of these traditions available to the researcher in this area. These objectives were accomplished by a review of literature from diverse areas—sociology, systems theory, developmental psychology, nonverbal behavior theory, behavior exchange theory, nonbehavioral and behavioral approaches to family and marital therapy, and the methodology of observation. From this review, a Structural Model of marital interaction was proposed, and research was presented to test this model.

With this book, I hope to increase the interest of psychologists in research on marriage, the interest of sociologists in the quantitative study of social interaction, and the interest of clinical researchers in both.

Acknowledgments

I am extremely grateful for the support I have received from the National Institute of Mental Health's Applied Research Branch, Grant Numbers PHS R01 MH 24594 and PHS R01 MH 29910. Without this support, the work described in this book would not have been possible, because the time-consuming and tedious task of coding requires considerable resources.

This research has been supported throughout by active laboratories, both at Indiana University from 1973 to 1976 and at the University of Illinois since 1976. Cliff Notarius, Howard Markman, and I began working together when they were beginning graduate students and I was a beginning faculty member. We learned together, and I am grateful for their support and friendship.

Most coding systems I have designed have begun with an unteachable first draft and then have progressed to an unreliable second draft before evolving into a sound presentation; the Couples Interaction Scoring System (CISS) was no exception. The coding system was the collective work of the three of us, and it reached the enviable point where no one recalled which contributions were whose. From 1972 to 1976 the three of us were a team, and this alliance provided much of the energy for our work.

An important event in our early collaboration was Mary Ellen Rubin's decision to do her dissertation in our laboratory. Her study proved to be of monumental proportions: The data took 6 months to collect; it took 10 coders 18 months to code the tapes; and it took several months to analyze the data. Mary Ellen's dedication to the research problem was far beyond that of most graduate students. The same is true for Howard Markman. He decided to undertake a $2\frac{1}{2}$-year longitudinal study on couples planning to marry, a study that should prove to be one of the most important in the field.

In short, I have been blessed with three excellent students, and all of us were equally fortunate in the quality of our laboratory staff. Nita Arnove, Carla Comarella, Audrey Heller, and Colleen Turner formed the core of our initial staff of coders, and they later became our core of paraprofessional therapists. In 1976 Susan Toler and Colleen Turner undertook the management of an extensive research project designed to test the classification system of clinic couples (see Chapter 9). It was an ambitious and well-managed research project.

I am grateful to Harold Raush for his support and for his generosity in sharing his data with us for recoding with the CISS and for reanalysis with a non-first-order Markov program. Such collaboration is highly unusual, and his support was a morale boost for all of us when we were just beginning this work.

I am also grateful to Roger Bakeman and Jim Sackett for the invaluable assistance they provided in thinking through methods and issues in sequential analysis. I am also grateful to Roger for sharing his sequential analysis program, JOINT. Jim Sackett's conference in the summer of 1976 at Lake Wilderness was an extremely important learning experience. He brought together educators, psycholinguists, linguists, anthropologists, clinicians, cognitive psychologists, ecological psychologists, developmentalists, primatologists, and ethologists to work on the problems of observational methodology. Sackett has been extremely influential both in articulating problems and issues in this area and in making important creative advances. His work has an unusual and valuable clarity.

Several computer programmers have been helpful to the project. George Cohen wrote our original first-order Markov program before we began using Roger Bakeman's program JOINT. Esther Williams, Ruth Ann Berck, John Bargh, Howard Miller, and Duane Steidinger have been extremely helpful. Duane provided needed expertise in the computations of spectral time-series analysis.

I want to acknowledge the assistance of the Psychology Departments of Indiana University and of the University of Illinois, of the Indiana University Foundation, and of the University of Illinois Research Board. I also want to acknowledge the assistance of the Psychology Department at the University of Wisconsin, particularly that of Richard McFall of that department, and of Robert Clasen of the University of Wisconsin Extension, for making it possible for me to work on the first draft of the book in the summer of 1977. I would also like to thank Gerry Patterson and Roberta Ray for talking to me about the history of the Oregon Social Learning Project.

I am grateful for the assistance of my tireless crew of intelligent coders at the University of Illinois, Linda Bruene, Gayle Fitzgerald, Mike Glickman, Ted Groves, Ann Johnston, and Jean Walter, and for the superb assistance of my student, capable research assistant, coder coordinator, and reliability checker, Gwendolyn Mettetal. I would like to thank my students Dorothy Ginsberg, Gwendolyn Mettetal, and Martha Putallaz for their helpful comments on the manuscript. I would also like to thank my loyal, hardworking, and capable secretary, De Bryant, for all her help in transcribing tapes and in keeping my professional life running smoothly.

MARITAL INTERACTION

Experimental Investigations

CHAPTER 1

Historical Traditions

It is difficult to write a history of research in this area. The task is difficult because of the way knowledge is transmitted in the behavioral sciences: Concepts are rapidly disseminated regardless of how well-established they are in fact. This is not the case in the physical sciences; despite repeated attempts at popularizing the idea of a finite, expanding universe bounded by the curving motion of light bending in gravitational fields or the concept of the nondeterministic nature of physical events on a microscopic scale, the general intellectual community has easily been able to avoid discussing these ideas over cocktails. Likewise most of us are quite content to be done with our mathematics requirements; we do not spend much leisure time exploring the implications of Gödel's proof, even though he proved the remarkable fact that in any axiom system there are unprovable statements that are true in every case. Perhaps we ought to care about Gödel's proof, but most of us do not.

This is not the state of affairs in the behavioral sciences. Psychological, sociological, and anthropological ideas are accepted and become a part of our language long before they have been demonstrated empirically; and, in fact, psychological concepts do not die even when they have been found to receive no empirical support whatsoever.

Behavior is the laboratory of all humans, and, because the culture is hungry for knowledge of itself, it absorbs psychological concepts rapidly; jargon soon becomes part of the language we all learn. For example, phrases from psychoanalysis, such as unconscious defenses, Oedipal complex, and inferiority complex, as well as concepts, such as the importance of dreams, began to become part of our linguistic and cognitive heritage as soon as psychoanalysis was widely disseminated. Psychoanalytic terms and concepts are now part of the language we grow up learning. The same kind of cultural osmosis makes us give credence to any kind of psychological concept that can be explained and that makes some kind of sense. The discussion here is not a polemic; it is merely a statement of why it is so difficult to construct a decent history in this area.

Despite the rapid diffusion of concepts, research in marital and family interaction has been characterized by several distinct traditions, distinct because researchers in each tradition have not read widely, and, therefore, scholars have tended to cite only their colleagues working in the same tradition. Somehow, amazingly, everyone has been influenced to some extent by everyone else. This is an advantage, but it is also a drawback because we maintain, without knowing their origin, implicit assumptions about what is true of marriage.

In order to describe the historical context for the work outlined in this book, this chapter will review research from four research traditions—the sociological tradition, the family therapy tradition, the social learning tradition, and the developmental tradition.

THE SOCIOLOGICAL TRADITION

Early Investigations

By far the oldest research tradition in the study of marriage and of the family is sociological. The earliest work in this area began in August, 1924, a decade before Kinsey initiated his research on the sexual behavior of the male, when a psychiatrist, G. V. Hamilton, began secretly investigating the sexual behavior of couples. Hamilton interviewed 100 couples in New York City who were mostly under 40 years old and were "classifiable as having attained a relatively high level of culture [p. 1]." Hamilton asked 372 questions of women who had been pregnant, 357 questions of women who had not, and 334 questions of all men. He found "evidence for a greater degree of [marital] satisfaction of the men [p. 79; material in brackets added]" than of the women. "The women," he wrote, "taken as a group, had been more seriously disappointed in their marriages than had the men [p. 80]." He also found that "marital satisfaction of the men of my study is much less dependent on size of income than is that of women [p. 98]" and that "wage earning by wives unfavorably affects the contentment of both spouses [p. 99]." His book also contained an analysis of 1358 love affairs, and he reported that extramarital affairs were related to marital dissatisfaction.

While Hamilton was conducting his research in secret, Terman, Buttenweiser, Ferguson, Johnson, and Wilson published their work in 1938. Thus, theirs was the first *published* study of marital happiness, and at the time it set a high water mark for methodological sophistication. Terman *et al.* (1938) reported the results of their questionnaire study with 1133 married couples, 109 of whom were divorced. Terman et al. began their volume with a section called the "chaos of opinion on the determiners of marital happiness" and cited writers who underscored the crucial importance of "satisfactory sexual relations," "knowledge of sex techniques," the deleterious "effect of shock at first intercourse," the harmful effects of the "wife's employment outside the home," the "effect of same or opposite temperaments," or the value of "the comradely marriage." They summarized:

> Contradictions of the kind we have set forth sometimes have their origin in an emotional bias. Authors of treatises on marriage orally base more of their conclusions upon opinion than upon experimental findings, and opinion is notoriously unreliable in a field when every individual has formed convictions based upon his own personal experiences [p. 10].

It was their intention to test the numerous myths about marital satisfaction and to discover the basic truths. For example, they examined the relationship between personality traits and happiness but did not find it to be significant. They also found no relationship between the frequency of sexual intercourse and marital happiness. Perhaps they had their own set of unstated assumptions about marital satisfaction, because they were surprised by many of their findings. They expressed their amazement as follows: "One might suppose that a high degree of congeniality between mates would tend to express itself in a relatively high frequency of copulation, a lack of congeniality in a relatively low frequency [p. 275–276]." However, they did find a strong relationship between the *discrepancy* between desired and actual frequency of sexual intercourse and marital happiness. Their findings led them to recognize the importance in predicting marital satisfaction of variables that describe the marital relationship. For example, they reported: "The highest ranking item is the one about avoiding arguments. From these data it appears that among the 545 items the greatest single danger to marital happiness is for one spouse to like and the other to dislike to argue [p. 29]." In their investigation of "domestic grievances," they were amazed at the amount of consistency in their data. The rank order correlation between seriousness of grievances between husbands and wives was .76. They found that, of 220 comparisons between happy and unhappy couples (based on a median split), all but 7 were statistically significant. From a long list of gripes, the following were the most frequently cited across all marriages: *Husbands*—insufficient income, wife's feelings too easily hurt, wife criticizes me, in-laws, wife nervous or emotional; *Wives*—insufficient income, in-laws, husband nervous or impatient, poor management of income, husband criticizes me. They discovered a remarkable consistency in these results.

Burgess and Cottrell (1939) intensively studied 526 couples, once again with questionnaires, and their results were largely consistent with Terman et al. (1938). They were particularly surprised to learn that "the economic factor, in itself, is not significant for adjustment in marriage [p. 346]," but that "the outstanding features in marital adjustment seem to be those of affection, tempermental compatibility, and social adaptability. The biological and economic factors are of less importance and appear to be largely determined by these other factors [p. 349]." Once again, variables that described the marital relationship were most important. These findings were also largely corroborated in Burgess and Wallin's 1953 longitudinal study with 1000 engaged couples. In both cross-sectional and longitudinal research, the same patterns of results emerged.

Locke (1951) expanded the sample of couples studied to cover a broader range of socioeconomic levels and a broader range of marital happiness scores. To avoid the bias of relying on returned questionnaires, Locke's interviewers went door to door in a county in Indiana. In fact, in one case Locke reported interviewing a man while the man was working underneath his car:

> "Is this about my divorce?"
> "Yes."
> "I was afraid of that. I am awful busy right now. If you want me to answer the questions, you will have to read them to me, for I have to get under the car [p. 20].

Locke studied both a divorced and a happily married group. He did report some evidence that economic factors were connected to marital satisfaction, but these were primarily a correlation between marital satisfaction and the *perceived* adequacy of the husband's income by the wife. He found no connection between marital satisfaction and the wife's employment, but he did find an association between the husband's approval of the wife's working and marital satisfaction. Once again, the data pointed to the importance of variables descriptive of the relationship.

From the mid-1930s, five researchers dominated this area—Burgess, Cottrell, Locke, Terman, and Wallin. They began, logically enough, with questions of how people select a mate, what kinds of variables predict marital happiness and stability, and what stages a family moves through in a typical life cycle. Because they were influenced by sociology, their units of analysis were sufficiently large, they used concepts such as cultural norms, values, roles, and social class, and they conducted both large-scale cross-sectional and longitudinal research. In the process, they also laid the groundwork for some measures with excellent psychometric properties. Three useful introductory texts review this research tradition: Bell (1975), Burgess, Locke, and Thomes (1971), and Nye and Berardo (1973). The part of this research tradition that is most important to this book concerns the search for variables that predict marital happiness and stability.

Classification of Marriages

In describing the marital relationship, one thing that most people notice is that some marriages seem to be going along rather well, whereas others seem to be a terrible muddle of misery. In an attempt to understand this, marriages have been classified by sociologists according to demographic indices; for example, the stability and satisfaction they provide (Lederer & Jackson, 1968), the vitality and totalness of the relationship (Cuber & Harroff, 1965), the congruence of values (Tharp, 1963), and the complementarity of needs (Winch, 1958, for example, one spouse needs dominance and the other needs to dominate). The goal of classification is always to sort things into more or less similar groups, and most investigators in the sociological tradition began their research by asking couples to tell them about their marriages.

Initially, researchers thought that classifications might differ depending on how the couples were asked about their marriage; some researchers focused on "happiness," some on "adjustment," and some on "satisfaction" (Burgess & Cottrell, 1939; Locke, 1951; Terman & Wallin, 1949). However, the questionnaires constructed to assess each of these apparently different concepts correlated very highly. Burgess and Wallin (1953) then concluded that a general factor they called *marital success* could be defined on the basis of correlations in the high 80s and low 90s between Locke's measures of happiness and the Burgess–Cottrell measure of adjustment. Subsequent research has borne out their conclusion.

For example, a measure of the extent to which a couple reported being problem-ridden correlated well with the Burgess–Wallin scale of marital happiness in one study of 984 Catholic couples (Mathews & Milhanovitch, 1963). Also, the independent criterion of whether or not a family is seeking psychiatric assistance, not necessarily for marital distress, correlated .90 with Locke's Marital Relationship Inventory (Locke & Williamson, 1958; Navran, 1967). Terman and Wallin (1949) found that their inventory of marital happiness had moderate success ($r = .47$) in predicting marital stability. This is the largest correlation establishing predictive validity in this area (but see Chapter 12, the Markman study). Also, in ratings of marital happiness that were obtained under conditions in which pairs of raters could not collaborate, Burgess and Cottrell (1939) found that, when the ratings of outsiders were compared to the ratings of the couple, "of the 272 pairs of ratings only 24, or 8.8 percent, show a disagreement by two or more scale steps. The tetrachoric coefficient of correlation . . . is .91 [p. 41]." To summarize, we can conclude that *different operations designed to measure marital satisfaction converge and form one dimension.* This conclusion solves an important measurement problem in the assessment of marital satisfaction.

Mate Selection Research

Another large body of sociological research has investigated mate selection; part of this research is a search for which variables predict that a relationship will continue, and part of it is a search for which variables will predict whether a continuing relationship will be happy.

Complementarity of Need. Although the debate continues, Tharp's (1963) review of the mate-selection literature effectively eliminated the hypothesis that complementarity of need rather than homogeneity of values and background (like choosing like) predicts who will select whom as a mate. Research on complementarity theory has many methodological problems. The theory has largely been argued by Winch (1955, 1958, 1967), who, using content analysis of "need interviews," case histories, and projective tests, found that, out of 344 interspouse correlations, most were close to zero. These results did not support his theory. He then reanalyzed this data with nonparametric sign tests and (incorrectly) reported that it was amazing that so many of these correlations were not negative. Furthermore, studies using other kinds of measures, such as personality inventories (Schellenberg & Bee, 1960), did not replicate Winch's conclusions. In general, across studies the results seem to favor neither a homogamy nor a complementarity theory, but there is a slight tendency toward homogamy.

Sequential Filter Theories. More recently, mate selection researchers have been investigating sequential filter theories, in which one set of variables are initially predictive and another set are later (but not initially) predictive. Kerckhoff and Davis (1962) reported that the stability of a dating pair was predictable from social homogamy, then subsequently by value similarity, and then still later stability by need complementarity. The sequential filter theory of Kerckhoff and Davis has had considerable appeal, but their findings were not replicated by Levinger, Senn, and Jorgensen (1970). Also, Hill, Rubin, and Peplau (1976) found no evidence that couples who remain together are more similar in attitudes than those who do not, and Levinger and his associates (Levinger, 1970; Levinger et al., 1972) found that couples highly similar in values were *less* likely to continue their relationship than were those with low simlarity (see also Huston & Levinger, 1978).

Behavior Exchange Theory Formulations. Nye and Berardo (1973) pointed out that behavior exchange theory formulations (see Chapter 12) can account for consistently observed, important deviations from what one would predict from homogamy theories of mate selection. One of these deviations is the preference of women for men older and more educated than themselves. Nye and Berardo wrote:

> The homogamy model would suggest [that women would show] preference [for men of] the same age. However, women have stated that men a little older are better established in their jobs or professions and are more de-pendable and adequate providers. The same explanation is provided for their preference that the husband have more education. One study showed that only 1 percent of women preferred a husband with less education, 18 percent preferred the same amount and 81 percent preferred that he have more. However, men (82 percent) preferred wives with the same education as themselves [p. 120; material in brackets added].

Relationship Variables.   In general, there seems to be increasing support that variables that describe the functioning of the relationship are predictive of relationship stability and satisfaction. For example, Murstein's cross-sectional (1970) studies indicate that, after individuals are attracted to one another and begin dating, the future stability of the dyad through engagement and into marriage depends on discussions the dyad has in which the partners assess their fit in values and then assess their fit in perceiving role behavior. Further evidence for the contention that characteristics of the relationship are related to the continuation of the relationship comes from a study by Goodman and Ofshe (1968). Using the game of "Password" to measure communication effectiveness and to gauge empathy through semantic differential responses, they found that: "Communication efficiency is greatest for the marital pairs, less high for the engaged couples, and lowest between strangers. Empathy follows the same general pattern [p. 597]." Huston and Levinger's (1978) review of mate selection research also supported the importance of relationship variables. They wrote that:

> Research examining *relationship* characteristics to predict courtship progress has been more successful than that which focuses on combinations of the psychological attributes of the partners. Relationship research suggests that partners who "understand" each other and who agree in their definition of their relationship are more apt to escalate their commitment; thus, persons whose partners see them the way they see themselves are more likely to report having moved closer to marriage when queried about their relationship several months later [p. 46, ms.].

Marital Satisfaction

Resolution of Differences.   There appears to be some support that variables descriptive of the marital relationship are important in predicting marital satisfaction. However, it would be useful to find a more specific set of relationship variables that are related to marital satisfaction, and, toward this end, this review proposes that marital satisfaction is related to the couple's ability to resolve differences. Uhr's (1957) longitudinal study found that happily married husbands' and wives' values became more alike after 18 years of marriage, whereas unhappily married husbands' and wives' values became more different. Of course, it is unclear as to which is cause and which is effect. However, similarity of background may interact with the way changes in resolving differences occur. The couples in the Uhr study changed in an interesting direction. In the happy marriages, wives moved in the direction of their husbands, and in the unhappy marriages it was the husbands who moved in a direction away from their wives (see Barry, 1969).

Further support for the importance of being able to resolve differences comes from the fact that there does not seem to be any optimal profile of variables characterizing a marriage that predicts marital satisfaction. For example, we have mentioned Terman *et al.*'s (1938) finding that the sheer frequency of sexual activity does not discriminate on the dimension of satisfaction. This is also true for the stability of the relationship. In short, there does not seem to be an optimal frequency of sexual activity. However, the discrepancies between actual and desired frequency, as well as interspouse agreement on desired frequency, have been found to be powerful predictors in both longitudinal and cross-sectional studies (Burgess, Locke, & Thomes, 1971).

Additional evidence for the importance of resolving differences is given in David's (1967) study of families with marital and parent–child problems. He concluded:

> It appeared that differences in values between the two spouses were of much less importance in promoting marital satisfaction than was *inconsistency in the way in which norms reflecting these values were sent and perceived.* Inconsistency in communication, one might conclude therefore, is a greater incentive to marital dissention than inconsistency in the values themselves [p. 8; emphasis added].

Children as a Variable.   Further support for the lack of an optimal profile related to marital satisfaction concerns children. More important than the number of children or their spacing is how successful the parents feel they are in controlling these variables according to their consensual desires or in adjusting their desires to conform to reality. In short, once again there is no optimal number, spacing, or sex–birth order of children except as defined by the couple's consensual decision (Christensen, 1968; Luckey & Bain, 1970). Luckey and Bain found that couples with a satisfactory marriage felt that their marriage was enhanced relatively little by their children, whereas couples with unsatisfactory marriages relied much more on their children as a source of satisfaction with their marriage.

Income as a Variable.   The variables *education, occupation,* and *income* often have been put forth as important in the prediction of marital stability and satisfaction. From the results of a factor analytic study by Cutright (1971), it appears that the predictive value of education and occupation can be subsumed under that of income. *Income alone* allows predictions as accurate as using all three of these variables. There has been some disagreement on the *strength* of income in predicting marital success. Burgess and Cottrell (1939) found a moderate relationship. However, neither Bernard (1934) nor Terman *et al.* (1938) found such a relationship, but their samples may have been too restricted in the range of financial income. Levinger (1965) concluded that "When wider ranges of income and marital satisfaction are considered, as in studies of the entire U.S. population by the Census, there is a clear inverse correlation between income and divorced status, and even more between income and separated status [p. 426]." The obtained correlations have been moderate (e.g., −.32, Schroeder, 1939) and are probably also a *result* of divorce.

Levinger (1965) suggested that the wife's perception of the husband's income as satisfactory may be essential to the cohesiveness of the marriage. Beyond a necessary minimum income, this perception may be important as a predictor of marital success. This is consistent with Locke's (1951) results. Also, the wife's perception of her husband's income as inadequate was associated in one study with violence given as a cause for divorce (O'Brien, 1971). Therefore, it may be that the perception of income rather than income itself is an important predictor of relationship satisfaction.

Personality as a Variable.   Further support for the importance of relationship variables comes from the study of personality and marital satisfaction. Studies comparing happily married with unhappily married couples find low to moderate correlations between self-ratings of happiness and personality indices. For men, these correlations range from .28 (Dean, 1966) to .39 (Burchinal, Hawkes, & Gardner, 1957). For women, the correlations are slightly higher, ranging from .35 (Dean, 1966) to .42 (Burchinal *et al.*, 1957; Terman *et al.*, 1938). However, the variables that characterize happily married spouses tend to be interpersonal rather than intrapsychic in nature. For example, in Burgess and Wallin's (1953) summary of the earliest investigations dealing with the relationship between marital adjustment and personality scale variables, happily married couples were characterized as emotionally stable, considerate of others, yielding, companionable, self-confident, and emotionally dependent. Dean (1966) noted that the personality variable with the highest correlation with both the husbands' and the wives' marital adjustment scores was wives' positive rating of their husbands' emotional maturity. Thus it seems that the *perception* of a personality dimension by the spouse predicts marital satisfaction better than the dimension itself. Corsini (1956) noted that the only significant correlation between marital happiness and interspouse Q-sort predictions occurred when the wife predicted the husband's Q-sort. The Q-sort is a task in which a set of statements about someone's personality are sorted into categories ranging from "extremely characteristic" to "extremely uncharacteristic." In a Q-sort prediction, one person predicts how the other will describe himself or herself. Corsini's findings are consistent with Tharp's (1963) review of interpersonal perception among spouses: Tharp concluded that marital happiness is related to the wife's perception of the husband being congruent with his self-perception. This, again, may be interpreted in terms of the predictive value of perception of personality rather than of personality variables per se.

Conclusions on Variables.   The data on the concommitants of marital satisfaction point toward the importance of relationship variables. To summarize: In particular, from a review of the research done in the sociological tradition, *of all the relationship variables that could be selected for understanding marital satisfaction, the couple's ability to arrive at consensus in resolving differences may be of central importance.* There are two ways in which a couple could arrive at consensus. One possibility is that they share normative conflict resolution rules transmitted culturally or from parental models. The other possibility is that they are able to construct their own decision rules. The first possibility is sociological, and the second possibility involves the study of individual differences.

Consensus and Culture. Sociologists have suggested that at least two basic kinds of marital relationships coexist in the United States—the institutional and the companionship marriage. The institutional marriage has been characterized by adherence to traditional role specifications, customs, and cultural mores. Hicks and Platt (1970) summarized the institutional marriage as follows:

> This is a tradition-oriented marriage in which model roles exist, and are sex-differentiated. The husband's role is held to be more instrumental, the wife's role the more expressive–integrative. In this marital type since the wife is more accommodating and the husband more rigid in role needs, marital happiness is more a function of the husband's possession of the expected instrumental needs and capacities [p. 555].

The companionship marriage, on the other hand, places emphasis on the affective aspects of the relationship.

To what extent is there evidence that cultural groupings differ in styles of marital interaction? There is some evidence that decision-making styles may be consistent within cultural groups. Komarovsky's (1961) review of family decision making on expenditures suggested the intriguing hypothesis that autonomy in decision making may be a U-shaped function of income. She thus suggested that joint involvement in decisions may be highest for the middle-income socioeconomic groups. This hypothesis is more clearly supported for the upper end of the income level. Lower income couples are characterized as autonomous decision makers in some studies and as joint decision makers in other studies. Komarovsky cited a study of long-settled London working-class families. In these families working children lived at home, and the families were characterized by the spouses' mutual ignorance of each other's sources of income. The wife generally was ignorant of her husband's wages, and vice versa. Komarovsky wrote:

> When one man was asked how much his two (working) daughters paid in board money, he said, "They give it to Mom. I don't even know how much they give her." Women talk of financial arrangements between themselves and their children as though the husband was not a party to them at all [p. 262].

Strodtbeck's (1951) study suggests that in three cultures in Southern Arizona (Navaho, Texan, and Mormon) culture decision rules were reflected in patterns of dominance, talk, and silence during decision-making tasks. This may explain the findings in the marital success literature that indicate the strong attachment of the spouses to the respective parents prior to marriage coupled with a successful parental marriage is predictive of marital success. To the extent that parents serve as models, they may induce both the expectancy of success and the appropriate normative mechanisms to ensure success. There is also some (though scant) evidence that specific interactional styles have been transmitted over three generations in a mobile Protestant American family (Borke, 1967).

Consensus and Marital Satisfaction. There is, therefore, some evidence that interaction patterns are partly a function of cultural and of socioeconomic groupings. However, how is this related to marital satisfaction? Could it be that, if a particular culture strongly transmits normative conflict resolution patterns, the development of consensual skills may not be as important? This hypothesis suggests that strong cultural patterns in decision making will, to some extent, ensure marital satisfaction. However, as far as one can tell from the data available, this does not seem to be the case. Strodtbeck (1951) found that, regardless of cultural patterns determining which spouse talks more, the least-talking participants were characterized by "simple acts of agreement, aggressive acts designed to deflate the other actor's status, and simple disagreements [p. 293]." He added, "taken together, these characteristics suggest the passive agreeing person who from time to time becomes frustrated and aggresses [p. 293]." Normative decision rules may thus work in the sense that decisions are completed efficiently, but not in the sense of creating mutual satisfaction. If normative decision rules do not account for marital satisfaction, perhaps some aspects of the couple's communicative style (rather than of the culture's) are important.

When the couple's communication style has been assessed indirectly by questionnaire methods and then related to marital satisfaction, the results have been provocative. Navran (1967) found a correlation of .82 between his Primary Communications Inventory (PCI) and his measure of marital satisfaction, the Locke Marital Relationship Inventory (MRI). He studied 24 happily married couples and 24 couples who sought marriage counseling. Navran concluded that happily married couples:

> (a) talk more to each other, (b) convey the feeling that they understand what is being said to them, (c) have a wider range of subjects available to them, (d) preserve communication channels and keep them open, (e) show more sensitivity to each other's feelings, (f) personalize their language symbols, and (g) make more use of supplementary nonverbal techniques of communication [p. 182].

The verbal scores of the PCI correlated .91 with the inventory measure of marital adjustment (the MRI), thus accounting for over 80% of the variance. However, although Navran's inventory (the PCI) taps communication, his data are not based upon actual observations of the couple's interaction. Strong correlations obtained in the Navran study could, therefore, be a function of common method variance between the PCI and the MRI.

It is also interesting to examine the paradigms that have been used to test explicitly the notion that the extent of conformity to an institutional relationship predicts marital success. One would expect these studies to report that measures of conformity to traditional or cultural role expectations correlate with measures of marital satisfaction and stability. Instead, these studies report that what does in fact predict well to indices of marital success is the extent to which the couple's performance meets the *couple's* individualistic role expectations, not society's. In other words, these studies tap the consensual agreement each couple has reached. Ort's (1950) study found a correlation of .83 between perceived and desired role performance and marital satisfaction. Hawkins and Johnson (1969) found a correlation of .84. An example of an item on the Hawkins and Johnson (1969) measure of role expectation follows:

> How often should the husband and wife take a little time during the day or
> evening to caress and kiss each other?
> _____ 1. More than once a day
> _____ 2. Once a day
> _____ 3. Several times a week
> _____ 4. Once or twice a week
> _____ 5. A few times a month
> _____ 6. Less often   [p. 508]

An item on their measure of role performance follows:

> In the last four weeks, how often did the husband and wife actually take a
> little time during the day or evening to caress and kiss each other [p. 508]?

These studies are tapping the extent to which a couple's behavior fits expectations held by both spouses, not the extent to which adherence exists to traditionally defined stereotypic roles. A typical item from Navran's (1967) Primary Communication Inventory is:

> How often do you and your spouse talk over pleasant things that happen
> during the day?

This is similar to items used by Ort (1950) and by Hawkins and Johnson (1969). Whereas the latter studies are reported and reviewed as studies of institutional marriage (Hicks & Platt, 1970), it would make more sense to consider all three studies as tapping consensual agreement.

Of course, we have no idea *how* couples in these studies reach agreement. The absence of a discrepancy between questionnaire data about desired and actual role behaviors in the Hawkins and Johnson study may not have come about by an active "give and take." The partners may have *independently* arrived at the same point of view. Further research is, therefore, necessary before one can conclude that consensual skills are a key factor in happy marriages characterized by low discrepancies between desired and expected role performance. Nonetheless, some evidence is provided by the fact that Ort's (1950) happily married group claimed to have resolved conflict by discussion, whereas the unhappily married group claimed to use avoidance of the issue, as well as aggression. Also, Locke's (1951) divorced couples reported using "mutual give and take" much less as a way of settling disagreements. Whereas 9 out of 10 of the happily married said they never walked out on their spouses during a conflict, 7 out of 10 of the divorced reported doing so. Similar results were obtained by Phillips (1975) in our laboratory in a questionnaire study of the relationship between reports of fight style and marital satisfaction. These data suggest that an active "give and take" may be necessary for marital success (see also Chapter 12, the Markman study). Further research is necessary on the interaction of these couples.

Summary of Sociological Tradition Review

The variables that have been used in most of the sociological research to date have successfully accounted for nearly 30% of the variance in marital stability and satisfaction (Burgess, Locke, & Thomes, 1971). The Navran (1967), Ort (1950) and Hawkins and Johnson (1969) data are the highest obtained correlations in this field and would suggest that it may be possible to account for more variance in marital satisfaction by observing couples' interaction in resolving differences. However, sociologists do not usually observe and quantify social interaction. The idea seems foreign to this research tradition. For example, in testing a Bales hypothesis (Bales, 1950; Bales & Slater, 1955), Levinger (1964) simply asked couples to what extent they specialized or shared labor on tasks versus emotional areas of their relationship. Psychologists, perhaps partly from the discovery that retrospective reports of parents about their children were highly inaccurate (Yarrow, Campbell, & Burton, 1968), have learned too much distrust of self-report data, whereas sociologists have not learned enough distrust.

A balanced view was presented in a recent paper on the study of parent–infant interaction, in which Parke (1978) suggested that researchers view parental reports as a valuable source of information, not as a *substitute* for observing parent–infant interaction, but as data about parental knowledge, attitudes, stereotypes, and perceptions. These data are not available from an observational record. Parke reviewed research to support his recommendation. For example, mothers who believed that their infants could not see at birth were less likely to provide visual stimulation for their infants (Kilbride, Johnson, & Streissguth, 1971). Applied to the study of marriage, Parke's suggestion implies that the sociological methodology that taps the couple's perception of their relationship can be combined with an observational methodology.

This review of research from the sociological tradition has been constructed to suggest that it is possible to interpret findings in terms of the potential importance of good communication in achieving consensus for a mutually satisfying marriage. Of course, it remains for us to define what "good communication" might be and to solve the problem of how to observe and to summarize the interaction of couples. The impetus for quantifiable observation of social interaction is not to be found in the sociological tradition. Historically, the impetus for a focus on observational research of actual social interaction in couples came from a strange source, toward the end of World War II, and it all began with an interdisciplinary team that was formed to design a gun.

THE FAMILY THERAPY TRADITION

Contributions of Wiener and His Colleagues

Interest in family and marital interaction began with a group of psychiatrists who reacted against individual psychoanalytic therapy and began treating patients in a family context. The family therapy tradition owes a great deal to an MIT mathematician, Norbert Wiener. He had been working with Arturo Rosenblueth, a physiologist at the Harvard Medical School, on the functioning of neural networks. Wiener's thinking was fundamentally interdisciplinary; he wrote that he had "the conviction that most fruitful areas for the growth of the sciences were those which had been neglected as a noman's land between the various established fields [Wiener, 1948, p. 2]." Before World War II, Wiener had worked closely with Vannevar Bush on developing early computers and with his former student Yuk Wing Lee on the design of electric networks. He decided that some use of scanning similar to that employed in television was the answer for solving partial differential equations in more than one variable, and he made some basic recommendations to Bush for designing computers that were to shape the development of the digital electronic computer. They were suggestions such as the use of the binary number system rather than the decimal and the use of electric rather than mechanical networks.

During the war, Wiener's attention was turned to the improvement of antiaircraft artillery. He wrote, "It was clear that the speed of aircraft rendered all classical methods for directing fire obsolete so that it was necessary to build into the control apparatus all the computations necessary [p. 3]." It was necessary to shoot the missile at the point where the plane was expected to be, so Wiener and Julian H. Bigelow worked on developing operators for extrapolating from the history of a curve where it is likely to be in the future. Wiener and Bigelow introduced the term *feedback,* a term then used in the design of servomechanisms (MacColl, 1946). Wiener and Bigelow hoped to create a self-correcting device in which the error—the difference between a predicted pattern and the one actually observed—becomes part of the new input to cause the regulated motion to correct itself.

Wiener and Rosenblueth were similarly interested in the regulation of feedback for purposes of self-correction in understanding pathologies of the cardiovascular and nervous systems. They argued that, since abrupt feedback can send a system into wild oscillation, the various pathologies could be systems defects with respect to the regulation of feedback for purposes of self-correction.

Wiener concluded that the fields of control engineering, which is concerned with the regulation of systems (much as a thermostat controls a furnace), and communication engineering were inseparable. He wrote, "The message is a discrete or continuous sequence of measurable events distributed in time—precisely what is called a time series by the statisticians. The prediction of the future of a message is done by some sort of operator on its past, whether this operator is realized by a scheme of mathematical computation, or by a mechanical or electrical apparatus [Wiener, 1948, pp. 8–9]." The study of the transmission of information, which is the basis of communication, was pioneered by one of Wiener's students, Claude Shannon. Shannon's classic 1949 paper (see Chapter 2) written while he was at Bell Telephone Laboratories became the landmark paper in the mathematical definition of the amount of information transmitted in a communication channel.

At about this time, Wiener coined the term *cybernetics* from the Greek χυβερνήτηζ, which means *steersman,* a term that, like the term *governor* (derived from a Latin corruption of the Greek word), has to do with self-regulation. In 1942 the Macy Foundation devoted a conference to the problems of central inhibition in the nervous system. Wiener's interaction with physiologists and psychologists began to influence engineers and mathematicians, and he wrote, "Everywhere we met with a sympathetic hearing, and the vocabulary of the engineers soon became contaminated with the terms of the neurophysiologist and the psychologist [Wiener, 1948, p. 15]."

Double-Bind Hypothesis

Events Leading to the Hypothesis. In the late winter of 1943–44 John von Neumann organized a series of meetings on cybernetics at Princeton. In the spring of 1946 Warren McCulloch and Frank Fremont-Smith (of the Macy Foundation) organized a series of meetings to be held in New York on the problems of feedback. Fremont-Smith realized the potentially broad application of cybernetics and invited psychologists, sociologists, and anthropologists. Gregory Bateson, returning from the war, ran into Fremont-Smith just before the conference, and he and Margaret Mead were invited to attend by Warren McCulloch, who chaired the first conference. According to Bateson, the cybernetic concepts introduced at the Macy conference affected all his subsequent work (see Brand, 1974).

Bateson then worked with Jurgen Ruesch at the Langley Porter Clinic and was introduced to psychiatry (Ruesch & Bateson, 1951). From 1949 to 1962 Bateson had the title "ethnologist" at the Palo Alto Veterans Administration

Hospital. Bateson could study anything he thought interesting, and his interest was captured by a group of maverick psychiatrists who felt that psychoanalysis was meeting its theoretical limits in the treatment of schizophrenia (see Goldstein, 1969, Preface).

With a 2-year grant from the Rockefeller Foundation, Bateson formed a team with Jay Haley, John Weakland, and William Fry to study the role of paradoxes and abstraction in communication. The 2-year grant ran out and was not renewed, but the research team stayed on without pay. Bateson wrote, "The work went on, and, a few days after the end of the grant, while I was writing a desperate letter to Norbert Wiener for his advice on where to get the next grant, the double bind hypothesis fell into place [Bateson, 1972, p. xi]."

Double-Bind Paper. The famous paper on the double-bind hypothesis was published in 1956 by Gregory Bateson, Don Jackson, Jay Haley, and John Weakland. The hypothesis was based in part on Bateson's study of play in otters. From film footage of a play sequence of otters in the Fleishhacker Zoo, he noticed the fact that is now widely accepted (see Wilson, 1975) that a play sequence is initiated by a particular nonverbal behavior that qualifies the sequence that follows and in effect says "This is going to be play and not a real fight." Sociobiologists call this nonverbal message a *metacommunication,* because it is a communication that qualifies communication and is, therefore, a message of a different logical type.

The double-bind hypothesis proposed that the schizophrenic's deficit was partly an inability to read metacommunications, an inability to use *context* as a guide for knowing how to interpret a sequence of messages. It is a complex hypothesis, and it has probably never been adequately tested. The idea is that the schizophrenic's family teaches him the communication deficit by placing him in doubly-binding situations where he is damned no matter what he does.

This example has become classic: A mother visits her schizophrenic son in the hospital. She is fearful of closeness, but she wants, nonetheless, to be a loving mother. She approaches her son; he is glad to see her and impulsively puts his arm around her shoulders; she stiffens; he withdraws his arm; she asks, "Don't you love me anymore?"; he blushes; she says, "Dear, you must not be so easily embarrassed and afraid of your feelings." Bateson *et al.*'s analysis of this clinical illustration suggested that the son simply could not win in that situation. He was damned if he was affectionate (his mother was threatened) and damned if he was not affectionate. Bateson *et al.* suggested that a person could learn a variety of things by repeated applications of double-bind situations: He could mistrust messages and assume that there was something else behind them, thus developing a paranoid style; he could accept literally everything everyone said to him, regardless of whether tone or gestures contradicted the content of their messages—his acceptance could be passive and without affect (simple schizophrenia); or he could "establish a pattern of laughing off these metacommunicative signals. He would give up trying to discriminate between levels of message and treat all messages as unimportant or to be laughed at [p. 256]" (hebephrenic schizophrenia); or he could ignore all messages entirely and detach his interest from the external world (catatonic schizophrenia). In this way, the double bind was proposed as a hypothesis of the etiology of schizophrenia.

The double-bind hypothesis paper also presented the case of a Zen master who told his pupil to act but struck him with a stick no matter what he did. The pupil needed to solve the problem by changing levels, by transcending the problem in some way, or by shifting the rules (for example, by breaking the stick over the Zen master's head). However, Bateson et al. argued that the option of a rule shift is not open to the schizophrenic. They wrote:

> By preventing the child from talking about the situation, the mother forbids him using the metacommunicative level. . . . . The ability to communicate about communication, to comment upon the meaningful actions of oneself and others, is essential for successful social intercourse. In any normal relationship there is a constant interchange of metacommunications messages such as 'What do you mean?' or 'Why did you do that?' or 'Are you kidding me?' and so on. To discriminate accurately what people are really expressing we must be able to comment directly or indirectly on that expression. This metacommunicative level the schizophrenic seems unable to use successfully. . . . . Therefore, the child grows up unskilled in his ability to communicate about communication and, as a result, unskilled in determining what people really mean and unskilled in expressing what he really means, which is essential for normal relationships [p. 258].

It was an exciting theory, and Haley's observations of the hypnotic experiments of Milton Erickson showed that double-binding situations could induce schizophrenic symptoms. For example, when Erickson told a hypnotized subject that his hand must move on signal but remain in place, the subject hallucinated the motion.

Work Subsequent to the Double-Bind Paper. To follow up the theory, the research group began by developing a conceptual language for what it was that talented therapists did in untangling the communication knots they observed in families with a schizophrenic member. It was an energetic period; there were many talented therapists with strong personalities to observe, and the Bateson group hoped to systematize the behavior of these therapists. In fact, in the original double-bind paper, Bateson et al. (1956) described an episode from the therapy of Frieda Fromm-Reichmann and then concluded the paper with the sentence, "We share the goal of most psychotherapists who strive toward the day when such strokes of genius will be well enough understood to be systematic and commonplace [p. 264]."

A paper by Beels and Ferber in 1969 was an attempt to classify the family therapy styles that had multiplied and proliferated in the decade and a half since the double-bind paper. Beels and Ferber divided family therapists into "conductors," who had strong personalities, worked alone, were active, powerful, and persuasive, and "reactors," who were less directive and usually worked with a cotherapist. Several books are useful in describing the styles of these two therapist types: Ackerman's (1966) book, which is communications-oriented but still basically psychoanalytic, and Ferber, Mendelsohn, and Napier's (1973) edited volume, which is a representative collection, as is Guerin's (1976) edited volume.

Theories of family pathology other than the double bind were proposed. Lidz's theory of schizophrenia was basically psychoanalytic, with a central concern about the age–sex structure of the family and the blurring of age and generation boundaries. Lidz identified two types of schizophrenogenic marriages—one with a domineering pathological figure (usually mother) was called *marital skew,* and the other, in which the parents are chronically hostile and withdraw from one another, was called *marital schism.* He suggested that murderous and incestuous wishes are reciprocated by the parents, which leads to a great likelihood for schizophrenic breaks in adolescence (see Lidz, Cornelison, Fleck, & Terry, 1957).

Wynne's theory was more sociological. He hypothesized that the schizophrenic family's interaction pattern had either too rigid or too ambiguous a role structure for the child to select his own roles as part of identity formation. A lack of true complementarity of relationships was concealed in a facade Wynne labeled "pseudomutuality," with its pressures on the child to avoid recognizing the basic meaninglessness of the family's relationships. Wynne's formulation posited a family environment remarkably similar to many schizophrenic symptoms, such as interaction patterns that lack focused attention, that contain inappropriate affect, particularly with respect to interpersonal distance and closeness; underlying feelings of anomie; and a shared deviant way of construing reality (see Wynne, Ryckoff, Day, & Hirsch, 1958).

It should be clear to the reader that these and other theories were not designed to be tested empirically. They were derived primarily from psychotherapy sessions, interviews, or projective test protocols with small hospitalized populations (see Mishler & Waxler, 1966). It is important to recognize that the tradition begun by the double-bind hypothesis was really not a *research* tradition, despite the fact that a new journal, *Family Process,* was founded in 1962. Rather, the tradition was clinical. The quantitative study in this tradition was by far the exception. In most cases, the family therapists studied only clinical cases; therefore, their hypotheses about pathology could never be tested.

In his decade review paper, Olson (1970) wrote that both marital and family therapists lacked adequate training in research methodology, and he concluded that:

> both groups went to different sources for guidance and assistance. Marital therapists have generally turned to the theoretical work of family sociology or clinical psychology. Family therapists have tended to utilize either psychodynamic formulations or ideas espoused by eminent family therapists. Neither group has attempted much in terms of empirical investigations [1970, p. 505].

This is not entirely an accurate description, because some research in family interaction was stimulated by family therapists. I will discuss this research in Chapter 3. However, it seems fair to say that two lines of research were stimulated by the family therapists. The first line was the study of talented therapists, and the second was the study of family interaction.

History must judge the wisdom of this first course of research, but in other areas of psychotherapy it has not proven especially profitable (see Gottman & Markman, 1978). For example, this approach produced Scheflen's (1973) monumental analysis of one session of family therapy by Whitaker and Malone; Scheflen wrote that he spent 10 years analyzing one 30-minute therapy segment. Although his microanalysis is both overwhelmingly detailed and provocative, it does not represent a feasible approach for constructing a theory of therapy based on quantitative methods. Nonetheless, it may be that, as observational methodology finds suitably sized categories for both therapist and family behavior, this approach will prove useful (see, for example, Pinsof, 1976).

The double-bind hypothesis itself had little to do with what therapists do, and, in fact, the hypothesis stimulated most of the subsequent quantitative observational research on family interaction. In general, investigators found it difficult to operationalize the double-bind transaction so that independent observers could reliably agree that one had occurred. Studies that were based on clinical work with a few distressed families tended to report having observed the double-bind pathology, but they also reported a host of other pathologies, such as Bowen's mother–child symbiosis, Jackson's pathological family homeostastis, Lidz's marital schism and skew, and Wynne's pseudomutuality (see Goldstein, 1969, for a collection of the original papers introducing the definition of these pathologies). On the other hand, studies that investigated both normal and distressed families with quantitative methods and controls, such as leaving the observers blind to which family was which, found essentially no differences between normal and pathological families.

Olson's (1972) paper reviewing research on the double-bind hypothesis suggested that researchers had been put in a double bind by the double-bind hypothesis. It is interesting that, except for Haley (1968), none of the researchers who initially proposed the hypothesis subsequently conducted any research on it, and, in fact, Bateson's (1966) comments on a review paper by Mishler and Waxler (1966) of theories of interaction processes and schizophrenia even suggested that the double bind was not a testable hypothesis. Mishler and Waxler's purpose was to be constructive rather than overly critical, but they wrote that "Our persistent concern with whether we had fully understood the meaning of one or another concept is obviously related to what we feel to be an unnecessarily high level of ambiguity and imprecision in their writings [p. 409]." In the same journal, Bateson (1966) responded as follows:

> The authors have been generous and—so far as this was possible—have been understanding in their critique of the "double-bind" theory. They say with some justice that the phrasings of the theory are sometimes ambiguous. They might have gone further and said that (like much psychoanalytic

theory) the double-bind theory of schizophrenia is *slippery*—so slippery that perhaps no imaginable set of empirical facts could contradict it . . . unfortunately, but necessarily, there is a basic formal truth about all abstract premises, namely: *The more abstract the premise, the more likely it is to be self-validating* [pp. 415–416; emphasis added].

The double bind that Olson suggested researchers had been put in was the call to do research by Bateson in 1956, on the one hand, and his statement of the hypothesis' untestability in 1966, on the other hand. Bateson himself (1966) wrote, "Let me say first that, while I have cared for several schizophrenic patients, I have never been intellectually interested in them [p. 416]." His interest lay in the formal study of interaction processes and in the ideas of general systems theory, and not in the etiology of schizophrenia. Researchers in the area must have felt abandoned by their guru.

Olson's review illustrated the difficulty researchers had in testing the double-bind hypothesis; he judged most studies as having improperly operationalized the hypothesis in the first place. Olson felt that few studies came close. Ringuette and Kennedy (1966) capitalized on an observation by Weakland and Fry (1962) that mothers' letters to schizophrenics contained good examples of double-bind messages. Ringuette and Kennedy obtained letters written by parents to hospitalized schizophrenics, letters written by parents to nonschizophrenic patients, and letters written by hospital volunteers who pretended to write to a hospitalized child. Judges—persons considered highly expert in the double bind, first-year psychiatric residents, experienced clinicians trained or untrained in the double bind, or a naive, untrained group—rated the letters blind on a seven-point scale on the extent to which a letter was double binding. Intercorrelations were low even for the expert group (.19), and none of the groups could discriminate between letters received by schizophrenic and by nonschizophrenic patients.

Another line of research on the double bind concerned schizophrenics' ability to detect double-bind messages, an approach criticized by Watzlawick (1963), who wrote that "the double-bind is *not* a failure in discrimination [p. 137]." Nonetheless, it is a reasonable hypothesis to deduce from the double-bind hypothesis. Loeff (1966) tape-recorded statements with positive and negative content and varied the affect to be neutral, consistent, or inconsistent with the content. His subjects were normal, delinquent, or schizophrenic adolescent girls. The three groups *did not differ* in the predicted direction in being able to discriminate the inconsistent messages, and, in fact, the delinquent and schizophrenic groups did *better* than the normal groups, who apparently placed greater emphasis on the content component.

This generalization that normal groups emphasize content did not hold up in a study by Mehrabian and Wiener (1967) with normal subjects; they found that, when content and vocal components were inconsistent, the total message was judged according to the vocal component. This result is not surprising; for example, when a message like "thanks a lot" is said with a negative voice tone, the obvious meaning is sarcasm, which is negative. This research on channel inconsistency is interesting in its own right, despite Olson's (1972) conclusion that it omits a concept central to the double bind. "A crucial factor, which they failed to take into account," Olson wrote, "is the relationship component [p. 78]." In subsequent research on channel inconsistency, Bugental, Love, and Kaswan (1972) and Bugental, Love, Kaswan, and April (1971) reported that children also rely primarily on nonverbal cues to evaluate a message; they found that the visual channel carried the greatest weight in the evaluations, a result consistent with a regression equation Mehrabian (1972) had derived from research with adults. Bugental et al. (1970) found that children will describe a sarcastic message (positive content plus negative voice and negative face) as far more negative than adults, who will describe the same message as neutral or slightly positive. Moreover, children will rate the same message as more negative if the adult speaker is a woman.

Let us carefully consider the relationship between the double-bind hypothesis and research on channel inconsistency. Love, Kaswan, and Bugental (1974) found significant differences in inconsistent messages between referred and nonreferred mothers. Furthermore, they wrote:

> The conflicting messages produced by referred mothers included conflict between verbal content and facial expression, and between verbal content and tone of voice, but not between face and voice. . . . The finding that the mothers of referred children give simultaneous conflicting evaluative messages in different communications is consistent with aspects of the double-bind hypothesis [p. 111].

However, inconsistencies across channels may be processed without creating a double bind. A sarcastic tone to a message such as "thanks a lot" has a clear meaning to most adults. Most children (Bugental et al., 1970) ignore the positive components of such messages, which is appropriate. Where then is the inconsistency? Love et al. (1974) reported that a common type of conflicting message produced by mothers was a "cooed criticism," such as "That's not n-i-c-e," which was an attempt to soften the criticism (perhaps due to the fact that this was a public situation; see, for example, O'Rourke, 1963). The child would again correctly ignore the positive aspects of this message. Thus, it may be that the "inconsistency" exists only in the construct system of the experimenter, and the correct conclusion would not be that referred mothers were more inconsistent than nonreferred, *but simply more negative.*

Consistent with the opening comments of this chapter on the lack of relationship between general belief in a theory and empirical findings, the bubble of communication theory was hardly burst by disconfirming research. In fact, in a review paper published in 1965, Frank concluded that no factors had been found in 40 years of research that differentiated between normal and pathological families. He concluded that research in this area may be unfeasible because the processes under study are so complex as to "defy one's attempt to draw meaningful generalizations. . . . [p. 201]." Despite this, the double-bind hypothesis and the set of metaphors collectively called "general systems theory" that it spawned have thrived and become accepted.

On the other hand, empirical investigations produced findings (e.g., Haley, 1964) that often were not replicated (Haley, 1967) or were subsequently shown to be exceedingly complex (Waxler & Mishler, 1971). Also, those findings that seemed to hold up the differences between normal and distressed families seemed "theoretically" trivial. For example, Riskin and Faunce's (1972) decade review paper suggested that one consistent finding was that agreement-to-disagreement ratios greater than 1.0 characterized normal families and that ratios less than 1.0 characterized distressed families. These findings were boring and disheartening to everyone except the social learning theorists. They had been somewhat intrigued by cybernetic, or "general systems theory" concepts, but only after they had come to value the importance of measuring observable behavior and of producing testable hypotheses and after they had come to value the elegance of simplicity.

THE SOCIAL LEARNING TRADITION

Work with Families

In the mid-1960s Gerald Patterson and his associates at the University of Oregon and the Oregon Research Institute began reporting work with families having aggressive children that was based on a social learning model. Their idea was that, in effect, it was possible to discover a set of social events in the family's interaction that *initiated* or *accelerated* the base rates of antisocial acts by the child; these acts were called the *eliciting stimuli* and the *reinforcing consequences* of the deviant act, respectively.

The work of the Oregon group was different from that of the family therapists, not only in the behavioral basis of the Oregon group, but also in its commitment to *data, quantification,* and *testability*. Patterson (1976) described the history of his parent training program as follows:

> The present procedures for intervention and data collection in the home evolved gradually. The development was reflected in a series of single case studies. . . . These in turn led to a pilot study in which five consecutive referrals were treated . . . which was developed to provide baseline, treatment, and follow-up data. The training procedures were then adapted for working with groups of parents, "standardized," and taught to a new group of therapists. The details were outlined in the report by Patterson, Cobb and Ray (1973) [p. 192].

A major methodological breakthrough of the Patterson group was the use of *an observational system in the homes of families* with problem children. In the mid-1960s the Patterson group received a series of grants from NIMH's crime and delinquency section to study aggressive children. It is interesting that Patterson remembers that the basic approach of the group was not Skinnerian but was heavily influenced by cybernetic theory (Patterson, personal communication). Within 6 months after these grants began, the group was training parents and investigating the impact of other family members on the targeted child. Earlier, Patterson and Ray had begun training mothers of autistic children and had begun observation with families, using the Schoggen face mask system of anecdotal recording of ongoing incidents. Thus, the ecological methods used by the Barker, Wright, and Schoggen group (see, for example, Schoggen, 1978) influenced the Patterson group and began a tradition of naturalistic observation in the study of families.

The targeted children were characterized on Patterson's (1964) behavior checklist as noncompliant, negativistic, as having continued difficulties with siblings, temper tantrums, loudness, hyperactivity, an inability to relate to peers, and aggressive behavior. The referred boys had conduct problems, but none were severely retarded or psychotic.

In a series of methodological studies, an observational system with 29 categories was developed for coding family interaction (first developed by Reid, 1967, and modified by Patterson, Ray, Shaw, & Cobb, 1969). Observers were trained on videotapes to match the trainer's protocol 75% of the time, with a time-based agreement such that if two coders observed the same behavior within one frame (6 seconds) it was considered an agreement. The observational data were shown to have reasonable stability over time (Patterson & Cobb, 1971; Patterson, Cobb, & Ray, 1973), with a median correlation of .57 for ten families between the first three and the last seven baseline sessions and .66 between the first five and last five baseline sessions. Also, repeated measures of analyses of variance produced only 2 out of 116 significant F-ratios. Although these analyses had little power to detect small differences with few subjects, Jones's (1972) within-subject analyses also showed stability from the first to second halves of the observation periods. Therefore, the observation system demonstrated reasonable levels of reliability (see also Jones, Reid, & Patterson, 1975).

The observation system was also shown to have reasonable levels of validity. Patterson, Jones, and Reid (1973) obtained ratings from mothers on a 1 to 9 scale (1 = annoying, 9 = pleasing) of code categories of child behavior. The behaviors they had previously considered deviant on an a priori basis received a mean of 2.5, whereas those codes they had considered prosocial received a mean of 7.5 by the mothers. Also, Adkins and Johnson (1972) predicted that the behaviors of a child that parents rated as most deviant should be observed to receive the greatest proportion of aversive consequences, and they found a Spearman rank order correlation coefficient of .73 ($p < .01$) of behavior ranked by parents and ranked by proportion of aversive consequences. But Taplin (1974) pointed out: "It should be understood that the functional analyses which would be necessary to empirically demonstrate that the behaviors in these classes actually operate as reinforcers have not yet been conducted [pp. 37–38].'' Despite the shortcoming Taplin noted, the important point in our historical review is that the Oregon researchers were the only investigators of family interaction that bothered with systematic investigations of the reliability and validity of their observational measures.

They also were the only therapists who bothered with careful assessments of their effectiveness with families. There were 27 families in the original 1968 sample, 16 of whom continued through a 1972 follow-up. The parents were taught principles of behavior modification by using a programmed book (Patterson & Gullion, 1968), and they were seen frequently by the therapists. At termination, 74% of the treated children showed reductions in targeted deviant behaviors greater than 30% of the total baseline level of deviant behavior (Patterson, 1972). Follow-up data 1 year after termination on 16 families showed that 75% of those children were still improved. In both the total sample and the follow-up sample these changes in child deviant behavior were significant ($F = 8.64$, $p < .007$, total sample; $F = 4.55$, $p < .05$, completion sample). Eleven control families (6 waiting list controls and 5 attention placebo controls) did not change significantly in 5 weeks after baseline. Therefore, in contrast to the family therapists who were not concerned about producing disconfirmable hypotheses or evaluating therapeutic outcome, the social learning theorists had emphasized both and had demonstrated the utility of an empirical epistemology.[1]

Although it is not really based on social learning theory, the work of Alexander and his associates at Utah is an attempt to integrate behavioral and systems theory concepts. Alexander (1973a,b) found that families without a

---

[1] A dissertation by Taplin (1974) investigated the assumption that these effects are mediated by changes in the parents' consequation of the child's behavior. He found that, at termination, for the 16 families that completed the follow-up, there was a decrease in fathers' and mothers' positive consequation of deviant behavior ($F = 6.44$, $p < .05$; $F = 4.94$, $p < .05$, respectively), a decrease in mothers' aversive consequation of prosocial behavior ($F = 5.66$, $p < .05$), and a decrease in mothers' aversive consequation of deviant behavior ($F = 5.79$, $p < .05$). This was not due to less interaction with the child. But there were no changes in the positive consequation of prosocial behavior.

At follow-up, ''a large part of maternal treatment gains had deteriorated [Taplin, 1974, p. 50],'' with significant increases from termination to follow-up in mothers' aversive consequation of deviant child behavior ($F = 14.22$, $p < .01$) and increases in mothers' positive consequation of deviant child behavior ($F = 5.01$, $p < .05$). Fathers had not changed significantly from termination to follow-up.

These results throw into question the processes of the obtained change in child behavior and parental ratings. To understand these effects, Taplin (1974) performed a series of cross-lagged panel correlation analyses to determine the direction of causation between changes in deviant child behavior and changes in parental consequation. Figure 1.1 illustrates Taplin's results, which suggest that changes in the child's deviant behavior cause changes in the parental consequation (the upper diagonal correlations are larger than the lower), and not conversely. It may, therefore, be the case that the processes of change in the Patterson research have yet to be fully understood (see also Taplin & Reid, 1977).

delinquent member showed greater correlations in rates of supportiveness than did families with delinquent members. Alexander and Parsons (1973) and Parsons and Alexander (1973) then modified the family's interaction processes and found the lowest recidivism rates for delinquency in their short-term "behavioral systems therapy" group for both the target child and nontargeted siblings (Klein, Alexander, & Parsons, 1975).

Work with Couples

In the mid-1960s Robert Weiss became director of clinical training at the University of Oregon, and in 1969 Patterson, Weiss, and Robert Ziller collaborated on an Office of Naval Research grant to study small group conflict. In treating the families of aggressive children, Patterson noticed that these families were characterized by marital conflict, and Patterson and Hyman Hops began working with married couples. They altered their family interaction coding system to assess changes in marital interaction by coding videotapes, and this system eventually became the Marital Interaction Coding System (MICS) (Hops, Wills, Patterson, & Weiss, 1972), which was an important step in the study of marital interaction.

Hops and Patterson also had couples monitor the frequency of pleasing and displeasing events, an idea that Patterson got from a paper by Lindsley (1966). Subsequently, Weiss and his associates at the University of Oregon have continued research that has suggested a behavioral basis for marital satisfaction

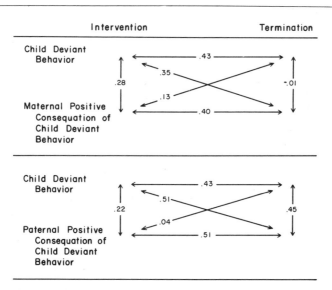

Figure 1.1 *Cross-lagged panel correlations from Taplin's (1974) reanalysis of Patterson's data (from Taplin, 1974, pp. 53 and 54. Reproduced with permission).*

(Birchler, Weiss, & Vincent, 1975; Patterson, Hops, & Weiss, 1975; Royce & Weiss, 1975; Vincent, Weiss, & Birchler, 1975; Weiss, Hops, & Patterson, 1973; Wills, Weiss, & Patterson, 1974). Their studies were a series of investigations based in part on the MICS codes and the pleases and displeases measures, and they have designed and begun testing on intervention program for increasing marital satisfaction (also see Jacobson, 1977).

Quid pro Quo Concept. It is interesting that, in the area of marital therapy, the theorizing of Don Jackson, a coauthor of the double-bind paper, was to have a great influence on the social learning theorists. In 1965 Jackson suggested that well-functioning marriages he had observed could be simply characterized as having established a family rule he called the *Quid pro Quo,* literally an exchange system that both partners had agreed was fair. Jackson cited a study by Leik (1963) that found that "the traditional male role (instrumental, nonemotional behavior) appears when interaction takes place among strangers. These emphases tend to disappear when subjects interact with their own families [p. 145]." As one example of a quid pro quo, Jackson (1965) suggested, "If A says to B, let us do X, spouse B assents because they have established a time-bound relationship in which the next move would be B's. The husband may suggest to his wife that they go to a movie; she says yes, and then she has the right to say, we can have a beer afterwards [p. 1538]."

In 1968 Lederer and Jackson published an influential book called *The Mirages of Marriage,* in which they elaborated on the quid pro quo concept and suggested a form of therapy called *reciprocal contracting* as a treatment for distressed marriages. Note that the quid pro quo interaction pattern had never been carefully established as a phenomenon by quantitative, observational research as characteristic of marriages that both partners consider mutually satisfying or as failing to characterize distressed marriages (see the review of reciprocity hypotheses in Chapter 3 of this book). The quid pro quo concept was, nonetheless, so intuitively appealing to behaviorally oriented therapists that it was rapidly adopted. In 1969 Richard Stuart published a paper with four couples reporting that a reciprocal contract had been established with all four. In 1976 he reported rather briefly and casually that he had obtained high rates of success (approximately 84%) with a large sample (200 couples), measuring improvement with his own Marital Precounseling Inventory. Therefore, the reciprocal contract, despite its lack of strong empirical support, began to be the treatment of choice of behaviorally oriented marriage counselors (see also Jacobson and Martin, 1976). The treatment was, however, considerably modified by adding training in negotiation and in other communication skills (e.g., Jacobson, 1977; Patterson, Hops, & Weiss, 1975; Weiss, Hops, & Patterson, 1973).

Another important and independent research tradition in family interaction research is the developmental tradition, whose focus was initially on the parents' effects on a child's development.

THE DEVELOPMENTAL TRADITION

Interest in children's socialization by parents accelerated in the 1950s with Robert Sears' move from Yale to Iowa and his studies of how parental practices affect child development. Through parental retrospection these studies reconstructed patterns of early feeding, toilet training, and parental handling of aggression and dependency. They considered the parental tasks of childrearing to be the curbing of the child's antisocial tendencies, a view inspired by psychoanalysis. Sears' subsequent move to Harvard eventually led to the important collaboration with Maccoby and Levin that produced the patterns of childrearing book (Sears, Maccoby, & Levin, 1957), which was based primarily on interview data.

This was a period described by Hartup (1977) as dominated by the "social mold theories," in which the child's personality was viewed as being molded by parental practices. It was also a period studying molar variables (such as parental warmth, tension, dominance, and consistency), in contrast to later research, which focused on more specific behaviors. Unfortunately, retrospective accounts of developmental milestones by parents were found to be unreliable and inaccurate (Yarrow et al., 1968), and laboratory studies became favored over interview and questionnaire methods.

The 15 years from 1955 to 1970 took developmental research into the laboratory and also into the mainstream of psychology. Studies in Iowa in experimental child psychology were essentially learning studies (rather than developmental studies) in the Hull–Spence tradition, which used children as subjects. The studies at Stanford by Bandura and Walters were in the social learning tradition. Parke has called it "an elegant era" in which miniature theories were constructed and tested with little regard for issues of the generalizability of results from one laboratory task to another or from the laboratory to natural settings (Parke, personal communication).

The 1960s were marked by the introduction by Elkind and Flavell of Piaget to American researchers; initially, Americans tended to treat Piaget as a normative developmentalist like Gessel, rather than as a hierarchical stage theorist. In this decade there has been an emphasis on information processing that replaced the Hull–Spence theory and an emphasis on the idea of the child as an active organism. This latter shift in viewpoint took place in diverse areas, such as psycholinguistic development and the early perceptual behavior of the infant.

Eventually, the recognition of the infant as an active and surprisingly competent organism challenged the social mold theories. This realization was crystallized in Bell's (1968) classic paper, in which bidirectional effects in the child's socialization were argued for.

The 1970s have seen renewed interest in the study of parent–child interaction as a dyadic process, and this research activity has recently been collected in an important book edited by Lewis and Rosenblum (1974), *The Effect of the Infant on Its Caregiver*, which presents research that demonstrates the complex patterning of adult–child social interaction.

An illustration of the infant's contribution in initiating and maintaining social interaction "bouts" with the mother was given by Bell (1974), who wrote:

> Jones and Moss in our laboratory (1971) have reported that infants in the awake–active state tend to babble much more when they are by themselves than when the mother is present. The mother who hears these episodes of noncrying vocalizations, even though busy, often cannot resist the appeal, and comes to the infant to enter the game. The infant's babbling thus may come to serve as a discriminative stimulus for a reciprocal "game." In such instances the infant often discontinues the babbling and shifts into a reciprocal relation in which the mother vocalizes or touches, and the infant responds by smiling and vocalizing.
>
> Often, a sitting infant gurgles and smiles when a mother passes on her way to do a household chore, thus inveigling her into interaction. One of the infants in our studies could emit a special noncrying vocalization which was quite effective in bringing the mother in from the kitchen to start an interaction . . . [pp. 8–9].

Brazelton and his associates (Brazelton, Koslowski, & Main, 1974; Tronick, Als, & Brazelton, 1977) have identified cycles of infant attention, affective involvement, and inattention and disengagement, with repeated loops through these behaviors. They observed that, over the course of development, mother and child show a greater range of behaviors and greater synchrony. Mothers learn to become sensitive to their babies' "away periods," and both partners learn how to engage and to stimulate one another.

Research activity in parent–child interaction has now been influenced by ethologists and primatologists, and recent investigations are characterized by renewed interest in observational methodology and sequential analysis.

SUMMARY

This chapter provided a historical context for the research reported in this book. Each tradition contributed important concepts. Research from the sociological tradition was reviewed to suggest the importance of studying a couple's communication in arriving at consensus. Theorizing from the family therapy tradition was reviewed to suggest that communication should involve concepts of cybernetic systems of verbal and nonverbal communication. Research from the social learning tradition suggested: (1) the importance of the quantitative study of interaction sequences using naturalistic observation; and, (2) behavior exchange concepts as exemplified by the quid pro quo. Research from the developmental tradition suggested the importance of a bidirectional view of interaction sequences. These concepts are the fundamental intellectual heritage of the research reported in this book.

CHAPTER 2

Sequential Analysis

THE IMPORTANCE OF SEQUENCE

There is a definition of communication that is intimately associated with the study of pattern in a sequence of observations. It dates back to the same era as the beginnings of family therapy. The seminal paper that presented the necessary mathematics (called *information theory*) for the sequential analysis of observational data was written by Shannon and Weaver in 1949. Family therapists recognized the importance of this paper, and it was even cited by Reusch and Bateson (1951). They wrote:

> The information sciences—perhaps the most exciting scientific and intellectual innovation of the twentieth century—emerged after World War II. The transactions of the early Macy Conference on Cybernetics, Wiener's *Cybernetics: Or Control and Communication in the Animal and the Machine* (1948), and Shannon and Weaver's *The Mathematical Theory of Communication* mark the beginning of a new era [p. v].

It was a strange twist of fate that none of the early family theorists knew how to use the mathematical concepts of this "new era," probably because they lacked the mathematical training to understand Shannon and Weaver's (1949) paper. Many other scientists shared this deficiency, and there were, therefore, subsequent excellent popularizations of information theory for psychologists by Attneave (1959) and for biologists by Quastler (1958).

It is unfortunate for the field of family interaction research that these popularizations were never applied, because, *whereas all the hypotheses of pathological family interaction concerned the patterns of interaction, none of the 57 research studies reviewed by Jacob (1975) were concerned with pattern.* They all presented analyses of the differences in *rates of various behaviors*. By their data analytic methods, these studies therefore assumed that the more of something good, the better, and the more of something bad, the worse. This was a tenuous assumption because, for example, not all interruptions in a dialogue may be the same; interruptions may initiate one kind of sequence, such as a negative affect cycle, in distressed families, and a different kind of sequence, such as humor, in nondistressed families. In other words, *the vast majority of research on family and marital interaction has not analyzed the relationship between codes over time,* and this seems to be a major shortcoming.

An excellent review of the relationship between family interaction and child psychopathology by Hetherington and Martin (1972) made precisely this point about sequence. Hetherington and Martin wrote:

> Most of the studies of family interaction have yielded separate frequency measures of parent and child behavior recorded while they were interacting. However, investigators are usually actually interested in the etiology, contingencies, and sequencing of these observed behaviors and often generalize to such questions on the basis of inappropriate methodology. . . . Such *studies should look sequentially at interchanges involving chains of interpersonal exchanges and should investigate shifts in probabilities of response in one family member to the specific behavior of others* [p. 36; emphasis added].

Somehow, researchers in family interaction remained uninfluenced by the social learning tradition's concern with sequence in a search for discriminative stimuli preceding a child's noxious behavior and reinforcing stimuli that follow and maintain it. Researchers in family interaction also remained uninfluenced by the following contributions:

1. Raush's (1965) paper, which used information theory to study the potential consequences of mixing aggressive and nonaggressive children
2. Altmann's (1965) seminal paper on interaction sequences among rhesus monkeys, which used information theory
3. Recent applications of sequential analysis to the study of bidirectional effects in parent–infant interaction (Bell, 1968; Lewis & Rosenblum, 1974)
4. Raush, Barry, Hertel, and Swain's (1974) work on interaction patterns in married couples (see Chapter 7 of this book for a recoding and reanalysis of Raush et al., 1974).

Part of the objective of this book is to change this lack of influence, which is probably a result of the fact that developmental psychologists, family interaction researchers, comparative psychologists and ethologists, researchers of nonverbal behavior, clinical psychologists, anthropologists, and sociologists simply do not have the time to read each other's work. Unfortunately, they tend to cite only their colleagues, and, as Wiener (1948) wrote 30 years ago:

Today there are few scholars who can call themselves mathematicians or psychiatrists or biologists without restriction. A man may be a topologist or an acoustician or a coleopterist. He will be filled with the jargon of his field, and will know all his literature and all its ramifications, but, more frequently than not, he will regard the next subject as something belonging to his colleague three doors down the corridor, and will consider any interest in it on his own part as an unwarrantable breach of privacy [p. 2].

COMMUNICATION AND SEQUENCE

The basic concept of communication as it relates to sequence is very simple. A good illustration is the following example on the social behavior of spider crabs. Spider crabs have a relatively simple behavioral repertoire (see, for example, Hazlett & Estabrook, 1974), and for the purpose of this illustration I shall further simplify that repertoire. These crabs can move or remain fixed in one place, and they can move their chilepids (arms) in a single side chilepid raise (right or left chilepid), a double chilepid raise, or by a forward chilepid extension. They also occasionally, but rarely, fight or flee. Let us denote these behaviors as *Move, Single Chilepid Raise, Double Chilepid Raise, Forward Chilepid Extension, Fight,* and *Flee.*

Suppose we want to discover the "language" of the spider crab; that is, we want to know what, if anything, these behaviors "mean" or communicate socially to other spider crabs in the vicinity. We need to know the communicative value of each of the crab's behaviors. This leads us to our fundamental definition:

> *A behavior of one organism has communicative value in a social sense if it reduces uncertainty in the behavior of another organism.*

We notice, for example, that the probability of a crab's moving is very low; that is, it rarely moves. Let us assume we discover that p (Move) = .06. This means that the average crab in our tank was observed to have moved in 6% of our observational coding units.

Now we look at the proportion of times that Crab B moved after Crab A did a Single Chilepid Raise. This is a conditional probability, written p(B moved | A's Single Chilepid Raise), and it is verbalized as "the conditional probability that B moved given that A did a Single Chilepid Raise." We note in our data that A raised a single chilepid 100 times and that, of those, B moved 6 times. The conditional probability was thus 6% (6/100), and it is, therefore, no different from the unconditional probability of a move. As a result, we have gained no information, that is, no reduction of uncertainty in B's having moved by prior knowledge of A's Single Chilepid Raises. This leads us to the statement:

> *Reduction of uncertainty is assessed by the difference between conditional and unconditional probabilities.*

Suppose we look at the double chilepid raises of A and again find that p(B moved|A's Double Chilepid Raise) = .07. We would probably conclude that, again, the double chilepid raise did not reduce uncertainty in our ability to predict B's having moved. However, if we were to look at all the times A performed a Forward Chilepid Extension, we would see that p(B moved|A's Forward Chilepid Extension) = .65. If the two crabs were facing one another, we would then wonder if the Forward Chilepid Extension means, "Get out of my way, you crab."

We might investigate further by looking at what happens to the 35% of the occasions when A did a Forward Chilepid Extension and B did not move. We notice that a fight occurred on 60% of those occasions. Suppose that the unconditional probability of a fight is .02 (it would have to be lower than the unconditional probability of a move). We are beginning to detect an elaborate sequence. This latter probability p(Fight|B did not move after A did a Forward Chilepid Extension), is called a "lag-2 conditional probability with A's Forward Chilepid Extension as the criterion behavior," because something else intervened between Flight and A's Forward Chilepid Raise. We can continue in this manner to conditional probabilities of lag 3, lag 4, and so on, in each case comparing conditional to unconditional probabilities.

Patterson (1978) used an analysis comparing conditional to unconditional probabilities to investigate those behaviors of a mother that were antecedents of two of a child's coercive behaviors—arguing or whining. The unconditional probability of the child's coercive behaviors was about .01, and the conditional probabilities of coercive behaviors given the mother's prior disapproval was .12 for the child's arguing and .15 for the child's whining and, given the mother's prior command, was .19 for arguing and .05 for whining. We can see from this example that we need some statistical test or some guidelines for making inferences from our sample of observations to the universe of observations. Such a test is given by the normal approximations to the binomial probability distribution.

Suppose that we look at the unconditional probability that a husband's nonverbal behavior was coded as positive during a discussion of a marital issue with his wife and notice that p(H+) = .15. We calculated this by noting that his affect was coded neutral 800 times, 50 times it was coded negative, and 150 times it was coded positive, so that

$$p(\text{H}+) = \frac{150}{800 + 50 + 150} = .15.$$

Now we observe that, out of 320 occasions that the wife's previous (lag-1) nonverbal behavior was coded positive, on 100 occasions the husband's subsequent affect was coded positive. We calculate the conditional probability as p(H+|W+, lag 1) = 100/320 = .31. To test the difference between .31 and .15, we use the following statistic:

$$Z = \frac{x - NP}{\sqrt{(NPQ)}},$$

where x = the observed joint frequency of husband's positive and wife's positive affect = 100, N = the frequency of the wife's positive affect = 320, P = the unconditional frequency of the husband's positive affect = .15, and $Q = 1 - P = .85$. In our example,

$$Z = \frac{100 - 320(.15)}{\sqrt{320(.15)(.85)}} = \frac{52}{6.39} = 8.14.$$

Sackett (1977) wrote:

> If the Z equals or exceeds ± 1.96, the difference between observed and expected probabilities has reached the .05 level of significance. If Z is positive, the matching behavior occurred *more* than expected by chance (an excitatory or positive dependency). If Z is negative, the observed probability occurs less than expected by chance (an inhibitory or negative dependency). The variability about the expected probability is estimated by ($I = P_{exp} \pm (1.96 \times SD)$, is the upper and lower 95% confidence points [p. 7].

Sackett's P_{exp} is what we have been calling the unconditional probability, and the standard deviation, SD, is $\sqrt{PQ/N}$.

The normal approximation to the binomial distribution states that the preceding Z-statistic approximates a standardized normal distribution, an approximation that is good only when N is larger than 25 (see, for example, Siegel, 1956, p. 40), but the convergence of the binomial to the normal distribution is more rapid when P is close to .50 and slower when P is near 0 or 1. Siegel (1956) suggested that "when P is near 0 or 1, a rule of thumb is that NPQ must be at least 9 before the statistical test based on the normal approximation is applicable [p. 40]." The formula proposed by Sackett was derived by Gottman (1979), using methods of time-series analysis.

The approach may also be used for testing sequential patterning in a single organism. For example, Bakeman and Dabbs (1976) presented the example of an infant who had his eyes open more frequently during feeding (conditional) than unconditionally (all times).

These ideas form the basis of an uncertainty reduction definition of communication. We will now turn to a discussion of how they may be used to identify pattern in interaction sequences. To do this, it will be helpful for us to discuss *information theory*.

WHAT IS INFORMATION?

A doorbell is a two-choice information transmitter; it may ring or be silent. A doorbell that never rings is perfectly predictable, and it obviously sends no

TABLE 2.1

Information Conveyed by Three Independent Binary Codes, Depicted as
Three Doorbells

Possible	Doorbells		
Messages	1	2	3
Charlie's here	On	On	On
David's here	On	On	Off
Bob's here	On	Off	On
Tom's here	On	Off	Off
Mary's here	Off	On	On
Alice's here	Off	On	Off
Carol's here	Off	Off	On
Relax, nobody's here	Off	Off	Off

information. One doorbell provides us with an information channel that can transmit one bit (a binary unit) of information. Viewed as a group, three doorbells that can or cannot ring independently present the eight possibilities for transmitting a more complex set of codes shown in Table 2.1. There are eight possibilities, or $2 \times 2 \times 2$, in this system composed of elements each of which has one bit of information. If we counted the number of 2s in the product above, we could define the information of the three-doorbell system as the sum of the information of its elements, for a total of 3 bits. Carrying this mode of thinking further would suggest that an information system with a total of n equally likely messages would have information of the power to which we needed to raise 2 to get n, that is, $\log_2 n$. To understand this better, consider how many (yes–no) questions we would have to ask to find out on which particular square of the 64-square chessboard someone had placed a king. It would take a minimum of 6 yes–no questions such as, "Is the square on the left half?" to locate the king, and 6 is the $\log_2 64$, since $64 = 2^6$. Each answer provides one bit of information by reducing the remaining alternatives in half. The information, H, is thus $\log n$, where n is the number of equiprobable alternatives.

If the messages were not all equally probable, the total amount of information would have to be weighted by the probability of each message. (For more mathematical detail, see Appendix 2.1 and Gottman & Notarius, 1978).

WHAT IS REDUNDANCY?

To transmit messages in the English language, we require 26 letters plus the blank space, or 27 symbols in all. If all the 27 symbols were equally common, the information content of the English alphabet would be $\log_2 27 = 4.76$ bits per letter. However, the letters do not occur with the same frequency. If we were to generate messages with the equiprobable assumption that all symbols occur with equal frequency, we would get messages such as the following one Shannon (1949) generated:

XFOML RXKHRJFFJUJ ZLPWCFWKCYJ FFJEYVKCQSGHYD QPAAMKBZAACIBZLHQD [p. 43],

which looks very little like an English sentence. If we were to assume that the symbols were independent but occurred with the frequencies of English text, we might obtain:

OCRO HLI RGWR NMIELWIS EU LL NBNESEBYA TH EEI ALHENHITPA OOBTTVA NAH BRL [p. 43].

Of course, we know that letters in English do not occur independently: X never follows J, U always follows Q, and so on. This dependency is a lag-1 dependency of pairs, and the rules of the dependency are called a *digram structure*. If we generate sentences with the frequencies of English and with the English digram structure, we would obtain sentences such as:

ON IE ANTSOUTINYS ARE T INCTORE ST BE S DEAMY ACHIN D ILONASIVE TUCOOWE AT TREASONARE FUSO TIZIN ANDY TOBE SEASE CIISBE [p. 43].

The next order of approximation adds the trigram structure of English, which tells us that THR is less probable than THE or THA or THI, etc. In this case, we would obtain a sentence such as:

IN NO IST LAT WHEY CRATICT FROURE BIRS BROCID PONDENOME OF DEMONSTURES OF THE REPTAGIN IS REGOACTIONA OF CRE [p. 43],

which is reasonably pronounceable English gibberish. The real information content of English turns out to be about 2 bits per letter rather than the 4.76 we originally estimated. One minus the ratio 2/4.76 is a measure of the redundancy, or degree of sequential patterning, in the English language.

When we collect observational data, we are in a position similar to an intelligent non-English speaker who receives incomprehensible messages, such as the sequence of symbols in this paragraph. In decoding a string of observational codes, what we obviously have to do is to use the sequence of symbols to figure out the frequencies of the symbols, the digram structure rules, the trigram structure rules, and so on. In observational research, we also are at an advantage because we have a code book (which is like a dictionary) that tells us what each symbol means in terms we can comprehend.

We are now in a position to discuss how pattern can be identified using the concepts of information, redundancy, and uncertainty reduction.

STRUCTURE AND PATTERN IN A SEQUENCE OF CODES

An excellent example of how to use the preceding concepts to detect structure and pattern in a sequence of codes was given by Attneave (1959), so we will continue our discussion with Attneave's example.

Suppose we have a sequence of codes that represent successive selections of black and white balls from an urn, and suppose that we ask someone to guess the obtained sequence and that we obtained the following pattern of 203 guesses:

```
          . . .
W B  W W B  B  B  W B  W B  B  W W W B  B  B  W W B  B  W B  B  B  W W
B  B  W B  B  W W W B  W W B  B  W W B  W W W W B  W W W B  B  W W
W B  W W B  B  W W B  W W B  B  B  W W B  W W B  B  B  B  W W B  W W
W W B  B  B  W B  W B  W W W B  W W W B  B  W B  W W B  W W W B  W
W W W B  B  W W B  W W W B  B  W W B  B  B  W W W B  W B  B  W W B
W B  B  W W W B  W W W B  B  W W B  B  W W B  B  W W W B  B  W W B
B  W B  B  W W B  B  B  W W B  B  W B  B  W W B  B  W W W B  W W B  B
W W B  B  B  B  W  . . .  [Attneave, 1959, p. 22].
```

There are 203 observations. What properties would the sequence possess if it were totally random? The absence of a first-order structure would be demonstrated by the fact that B and W were equally likely. The actual numbers are 109 and 91, which turn out to be extremely close. In fact, the information value for the assumption that both codes are equally likely is $H_0 = \log_2 2 = 1.0$, and for the two actual frequencies we would obtain $H_1 = .995$, which is very close to 1.0. The first-order approximation weights each logarithm by the probability of occurrence of each of the codes, B and W in the sequence of guesses, for the first-order approximation of the amount of information, H_1. If $H_0 = H_1$, nothing is gained by the first-order approximation.

If we now search for a digram structure, we count the frequency of all *overlapping* pairs; by overlapping pairs we mean that the starting string–W–B–W–W gives the pairs W–B, B–W, and W–W and that we continue through the observed sequence in this fashion. We would count 58 W–W pairs, 51 W–B pairs, 50 B–W pairs, and 41 B–B pairs. Once again, these are very close to being equally likely, so we would not expect much digram structure, and, thus, our recalculation of H would not differ much from the .995 value we previously calculated; in fact, H turns out to be .994, so this surmise is correct.

We are searching for an *imbalance* in frequencies, and we find it first at the trigram level. We would discover by counting trigrams that B–W–B and B–B–B do not occur as frequently as the others. The frequencies are 19 W–W–W trigrams, 39 W–W–B trigrams, 20 W–B–W trigrams, 31 W–B–B trigrams, 39 B–W–W trigrams, 11 B–W–B trigrams, 30 B–W–B trigrams, and 11 B–B–B trigrams. This imbalance results in an H of .873, which is different from our previous .994. Thus, our first drop in uncertainty occurs at the trigram structure.

If there is an imbalance in trigram frequencies, would it not continue to the tetragram level? The answer is yes. Because of this, we really want to know how much *new* imbalance in frequencies is met at the next level, so we keep comparing the information at each order with the information of the *previous* order.

The first-order approximation to the average information per symbol assumes no history, but the digram structure produces a new approximation, which is the information left in H_1 after we subtract out H(digram); this is H_2. The third-order estimate is the new information that the third symbol adds to the digram preceding it, or, $H_3 = H$(trigram) minus H(digram), and so on.

At each step of the way the previous approximation becomes the null hypothesis for the next step. In the preceding data, we could plot H_N as a function of the order of approximation, N, and, "through the first two orders analyzed, we find very little deviation from randomness, since neither symbol nor diagram frequencies are disproportional at any great extent. At $N = 3$, however, a sharp drop occurs, indicating that a knowledge of the two guesses which have just occurred reduces considerably the uncertainty of the next [Attneave, 1959, p. 25]." To avoid complex formulas, this chapter presents only the concepts of the calculations; the mathematics are presented in Appendix 2.1. The reader should be aware of the existence of a statistical test at each order, also discussed in the appendix, and of the modern treatment of the same problem by a method called *log likelihood analysis* (Bishop, Fienberg, & Holland, 1975; Fienberg, 1978). Additional exposition of the concepts in this chapter are available in Gottman and Bakeman (1979) and Gottman and Notarius (1978).

We can note one limitation in the information theory method for detecting sequences. Usually we are not interested in many imbalances in frequency because we know what each code means. For example, we may know that smile and frown are not likely to immediately follow one another, and, for our purposes, this kind of pattern may be trivial. Or it may be the case that it is illogical for two codes to follow one another given the construction of the coding system, and this knowledge may, therefore, be uninteresting. In these cases, knowledge that there is a digram structure may result from many zero frequencies among certain pairs of codes, but the result will not be interesting to the experimenter. In these cases, the experimenter is interested in which sequences are most common and in how *particular* codes of interest are sequentially related. The experimenter may be interested in sequences in which code A precedes code B, even if other indefinite elements intervene; that is, the experimenter may wish to detect sequences of the form A–B, A–X–B, A–X–Y–B, and so on, where X and Y are not predictable definite codes. For these and other reasons to be discussed, an alternative analysis developed by Sackett (1977) is extremely useful.

SACKETT'S LAG ANALYSIS

Unfortunately, for more than even a handful of codes and for long sequences, the preceding method becomes extremely unwieldy. For example, for a 20-symbol coding scheme there would be 800 triads and 160,000 tetrads. Some alternative system is needed, and Sackett (1974, 1977) has suggested an extremely useful one. Each behavior, C, in the coding scheme plays a role as the "criterion behavior"; for each other behavior, X, the conditional probability is calculated as a function of the lag of X from C, for lags 1, 2, 3, 4, and so on. This produces a probability profile of X, given C at some lag.

Bakeman and Dabbs (1976) summarized an example of this method applied to the study of primate interaction between mothers and infants.

Sackett observed a crab-eating macaque mother and her infant; his . . . code catalog included such behaviors as "infant acitve," "Mother pat–stroke–jiggle," "mother nurse," "mother groom," and "passive contact." The analysis begins by designating one behavior the "criterion behavior" (this procedure can be repeated as many times as there are behaviors, so that each behavior can serve as the criterion). Then for every other behavior a "probability profile" is constructed; each profile shows the lagged conditional probabilities that the behavior will follow the criterion immediately (lag 1), follow as the second behavior (lag 2), follow as the third behavior (lag 3), and so forth. [see Figure 2.1] Peaks in the profile indicate sequential positions following the criterion at which a given behavior is more likely to occur, while valleys indicate positions at which it is less likely to occur. If a behavior is sequentially independent of the criterion, then its conditional probabilities at various lags should be about the same as its simple, or unconditional, probability [indicated with dashed lines in Figure 2.1]. The extent to which observed and predicted values differ from one another can be gauged, as before, with z-scores.

Now, several profiles can be examined together to determine which behavior is most likely at each lag after a particular criterion behavior. This information in turn would suggest probable sequences even though actual sequences are not observed for more than two behaviors at once. For instance, the rightward shift of the peak in the first three frames [of Figure 2.1] suggests the sequence, "infant active, mother pat–stroke–jiggle, mother nurse, mother groom." This particular sequence seems quite strong and undoubtedly would have been detected by an absolute approach as well. The probabilistic approach, however, detects sequences with indefinite elements which might well be missed with absolute methods. For example, the bottom frame [in Figure 2.1] suggests that after activity on the part of the infant, it is unlikely that the third behavior following will be passive contact. This ability to detect sequences with indefinite elements seems a real strength of this approach [p. 339; material in brackets added].

By "indefinite elements" Bakeman and Dabbs mean that it is possible to identify sequences such as "Code A, something else, and then Code B" as a likely chain, where the "something else" could be any other code. Thus, Sackett's method offers a flexible and powerful alternative to the informational

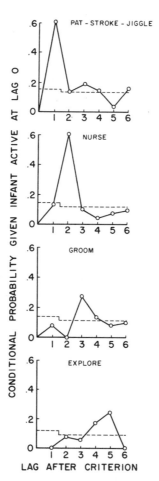

Figure 2.1 *Lagged conditional probabilities for four behaviors given previous infant activity (data from Bakeman, 1978). Dashed lines represent unconditional probabilities of each of the four behaviors. Since with the kind of data used (called Type I by Bakeman, 1978) the criterion cannot follow itself, the number of behaviors that can occur at lag 1 is one less than for other lags; unconditional probabilities are thus a bit higher at lag 1 than for other lags. (Reproduced with permission)*

approach, and it provides for extracting most of the information from the data.[1]

We can think of communication as being similar to a chess game where the moves of one player constrain the alternatives available to the other player and,

[1] One limitation of Sackett's lag sequential analysis is that the exact frequencies of specific sequences cannot be derived from the set of all lagged conditional probabilities from every code. Thus, the detection of common sequences requires inferences, and a method for making such inferences is outlined in this chapter. Lag-sequence analysis itself, in addition to its specificity, thus performs an information reduction function, which is much needed in reporting sequential analytic results.

therefore, reduce uncertainty in his behavior. Not all moves create equal constraint; for example, in the middle game the activity of a queen is, in general (but not always), likely to provide more information than the activity of a pawn. The task of the experimenter who analyzes sequential data is, in effect, to discover the rules of the game. The participants in an interaction usually are unable to state the rules of the game; for example, people seem to be unaware of personal space invasion rules (see Sommer, 1969) and of the intricate dance of gaze and gaze aversion in conversation (Kendon, 1967). To accomplish the objective of determining the implicit rules of interaction, it is necessary to have some method for obtaining common sequences in the data.

Obtaining Common Sequences from Lag Analysis

Sequences can be identified in three steps. First, suppose the code with the highest lag-1 conditional probability from the criterion behavior C is code A, the code with the highest lag-2 conditional probability from the criterion is behavior B, and so on. Then a probable sequence C → A → B is identified. The second step in identifying a sequence is to note that this would be a likely sequence only if the lag-1 transitional probability of behavior B with behavior A as the criterion showed a peak. The third step in identifying a probable sequence is to determine, at any lag, the Z-scores of the codes with highest conditional probabilites. This operation tests whether these conditional probabilities differ from unconditional probabilities. Thus, if a code is the most probable code at some lag from the criterion, but no more probable than at any other time, it does not enter into the identified *common sequence*. To summarize, the three steps in identifying a common sequence are:

1. Select a criterion behavior code, C, and compute the conditional probabilities of the other codes at each lag. If behavior code A has the highest conditional probability with respect to C at lag 1 and B has the highest conditional probability with respect to C at lag 2, a possible sequence, C → A → B, is suggested.
2. To test the sequence C → A → B, make A the criterion behavior and see if the transition probability of B with respect to A at lag 1 from A shows a peak (i.e., is above the transition probabilities of other codes).
3. Z-scores that test conditional against unconditional probabilities should be greater than 1.96, or the transition probabilities are at base rate level, which would argue against a *sequence* (i.e., some reduction in uncertainty in a code, given knowledge that the criterion has occurred at some prior lag).

In practice, a matrix such as the one in Table 2.2 is generated. A sequence C → A → Y → X → C is identified if and only if the lag-1 Z-scores (greater than 1.96) connecting intermediate codes suggest that A and Y, Y and X, and X and C are connected. A measure of the probability of the chain is given by the conditionals of each behavior in the chain with respect to the criterion code,

TABLE 2.2

Matrix Generated by Sackett's Lag-Sequence Analysis Using a Lag-One
Connection Rule

Criterion = C	Lag			
	1	2	3	4
	A	B	A	C
	B	Y	X	
	X			
	Y			

and a measure of connectedness in the chain is given by the Z-scores. As a rule
of thumb, the data sequences with lag-1 conditionals anywhere in a chain
($p(A/C)$ at lag 1) less than .07 are too infrequent to be reliably reported. This
would not be the case with a great deal more data than the experiments reported in this book (i.e., more subjects or longer strings within subjects). Also,
more than one chain can be associated with any criterion behavior. Another
useful decision rule and a device for reducing complexity for data that are not
long enough to permit analysis at lags longer than 20 (which would make it
possible to identify cyclicity even with categorical data) is that, when Z-scores
are less than 1.96, consider the sequence to have ended, since conditional
probabilities have returned to unconditional base-rate levels.

Notation for Sequential Diagrams

This book will introduce a notation for summarizing the sequences obtained. The diagram below illustrates this notation (see Figure 2.2). In the diagram, code A is the criterion code. The arrows between codes A and B, B and C,
and B and D indicate Z-scores greater than 1.96 and conditional probabilities
greater than .07. Where there is a branch at B the numbers near the arrows are
the conditional probabilities with respect to the criterion. Thus, $.326 = p(C|A;$
lag 2). The decision rules described in this section are used throughout this
book. They are helpful in coping with the major problem of sequential analysis,
which is the incredible overload of data that must be conveyed in some com-
prehensible form to the reader.

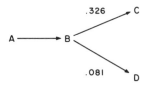

Figure 2.2 *Notation used in this book for inferred branching based on lag sequential
analysis. Probabilities represented are conditional with respect to the criterion code; A.*

APPENDIX 2.1

The information with K equally probable alternatives is $H = \log_2 K$, and each of the alternatives has probability $p = 1/K$; therefore, H can be rewritten as $H_1 = \log_2 1/P$. When the K alternatives are not equally probable, and each alternative has probability P_i, ($i = 1, 2, \ldots, k$), H is given by $H_1 = \Sigma_{i=1}^{k} P_i \log P_i^{-1} = -\Sigma_{i=1}^{k} P_i \log P_i$, which is the classic Shannon measure of information.

For digrams, H (digram) $= -\Sigma_i\, p(\text{digram}_i) \log p(\text{digram}_i)$, and the new approximation to H is $H_2 = H(\text{digram}) - H_1$. In general, the Nth order approximation is $H_N = H(N\text{-gram}) - H((N - 1)\text{-gram})$.

For computational purposes, if there are N total N-grams and N_i of the ith N-gram, the formula for $H(N\text{-gram})$ is

$$H(N\text{-gram}) = \log N - \frac{1}{N} \Sigma N_i \log N_i.$$

To calculate how many of a particular digram there are, we use a moving window as follows:

There are two (WB)'s above, one B–W, one W–W, and two B–B's. The window for the N-gram encloses N symbols.

Table 2.3 illustrates these calculations, and Figure 2.3 is a plot of the various estimates of the average information per symbol as a function of the order of estimation.

It can be shown that the reduction of information, $T_n = H_n - H_{n+1}$, given by each order of estimation can be used to test statistically the order of sequential constraint inherent in a sequence. It can be shown (Attneave, 1959, pp. 28–30) that $\chi^2 = 2(\log_e 2) k\, T_n = 1.3863\, k\, T_n$, where k is the number of symbols in the sequence ($= 203$ in our example), with $df = C^{n-1} x(C - 1)^2$, where C is the number of symbols in the sequence (which $= 2$ in our case).

TABLE 2.3
Calculation of Reduction of Information Provided by Each Assumption of Increasing Structure, Digram, Trigram, etc. (from Attneave, 1959, p. 23)

Tetragram	n_i	$n_i \log n_i$	Trigram	n_i	$n_i \log n_i$	Digram	n_i	$n_i \log n_i$	Symbol	n_i	$n_i \log n_i$
WWWW	3	4.755	WWW	19	80.711						
WWWB	16	64.000				WW	58	339.763			
WWBW	15	58.603	WWB	39	206.131						
WWBB	24	110.039							W	109	737.733
WBWW	16	64.000	WBW	20	86.439						
WBWB	4	8.000				WB	51	289.294			
WBBW	22	98.108	WBB	31	153.580						
WBBB	9	28.529									
BWWW	16	64.000	BWW	39	206.131						
BWWB	23	104.042				BW	50	282.193			
BWBW	4	8.000	BWB	11	38.054						
BWBB	7	19.651							B	91	592.209
BBWW	23	104.042	BBW	30	147.207						
BBWB	7	19.651				BB	41	219.660			
BBBW	9	28.529	BBB	11	38.054						
BBBB	2	2.000									
Sum	200	785.949	Sum	200	956.307	Sum	200	1130.910	Sum	200	1329.941

$\hat{H}$(tetragram)

$= 7.644 - \dfrac{1}{200} \times 785.949$

$= 7.31$

$\hat{H}$(trigram)

$= 7.644 - \dfrac{1}{200} \times 956.307$

$= 2.862$

$\hat{H}$(digram)

$= 7.644 - \dfrac{1}{200} \times 1130.910$

$= 1.989$

$\hat{H}_1 = \log n - \dfrac{1}{n} n_i \log n_i$

$= \log 200 - \dfrac{1}{200} \times 1329.941$

$= 7.644 - 6.649$

$= .995$

$\hat{H}_4 = \hat{H}$(tetragram) - H(trigram)

$= 3.714 - 2.862$

$= .852$

$\hat{H}_3 = \hat{H}$(trigram) - $\hat{H}$(digram)

$= 2.862 - 1.989$

$= .873$

$\hat{H}_2 = \hat{H}$(digram) - $\hat{H}_1$

$= 1.989 - .995$

$= .994$

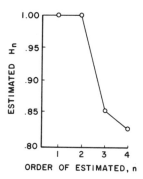

Figure 2.3 *Average information per symbol as a function of the inferred order of structure present in the sequence. (based on Attneave, 1959; p. 25. Reproduced with permission)*

CHAPTER 3

The Structure of Interaction

THE SEARCH FOR STRUCTURE

The most consistent set of investigations of pattern in family interaction has involved the simplest possible category system for describing interaction. A system that looks only at sequences of talk and silence requires no human observer and can be automatically measured. At first glance, one might think that such a system would provide an overly simplified summary of complex processes, but Jaffe and Feldstein (1970), using only talk and silence codes, reported a series of investigations on conversation between strangers that was surprisingly interesting in its ability to construct mathematical models of dialogue.

Strodtbeck (1951) found that three cultures in Southern Arizona (Navajo, Texan, and Mormon) had three distinctively different family decision-making styles. In his analysis of decision-making, he found patterns one would expect from anthropological descriptions of the three cultures. In the female-dominant Navajo culture, the husband moves in with his wife's parents after marriage, works for 7 years for her parents before he and his wife leave her parents' household, and property is in the wife's name. In this culture, the wife won 58% of Strodtbeck's decisions. In the more equalitarian Texan Anglo culture, the wife won 46% of the decisions. In the male-dominant Mormon culture, the wife won 41% of the decisions. Strodtbeck also found that the spouse who talked the most won most of the decisions (see Table 3.1).

Haley (1964) studied talk patterns in three-person (two parents and a child)

TABLE 3.1

Decisions Won and Talking Time for 34 Married Couples (from Strodtbeck, 1951)

Spouse who talked most	Spouse who won most	
	Husband	Wife
Husband	14	5
Wife	5	10

"disturbed" and "normal" families. The disturbed group of 40 families included those in which some member (a) was diagnosed schizophrenic; (b) had committed a delinquent act; or (c) had been referred for a school problem. Also included in the disturbed group were families in which a member sought help for "a neurotic problem" or in which the parents sought marriage or family therapy. The normal group was selected randomly using a high school directory. They were considered normal because they had not come to the attention of the community as having problems. Children ranged in age from 10 to 20 and were living at home with their natural parents.

Haley did not place importance on the tasks the families were given. The task situations used were (a) making decisions as a family (after choices had been made individually by each member) about such items as the choice of food for dinner or countries to visit if one makes a trip, the color of the next car to be purchased, and so on; and (b) making up composite stories by putting together the three cards of each of three sets of Thematic Apperception Test TAT cards. The ratio of agreement to disagreement is a useful index of the amount of conflict introduced by a task, and, using this measure, these tasks were found to be low-conflict tasks by Gottman, Notarius, Markman, Bank, Yoppi, and Rubin (1976).

The process measure that resulted in the greatest separation of disturbed and normal families on Haley's tasks was obtained by using a "Family Interaction Analyzer" devised by the Alto Scientific Company of Palo Alto. Using lavaliere microphones, the interaction analyzer automatically records the frequency with which each member's talk is immediately followed by that of another family member. When father speaks, for example, nothing happens until mother speaks; then a click is recorded on the father–mother (FM) counter.

Haley's process measure, called *R-deviation*, was the extent to which the sum of the percentage of speech in each of the six categories (FC, FM, MF, MC, CM, CF) deviated from what would be expected in a random talk pattern (16.66 in each category). Note that the R-deviation measure is a naive approximation to an information theory search for digram structure. Haley is not controlling for imbalance in the frequencies of M, C, and F. Haley hypothesized that one would expect to find greater rigidity, more limited response alternatives chosen, and, therefore, greater R-deviation scores in pathological families.

The results of this experiment are provocative (see Figure 3.1). Furthermore, Haley found that analyzing individual sequences of three, four, five, six, and seven speech patterns (for example, the series of three would be FMC, FMF,

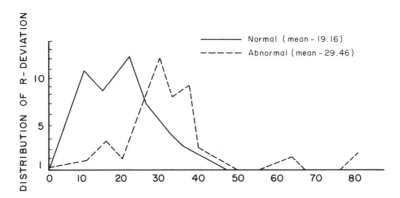

Figure 3.1 *Distributions of R-deviation for normal and abnormal families. (from Haley, 1964. Reproduced with permission)*

etc.) in terms of R-deviation produced significant but weaker differentiations of the two groups than the digram R-deviation. This finding is consistent with Jaffe and Feldstein's (1970) results that a first-order Markov model was an adequate fit to their data (see Gottman & Notarius, 1978, for a discussion of Markov models).

Haley's (1964) results did not extend to four-person families with two children, considered in a later study (Haley, 1967; selected on the same criteria as the 1964 study). In fact, if one reanalyzes Haley's results in the 1964 study for only those families with marital problems, there is a mean R-deviation of 21.45, which is not significantly different from the normal mean of 19.16, since the critical difference value of R-deviation is 4.42 for two speech sequences.

Waxler and Mishler proposed a T-statistic that may be a more useful measure than R-deviation with well and problematic family triads in four-person families. Using the task of the family's discussion of questionnaire items, Waxler and Mishler (1970) also did not succeed in replicating Haley's (1964) results. They suggested a procedure for controlling for relative participation rates and again found (as did Haley, 1967) that there was no difference in predictability of talk sequences. However, there was one important exception. "The exception occurs," they wrote, "when the parents of a schizophrenic child interact with that child (rather than with a well child from their own family). In this case, the sequence of *three* speakers is more predictable than that for normal families [p. 219]." Thus it may be that, with respect to potentially conflict-producing interaction, distressed families have developed structured interaction rules for family subgroups and that R-deviation (or Waxler and Mishler's T-statistic) is tapping this interaction structure.

Haley's (1964) three-person disturbed families may have ritualized the sequence of exchange to a great degree in order to avoid conflict. This hypothesis would be consistent with the Waxler and Mishler replication. High R-deviation scores for disturbed families or for disturbed triads in four-person families may tap this ritualized quality of interaction designed to avoid conflict.

It is typical, though not very functional, to assume that conflict-avoiding strategies are unhealthy. However, Raush *et al.* (1974) found a polite, conflict-avoiding style in couples who were functioning successfully. It may, in fact, be very functional for families with a schizophrenic child to develop ritualized modes of interaction, and the child may contribute to the development of these rules by selective reinforcement (see, for example, Patterson & Reid, 1970). It would seem essential to investigate the dynamics of the particular triads described by Waxler and Mishler by using more detailed content coding of these sequences.

The area of conflict-avoidance was studied more carefully in the tasks used by Ferreira and Winter (1968). They found that information exchange was greater in normal than in problem families and that there was less silence in normal families. However, they also found that, when each family member talked, the speech lasted longer in problem families, and there was less spontaneous agreement. This may suggest a "monologue–silence–monologue–silence" sequence for problem families in which each family member states an opinion with little engagement or subsequent follow-up by other members. Family members in problem families may, thus, be more isolated, and the group may be less cohesive. This hypothesis is consistent with Cheek and Anthony's (1970) result that there is a greater frequency of singular personal pronoun usage (less "we" or "us" phrases) in families with a schizophrenic member.

To summarize, it may be the case that *indices of the extent to which talk and silence patterns are ritualized will be high in distressed families and, specifically, in interactions with an identified patient in a distressed family.*

The Active–Passive Continuum

The research on talk and silence just reviewed can be considered in terms of an active–passive continuum, and the general findings are that nondistressed families are more active and more randomly patterned than distressed families. Jacob's (1975) review of family interaction in disturbed and normal families also suggests that in normal families people tend to interrupt one another more than they do in families with a schizophrenic member. Although Jacob concluded that these differences were not as clear in studies attempting to differentiate normal from disturbed nonschizophrenic families, we can, in general, conclude from our review *that nondistressed couples and families should be placed on the active end of an active–passive continuum and that greater activity is associated with less deviation from randomness.*

These findings are reminiscent of the Second Law of Thermodynamics that relates greater energy in a physical system with greater degrees of disorder. The Second Law of Thermodynamics also associates high energy (and, hence, less order and patterning) with the capacity of a system to undergo spontaneous change. In other words, systems that are highly patterned are more difficult to change than more randomly patterned ones.

Metaconcept about Interaction

This primitive search for pattern (using only talk and silence) in family and marital interaction therefore suggests that *the degree of patterning is itself an index of how poorly the system is functioning.* The major overarching construct is the amount of information that any act in a family adds to a sequence of acts, and the amount of information is less in distressed families. The amount of information added by an act is, thus, inversely related to the tightness of the interaction structure. The tighter the structure, the less information each new event provides; that is, the more certain we are of pattern and the less the information we expect at each point in the sequence. The amount of pattern is, thus, a "metaconcept" about interaction structure, and it is measured by the size of the Z-scores discussed in Chapter 2. The greater the reduction of uncertainty provided by conditional probabilities over unconditional probabilities, the greater the degree of patterning.

THE CONTENT OF THE PATTERNING

Description of Pattern Content through Codes

Although a simple talk–silence category system is useful as a first step in the search for pattern, more complex category systems are necessary to describe the *content* of the patterns. This category system for describing interactions is usually called the *coding system.*

The coding system is the most important aspect of studies analyzing family and marital interaction. It is the vehicle for summarizing the rich data of verbal and nonverbal behavior; therefore, any coding system is a data reduction device that is based on a set of assumptions about the nature of social interaction.

Units Used in Coding.   One important assumption concerns the way an interaction sequence is segmented for coding. Riskin and Faunce (1972) classified the variety of units that have been used for the analysis of family interaction. The coding unit may be an *act,* which is a grammatical sentence that expresses a simple idea. This unit was first used by Bales, but it is now used by other researchers who do not necessarily use the Bales Interaction Process Analysis coding system (for example, Mishler & Waxler, 1968). The *speech* is also used as a unit. It represents all the words between floor switches, that is, until another person begins speaking and has the floor. Special decisions are usually made for the case of simultaneous speech (Raush et al., 1974; Riskin & Faunce, 1970). Longer units, such as *idea, theme,* or *style,* also have been used. Weiss, Hops, and Patterson (1973) have observers code without a typed transcript for 30-second blocks, and they then collapse codes into *behavioral units.* A behavioral unit continues until a new code occurs; hence, the unit is defined by a shift in code, and so no code can follow itself. The behavioral unit can last a sentence or a paragraph, or it can be a brief nonverbal gesture.

Categories Used in Coding.   Coding systems also vary in the categories they use, and these categories are often a function of the task the family or couple is given by the experimenter. Some coding systems have been developed for the study of decision making (Olson & Ryder, 1970; Winter & Ferreira, 1969) and some for clinical applications (Alexander, 1973a,b; Weiss et al., 1973). As a function of our current approach to studying family interaction, nearly all coding systems have been designed to study conflict resolution; there are very few exceptions.

Because of the variety of units and code categories, the comparison of results of studies that have used different coding systems is difficult. Riskin and Faunce (1972) pointed out that Mishler and Waxler (1968) concluded that normal families scored high on "fragmentation," whereas Wynne and Singer (1963) concluded that "fragmentation" was characteristic of families with schizophrenic children. The two research groups had slightly different meanings for "fragmentation," but, for an even more precise category such as disagreement, Lennard and Bernstein (1969) use several fairly complex categories, whereas Riskin and Faunce (1970) have a single category. Investigators have rarely published their coding schemes with specific examples and instructions, and the summaries different investigators provide for categories such as "acknowledgment" seem the same, when actually they are often entirely different (see Riskin & Faunce, 1972, pp. 397–399).

A delicate balance must be reached in the construction of coding categories. Fine discriminations may be accomplished with high reliability, but very little data reduction may be the result. For example, Birdwhistell (1952) reported that it takes several hundred hours to code 1 minute of film with his coding system, and the same is true for research that follows Hall's (1974) proxemic handbook. Hall's codes, in fact, are cartoon sketches of minute movements of body and face, which results in a data overload. On the other hand, coding categories may be so broad that they lose their descriptive power. For example, it is only the ingenious writing ability of Raush et al. (1974) that makes it possible to understand their findings when complex codes such as "cognitive" include such diverse subcodes as "giving information," "withholding information," "agreeing with the other's statement," and "denying the validity of other's argument with or without the use of counterarguments." The summary code "cognitive" is simply too large and thus not functional enough to provide even a simple journalistic description of what happened in a particular coding unit. It should be possible to reconstruct the gist of an interaction from a sequence of code symbols.

Evidence Indicating Differences in Marital and Family Interaction

In reviewing the research findings on coding systems of family and marital interaction, we need to keep in mind a basic question about marital and family interaction: "What, if anything, is different about the way people interact in marriages and families?" This is partly a question about whether the nature of social interaction is different in groups that have a history and partly a question of whether families, as a particular kind of group with a history, are especially distinct.

Problems in Using the IPA. Researchers initially assumed that the versatile category system developed by Bales (1950), called Interaction Process Analysis (IPA), could be adapted for the study of interaction in families. However, many investigators found that too much judgment was involved in coding statements made by families, thus making it difficult to establish decent levels of agreement between independent observers. Winter and Ferreira (1967), Waxler and Mishler (1965), and Raush et al. (1974) reached the same conclusion in separate attempts to apply the IPA. For example, Winter and Ferreira wrote:

> We are forced to conclude that the Bales IPA system in its present form is not suited for work with families. Even with presumably adequate training of raters, neither we nor Waxler and Mishler have been able to achieve reassuring reliability levels. The major difficulty seems to be that the categories are multidimensional in meaning, and the raters are required to classify the items on the basis of higher order inferences. . . .
>
> In addition to the problem of shared similarity of behavior in families, one might also mention the subtle pattern of nonverbal and verbal communication within a family, and the immensely rich contextual historical background against which a remark by one family member is judged by the others [1967, pp. 170–171].

In addition to unreliability, the problem in applying the IPA was that it seemed to these researchers that family interaction was different from group interaction—it was somehow more private and harder to judge.

History and No-History Groups. There is, in fact, some evidence to suggest that interaction in groups of people who are well acquainted differs markedly from the interaction of strangers. Hall and Williams (1966) found that intact groups of management trainees who had a history had different styles of decision making and conflict resolution and made different types of decisions than did groups with no history outside the laboratory. They used a task called "12 angry men" in which subjects, after seeing 38 minutes of the feature film by that title, had to predict the order in which other jurors in the film will change their verdict from guilty to innocent. This task makes it possible to compute an accuracy criterion as the discrepancy between the person's rank order and the true rank order. Subjects completed the task individually and then arrived at a group consensual ordering.

The individual rankings of the two kinds of groups showed equal levels of expertise, and the two types of groups did not differ on the time it took to reach a decision. However, the final scores of the established groups were superior to the scores of the ad hoc groups. All groups improved significantly over their average individual member's pre-scores, but "established groups tended to improve more when there was conflict among members than when there was fairly close agreement, while ad hoc groups did not differ significantly as a function of level of conflict [p. 217]."

Hall and Williams concluded that "it appears that ad hoc groups respond to conflict in a manner designed to bring about compromise and, thereby, to short-circuit disagreements. Established groups, on the other hand, seem to view conflict as symptomatic of unresolved issues and adopt procedures designed to bring about constructive resolution of differences [p. 21]." The Hall and Williams study suggests that a social psychology based on the study of stranger interaction may be limited in its ability to generalize to relationships with a history.

Interaction Distinctive to Marriage. There is additional evidence that social interaction varies with acquaintanceship. Ryder (1968) asked the question, "What, if anything, is demonstrably distinctive in interaction between husbands and wives?" Using a decision-making task (The Color Matching Test), he paired husbands with their wives or with female married strangers, and he found that:

> Husbands are more likely to take the lead in conversations with their wives than with strangers, suggesting more task orientation with wives. Wives laugh less with spouses than with strangers; but they also use more disapproval of spouse, as do husbands. . . . The differences between married and split dyads seems much better described by noting that Ss treat strangers more gently, and generally more nicely than they do their spouses [p. 237].

The effect was replicated by Birchler et al. (1975) for a high conflict problem-solving task (the IMC) and for simple conversation in a comparison of stranger dyads and nondistressed couples.

Winter, Ferreira, and Bowers (1973) used their standard decision-making task to study interaction in married and unrelated couples. Replicating Ryder (1968) and Birchler et al. (1975), they found that "unrelated couples were more polite to each other than were married couples [p. 91]." They also found that married couples intruded upon and interrupted each other more often than unrelated couples and that unrelated strangers listened respectfully to one another, whereas married couples were often rude. Also, interruptions in married couples decreased subsequent talk by the spouse who was interrupted, whereas in strangers interruptions increased subsequent talk.

There seems to be something different in these results and those obtained by Hall and Williams. Conflict in marriages may not always be quite as productive as conflict was for established groups of managerial trainees. Familiarity in marriage may breed some vulnerability to disagreement.

Parent–Child Interaction. These findings on interaction between spouses also hold for parent–child interaction. Halverson and Waldrop (1970) studied the behavior of mothers toward their own and toward other preschool children. They found that, "while maternal behavior tended to be consistent with both children, mothers used significantly more positive, encouraging statements with other children and significantly more negative sanctions with their own children [p. 839]." Unfortunately, from their data it is not possible to tell how the children differed in behavior *they* initiated with strangers and with their own mothers.

The results of Halverson and Waldrop, however, are consistent with a general hypothesis that *human behavior in marriages and families is generally less positive and less polite than it is with strangers.*

It thus appears that positiveness is the first dimension that must be included in any basic conceptual model about the content of interactional structure in marriages and families, and we now turn toward a review of the literature with respect to this important dimension.

PATTERNS OF POSITIVENESS

Difficulties in Operationalizing Positiveness

The increase in complexity introduced by this first dimension— positiveness—is astronomical, because positiveness is so difficult a dimension to operationalize. There are two difficulties. First, messages sent by one family member to another are not intended for strangers; observers are always strangers. As Winter and Ferreira pointed out in the quotation reproduced earlier in this chapter, these problems involve "the subtle pattern of nonverbal and verbal communication within a family, and the immensely rich contextual historical background against which a remark by one family member is judged by others [p. 171]."

A second difficulty in coding positiveness involves the separation of verbal and nonverbal behavior. For example, Schuham and Freshley (1971) employed two coders experienced in using the Bales IPA to score the interaction of four families using either only verbal information or verbal plus nonverbal. Two totally different profiles of the families were obtained under these two conditions of information availability. This review on positiveness will begin by ignoring the distinction between verbal and nonverbal behavior and then discussing the coding of positiveness specifically from nonverbal behavior.

Positiveness in General

There is considerable evidence to suggest that the interactions of distressed and nondistressed couples and families can be discriminated using a simple measure, the ratio of agreement to disagreement. The ratio is generally higher in nondistressed populations (Cheek, 1964; Lennard & Bernstein, 1969; Mishler & Waxler, 1968; Riskin & Faunce, 1970). In their decade review paper, Riskin and

Faunce (1972) wrote: "There appears to be a general opinion that a ratio of more than 'one' is healthy, i.e., families should have more agreements than disagreements for healthy functioning [p. 402]."

Similar results have been obtained for married couples. Bircher et al. (1975), using the Marital Interaction Coding System, combined their categories of positive verbal and nonverbal behavior and negative verbal and nonverbal behavior. They were able to discriminate distressed from nondistressed couples on the mean rate per minute of negative codes in both a problem solving (IMC) task ($t = 1.724, p < .05$) and in conversation ($t = 1.982, p < .05$). They were also able to discriminate distressed from nondistressed couples on positive codes, but only on the problem-solving task ($t = 2.164, p < .025$). These findings are consistent with other research on family interaction. There is more humor and laughter in nondistressed families (Mishler & Waxler, 1968; Riskin & Faunce, 1970), and there is more support and less defensiveness in nondistressed marriages and families (Alexander, 1973a,b; Caputo, 1963; Cheek, 1964; Mishler & Waxler, 1968; Riskin & Faunce, 1970).

Jacobson (1977) reported an increase in marital adjustment scores of positive Marital Interaction Coding System (MICS) codes and a decrease of negative MICS codes after therapy with five couples; changes in marital adjustment were maintained 1 year following; five control group couples did not change on the MICS codes at post-test.

In a study of couples' behaviors at home, Weiss, Hops, and Patterson (1973) computed a pleases to displeases ratio using a behavioral checklist kept daily by couples as an outcome measure of their marital therapy program. They reported that the seven couples seen in their program (who were shown to have improved on other variables) increased their pleases to displeases ratio. Wills et al. (1974) showed that pleases and displeases were able to account for substantial portions of the variance in a daily global one-item rating of marital satisfaction in seven nondistressed married couples. They also reported that pleases and displeases are essentially unrelated, and they found no relationship when these events were further classified as instrumental (e.g., helping with household chores) or affectional. Affectional event records were kept with a wrist counter worn by each spouse, since these events were considered too brief to be remembered for subsequent recordings on a checklist. Wills et al. (1974) found that instrumental and affectional behaviors over 14 days accounted for 65% of the variance in the global daily rating of satisfaction but that pleasurable behaviors accounted for only 25% of the variance. They also concluded that "husbands tended to emphasize the instrumental dimension and wives the affectional [p. 807]."

Alexander (1973a) found that parent–child interactions in families without a delinquent child were more positive ("supportive"), or less negative ("defensive"), than in families with a delinquent child. Family therapy designed to change the interaction from defensive to supportive produced impressive results on the delinquency of both targeted children and untargeted siblings, as compared to control groups (see Alexander & Parsons, 1973, and Parsons & Alexander, 1973). Stuart (1971) reported that interactions between parents and their delinquent children were three times as negative as in matched control families and that delinquent behavior decreased when the balance of positive and negative interactions was restored.

To summarize, in reviewing literature on family interaction, there is remarkable consistency in the general conclusion that *distressed couples and families are far more negative to one another than nondistressed couples and families, and there is some (though less) support for the conclusion that distressed couples and families are less positive to one another than their nondistressed counterparts.*

Coding Positiveness from Nonverbal Behavior

The following review of nonverbal behavior will suggest that it is possible to code separately positiveness in interaction by using nonverbal behavior. For some reason the vast research literature on nonverbal behavior has been largely ignored by researchers in the study of family interaction. Perhaps this is partly a reaction against the Bales IPA. The Bales IPA codebook stated that "All kinds of behavior—overt, skeletal, verbal, gestural, expressive, are included, provided that the observer can assign a meaning to the behavior in terms of the categories [1950, p. 7]." However, investigators such as Mishler and Waxler (1968) created an "expressiveness dimension" that ignored nonverbal behavior. They wrote:

> The point of view used to make a judgment about affect is the point of view of the common culture, not the affective meaning implied by the context of the interaction or the tone of voice used. . . . For example, when the verb 'to like' is used in a sentence this is coded as positive affect, no matter in what context it occurs or what tone of voice is used [pp. 366–367].

Mishler and Waxler thus preferred to rely on the content of messages rather than on the manner of their nonverbal delivery. This decision thus ignored voice tone, facial expressions, body cues, and movement. The decision was characteristic of family interaction research, and it may be responsible for the schism between the literature on nonverbal behavior and the literature on family interaction.

This avoidance of nonverbal behavior is unfortunate, but we must begin the review of the literature with a word of caution. Conclusions will be tentative, since the research on nonverbal behavior, when it considers interaction at all, is based on brief interactions between strangers; thus, findings need to be used primarily to generate hypotheses for coding nonverbal behavior in couples and families.

In Mehrabian's (1972) research on nonverbal behavior, the positiveness dimension contained a cluster of behaviors he called *immediacy*. Immediacy includes behaviors that increase physical proximity and sensory stimulation between interactants, such as touching, forward lean, eye contact, facial observation, and an orientation of the torso toward the other person. These behaviors are positively correlated with positive evaluation. This conclusion is restricted to the range of social situations and acquaintanceship studied by Mehabian, that is, brief interactions between strangers in a waiting room; hence, Mehrabian's situations may have limited generality. Couples and families resolving a problem will probably exhibit a greater range of emotions than strangers in a waiting room situation; we are likely to believe that eye contact is positive, but we are more likely to observe a hostile glare in families than in the polite interaction of strangers. Although a glare will increase immediacy, it is not likely to be evaluated positively by its recipient. Therefore, immediacy cues will be good only as rough guides for observers to use in judging whether behavior in families is positive. This is one example of the caution that needs to be exercised in generalizing from the literature on nonverbal behavior.

Despite these cautions, an examination of nonverbal behavior will, undoubtedly, suggest modifications of previous coding systems of marital interaction that have integrated some selected nonverbal behaviors with verbal behaviors. Nonverbal behaviors are implicit in many coding systems of marital and family interaction. For example, Weiss, Hops, and Patterson (1973) use two codes in coding marital interaction, *problem description* and *complaint*. It is likely that the verbal content of both complaints and problem descriptions are the same but that complaint would receive a negative nonverbal code because it would be a problem described with an angry, blaming, or whining voice tone, sour facial expression, and, perhaps, a pointing finger. Similarly, *criticize* and *disagree* in the Weiss, Hops, and Patterson system would probably be distinguished by the nonverbal code of a message.

Our review will use a guideline for discussing components of positivity suggested by Mehrabian's (1972, p. 182) equation for the transmission of emotional messages in his study of brief interaction between strangers. The equation is as follows:

$$\text{Total affect} = 7\% \text{ verbal} + 38\% \text{ vocal} + 55\% \text{ facial.}$$

Although body position and body movement cues are not represented in Mehrabian's regression equation, these cues are implicated as part of positiveness in other reviews of nonverbal behavior. With this modification, the elements in Merabian's regression equation constitute a good way of organizing the literature on components of nonverbal behavior, and the following review is, therefore, divided into sections on the face, the voice, and the body.

The Face.   Obviously, not every movement of a facial muscle is intended to convey a message. There are brief twitches, tics, and responses to internal events, such as gas pains, that result in some kind of facial display indicative only of some brief biological autoinvolvement. One useful way of organizing facial displays is in terms of the permanence of the display.

STATIC FEATURES. Coders of facial expression will need to be aware of the cultural stereotypes they possess that result in impression formation, and they will need to calibrate their coding of a face in motion to zero-out impressions based on static features. There are static features of every face that may or may not be related to a person's character but are certainly related to the formation of first impressions based on the stereotypes in our culture. Table 3.2 presents some of these stereotypes, taken from popular writing on reading character from the face. Many of these stereotypes go back to the writings of Aristotle. These stereotypes are reminiscent of Sheldon's work on body types. For example, one book reviewed in preparing Table 3.2 suggested that if a person with full lips and large eyes is on time for a date, this demonstrates extreme interest; the stereotype is that the sensuous person tends to be disorganized and inefficient, so any sign of following a schedule has extra meaning.

TABLE 3.2

Cultural Stereotyped Impression of Static Facial Features

Feature	Quality	Impression
Shape of face	1. Vertical oval	1. The indoor type
	2. Square	2. The rugged type
	3. Horizontal oval	3. Tolerant, happy
Eyes	1. Can't see whole iris	1. Emotionality
	2. Can see whole iris	2. Hidden emotionality
	3. Eyes far apart	3. High tolerance
	4. Eyes close together	4. Low tolerance
	5. Small eyes	5. Feelings deeply buried
	6. Large eyes	6. Expressiveness
	7. Turned down lines	7. Melancholy
	8. Extra white between iris and lower eyelid	8. Weighed down with problems
	9. Shifty eyes	9. Deceitful
	10. Eyes slant downward to outer corner	10. Critical: The inspector
	11. Can see much of upper eyelid	11. High action & impulsive & low analytical
	12. Can't see much of upper eyelid	12. Analytical
	13. Lines in corners of eyes fan out symmetrically	13. Laugh lines, happiness, humor
	14. Lines in corners of eyes fan down toward mouth	14. Appreciation for rhetoric
	15. Lines from nose grooved and pronounced down around mouth	15. Talker (lawyer type)
Lips and lines	1. Tight, thin lips	1. Efficient, business-like, not wasteful, concise, & terse
	2. Full lips	2. Generous, sensuous
	3. Mouth drops at corners	3. Sour puss, pessimistic
	4. Mouth and eye lines down	4. Depression
	5. Mouth turned up at corners	5. Optimism
Brow	1. Furrowed horizontally	1. Worried
	2. Furrowed vertically	2. Suspicious
Nose	1. Hawk nose convex	1. Good general and administrator
	2. Concave nose	2. Nurturant, helpful
Arc of eyebrow	1. High upsweep	1. Dramatic
	2. Down sweep	2. Esthetic
	3. Eyebrows close to eyes	3. Affable
	4. Eyebrows far from eyes	4. Discriminative, critical
	5. Ledge above eyebrows	5. Methodical, concern for detail

Clearly, it is important for coders of nonverbal behavior to be aware of their cultural stereotypes and to avoid using these perceptions of the static features of the face for coding the positivity of nonverbal behavior.

THE FACE IN MOTION.   Moods can be conveyed by features that resemble an emotional disposition. A mood will usually sustain only some of the features of an emotional expression of the mood. For example, if someone is in an irritable mood, we will notice only some of the features of anger, such as a tightened jaw, tightened, compressed lips, or brows drawn down and together. In an irritable mood that continues for some time, the full facial expression of anger will flash on and off periodically (Ekman & Friesen, 1975).

Expressions that last longer than emotional displays may not be moods but, instead, communications of another sort. An example of this is the exaggerated expression, or pantomine. For example, at a party a look of boredom flashed to a spouse means, "Rescue me from this dull conversation." A look of tiredness or pantomined yawn may mean, "Let's leave." These messages have meanings different from their simple meaning as facial expressions.

The study of facial expressions has been discredited in psychology since a review by Bruner and Tagiuri appeared in the 1954 *Handbook of Social Psychology*. However, Ekman, Friesen, and Ellsworth (1972) critically reevaluated the evidence before and since the Bruner–Tagiuri review. They made several points. First, the research evidence was misrepresented and distorted by Bruner and Tagiuri. Ekman *et al.* (1972) wrote that "Bruner and Tagiuri were factually incorrect and misleading. They enhanced the credibility of negative findings on accuracy by saying that all of those experiments utilized photographs of real emotion elicited in the laboratory. This is true only of Landis and Sherman [p. 78]." Second, the studies in which subjects could not accurately identify emotion from facial expressions suffered from several methodological weaknesses. For example, early investigators of facial expressions expected to find an isomorphism between emotionally arousing situations and universal facial expressions. However, several factors may intervene to ruin this one-to-one relationship. For example, not everyone laughs at a standard set of jokes, nor reacts with fear to the threat of shock. Therefore, the assumption that a particular experimental event will produce the same internal state in all subjects is unwarranted. Third, in some studies (Landis, 1924, 1929) the subjects were colleagues of the experimenter, and he marked their faces with burnt cork to highlight facial features. They were, thus, aware of what was being measured, and in most situations (such as suddenly placing excrement under their noses) they produced the same expression—a pained, polite smile. Since subjects were asked to pick out which situation produced which photograph, it is predictable that they did no better than chance. Fourth, the situations followed one another in rapid succession, which may have contributed to subjects' producing blends of various affects. Ekman *et al.* (1972) show that, when these methodological problems are controlled, subjects can accurately identify facial expressions. This result has been replicated in many investigations by several researchers (for example, Izard, 1971).

Most facial expressions are blends of a few basic emotions. Ekman and Friesen (1975) listed six basic emotions, and Izard (1971) listed nine.

Ekman and Friesen (1975) discussed three basic areas of the face: the *brow area*, the *eye area*, and the *lower face*. They suggested that it is possible to have blends of various emotions by combining parts of different emotions displayed on different regions of the face. For example, an angry husband who wants to appear reasonable to his wife may display a pained grin, which is a combination of an angry brow and a slight smile. A detailed summary of Ekman and Friesen's work on the various areas of the face is presented in Table 3.3.

Although it may seem easy to use Ekman, Friesen, and Tomkins' (1971) Facial Affect Scoring Technique (FAST) with videotapes of families, it must be pointed out that *Ekman and Friesen obtained reasonable levels of reliability only on still photographs of trained actors posing pure emotions*. These expressions are dramatically pronounced, and, using a similar set of photographs, Izard (1971) found that even most 2-year-olds do very well in recognizing these pure emotions.

Most of the facial expressions of couples on our videotapes are neutral or attentive, and the remainder are affect blends rather than the extreme emotions in the Ekman and Friesen study. At first glance, this may make it seem difficult to use Ekman and Friesen's coding system, but that is not the case. There are several reasons why this is true. First, there is an incredible degree of redundancy on videotape, which contains 40 frames per second. Since most facial expressions last several seconds, there are a large number of frames per expression. Furthermore, an expression builds up in intensity, reaches a crest, and then dies out. It is, thus, easier to code the face from videotape than from the still photographs Ekman and Friesen use. Also, the coding system used in this book does not make the fine discriminations that Ekman and Friesen make. Despite the complexity of affect blends, observers can agree at high levels of reliability by using a more subjective coding scheme with only three codes—positive, negative, and neutral—and by using cue words to denote facial expressions, such as those reproduced in Table 3.4.

The Voice. The voice is as important a channel of emotional expression as is the face. There is no set of physical cues that can be listed as isomorphic to adjectives that describe emotional content in the voice. Nonetheless, it is remarkable that human observers can agree on emotional tone even when they cannot hear the content of the speech, either because it has been electronically filtered or because the alphabet or nonsense syllables compose the content (Davitz & Davitz, 1959).

Emotional content in the voice has generally not been coded from the actual speech of interacting people. Because verbal content and vocal cues have been varied separately, actors have usually read programmed phrases

TABLE 3.3

Emotions and the Three Areas of the Face

Emotions and Subtypes	Brow	Eyes	Lower Face
Surprise			
1. Questioning surprise (has neutral mouth)	Eyebrows curved and high Brow furrowed horizontally	Wide White of eye showing below the iris	Jaw drops Relaxed open mouth
2. Astonished surprise (has neutral brow)			
3. Dazed surprise (has neutral eyes)			
Fear			
1. Only fear brow or mouth connotes worry or apprehension	Raised and straightened corners of brow drawn together	Upper eyelid raised, lower eyelid tense Eyes opened and tense	Mouth open but lips not relaxed Tension in upper lip Corners of lips may be drawn back
2. Apprehensive fear differs from horrified, frozen fear—Shock			
Disgust			
1. Disgust	Eyebrows are down	The opening of the eye is narrowed, producing lines and folds below the eye	Upper lip is raised Tip of nose changes Lower lip slightly forward Nose wrinkled Cheeks are raised
2. Contempt			
Anger	Eyebrows drawn down and together Brow lowered No horizontal wrinkles unless they are permanent	Lids are tensed Eye seems to stare out Upper eyelid is lowered	Two types of mouth: lips pressed together or open, square mouth depends on whether person is speaking or trying to gain control
Happiness	Not necessarily involved in this expression	Cheek is raised Crowsfeet wrinkling Eyes not important Lower eyelid has wrinkles below it	Corners of lips drawn back and slightly up Intensity related to amount of teeth showing Nasolabial grooves visible
Sadness	Inner corners of the eyebrows are raised and may be drawn together Sadness triangle between eyebrow and upper eyelid	Raised lower lid increases sadness expression Gaze is often down	Corners of lips down Lips will be loose and trembling if person is near crying or trying to hold it back

TABLE 3.4

Cue Words for Coding Affect in the Face

Positive Face	Negative Face
Smile	Frown
Laughter	Sneer
Empathetic face	Fear face
Head nod	Cry
Eye contact	Mocking laughter
	Smirk
	Angry face
	Disgust
	Glare

with different contents. Two major methods have been used to code vocal cues—the ignore-content method and the electronic filtering method. Instructing coders to ignore content has been shown to be largely, but not entirely, successful. Overall, more weight is given to vocal cues than to verbal content; for example, vocal cues accounted for 1.39 times the variance in judgments than did verbal content in one study (Zahn, 1975).

Electronic filtering removes all cycles greater than a certain frequency; although the literature is not consistent about the cutoff frequency, the most common cutoffs are 400 CPS and 250 CPS. Electronic filtering is usually called *content filtering* in the literature, but such labeling draws a conclusion that has yet to be tested. The assumption inherent in this term is that emotional content remains unchanged by electronic filtering. However, there may be considerable emotional content in the higher frequencies or in oscillations from lower to filtered higher frequencies that could be lost because of electronic filtering. A further drawback of electronic filtering is that most investigators report that, with increased coding experience, coders can eventually recognize the content of the speech; most investigators instruct coders to ignore this content. A variable that has not been described in the literature on electronic filtering is the slope of the filter, that is, the amount of energy removed from the voice beyond cutoff frequencies. A 3db filter is inadequate; a 20db filter removes most of the energy. With a 20db filter our (Gottman and associates) experience is that we can still discern the content, but we can train ourselves to ignore it. However, with this filter there appears to be some distortion of emotional content. Crying is often lost, but anger and depression are not. This may be because anger and depression cues involve intensity and tempo as well as pitch. In general, the decision about whether to use electronic filtering or merely to ignore content remains unresolved. If the coding involves only judgments of positive, negative, and neutral (which is most common in this literature), then the methods would probably give similar results.

In a study of the complexity of cues in judgment of emotional content from vocal information, Scherer (1974) used a Moog synthesizer to create voice-like sounds and investigated whether a specific set of cues in the sounds were associated with emotions by listeners. Some of his results were:

Happiness	Moderate amplitude variation
Fear	Extreme amplitude variation
Happiness, surprise	Extreme pitch variation
Anger, fear, surprise	Pitch contour up
Sadness	Pitch contour down
Sadness, boredom	Pitch low
Anger, fear, surprise	Pitch high
Boredom, disgust, sadness	Tempo slow
Pleasantness	Tempo moderately fast
Fear, anger, surprise	Tempo very fast
Disgust	Tones atonal or minor key
Anger	Tones minor
Happiness	Tones in major key
Fear, surprise	Rhythmic
Boredom	Arhythmic

Scherer's complex results suggest that some cues are likely to be unaffected by electronic filtering, whereas other cues are likely to be affected (e.g., major–minor key judgments, pitch contours).

Although the evidence is scant, judgments of emotional content in vocal cues with verbal content electronically filtered have been shown to have some predictive validity. For example, judgments of anger in a doctor's voice in an interview, electronically filtered, were excellent predictors of whether or not alcoholic patients later sought treatment (Milmoe, Rosenthal, Blane, Chafetz, & Wolf, 1967).

Another important aspect about the voice is speech disturbance. There are two kinds of speech errors: Errors such as "ah" or "um" or "er" have been called *ah-disturbances,* and other speech errors are *non-ah disturbances.* Examples of non-ah disturbances are sentence change in the middle of a sentence, repetition, stuttering, omissions, slips of the tongue, and intruding incoherent sounds. Non-ah disturbances seem generally to be related to a speaker's tension, whereas ah-disturbances are requests for thinking time and for wanting to keep the floor of conversation while thinking (Knapp, 1972).

The Body.   Unfortunately, the body is a far less reliable channel of expression. For example, it is subject to many situational, ethnic, and cultural influences. Efron (1941) found that Jewish immigrants are more likely to use their hands to emphasize a point, whereas Italian immigrants use their hands to describe the shape of the object they are talking about. Cultural groups vary a great deal in how close their members stand to the other persons when talking or in how much they touch (Argyle, 1969). In our culture, for example, the distance from the elbow to the hand is as close as most persons feel comfortable in standing to others at parties. A move closer than this will be taken as an invasion of personal space, and the other person will usually eventually back up (Hall, 1969).

Despite these problems with coding positivity from body cues, there are some useful cues. Mehrabian's immediacy behaviors are those that increase sensory stimulation between people. These behaviors include physical proximity, touching, eye contact, a forward lean of the body rather than a reclining position, and an orientation of the torso toward rather than away from the listener. Immediacy behaviors were related to the positiveness dimension in strangers. However, it may be that the set of nonverbal behaviors on a relaxation–tension continuum, which are related to status in stranger interaction (higher status people assume more relaxed postures than lower status people), are related to a positiveness dimension in marital family interaction. With families, relaxation may simply indicate closeness. The cluster of relaxation behaviors includes arm and leg position asymmetry, recline or sideways lean, and hand and neck relaxation. An arms akimbo position (arms folded across the chest) that is symmetrical would indicate tension and would thus be coded negative.

To summarize, *it is likely that positiveness can be coded separately from the content of messages by using nonverbal cues.* A second dimension that has received a great deal of attention in social interaction theory is the dimension of *reciprocity.* The word "reciprocity" has, in fact, been so appealing to researchers that it has been defined in two different ways. The following discussion will review the concept and attempt to sharply define it as a dimension in the search for structure in the social interaction of couples and families.

A REVIEW OF LITERATURE ON RECIPROCITY

Contingency-Based Reciprocity

In literature on social interaction in nonhumans, the term *reciprocity* emphasizes the contingent nature of the interaction between two conspecifics (for example, see Wilson, 1975, pp. 120–121 on reciprocal altruism). This means that, if we know that organism Y has given behavior A to organism X, there is a greater probability that organism X will, at some later time, give behavior A to organism Y than if the prior event had not occurred.

Brazelton, Koslowski, and Main (1974) discussed the origins of reciprocity in a paper describing the cycle of inattention, initiation, orientation, attention, acceleration, excitement, deceleration, withdrawal, and turning away in mother–infant interaction. In their description of the dyads in their study, they specified what they meant by "reciprocity":

> One of our mothers was particularly striking in her capacity to subside as [her infant] decreased his attention to her. She relaxed back in her chair smiling softly, reducing other activity such as vocalizing and moving, waiting for him to return. When he did look back, she began slowly to add behavior on behavior, as if she were feeling out how much he could master.

> She also sensed his need to reciprocate. She vocalized then waited for his
> response. When she smiled, she waited until he smiled before she began to
> build up her own smiling again [p. 67].

The reciprocal mother, thus, does not continue until the infant returns her
smiling, and, therefore, the infant's smiling increases the probability of subsequent smiling by the mother. We see then that "reciprocity" as defined by
Brazelton et al. (1974) is identical to the definition used with nonhumans, as
described previously. In fact, this is the ubiquitous sense of the term *reciprocity*
in literature on infant–caretaker interaction (see Bell, 1974, p. 7), namely, that
reciprocity involves one person's behavior's changing the probability of subsequent behavior by the other. Reciprocity is, thus, a *probability change* concept.

Noncontingency-Based Reciprocity

The use of the term *reciprocity* by social learning theorists is considerably
more complex. Patterson and Reid (1970) wrote. " 'Reciprocity' describes
dyadic interaction in which persons A and B reinforce each other, at an equitable rate. In this interaction, positive reinforcers maintain the behavior of both
persons [p. 133]." There are several components in this use of the term reciprocity. It is apparently still possible in this definition to judge reciprocity from the
interactions of one dyad. This is consistent with the use of the term in other
literatures. A seemingly new addition is the term *reinforcer,* but, by definition,
for a behavior emitted by one person in the dyad to be a reinforcer, it must first
follow the behavior of the other person, and, second, it must alter the probability of that behavior's taking place. Hence, the two definitions of reciprocity are
equivalent so far. However, the notion of equitable rates is a new concept, and
Patterson and Reid (1970) further explicate this idea as follows:

> [Reciprocity] . . . would require that, over a series of interactions, two
> persons reinforce or punish each other for approximately the same propor-
> tion of behaviors. For example, if person A reinforces B for 50 percent of the
> interactions which B has with A, then A, in turn, will *receive* about the same
> proportion of positive reinforcers from B [p. 140].

This concept is really one of *similar rates* of positive behaviors in the two
members of the dyad, and *this concept is logically independent of the notion of
contingency* that is central to other uses of the term reciprocity. The similar rate
idea is one that Patterson and Reid called "social economics" (p. 139) in
referring to behavior exchange theory (Thibaut & Kelley, 1959).
     Stuart (1969) had a similar concept in mind when he described the *quid
pro quo* arrangement. He wrote:

> In effect, a quid pro quo or "something for something" arrangement under-
> lies successful marriage (Jackson, 1965, p. 591). The exchange of rewards in

a marriage may be viewed as a quasi-legal contract affording distinct safeguards to each partner. Whenever one partner to a reciprocal interaction unilaterally rewards the other, he does so with the confidence that he will be compensated in the future [p. 675].

In addition to the difference between a *rate matching* definition and a *probability change* definition, the time periods involved in the two definitions are vastly different. Brazelton *et al.* (1974) referred to a more moment-to-moment definition, whereas Stuart (1969) proposed the following illustration: "For example, if the husband agrees to entertain his wife's parents for a weekend, he does so with the expectation that his wife will accompany him on a weekend fishing trip at some time in the future [p. 675]."

Nonequivalence of the Two Definitions

Social learning theorists have at times discussed the concept of reciprocity as a probability change definition but measured it by rate matching. For example, Azrin, Naster, and Jones (1973) wrote:

The strategy may be summarized as "reinforce the reinforcer (person)." . . . Since the nature of the reinforcing interactions is changeable, each partner must continuously rediscover the reinforcers. Secondly, *the relationship must be contingent:* the reinforcers are to be given when, but only when, reinforcers are received. This contingent relation is adequately described by the term "reciprocity," a concept which was also central in Stuart's (1969) marital counseling procedure [p. 367; emphasis added].

Weiss, Birchler, and Vincent (1974) described their intervention procedure with married couples as a means for developing *"mutual gain or reciprocity"* [p. 321; emphasis added] but never assessed it by probability change methods.

The two definitions of reciprocity are not equivalent. It is easier to see this if we consider nonsocial behaviors, such as eating or typing. A husband may eat or type at a rate similar to his wife's without any contingency between these two activities; they may, for example, have similar physical tempos. In this case, we would merely report that eating or typing took place at similar rates, not that they were reciprocal. If a mother smiles at a rate similar to her infant, their interaction may, nonetheless, be totally unconnected and noncontingent; the mother's smiling and her infant's smiling would be considered reciprocal only if they were somehow connected in the probability change sense.

Inadequate Tests of Reciprocity

The two definitions would be similar only if the term *reinforcement* were used strictly in the sense of altering probabilities *within* a dyad. In fact, in research on reciprocity by social learning theorists, the term *reinforcement* has been used to mean positive behavior defined as positive on a priori grounds. There has been no demonstration that positive behaviors are reinforcers in the probability change sense. Furthermore, in every case but one the empirical test of reciprocity has been inadequate: Husband–wife correlations of positive act rates *across* couples or correlations between family members *across* families were calculated. This test of reciprocity has abandoned the individual dyad in the definition. The correlation of husband–wife rates of positive behaviors *across* couples also does not deal with base-rate differences of positive behaviors between couples, and it is thus invalid as a test of a reciprocity hypothesis.

Birchler (1972) found a husband–wife correlation of .97 across 12 nondistressed couples for mean frequencies of positive items checked and .74 in 12 distressed couples; the correlations for negative items checked were .26 and .54, respectively. Alexander (1973a) analyzed his data in a similar manner. He obtained high correlations between father-to-son supportiveness and son-to-father supportiveness (.69) across families and a similarly high correlation for mother-to-son supportiveness and son-to-mother supportiveness (.59), but the equivalent correlations for defensiveness were not significant. He concluded that "To have developed and maintained these differential rates, the families would have had to reciprocate supportiveness but not defensiveness, which was exactly the finding of the present study [p. 616]." In fact, rate differences between families, not reciprocity, was exactly what was tested by the correlations. The point is similar to one that states that analyses of husband–wife correlations across couples is an inadequate test of a reciprocity hypothesis. Gottman *et al.* (1976) wrote:

> Although nondistressed couples may seem to be reciprocating positive behavior more frequently than distressed couples, that may only be an artifact of the higher probability of positive behaviors in nondistressed couples. By emitting more positive responses, nondistressed couples increase the probability that one partner's positive response will be followed by the other partner's positive response [p. 14].

High (noncontingent) positive frequencies in some couples and not in others could also be an artifact of many other variables, such as similar physical tempos (couples are more similar to one another than they are to strangers on most variables), or an artifact of the amount of time spent together (for couples who spend more time together each day, both husband and wife will have more items checked on their behavior checklist than couples who spend less time together).

Evidence of Reciprocation of Displeasurable Behaviors

The one test of correlations of positive and negative checklist items *within* couples was made by Wills, Weiss, and Patterson (1974), who correlated these variables for seven nondistressed couples between each husband and wife across 14 days.[1] Husbands had been instructed (as a validity check) to double their output of positive affectional behaviors on Days 13 and 14. Wives' recording of their husbands' behaviors on these days showed a significant increase in pleasurable instrumental events, but not in pleasurable affectional events. In six out of seven couples, there were no significant correlations between husbands' and wives' records of pleasurable behavior, but in four of seven couples there were significant correlations between husbands' and wives' records of displeasurable behavior.

The Wills et al. (1974) study concluded that *there was evidence for the reciprocation of displeasurable but not of pleasurable behaviors.* They wrote: "The within-couples analysis provides an index of immediate reactions to behavioral events and indicates that in day-to-day affectional interaction, a displeasurable behavior is more likely to be reciprocated than a pleasurable behavior [p. 809]." There is, thus, evidence to support negative reciprocity but no evidence to support the positive matching or quid pro quo model of nondistressed marriage proposed by Azrin et al. (1973), Patterson and Reid (1970), and Stuart (1969).

The within-couple analysis of displeasurable events for these four nondistressed couples also does not constitute support for the conclusion that the *matching* of displeasurable events across days is necessarily related to marital dissatisfaction. This test has never been conducted; however, Murstein, Cerreto, and MacDonald (1977) recently reported that adherence to a quid pro quo belief, particularly by husbands, was negatively related to marital satisfaction, $(t(32) = 2.78 \ p < .01)$. The correlation between an exchange orientation and marital satisfaction was $-.63$ $(p < .01)$ for men and $-.27$ $(p < .06)$ for women. The correlations between each person's exchange orientation score and her or his partner's marital satisfaction score were also negative and significant.

Summary of Points on Reciprocity

To summarize, the term *reciprocity* has been used in two different ways in the literature on social interaction. Furthermore, its use by social learning theorists in describing marital interaction has been confused, and their proposal

[1] There is a methodological problem in using regression analysis to correlate two time series (husband and wife frequencies) if the time series are autocorrelated. Hibbs (1974) pointed out that "if an equation is estimated via ordinary least squares when regressors and disturbances are (positively) autocorrelated, the researcher will obtain a spurious underestimate of the error variance and an inflation of R^2 [p. 259]." This is true for even moderate autocorrelations. Although Wills et al. (1974) tested the first-order autocorrelations, 14 points are not enough to detect significant moderately sized autocorrelations, and it is possible for autocorrelations at lags other than 1 (all of which enter into a time-series regression equation—see Hibbs, 1974, p. 256) to have been significant. Theoretically, what we want to show is that the husband's past behavior is a *better* predictor of his wife's current behavior than her own past behavior. We, therefore, want to subtract the prediction we can make based on autocorrelations.

that nondistressed marriages are characterized by a quid pro quo exchange of positive reinforcers has received no support whatsoever. Nonetheless, the concept of negative reciprocity has received some support, and thus reciprocity remains an important dimension in the search for structure in marital and family interaction.

The third substantive dimension of interaction in the search for structure is *dominance.*

REVIEW OF LITERATURE ON DOMINANCE

Distinguishing Distressed from Nondistressed Families

The concept of *dominance* has played a central role in theorizing and research on family interaction, although the role investigators have proposed for dominance is by no means unambiguous. In fact, some theorists have argued that the lack of a clearly defined power structure is characteristic of distressed families, and other theorists have proposed the opposite position. Unfortunately, research evidence is equally ambiguous. Some researchers have suggested and have found evidence that normal families are equalitarian (Haley, 1964; Murrell, 1971), whereas other investigators have suggested and have found evidence that normal functioning implies a clear power hierarchy (Schuham, 1972).

Jacob's (1975) review of family interaction concluded that in differentiating *schizophrenic* from *nonschizophrenic* (but nonetheless distressed) families, measures of dominance and power produced no clear-cut results. Of 17 studies, 10 produced significant differences, but the pattern of findings was inconsistent and inconclusive. In discriminating disturbed *nonschizophrenic* families from *normal* families, the results were once again complex, but in this case Jacob concluded that "family power structures are more often differentiated (hierarchical versus equalitarian) in normal than in disturbed families [Jacob, 1975, p. 51]" and, furthermore, that "fathers are more influential (especially vis-a-vis the child) in normal than disturbed family groups [p. 51]." Considering all the research to date, however, we would be wise to conclude that the concept of dominance has provided little insight in distinguishing well-functioning from distressed families.

In the area of marital interaction, the predominant *sociological view* is that well-functioning marriages are equalitarian rather than characterized by a fixed dominance pattern. This is consistent with social learning theories that view dominance as an example of coercive control (Patterson and Reid, 1970) rather than reciprocity, which suggests symmetry in interaction patterns. This view of dominance as symptomatic of dysfunctional marital relationships has also been proposed by communication theorists (see Watzlawick et al. 1967), who suggested that "symmetrical" relationships were less dysfunctional than "complementary" relationships. Until now, this hypothesis has not been tested directly in observational research on marital interaction. Such a test is the objective of Chapter 10. However, before this hypothesis can be operationalized, alternative definitions of dominance that have been used in observational research must be reviewed.

Difficulties in Operationalizing Dominance

Frequency versus Consequences. In research on *family interaction,* dominance always seems to refer to some *asymmetry* in the frequency of a variable presumed to reflect power. The variables implicated in the asymmetry have been diverse. Jacob (1975) wrote that:

> measures of dominance can be separated into quantitative process measures (verbal frequency measures) and qualitative process measures (rater judgements of dominance and dominance-related dimensions). In addition an outcome measure of domination can be identified in terms of the relationship between a family's questionnaire responses (completed as a group) and responses to the same questionnaire previously completed by each member individually [p. 47].

Heatherington and Martin (1972) listed among the verbal frequency measures (a) who speaks first; (b) who speaks last; and (c) passive acceptance of a solution. Jacob (1975) listed talk time, number of communications, successful interruptions, and acts directed toward a particular family member.

There are several problems with these methods of operationalizing the concept of dominance. First, these operational definitions assume that an isomorphism exists between asymmetry in the *frequency* of these behaviors and dominance. However, in some families the dominant member may be a person who does not speak very often, who rarely interrupts, but who is highly influential. If this were the case, the asymmetry we would expect would be an asymmetry in *patterns* of interaction rather than in frequencies. For example, when the dominant member called for compliance, a compliance would be more likely than when less dominant family members called for it. The asymmetry would thus be in the amount of predictability (or reduction of uncertainty) gained by knowing the behavior of the dominant, compared to the less dominant, member. A second problem is that dominance may not be reflected in one variable but instead in overall patterns across several coding variables. For example, it seems conceivable that, at times, well-placed agreement, a variable not utilized in definitions of dominance, can be an influential mechanism during decision making. To summarize, it may not be one kind of variable and it may not be the variable's frequency, *but, rather, it is the asymmetry in its consequences that is related to dominance.*

Application to Observational Studies. A third problem with the operational definitions of dominance is that they are difficult to apply to the naturalistic observational study of family interaction. The problem is one that family interaction researchers share with ethologists. In the animal ethology literature, dominance has been defined variously in terms of asymmetries in resource utilization, territory, freedom of mobility, and outcomes of aggressive bouts. However, in the ethology literature the concept of dominance has been difficult to observe. For example, Wilson (1975) wrote that:

> Serious difficulties in the dominance concept appeared as soon as the idea was extended to the more complex life of primates. . . . Some writers then recognized that in both primates and wolves a rich repertory of signals is used to denote status in a manner not directly coupled with aggressive interactions. Status signs were seen to be metacommunicative, indicating to other animals the past history of the displaying individual and its expectation of the outcome of any future confrontations [p. 281].

Dominant behaviors are, thus, exceedingly complex in higher-level organisms that have already established a dominance pattern. The signals are varied, perhaps even somewhat abbreviated and telegraphic, and may only be displayed in specific situations.

There is also some evidence that primate groups with a history of interaction develop "dominance dialects" in the sense that specific behaviors related to dominance may be idosyncratic to a particular group. Stephenson (personal communication) found evidence for this in a troop of rhesus monkeys. He periodically assessed the dominance structure of a rhesus troop by depriving the group of water for 2 days and observing the lineup at the water tap when the water flow was restored. He observed that in one troop the alpha male had a peculiar spastic motion of one arm out to his side. This animal died suddenly and the beta male became the new alpha; surprisingly, he then began to exhibit this same behavior even though he had never before been observed to display it. In an experiment, the new alpha male was removed and, when the new beta became the dominant alpha, he also began displaying this movement. Obviously, observation of specific behaviors in groups of monkeys would ignore this extremely salient behavior.

Defining Dominance as Asymmetry in Predictability

The problem is likely to prove more difficult in naturalistic observations of marital interaction, particularly those based on a brief slice of interaction, such as those usually obtained from laboratory video- or audiotapes. An alternative approach for operationalizing the concept of dominance is to search for definitions that involve an asymmetry across a range of coding variables and to employ a definition related to patterns of interaction rather than to frequencies of a specific variable. Information theory provides one such approach, and we propose the following definition of dominance:

> *In a dyad, if B's future behavior is more predictable from A's past behavior than conversely, then A is said to be dominant.*

The asymmetry suggested in this definition is predictability. This definition can be shown to have considerable generality in the sense that observations by other researchers about the dominance construct are consistent with this definition.

In human social groups, dominance has been noted to be partly related to "the powerful person having greater freedom of action, or permission to deviate [Argyle, 1969, p. 234]." This implies that the behavior of the more powerful person in the group is less predictable from the normative behavior of subordinates than conversely, and this is, therefore, an asymmetry in predictability. The asymmetry in the predictability definition is also consistent with the finding by Bandura, Ross, and Ross (1963) that there is more voluntary imitation of powerful than of less powerful confederates.

Mehrabian's (1972) result that in factor analyses of interaction among strangers nonverbal relaxation behaviors load on a status factor suggests that subordinates are more tense than people of higher status. It may be that this differential in tension is related to lower status people's tendency to be more attentive and more responsive to their more powerful cohorts than conversely, which is consistent with the asymmetry-in-predictability definition. There is evidence to support this interpretation. Exline (1963) and Exline, Gray, and Schuette (1965) found that people high in affiliative motivation look more at the person with whom they are interacting than people low in affiliative motivation.

Most research on dominance view it as a trait as opposed to the relationship-specific and situation-specific definition proposed in this chapter. Research would have to be designed specifically to address this issue. However, in general the findings with trait measures of dominance are consistent with the asymmetry-in-predictability definition of dominance. For example, Exline and Messick (1967), using trait measures of dominance, found that during an interview *dependent subjects* who were given low verbal reinforcement for looking looked more at the interviewer, whereas *dominant males* in this condition decreased their amount of looking.

The use of the definition of dominance as asymmetry in attention (usually assessed by gaze) is an attempt to deal with the problem that one function of dominance hierarchies is to minimize the occurrence of aggression. The existence of a dominance hierarchy means that aggressive encounters will be rare. The use of asymmetry in attention is, thus, an extension of the dominance concept to nonaggressive interactions. Chance suggested that the asymmetrical patterning of attention could be widely applied as an index of dominance (Chance, 1967; Chance & Jolly, 1970; Chance & Larsen, 1976). This suggestion is entirely consistent with the asymmetry in predictability definition, although the predictability definition is more general. This is true for two reasons. First, the measure need not be attentional; it could be activity level or a positiveness dimension. Second, the predictability definition considers pattern over time, rather than rates. Another issue, one that I will not discuss here, has to do with the problem of inferring cross-correlation when autocorrelation exists (see Gottman & Ringland, unpublished). The asymmetry-in-predictability definition is, thus, more general than the asymmetry-in-attention definition.

The definition of asymmetry in predictability is consistent with other uses of dominance. Patterson (1978) and Patterson and Reid (1970) discussed an aggressive child's "coercive power" in terms of a deviant act's ability to command a response. The aggressive child is powerful in the sense that it reduces the range of alternative responses from its parents, and, therefore, the parents' behaviors are made more predictable given an antecedent deviant act by the child.

Thibaut and Kelley's (1959) definitions of power (e.g., "fate control" and "behavior control") are also consistent with asymmetry in predictability. In fate control, the rewards that one person obtains from an exchange are controlled by the other, but the converse is not the case; in behavior control, the rewards in the exchange vary as a function of the subordinate's behavior when the dominant person exhibits a particular behavior. In both fate and behavior control, there is an asymmetry in predictability (of rewards or of behavior).

The definition of dominance as asymmetry in predictability is also consistent with other research on dominance across a variety of species. As early as 1936, Maslow defined the dominant primate as:

> one whose sexual, feeding, aggressive and social behavior patterns are carried out without deference to the behavior patterns of his associates. The subordinate animal is the one whose sexual, feeding, aggressive and social behavior patterns are suggested, modified, limited or inhibited by the behavior pattern of its more dominant associations [p. 263].

The dominant fowl has greater spatial mobility (Wilson, 1975), and it is the lower-status fowl who moves away when the dominant animal approaches, not conversely; that is, there is differential predictability.

STRUCTURAL MODEL OF MARITAL INTERACTION

The foregoing review of literature has led this author to propose a structural model of marital and family interaction. This model has one general "metaconcept," which concerns the degree of patterning or structure in marital and family interaction—this concept is independent of the specific kind of variable used to assess the degree of patterning; the model also has three dimensions of the content of that structure: *positiveness, reciprocity,* and *dominance.*

HYPOTHESIS 1:   *Degree of Structure.* There is more patterning and structure in the interaction of distressed couples than in the interaction of nondistressed couples.

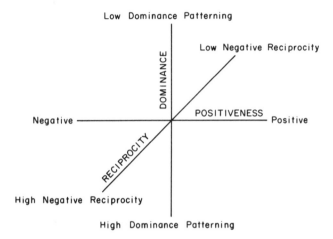

Figure 3.2 *Structural Model for marital interaction.*

HYPOTHESIS 2:   *Positiveness.* Nondistressed couples are more positive and less negative to one another than distressed couples. The differences should be greater for negative than for positive interaction, and greater for nonverbal than for verbal behavior.

HYPOTHESIS 3:   *Reciprocity.* The reciprocation of negative behavior will discriminate distressed from nondistressed couples, with more reciprocity of negative behavior in distressed than in nondistressed couples. I do not expect similar discrimination in the reciprocation of positive behaviors. This discrimination would have been predicted by quid pro quo theory.

HYPOTHESIS 4:   *Dominance.* The interaction of distressed couples will show more asymmetry in predictability than will the behavior of nondistressed couples. This greater asymmetry of predictability, which is in itself a type of patterning in interaction of distressed couples, is also consistent with my hypothesis about the differential degree of structure in the two groups.

These last three hypotheses are illustrated in Figure 3.2. In this three-dimensional model, nondistressed marriages would be in the upper right corner in these coordinates, and distressed marriages would be in the lower left.

COMPARISON WITH OTHER MODELS

The model we have been considering is similar, to some extent, to other models of interpersonal interaction proposed by others in a variety of substantive research areas, and these models have appeared repeatedly in the study of personality, person perception, and developmental psychology and also in observers' judgments of overt behavior.

In the early 1960s studies of parental childrearing practices, as perceived by both parents and children, consistently produced circumplex models with orthogonal axes of positiveness ("love–hostility") and control ("autonomy–control") (see Schaefer, 1971 and Becker, 1964). Similar patterns of correlations emerged from observations of mother–infant interaction (see Schaefer, 1971, p. 141), and ratings on a positiveness dimension "suggested that such ratings have relatively good validity for predicting child behavior [Schaefer, 1971, p. 141]." Positiveness ratings predicted the child's social, emotional, and cognitive development, using data from the Berkeley Growth Study and predicting from infancy to adolescence. Similar circumplex models with similar orthogonal dimensions were obtained cross-culturally, and also from different measurement operations, including ratings based on interview data, behavior checklists completed by parents and teachers, and questionnaires.

Becker's (1964) model of parental discipline is a circumplex model with three axes: a control axis (restrictive–permissive), a positiveness axis (warmth–hostility), and a tension axis (calm detachment–anxious emotional involvement). The model was used to make some clear predictions about children's moral development (resistance to transgressions and temptation), aggression, dependency, sociability, and intellectual striving in school settings (see Becker, 1964). Clausen and Williams (1963) reviewed research on similar dimensions that showed relationships between parental punitiveness and teachers' ratings of children's impulsivity, aggressiveness, and initiation of friendships, as well as peer ratings of the child's influence (Clausen & Williams, 1963, p. 93). The "actual balance of power" (p. 93) in the marital relationship vis-à-vis authority over the child was also found to affect the child's self-concept.

Therefore, at one time in the recent history of the developmental tradition's study of the family, dimensions similar to positiveness and dominance were used to organize the data of parents' and children's perceptions of the family and to predict observers' ratings of interactions, interviewers' ratings of behavior, teachers' ratings of child behavior, peer sociometric data, and indices of cognitive, social, and moral development.

Dimensions similar to those proposed in the Structural Model have also emerged in other areas of research. Wiggins (1973) reviewed models underlying methods of personality assessment. One of these models was the *interpersonal model* (p. 475ff.). Wiggins reviewed the Interpersonal System of Personality Diagnosis, which, he wrote, "must be considered a milestone in the development of interpersonal assessment models [p. 479]." The circular arrangement of variable correlations known as a circumplex was presumed to be "generated by two orthogonal axes representing *power* (dominance versus submission) and *affiliation* (love versus hate) [p. 479]." These two dimensions are also similar to my dominance and positiveness dimensions.

Clore and Byrne (1974) reviewed research that supported their reinforcement–affect model of interpersonal attraction, a model that emphasizes the predictive value of the positiveness dimension. In their review, they summarize Osgood's three-dimensional model of human judgments (see Osgood, 1966). They wrote:

> According to Osgood (1969), the meaning structure of human language reflects innate emotional responses of considerable evolutionary significance. When one is confronted by a novel stimulus, the first order of business is to determine whether it is good or bad (*evaluation*). After that, one needs to know whether it is strong or weak (*potency*) and whether it is approaching fast or slow (*activity*) [p. 144].

A model of nonverbal behavior proposed by Mehrabian (1972) is also similar, although not identical, to the model I have proposed. Mehrabian's model consists of three dimensions: a positiveness dimension, a status dimension, and an active–passive dimension. Mehrabian's positiveness dimension represents a basic evaluation dimension that determines approach or avoidance tendencies toward persons, situations, or objects. It was applied in Mehrabian's work to the study of interpersonal attraction and evaluation, and it is similar to the general evaluation dimension proposed in other psychological research (for example, Osgood, 1966; Williams & Sundene, 1965).

Mehrabian's active–passive dimension represents the nonverbal social counterpart of the orienting reflex, the basic response of attending to novel stimulation. This dimension, in the context of social interaction, can be subsumed in a reciprocity dimension. Status in Mehrabian's model relates to social control, social influence, and territoriality.

A similar three-dimensional model of interpersonal behavior was proposed by Schutz (1960) as *affection, inclusion,* and *control.* Schutz proposed that personality research and person perception research can be organized by considering interpersonal needs people have to receive and to extend affection (which is similar to positiveness), inclusion (which is similar to reciprocity), and control (which is similar to dominance) to others. Schutz's dimensions of inclusion, affection, and control have been used successfully to predict sociometric indices of attraction and liking in college students' ratings of roommates and in selections for a cross-country driving vacation (Schutz, 1960).

Not all the dimensions proposed in these models are conceptually distinct or unrelated. For example, the tense–calm dimension in Becker's (1964) model appears in Mehrabian's (1972) model and was obtained from factor analyses as loading on a dominance dimension. If there is a status differential in a relationship, the high-status person will be more relaxed and the low-status person more tense than in relationships without a status differential.

The *active–passive* dimension is probably not independent of the degree of patterning and structure inherent in the sequencing of interaction. Less activity is associated with greater patterning, a result I have noted in my review of talk–silence sequences with the identified patient triad in a family, and in negative affect reciprocity. More activity is associated with less patterning, much as in the Second Law of Thermodynamics: Ice crystal molecules are less active and more patterned than steam molecules; both are states of the same substance that differ in *both* structure and activity of the elements. In family interaction this implies that in distressed families and couples there is less activity and, when it occurs, it is simultaneously more structured, predictable, and ritualized than in nondistressed families and couples.

The differences between the Structural Model proposed in this book and the other interpersonal models are that all dimensions in the Structural Model are derived from observational data, positiveness is reconceptualized specifically in terms of the role of agreement and positive and negative nonverbal behaviors, reciprocity is reconceptualized specifically in terms of the contingent nature of (primarily) negative nonverbal behavior, and dominance is reconceptualized specifically in terms of asymmetry in predictability of one person's behavior from the other's.

In the next two chapters, the methodological preliminaries necessary to test the foregoing four hypotheses will be presented. In subsequent chapters, work done to test these hypotheses will be described. Because additional statistical methodology must be introduced to operationalize the dominance dimension, the testing of Hypothesis 4 will be deferred until Chapter 10.

CHAPTER 4

The Couples Interaction Scoring System

This chapter will introduce the Couples Interaction Scoring System (CISS, pronounced "kiss"), which is based on the idea that every message has several components, one of which is the *content*. Content refers to the printed word, that is, the literal aspect of the message, and it often cannot by itself convey meaning. Anyone who studies marital interaction and prepares a verbatim transcript of the conversation will immediately want to annotate the transcript with notes about the way things were said, the voice tones, the facial expressions, the bodily movements, etc. and also to annotate the transcript with notes about the listener's nonverbal behavior. It is nearly impossible to read a transcript without imagining these cues, because they give life to a conversation. For example, consider the following excerpt:

H: *You'll never guess who I saw today at the Hour House, Frank Dugan.*
W: *So, big deal, you saw Frank Dugan.*
H: *Don't you remember I had that argument with him last Wednesday?*
W: *I forgot.*
H: *Yeah.*
W: *So I'm sorry I forgot. All right?*
H: *So, it **is** a big deal to see him.*
W: *So, what'dya want me to do, jump up and down?*
H: *Well, how was **your** day, honey?*

The aspects of the message that concern its nonverbal delivery in the CISS are called *affect,* and the nonverbal behaviors of the listener are called *context.* The meaning of a message in a social interaction will change as a function of its content, affect, or context.

EARLIER WORK IN IDENTIFYING COMPONENTS

The idea of partitioning a message into component parts is not new. Bateson (1968) suggested that every message has a report and a command aspect. He wrote, "On the one hand the message is a statement or report about events at a previous moment, and on the other hand it is a command—a cause or stimulus for events at a later moment [p. 179]." Watzlawick, Beavin, and Jackson (1967) proposed a different way of dividing messages into components. They wrote, "Every communication has a content and a relationship aspect such that the latter classifies the former and is therefore a metacommunication [p. 54]." Watzlawick et al. were particularly interested in paradoxes within and between levels of a message (as in a notice that reads "Disregard this sign.") because they were trying to elaborate on the double-bind hypothesis. In pursuing the concept of a relationship component of a message, they suggested that a sequence of messages has two components, digital and analogic. They wrote, "Digital language has a highly complex and powerful logical syntax but lacks adequate semantics in the field of relationship, while analogic language posesses the semantics but has no adequate syntax for the unambiguous definition of the nature of relationships [p. 67; italics removed]." This is a confusing dichotomy. In a further clarification, they asked, "What is analogic communication?" and they replied, "The answer is relatively simple: It is virtually all nonverbal communication [p. 62]." The digital–analogic distinction may be similar to the distinctions made by the CISS. However, the distinction was somewhat more complex than a verbal–nonverbal split.

Part of the idea is that any message communicates both its content and the statement "I have the kind of relationship with you that allows me to say that." In other words, a message transmits information and simultaneously defines the relationship. This concept of the relationship component of a message is an intriguing idea, but one that has been difficult to operationalize in coding any particular message; therefore, investigators have operationalized the relationship aspects of messages by searching for specific kinds of sequences in a stream of messages. These investigators thus code the relationship aspect of messages by changing the size of the coding unit, that is, coding sequences of messages (see Ericson & Rogers, 1973; Mark, 1971; and Rogers & Farace, 1972).

THE CISS SCHEME FOR IDENTIFYING COMPONENTS

An alternative to applying one code to a *sequence* of messages is to code each message separately and to assess empirically the way these messages are sequenced, using the techniques that were described in Chapter 2. This is the approach taken in this book. The CISS assumes that a message has two components, *affect* and *context,* in addition to its content.

Defining Affect and Context

Affect does not refer to an inner emotional state, but to the nonverbal behaviors of the speaker during message transmission. For example, a message may be delivered neutrally, sarcastically, fearfully, affectionately and tenderly, angrily, disgustedly, and so on. Affect on any videotape is coded by a separate group from those who code content on that tape. The affect coders follow a hierarchical decision rule based in part on Mehrabian's regression equation (see Chapter 3); thus, they scan for specific cues involving facial expressions, voice tone, body position, and movement (in that order). The same persons also code the nonverbal behaviors of the listener during the coding unit, and they use the same decision rules as in coding affect. By the word *context* I thus mean the nonverbal behaviors of the listener during the coding unit.

Using the Thought Unit

Each videotape is transcribed verbatim, as the following example illustrates:

W: *Honey, if they could afford it / That's what I mean /*
35   36

H: *Okay /*
43

W: *If they could afford it I know they would /*
37

H: *Okay / Let's leave the money matter aside for now /*
44   45

This transcription allows us to obtain a sequential record of a couple's conversation. The couple's statements are divided into what most researchers who code speech (developmentalists, sociolinguists, psycholinguists, and clinical psychologists) have variously called "thought units," "speech acts," or "utterances" and are indicated in the example by the numbered slash marks. The unit is not fixed: Sometimes the thought unit is a phrase; sometimes it is a sentence; and sometimes it is a speech fragment. A thought unit is usually grammatically separated by pauses, commas, ands, buts, and periods. The coders code each thought unit, using both the written transcript and the videotape. The thought unit may appear, at first glance, to be a relatively soft unit, perhaps not as objective as, for example, an N-second interval, which is used by some systems. Coding systems that do use time to segment speech most frequently employ $N = 6$ or $N = 30$. Thus, the coder must make a selection every N-seconds. It does not require much experience in coding speech to learn that a fixed time unit is extremely inappropriate. Sometimes the time unit is too long because several utterances, facial expressions, and voice tone shifts have occurred within one interval. Sometimes the fixed time interval is too short, so it cuts an utterance before it is completed. Such an occurrence is a frustrating experience for a coder. However, coders using the thought unit to divide a transcript with slash marks can do so independently with nearly perfect reliability. After discovering this fact in two pilot studies, the group developing the CISS established the thought unit as the reliability checking unit for the CISS.

The slash mark reliability check has recently been repeated with similar results. Furthermore, the thought unit is a good guess at how information is actually processed by listeners, and therefore it seems to be more realistic than a fixed time interval.

Each thought unit receives only one content code unless it is a question, in which case it is double coded: Q/ and another content code.

Part of the intention in using thought units was to be able to shift to *behavioral units* in the data analysis phase, but not before. A behavioral unit is defined by a change in codes (see Weiss, Hops, & Patterson, 1973). Thus, consecutive thought units coded the same on content, affect, and context are parts of one behavioral unit for reliability checking.

A rough estimate of the coders' agreement on the training tapes is derived by comparing codes assigned for each thought unit. A criterion of 70% of the coders agreeing 70% of the time was initially the minimal level of agreement acceptable before the coders were allowed to begin working with actual data. Levels of agreement were considerably higher than this minimum. If there were only three codes, each equally likely, the probability of obtaining this minimum level of agreement for 10 coders independently and randomly coding 10 thought units can be calculated as approximately .024, so the minimum criterion is more exacting than it may seem. In the early stages of the research program, a reliability checking method was used in which periodically and randomly all the coders independently coded the same reliability tape in order to control for slippage (decay and drift) over time; the same criterion was maintained for the duration of the coding. In the later stages of the research program, the procedure for reliability checking was modified so that all coders in training had to reach agreement to agreement-plus-disagreement percentages of 85% on two successive tapes with one staff member who served only as the reliability checker. The reliability checker codes randomly selected segments of transcript of varying length on every transcript except those used in training. Because the study initially conducted and repeated twice on the independent placement of slash marks found that separate thought units produced nearly perfect agreement, for each tape the coder slashed two copies of the transcript: The coder uses one copy and the second copy is for the reliability checker, who codes a random segment of the transcript. This new procedure for reliability checking proved itself to be superior to the earlier procedure when both methods were compared on the same set of tapes.

TRAINING CODERS

Initially, coders were trained separately to code either content or affect. Although an individual can be trained to code both components of a message, it is best to have different people code content and affect on a given tape, since the affect codes require careful attention to the nonverbal behaviors of the couple. It is possible to train the same group of coders on both nonverbal components of messages, although affect and context on a tape should be coded by a person different from the one who codes content. Coders find it a welcome relief to change from one system to another.

Coders are always blind to whether or not a couple is distressed or nondistressed. As an added precaution, when processing tapes of a therapy study, coders also are unaware that a therapy study has been conducted and do not know the time order of the tapes (pre, post, or follow-up).

Coders are male and female graduate or undergraduate psychology majors, or they are nonstudents. Five generations (separate groups) of coders—a total of 38 persons—have been trained. A codebook gives an initial introduction to the CISS, and it is accompanied by mini-programmed instructional units designed to teach specific discriminations. The codebook avoids overwhelming the beginning coder. Although this chapter is based on the codebook, it does not include the instructional units for more fine-grained discriminations.

Training sessions are similar to a course in that coders progressively learn the components of the task. These components are listed sequentially in the following.

Content coders must be able to:

1. list (from memory) the code abbreviations and describe what each code means.
2. code correctly a set of printed word examples from the codebook that are presented in random order.
3. code a tape with the trainer.
4. code sections of other tapes, discussing each code with the trainer.
5. code a series of audiotapes or videotapes until criterion is reached.

During this training, it is important to check the progress of coders. Reliability will be low if coders have not *memorized* the entire codebook. There is a tendency for coders to remember some categories better than others and to use their favorite ones more frequently. These favorite categories will vary from coder to coder. If complete memorization is required and tested, this type of faulty coding can be avoided. It is also important to check agreements between coders to make sure that a consensual "garbage category" does not emerge. Garbage categories will give high reliability at the cost of validity. The reliability checker always keeps a record of common sources of disagreement for each coder so that particular misunderstandings can be corrected, or so that occasional ambiguities in the codebook can be clarified. It takes approximately 28 hours to transcribe and code content, affect, and context (including time for reliability checking) for each hour of videotape.. Thus, coding is an expensive and slow process.

Learning to code is a grueling and frustrating experience for most persons. We have found that it is a good idea to issue a disclaimer at the beginning of training that recognizes the difficulty coders will experience in making some discriminations that are difficult.

DERIVING CISS CONTENT CODES

Our content codes were derived partly from the work of others and partly from our own experience. One major influence was the Hops, Wills, Patterson, and Weiss (1972) Marital Interaction Coding System (MICS), whose orientation is the assessment of a problem-solving form of couples therapy. We also drew from the Olson and Ryder (1970) Inventory of Marital Conflict (IMC) coding system, whose orientation is the assessment of decision-making on specific problems that contain varying degrees of programmed conflict.

Specific Content Codes

Agreement (AG).   There are five types of agreement:

1. *Direct agreement* is a statement of direct acknowledgment of agreement with the other person's views, such as "You're right," "OK," "I think that was very well put," or "It is certainly true that our lives could be affected by these global sorts of things." Direct agreement requires some preceding point of view to have been expressed with which the speaker agrees, such as "I think we have a problem with the kids." "Yeah (AG)." Note that the type of agreement represented by the "Yeah" is different from a response to a request for information, as in "Do you think we have a problem with the kids?" Yeah." The last "yeah" is not an agreement; it is a response to a request for information. This distinction illustrates the fact that coders do not simply proceed through a transcript coding every "yeah," "right," and "OK" as an agreement.

2. *Acceptance of responsibility* involves a past or present problem. Examples are "You're right, I have been putting wet towels in the hamper" and "Yes, I suppose we both need to budget our time better." Any apologetic statement or an acceptance of a criticism is also an example of accepting responsibility; for example: "I'm sorry for the way I acted" and "John, you're so messy; you put your junk all over the place." "Yeah, you're right (AG)." However, a speaker's recognizing that he or she ought to accept more responsibility for behavior necessary to solve a defined problem is not coded AG. For example, "I really feel I ought to be doing more to help you around the house" is not coded AG.

3. *Acceptance of modification* is a change of opinion resulting from the influence of the other person. The speaker must have previously stated an opinion and then changed as a function of the spouse's opinion or arguments; for example: "OK, you're right, I'm wrong" and "I never saw it that way before, Bill; the kids can take care of themselves while we're at the movies" and "Yeah, you're right. I see now how curiosity can get you into trouble."

4. *Compliance* is a statement that complies with a preceding request or command. Here is an example: "Please don't interrupt." "OK, go ahead." Agreeing with a request for delayed compliance is also compliance; for example: "Oh, pick up some bread on your way home." "OK, I will."

5. *Assent* is a brief verbal response, such as "Mmhmm" or "Yeah," made while the other person is talking. It acknowledges listening or attention rather than indicates explicit agreement. Repetition of the other person's statement or a fragment of a statement in a neutral voice tone is also an assent.

Disagreement (DG). There also are five types of disagreement:

1. *Direct disagreement* is a simple disagreement with a spouse's viewpoint (for example, "No, it's never been twice a week.") or a denial of responsibility [for example, "You don't clean the cat box." "Well, I never said I would." (DG)]. Also, any statement denying the responsibility of both people for a problem is coded DG [for example, "Perhaps we're both at fault." "No, we had nothing to do with that problem." (DG)].

2. *Yes–but* is a statement of qualified agreement or apology that can be either explicit or implicit; for example, "I'm sorry I made you mad, but I really felt that I had to make my point." and "There is nothing upsetting me." "Yeah, but it sure seems like there is." (DG).

Yes–but is an interesting code. Our clinical experience has shown that the speaker usually views such a statement as basically an agreement, whereas the listener views it as basically a disagreement. The speaker feels as if she or he is only being logical and helpful, but the listener feels criticized.

3. *Disagreement with rationale supplied* occurs when a speaker provides a rationale, justification, reason, or explanation for disagreement; but, the statement is still coded DG (for example, "No, we have to go see Mom. She really appreciates our visits." and "You're wrong; it's important to save money in case of an emergency.").

4. *Command* is a statement ordering the partner to do something or not to do something, such as "Please don't smoke."

5. *Noncompliance* is a failure, either by making a direct statement or by ignoring the command, to fulfill the requirements of an immediately preceding command or a request for clarification (see the following code, CT, type four).

Communication Talk (CT). There are four types of communication talk statements, all of which are communication about communication or a comment on the process of the transaction.

1. *Back on Beam #1* is a statement that directs the conversation back to a topic from which the couple has strayed. This included a restatement of a problem or a redescription of a problem intended to refocus the discussion. Examples: "John, that's getting away from the issue." and "Come on, we don't have to discuss the world's economy." and "Aren't we supposed to be discussing the in-laws?" and "That's all fine and good, but getting back to the issue of the budget book. . . ."

2. *Back on Beam #2* is a statement directing the couple's discussion toward a resolution of a problem. It is a statement that serves the function of beaming the couple toward resolution. Examples: "We have to reach a decision on that issue." and "Let's wrap this up in 5 minutes." and "It's getting late and we have to decide how to solve this."

3. *Metacommunication* is a statement about a discussion. It is a critique, an evaluation, an examination of a conversation. These statements often involve a stop in the action of a conversation in order to comment on it. This category also includes statements that communicate understanding or lack of understanding on the part of the speaker concerning previous statements of the partner. Examples: "I don't think we're getting anywhere." and "I like the way we're relating to each other." and "I'm afraid I don't really understand what you're saying." and "Gerry, I just can't get my thoughts out today."

4. *Clarification request* is a question or statement requesting clarification, repetition, or rephrasing of a previous statement when the speaker does not hear or understand the partner's statement. Examples: "I didn't get that." and "Would you say that again?" or "Huh?"

Mindreading (MR).   There are two types of mindreading statements:

1. *Mindreading feelings, attitude, or opinion* are statements that attribute feelings, attitudes opinions, or motives to the spouse or to both partners. Examples: "You hate to go to my mother's." and "You don't care about how we live." and "You're lying."

2. *Mindreading behaviors* are statements that attribute past, present, or future behaviors or facts *solely* to the other person. These are statements like "We haven't eaten well for a long time," which is a relationship information exchange statement. Examples: "You didn't study at all last weekend." (attributes past behavior), "You never went to that party." (attributes past behavior), "You won't go to the library to study." (attributes future behavior), "You're not spending weekends with me anymore." (attributes present behavior), "You were spending a lot of time with that woman at the party last night." (attributes past behavior), "You have a hard time getting up in the morning." (attributes present behavior). Mindreading behavior statements should not be confused with "we statements," which are coded PS (see next code).

Problem Solving and Information Exchange (PS).   There are two types of problem-solving statements and two types of information statements:

1. *Specific plan* is a plan or a method for arriving at a solution to a specific problem. The plan must speak to the issue at hand. Examples: "You had your way last time, so it's my turn." and "Let's write down all possible solutions and then discuss each one separately." and "I think we should go out to dinner if you're feeling so rushed."

2. *Nonspecific plan* is a solution in nonspecific terms. Examples: "I think you shouldn't be late again." and "Let's be happy." and "We'll just stay within the budget." and "I'll just have to be more consistent." This kind of statement is more a recognition of the problem than a concrete solution; it suggests a desired final outcome rather than an actual method for arriving at the outcome.

3. *Relationship information* presents information or facts related to the couple or to the speaker, stated in past, present, or future tense. Examples: "We're taking the kids to the park this Sunday." and "I have a 2 p.m. appointment in the clinic this afternoon." Sensory reports also are included in this category; for example:"I saw you talking to Stella." and "I heard what you said."

4. *Nonrelationship opinion, feeling, or attitude* is a subjective expression about the speaker's preferences or evaluations concerning issues totally unrelated to the couple's relationship. Examples: "That print over there is really beautiful." and "I think God is a woman."

Summarizing Other (SO). There are two types of summary statements that are coded SO:

1. *Summarizing other* is any statement by the speaker that summarizes the previous statements of the other person; for example, "It seems to me what you're saying is. . . ." and "To put it in a few words, you're tired of the way things are."

2. *Summarizing both* is a statement that prevents a review of the conversation; for example, "What we're both saying is that we want to move."

Summarizing Self (SS). Is a statement that reviews the speaker's previous statements. These statements tend to occur at the end of a long series of statements. Verbatim repetition of a speaker's previous statement is also included; for example, "So all I'm saying, Ted, is that I do not want to take responsibility for the house."

Expressing Feelings about a Problem (PF). There are four types of PF statements:

1. *Generalized problem talk* is a statement directly concerning the relationship, but it is phrased in abstract terms (depersonalized) or it can be generalized to a whole population or subgroup. Examples: "Most people are selfish about how they want to spend their free time." and "There isn't a place in the world where there isn't a war going on part of the time."

2. *Relationship issue problem talk* is a statement concerning a relationship problem the couple is discussing: opinions, attitudes, evaluations, or thought processes of the speaker, directly related to the problem. Examples: "We have a

problem with the kids." (existence of problem). "Our financial situation is pretty bad because of your doctor bills and becaus₋ of the new brakes and tires for the car; we also have to save for next year's tuition." (nature of problem). "Maybe we have a problem with the children because I tell them to do one thing and you tell them to do another" (cause of problem). "I've been trying so hard to prove to everyone how capable I am so that I would have a chance at the fellowship that I'm almost at the point of a nervous breakdown." (effect of problem). "If you continue to work yourself so and deny me attention, it's bound to destroy our relationship." (implications of problems or predictions). "The way I see it, we should have made it clear to your parents how long we could stay with them before we went." (attitudes or opinions about problem).

3. *Feeling* is a statement that *directly reveals* the immediate affective experience of the speaker, occurring in the past, present, or future. The statement must make it possible to describe the *feeling being communicated,* the situation in which the feeling occurs, or the problem to which the feeling refers. In the case of a present feeling, the situation may be implicit. (*Note:* Feelings can be expressed through the use of a metaphor.) Examples: "I'm very nervous right now." "I've gone to those parties with you before and I've been miserable." "I'm happy about going to my folks." and "I have butterflies in my stomach."

4. *Blurp* is any statement that cannot be coded because it is inaudible or unintelligible. Examples: "Well, I . . . er . . . I'm not . . . why don't . . . ." and "Uh, well, I just . . . ."

TABLE 4.1

Eight Summary Content Codes of the C.I.S.S.

Code	Definition	Example
AG	Agreement	(a) Yeah. (b) You're right.
DG	Disagreement	(a) No. (b) Yes, but. . . (c) No, because it's too late.
CT	Communication Talk	We're getting off the issue.
MR	Mindreading: Attributing thoughts, feelings, motives, attitudes, or behaviors to spouse	You always get mad in those situations.
PS	Proposing a solution to a problem or information exchange	Let's take out a loan.
SO	Summarizing other	(a) What you're saying is I drink too much. (b) We're both suggesting that we take a vacation.
SS	Summarizing self	(a) I told you that I'm not going because it's too far to drive. (b) What I'm saying is that it's just too late.
PF	Problem information or feelings about a problem	(a) The problem is that we don't have enough money. (b) That makes me sad.

Table 4.1 presents an overview of the eight summary content codes of the CISS.

NONVERBAL CODES OF THE CISS

Assigning Affect and Context Codes

There are two categories of nonverbal codes—affect and context. Affect codes for a thought unit classify the speaker's nonverbal behavior, and context codes indicate the listener's nonverbal behavior. Only one affect code and one context code are assigned for any thought unit. Affect and context codes are given ratings of +, 0, or − (positive, neutral, or negative).

Using both the transcript and the videotape, the coder considers each thought unit, scanning down the list of positive or negative cues for the *face* presented in Table 4.2; if the person is unable to code it positive or negative, he or she scans the list of *voice tone* cues; if the coder is still unable to judge the affect positive or negative, he or she scans the list of *body* cues; if the coder is still unable to assess affect as positive or negative, he or she codes the affect neutral. Our experience is that the process of assigning an affect code is by no

TABLE 4.2

Cues Used to Code Nonverbal Behavior in the C.I.S.S.

Nonverbal Channel	Cues			
	Positive		Negative	
Face	smile		frown	
	empathetic expression		sneer	
	head nod		fearful expression	
			cry	
			smirk	
			angry expression	
			disgust	
			glare	
Voice	caring	satisfied	cold	blaming
	warm	buoyant	tense	sarcastic
	soft	bubbly	scared	angry
	tender	cheerful	impatient	furious
	relieved	chuckling	hard	blaring
	empathetic	happy	clipped	hurt
	concerned	joyful	staccato	depressed
	affectionate	laughter	whining	accusing
	loving			mocking
				laughter
Body	touching		arms akimbo	
	distance reduction		neck or hand tension	
	open arms		rude gestures	
	attention		hands thrown up in disgust	
	relaxation		pointing, jabbing, slicing	
	forward lean		inattention	

means as mechanical as the code manual's hierarchy would suggest. For example, a smile can be indicative of many things, including tension and anger. Therefore, in practice the hierarchy is a very rough guide, and all cues are used in conjunction to produce an affect code. Perhaps the most useful procedure in training coders is to suggest the concept of an affect climate in the interaction that is either positive, neutral, or negative. Each thought unit is then assessed in terms of its contribution to the affective climate. Coders are first trained to come to agreement on voice tone, then on facial expressions (using Ekman & Friesen, 1975), and then on body cues such as those that indicate tension and immediacy. However, this training is inadequate by itself. Coders must be trained to integrate all three channels into one judgment. The judgment is an overall impression, and it is likely that coders' decision rules vary to some degree from couple to couple. In fact, such an adjustment is often necessary, since there is so much variability both in the style that people use to express affect and in the amplitude (intensity) of the expressions. The coder's decision is, therefore, complex. The coder needs to use relatively absolute cues and simultaneously to be able to calibrate the coding to fit each couple. To facilitate this calibration, the affect coder watches the entire tape through once, noting rises and falls in affective climate before beginning to code.

Although the code manual stresses facial cues in the hierarchy, it is our experience that coders report stressing voice tone cues in coding. This discrepancy with Mehrabian's (1972) equation is probably a function of Mehrabian's restricted range of emotional expression. Strangers in a waiting room do not laugh bitterly or smile while making a sarcastic comment. In these cases, the smile and the laughter are obviously not examples of "channel inconsistency" but of tension, uneasiness, and perhaps even desperation. It would not make sense to code the thought unit's affect as positive in these cases. The body cues that have proved most useful are tension and relaxation cues. In most cases, however, all channels are either positively or negatively on or off together; in the common thought unit, affect contains more redundancy across channels than what may at first glance seem like inconsistency. We are currently developing codes for voice tone and facial expressions taken separately in an attempt to provide more specific and more detailed information about each channel.

Coders are instructed to be sensitive to the interaction and not to expect exaggerated affect. For example, a brief smile is sufficient for a positive code; another example is a statement such as "I never knew you felt this way," said with tenderness and concern. The concept of "affective climate" is thus sometimes helpful to coders; it suggests that they view each nonverbal cue as a contribution to the overall affective climate.

Coders encounter problems when they attempt to assess the speaker's *intention* instead of adhering to the cues displayed during message delivery (or listening, for the context codes). Coders are instructed to ignore content and to avoid negative or positive halo judgments. The code manual states:

It is not necessarily a 'bad' sign to have a high frequency of negative codes—perhaps it just represents an ability to express one's feelings. Likewise, it is not necessarily a 'good' sign to have a frequency of positive codes—it may reflect an inability to confront negative feelings. The coders must avoid attributing significance to either positive or negative codes. The couple's behavior should be coded as objectively as possible and this can be accomplished best by adhering closely to the cues specified in the manual.

PROCESSING A TAPE

All coders (content and nonverbal coders) view the entire videotape once before beginning to code. Coders of nonverbal behavior mark specific segments of the transcript that seem (upon initial viewing) to contain sections of nonverbal positive or negative codes; they return to these sections for closer viewing the second time through. Another purpose of the first viewing is to give the coder a sense of the style of both people before beginning to code. A particularly nasal voice tone, for example, will be coded negative unless the coder adjusts to that particular style of speech; the same problem exists for dialects, facial expressive styles, gestures, personal tempos, and rhythms. In some studies, we have coded only audiotapes or only the soundtracks of videotapes. Thus, in these cases only voice tone cues were used in affect coding, so it was impossible to code context.

I will present a specialized coding system for voice tone (and a generalizability study) in Chapter 13.

CHARACTERISTICS OF THE SUMMARY CODES

Howard Markman, Cliff Notarius, and I developed our initial system, which proved to be unteachable and unusable during a frustrating summer (1973). We subsequently revised the system into the 28 content codes and 3 nonverbal codes, which were in turn revised to the 8 content and 3 nonverbal codes being currently used. The 8 content code lumping scheme was accomplished by using two criteria. First, 2 codes were lumped together if they were semantically similar. For example, 2 codes that served to comment on the process of communication would be placed in the summary category "communication talk." Second, if first-order conditional probabilities related 2 codes significantly (see Chapter 2: Z-score > 1.96), they were considered to have the same function. For example, the "yes–but" code functions in a way similar to simple disagreement, so they would be lumped together in the "disagreement" summary code.

Any coding system is an entity that changes with use and with increasing knowledge of how it functions. A basic question of any coding system is "when to lump," that is, to combine subcodes, and "when to split," that is, to distinguish between two types of one code (see, for example, Hutt & Hutt, 1970). The CISS has gone through several versions: It began as a system that had 28 codes for designating content; these 28 codes were lumped for analysis as a data reduction procedure into 8 summary codes. Later coders worked directly from a revised manual which contained only the eight summary codes. Data in this book will always be presented in terms of these 8 summary content codes.

Conditional probabilities were used to cluster codes into summary content codes. The logic of this clustering method is that codes having a "similar function" should be considered part of the same summary code category if they have similar semantic functions (e.g., are both logically forms of disagreement). By "similar function" I also mean that a similar sequence results. I base this decision on the notion of Z-score between conditional and unconditional probabilities, discussed in Chapter 2.

To operationalize this concept of creating summary codes, a priori summary categories were constructed based on similarity in meaning, and then first-order (lag-1) conditional probabilities and Z-scores were used to examine sequences. The data described in Gottman et al. (1977) were used in this analysis; sequences were analyzed separately for clinic and nonclinic couples.

Beam statements (BM), metacommunication statements (MC), and clarification requests (CL) are all linked in chains by Z-scores greater than 1.96 (see Figure 4.1). This is one of several networks that link the three codes.

In the same way, accepting modification, assent, and agreement are linked. Compliance occurred too infrequently even for first-order sequential analysis, but compliance seemed logically related to agreement, so it was included in the summary code for agreement.

Simple disagreement, yes–but, disagreement with a rationale provided, commands, and noncompliance with a command were all linked in first-order chains, except for noncompliance, which occurred too infrequently for sequential analysis, but again seemed logically related to disagreement.

This simple system for creating summary codes worked well for all summary codes except the ones designating problem-solving and information exchange, where things were more complex. Although these two code types are logically connected and occur in approximately the same blocks of transcript, they are usually separated by agreement and disagreement codes. This is true because the usual reaction to a plan seems to be to agree or disagree before

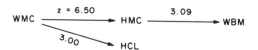

Figure 4.1 *Decision rule for empirical lumping of metacommunication subcodes based on their sequential connection and logical interrelatedness.*

Figure 4.2. *Illustration of sequential connectedness of problem solving and information exchange, with agreement and disagreement codes as the intermediaries.*

adding information. Hence, plans are followed by other plans, agreements, or disagreements before they are followed by information exchanges. Nonetheless, it seems that *information exchange* codes are close cousins to *problem-solving* codes. They are logically similar, and they are related by the chains depicted in Figure 4.2. Because of the linkages described in Figure 4.2, they are lumped together.

The two forms of *mindreading (feelings, attitude, or opinion and behavior)* seem logically distinct, but they have identical functions, depending entirely on the affect with which they are delivered. Neutral or positive *mindreading* codes lead to agreement, whereas negative mindreading codes lead to disagreement. This will become clear in Chapter 6 when the "feeling probe" sequence is discussed.

The three forms of *summary* were infrequent, but *summarizing both people* in clinic couples led most commonly to agreement, whereas *summarizing self* led most commonly to disagreement. Hence, they were put into different summary categories. Where were we to put *summarizing the other?* For clinic couples, it led most commonly to disagreement, whereas for nonclinic couples it led most commonly to agreement. The pattern was strongest (largest Z-scores) for putting it with *summarizing both,* and it seemed most appealing clinically, so it was classified with *summarizes both* rather than *summarizes self.*

The method described is in sharp contrast with the most commonly used technique for combining and separating codes, namely, factor analysis (see Gottman, 1978). The problem with factor analysis in this application is that it lumps two codes on the basis of high correlations between these two codes across subjects. However, just because subjects who do a lot of code A also do a lot of code B does not imply that these two codes are functionally equivalent. For example, children who frequently hit their peers also frequently help their peers, probably because they frequently interact with their peers. The mediating variable is the rate of social interaction with peers. We would be reluctant for many applications to combine prosocial and antisocial behaviors into one functional, descriptive code. This might be appropriate if frequencies were our primary summary statistic, but not if pattern and sequence are important.

Social learning theorists who are searching for interaction sequence units use similar temporal patterning methods for lumping together behaviors that have similar classes of antecedents or similar classes of consequents (see Patterson, 1974, and Patterson, 1978).

Another important criterion for deciding to combine subcodes into a larger category is the extent to which coders are able independently to distinguish among subcodes. No coding system can exist independently of its ability to be usable by coders, which implies that the coding system must have acceptable levels of reliability. Reliability is, thus, an issue that cannot be separated from the design of a coding system. Because reliability is so important and also because it is so widely misunderstood, the next chapter addresses this issue.

CHAPTER 5

Reliability for Sequential Analysis

This chapter will review concepts of reliability on observational research because these ideas may not be familiar to readers who have not worked in a behavioral tradition or who have not dealt with current conceptions in psychological measurement. At the outset we need to discuss the most important advance in the theory of reliability and validity in the last decade, namely, Cronbach, Gleser, Nanda, and Rajaratnam's (1972) monograph, which presented the *theory of generalizability*. The great contribution of Cronbach et al.'s work is that it has integrated the disparate concepts of reliability and validity into an eminently sensible and very practical theory. The older theory of reliability has come to be called "classical theory."

DIFFERENCES BETWEEN CLASSICAL RELIABILITY THEORY AND GENERALIZABILITY THEORY

The reader may recall some terms from classical theory, such as "internal consistency" reliability, "alternate forms" reliability, "parallel forms" reliability, "split-half" reliability, and "test–retest" reliability. Classical theory was developed for psychological tests, and the creators of a new test were urged to assess all possible forms of reliability so that the test could have the widest possible use. For each potential application of a wide variety of item types, different reliability coefficients (usually mathematically equivalent) were proposed, and the student of reliability was confronted with a plethora of formulae with names like "Spearman–Brown." The student was often left with the question "Yes, but what is in fact *the* reliability of the test?"

Generalizability theory dispenses with the concept of *the* reliability of a test by noting that all reliability assessments are statements of the extent to which one may generalize along some dimension. Coefficients of internal consistency, for example, assess the extent to which one may assume that the test items come from the same item domain (Nunnally, 1967), that is, measure the same basic dimension. If one were to randomly sample items from the domain and construct several tests, coefficients of internal consistency would assess the extent to which one could generalize across parallel forms of the test. Coefficients of test–retest reliability assess the extent to which one can generalize across repeated occasions of administration of the test. In each case the reliability coefficient assesses the extent to which one may generalize across some facet (parallel tests, or time). If an investigator constructs a test for a specific purpose, a particular generalization is automatically suggested, and thus *the work that the measurement instrument is to perform suggests the reliability assessment that is relevant.*

The equations that result from either the domain sampling (Nunnally, 1967, pp. 176–177) version or the parallel test (Nunnally, pp. 182–183) version of classical theory are based upon the assumption that a person's score on a test is the sum of two scores—*true score,* which can be thought of as the person's average score on all items in the domain, and *error,* which can be thought of as the error due to having sampled only some items from the domain. The classical equations in the parallel test version also make some assumptions about the distributions and independence of the errors from the two tests (Nunnally, p. 182).

Two equations are important to review from classical theory. The first is that the reliability of a test can be estimated as the square root of the average interitem correlation, and the second is the Spearman (1910) and Brown (1910) formula for estimating the increase in reliability with increasing test length. Given that a new test has N_2 items and the old test had N_1 items, the old test had reliability coefficient α_1, and K is the ratio of the two item lengths, then $K = N_2/N_1$, and the reliability of the new test (see Wiggins, 1973, p. 292) is

$$\alpha_2 = \frac{K\alpha_1}{1 + (K - 1)\alpha_1}$$

If $\alpha_1 = .70$ and the test were doubled in length, then α_2 can be calculated as .82. This is an intuitively sensible result similar to the law of large numbers. As we sample more items, we reduce sampling error. Since reliability is defined in classical reliability theory as the ratio of true score variance to observed score variance (Wiggins, p. 282), the more we reduce error, the closer the observed score approaches true score, and therefore the closer the reliability ratio must approach 1.0.

In generalizability theory, reliability is the extent to which one can generalize to some universe of interest, and "Since a given measure may be generalized to many different 'universes,' the investigator must be able to specify the universe in which he is interested before he can study 'reliability' [Wiggins, p. 285]." The investigator may wish to generalize across *persons* or across any of a set of *conditions*. The term condition is general; it may refer to test items, stimuli, settings, observers, times of observation, or situations of the observation. If we want to generalize across occasions, we must sample across occasions of interest just as we would in an analysis of variance design. For example, in an analysis of variance in which we wish to generalize across age, we would include samples of different ages.

An interesting thing about this idea in generalizability theory is that it purposely merges the concepts of reliability with the concepts of validity, because validity is simply a slightly different kind of generalization. To complete the conception mathematically, Cronbach *et al.* use familiar analysis of variance models. Analysis of variance models partition the total variance around the grand mean into whatever independent sources of variance the investigator chooses, plus error variance. One such model partitions variance into a person effect, a condition effect, and a residual (error) effect. Any other partition is possible to remove systematic sources of variance from the residual, so that error variance can be reduced. As in analysis of variance, the partitioning of variance produces a mean-square term between persons (MS_p), a mean-square term between conditions (MS_i, where N_i is the number of conditions), and a residual (error) term (MS_r). The reliability coefficient is an intraclass correlation coefficient obtained from the analysis of variance,

$$\alpha = \frac{MS_p - MS_r}{MS_p + (N_i - 1)MS_r} \quad .$$

EXAMPLE. Suppose that the two observers code the same set of fourteen videotapes, counting instances of agreement as defined by the CISS, and that the data in Table 5.1 are obtained. The investigator is interested in generalizing across observers, which becomes the occasions source of variance. This generalization says, in effect, that most of the variance is accounted for by variance in agreement across couples, and not across coders or by coder-by-couple interaction. That is what the generalizability statement means. The investigator calculates α as

$$\alpha = \frac{MS_p - MS_r}{MS_p + (2 - 1)MS_r} = \frac{MS_p - MS_r}{MS_p + MS_r} = \frac{22.07 - 1.52}{22.07 + 1.52} = .87 \quad .$$

If the investigator had wanted to have observers code segments of the videotape and wanted to generalize across segment length (a statement that it does not matter which segment length he uses), two randomly selected segment lengths could have formed another facet of the analysis of variance design. This could

TABLE 5.1

Sample Data for Generalizability Study

Tape Number	Observers	
	1	2
2	0	0
4	4	7
6	0	0
8	0	0
10	11	12
12	3	3
14	7	7
16	2	2
19	5	5
22	1	1
25	0	1
26	1	1
29	5	6
31	1	1

be expanded to generalizations across location of the segments, male or female coders, and so on.

Jones, Reid, and Patterson (1975) reported the first generalizability study ("G study") with observational data. They wrote:

> Generalizability theory (Cronbach et al., 1972) provides an elegant and comprehensive set of procedures for assessing the reliability, or more correctly, the generalizability, of behavioral observations which are obtained under varying conditions. Subjects' scores derived from observations are classified according to conditions within facets, which are analogous to levels within factors in the analysis of variance. Estimates of variance components for each of the facets, and their interactions, are obtained via the appropriate ANOVA model, and these variance estimates are used to obtain generalizability coefficients. These results comprise the generalizability, or G study, and are used to estimate the reliability of observations [p. 60].

OBSERVER AGREEMENT

In an excellent paper, Johnson and Bolstad (1973) discussed various problems in alternative methods of computing observer agreement; their discussion will be reviewed here in part. They pointed out that there should be no one way to assess observer agreement because the index must suit the purposes of each individual investigation. However, they suggested that an overall percentage agreement score over all codes is meaningless because the figure tends to overweigh those behaviors that occur most frequently (see also the discussion of Cohen's statistic "Kappa" in this chapter).

If agreement between observers is calculated separately for each code, then the next issue is what the time span is within which common coding is counted as an agreement. If the time unit is large, it is possible that two coders may have observed exactly the same number of a particular code but never have agreed as to when it was observed. Johnson and Bolstad wrote, "If one observer sees 10 occurrences of a behavior over a 30-minute period and the other sees 12, there is no assurance that they were ever in agreement [p. 13]." Furthermore, the total number of occurrences of a code summed over observations is useful for some purposes, but not for others. Johnson and Bolstad correctly pointed out that, for the study of sequence or pattern, this summing is not appropriate. They wrote:

> For some research purposes, this broad time span for agreement would be totally inadequate. For conditional probability analysis of one behavior (cf. Patterson and Cobb, 1971), for example, one needs to know that two observers saw the same behavior at the same time and (depending on the question) that each observer also saw the same set or chain of antecedent and/or consequences. *This latter criterion is extremely stringent, particularly with complex codes where low rate behaviors are involved, but these criteria are necessary for an appropriate accuracy estimate* [p. 12; emphasis added].

This is an extremely important point, and it suggests that *for sequential analysis agreement must be tied to specific codes on specific units of transcript.* In the preceding generalizability example, the two totals would have to be agreement in one column and agreement-plus-disagreement in the other column tied to specific thought units on a transcript in which one observer noted the occurrence of a particular code category.

The most commonly used index of observer agreement is the ratio of the number of agreements (in the numerator) to the number of agreements-plus-disagreements (in the denominator). However, this ratio ignores the base rate problem, that is, the amount of agreement that could be obtained by chance alone. An example Johnson and Bolstad cite, suggested by Hartmann, will illustrate the base rate problem. Suppose that there are only two possible codes for a husband's behavior, Nice and Nasty, and that this husband is Nice 90% and Nasty 10% of the time. If two observers coded independently and randomly at these base rates, they would obtain agreement 82% of the time by chance alone. This figure is computed by squaring the base rate of each code category and adding the results: $(.90)^2 + (.10)^2 = .82$. Note that if we computed observer agreement on only those segments in which one observer coded the husband as Nasty, the level of agreement by chance alone would be quite low, $(.10)^2 = .01$, whereas, if we computed observer agreement on only those segments in which one observer coded the husband as Nice, the level of chance agreement would be quite high, $(.90)^2 = .81$. See Appendix 5.1 for an extension of this example to multiple coders.

Statistical tests of the difference between obtained and chance agreement

TABLE 5.2

Table for Cohen's Kappa Computation

		Observer 2				
		Codes				
		A	B	C	Row Total	P_1
Observer 1	A	25	0	1	26	26/124 = .21
	B	1	30	2	33	33/124 = .27
	C	10	5	50	65	65/124 = .52
Column Total		36	35	53	124	
P_2	36/124 =	.29,	.28	.43		

$$P_0 = \frac{\text{sum of diagonal elements}}{\text{grand total}} = \frac{105}{124} = .85$$

$$P_c = \Sigma \ P_1 \ \text{x} \ P_2 = (.21)(.29) + (.27)(.28) + (.43)(.52) = .36$$

$$\text{Kappa} = \frac{.85 - .36}{1 - .36} = .77$$

can be computed; various tests were reviewed by Hollenbeck (1978), who recommended Cohen's (1960) statistic Kappa, which is the proportion of agreement after chance agreement has been removed from consideration:

$$\text{Kappa} = \frac{P_0 - P_c}{1 - P_c},$$

where P_0 is the observed proportion of agreement and P_c is the chance proportion of agreement. Kappa may be calculated across all the codes in a coding system, as follows; suppose the matrix of observations by two coders were given by Table 5.2.

As Hollenbeck pointed out, the matrix given is extremely useful for doing reliability checks because such a display makes it easy to detect confusion between coders on specific codes by scanning for pockets of off-diagonal elements, as in the confusion between C and A in Table 5.2. The statistical properties of Kappa have been worked out (e.g., Fleiss, Cohen, & Everitt, 1969) and have been generalized to more than two observers (Fleiss, 1971) and situations (Light, 1971). Another advantage of Kappa is that it can be computed separately for each transcript to indicate particular transcripts on which agreement was difficult for observers.

RELIABILITY DRIFT AND DECAY

A series of investigations by Reid and his associates (Reid, 1970; Taplin & Reid, 1973) and O'Leary and his associates (O'Leary & Kent, 1972;

Romanczyk, Kent, Diament, & O'Leary, 1973) indicates that interobserver agreement declines during periods when observers think that their coding is not being checked. Taplin and Reid found that this problem occurred least when observers thought random reliability checking was used as compared to when they believed there would be no checking or when they knew they were to be checked at two specific times. In their study, all the data had been checked in all three groups. The period spot-check group came up to levels of reliability higher than the random spot-check group on the days when it was checked, but it fell far below in between spot checks. This chapter will present evidence to suggest that if observers are trained to high levels of agreement on two consecutive tapes before coding begins and if a random segment of *every* tape is checked by a reliability checker, levels of observer agreement will not decay, and for some codes reliability will in fact *increase* over time rather than decay. The author has experienced the same phenomenon of no reliability decay with a coding system of tapes of children's social speech. This may be one advantage of coding taped records rather than coding live behavior.

O'Leary and Kent (1972) identified a phenomenon called observer "drift," in which pairs of observers modify the coding system and stay reliably together, but drift apart from other coders. The problem is complex (see Johnson & Bolstad, 1973, pp. 23–25), but it can be attenuated by a written code manual, by training sessions on coded material, by tapes that are coded unknowingly by everyone with subsequent discussion of disagreements, or by using one reliability checker who independently codes samples of every tape. All of these procedures have been used in the research reported in this book. The procedure that uses one reliability checker is best.[1]

RELIABILITY OF THE CISS

To simplify the presentation of reliability results on the CISS, the results of several generalizability studies will be presented at this point. Throughout this book generalizability studies will occasionally be presented for specific applications of the CISS, such as coding affect only from audiotapes. For the first generalizability study, transcripts and tapes from 28 couples were coded by one reliability checker and five coders using both the verbatim transcript and the videotape. Coders were trained following the procedure described in Chapter

[1] One problem can occur with the procedure of checking reliability of each coder with one coder coordinator. It is possible for coder 1's errors to be consistently in category A and coder 2's errors to be consistently in category B. In that case, both A and B would check within acceptable limits with the coordinator except on one code, but if they were ever checked out with one another they would not agree on two codes. To test for this possibility, we (Gottman and associates) periodically check coders with one another, paired randomly, and without their awareness that they are being checked. We have observed no such potential problem with any of the CISS coding categories.

TABLE 5.3

Design Matrix for Generalizability Study

	Code A	
Transcript	Agreements	Agreements-plus-Disagreements
1		
2		
•		
•		
•		
N		

4. For each code, the following analysis of variance design was used (see Table 5.3), with the stringent criterion of agreement tied to specific thought units of transcript; that is, the reliability checker and coder agreed only if they had independently coded the same thought unit in the same way.

For 14 transcripts (those with odd couple numbers), four pages were sampled, and for 14 couples (those with even couple numbers), two pages were sampled; clinic and nonclinic couples were included in both samples. The results presented in Table 5.4 show that all codes have high Cronbach alpha

TABLE 5.4

Generalizability Study Results with C.I.S.S. Content Codes

Code	Frequency	Mean Square Transcripts	Mean Square Residual	Cronbach Alpha
Four Pages				
Problem Feeling (PF)	281	242.63	1.66	.986
Mindreading (MR)	70	49.12	2.20	.914
Problem Solving (PS)	317	177.73	3.35	.963
Communication Talk (CT)	40	8.89	.28	.939
Agreement (AG)	126	42.38	.69	.968
Disagreement (DG)	99	34.50	.80	.954
Summarizing Other (SO)	11	1.67	.14	.842
Summarizing Self (SS)	9	1.22	.07	.897
Question (Q/)	80	14.22	.44	.940
Two Pages				
Problem Feeling (PF)	201	105.43	1.43	.973
Mindreading (MR)	48	14.19	.21	.971
Problem Solving (PS)	134	75.53	.85	.978
Communication Talk (CT)	13	2.54	.00	1.000
Agreement (AG)	46	22.07	1.52	.871
Disagreement (DG)	53	22.30	.42	.963
Summarizing Other (SO)	1	.07	.00	1.000
Summarizing Self (SS)	8	2.34	.04	.970
Question (Q/)	38	18.30	.00	1.000

*Frequency refers to how often this code was noted in the sample by one or both observers and is thus the diagonal plus off-diagonal total in the Cohen Kappa matrix over all fourteen transcripts.

generalizability coefficients even with an extremely stringent criterion of agreement between observers. This is true even for codes with relatively low base rates, such as the summary codes—Summarizing Other (SO) and Summarizing Self (SS).

On the same set of 14 transcripts for which content was coded, two coders coded affect and context for the same four pages previously sampled. Table 5.5 presents the results of this study. These results show that the nonverbal codes have high levels of reliability but that positive and neutral context are not quite as reliable as the other nonverbal codes. This is probably a function of the fact that all videotapes in this study involved a one-camera profile shot of the couple rather than a full-face or three-fourths shot of both faces; for example, negative affect listening (such as disgust, which involves the nose's wrinkling up) may be easier to detect in profile than positive affect listening.

These results suggest that the CISS is a reliable coding system in the sense of generalizability across coders and across sample lengths.[2]

To test for reliability decay with the CISS, a generalizability study was conducted by having the same group of coders consecutively code *three additional separate sets* of transcripts. Table 5.6 presents the results of that study. There is no evidence of reliability decay; in fact, reliability for most codes increased slightly from the first occasion to the third occasion. When all transcripts are nested within occasions and the analysis of variance design spans the three studies (transcripts nested within occasions, and either two or four pages, crossed by the within-transcripts factor of diagonal and off-diagonal), the relevant interaction term (see Table 5.4) is not significant six times out of nine, and for two of the three times it is notable that the data indicate a *significant*

TABLE 5.5

Generalizability Study Results with C.I.S.S. Affect and Context Codes

Code	Frequency	Mean Square Transcripts	Mean Square Residual	Cronbach Alpha
Affect				
Positive	113	68.13	3.52	.902
Neutral	775	336.50	6.20	.964
Negative	145	76.33	.21	.995
Context				
Positive	107	53.17	6.67	.777
Neutral	874	421.30	37.35	.837
Negative	134	82.19	4.27	.948

[2] In one study (the Phase One study reported in Chapter 14), Cohen's Kappas for the content codes averaged .909 with a standard deviation of .040, and for the affect codes Kappas averaged .715 with a standard deviation of .169. If one matrix is computed for all transcripts, the Kappa for the content codes is .911 and the Kappa for the affect codes is .764.

TABLE 5.6

Generalizability Study Results over Three Separate Occasions to Access Reliability Decay (C.I.S.S. Codes)

Code	OCCASIONS 1 MS_T	MS_R	α	2 MS_T	MS_R	α	3 MS_T	MS_R	α	Interaction Term F-ratio Diagonal/Off-Diagonal by Occasions	Direction of Effect if Significant
Problem Feeling (PF)	166.63	1.19	.986	299.43	3.85	.975	959.94	1.40	.997	3.02(ns)	—
Mindreading (MR)	32.38	.29	.982	27.11	.43	.969	91.42	.72	.984	3.82*	3>2
Problem Solving (PS)	127.10	1.97	.969	507.31	5.40	.979	445.97	1.79	.992	1.59(ns)	—
Communication Talk (CT)	5.31	.14	.949	9.85	.62	.882	6.94	.07	.980	5.14**	3>2
Agreement (AG)	32.83	.32	.982	38.20	.69	.965	47.21	.23	.990	.21(ns)	—
Disagreement (DG)	28.40	.61	.958	334.56	2.14	.987	88.22	1.99	.956	1.33(ns)	—
Summarizing Other (SO)	.94	.10	.808	31.55	.05	.997	4.45	.27	.886	.08(ns)	—
Summarizing Self (SS)	1.78	.05	.945	12.64	.02	.997	6.67	.25	.928	6.74**	1<2>3
Question (Q)	17.16	.16	.982	34.41	.06	.997	41.97	.19	.991	.72(ns)	—

*p < .05
**p < .01

102

reliability increment, rather than decay. For the remaining F-ratio, for the Summarizing Self code (an infrequent code), reliability was highest on the *second* occasion, but again there is no evidence of a steady decay over time for the reliability of this code. Also, the size of the reliabilities shows that not only do they not decay, but they also remain at the initial acceptable levels.

APPENDIX 5.1

This appendix summarizes how to calculate Cohen's Kappa statistic for several coders; the presentation is taken from Fleiss (1971), but it is translated to apply to observational coding.

We let N = the number of thought units in a transcript or transcript segment

n = the number of independent coders

k = the number of code categories

n_{ij} = the number of coders who assigned the ith thought unit to the jth coding category.

Then we define

$$p_j = \frac{1}{Nn} \sum_{i=j}^{N} n_{ij} = \text{the proportion of all thought units that were coded into the } j^{th} \text{ coding category.}$$

To calculate agreement on a particular coding category, we compute the conditional probability that if one rater assigns a thought unit to category j, a second coder will also. Then this conditional probability averaged over thought units is given by

$$\bar{P}_j = \frac{\sum_{i=1}^{N} n^2_{ij} - Nnp_j}{Nn(n-1)p_j} .$$

Under the hypothesis of no agreement beyond chance levels, this number should equal the unconditional probability of an assignment to category j, namely, p_j, and Kappa is thus given by

$$K_j = \frac{\bar{P}_j - p_j}{1 - p_j} .$$

Fleiss (1971) also shows that the variance of Kappa is given by the expression

$$Var(K_j) = \frac{[1 + 2 \cdot (n-1)p_j]^2 + 2(n-1)p_j q_j}{Nn(n-1)^2 p_j q_j} ,$$

where $q_j = 1 - p_j$, and that $K_j/SE(K_j)$ is approximately distributed as a standard normal variate, which can be used to assess if agreement is significantly greater than chance. Kappa for the entire matrix is given in Fleiss, as well as an expression for the variance of this overall Kappa.

CHAPTER 6

The Topography of Marital Conflict

This chapter presents the nonsequential and sequential analyses of differences between distressed and nondistressed couples, and clinic and nonclinic couples, respectively. The definitions of these criterion groups are described below.

PROCEDURES AND METHODOLOGY

All couples were interviewed by a male–female team after husband and wife filled out a Standard Problem Inventory (see Appendix I), which required a rating of the preceived severity of a set of common marital problems. Using the Problem Inventory, the interviewers selected three problems that were rated highest in perceived severity by both husband and wife. The interview was introduced as follows:

> What we've been doing while you were filling out forms was determining which of the situations you both listed as problems. Now what we'd like to do is talk to you about each of the problems and find out what specifically happens in situations where that problem occurs.
>
> We'd like to get a play-by-play account of who said what and when in a typical example of a discussion of that problem. We'd also like to identify some key times in the conversation when things become particularly difficult for each of you. We will be tape recording the conversation and taking notes.
>
> Let's take the Number 1 problem that you identified: _____. Can you think of a specific situation that came up?

During this *play-by-play interview,* the following information was obtained: (a) the situational context of the discussion (kitchen, car, etc.); (b) the time of day; (c) the other people present (if any) and their relationships to the couple (e.g., in-laws, friends); (d) the interaction flow, that is, who said what when; (e) who got upset first; and (f) the points in the interaction flow that were particularly problematic for each person. The play-by-play interview for each of the three problems was conducted, and the interviews were recorded on audio cassettes. The play-by-play interview was useful in building rapport with the couple. After the interviews were transcribed, the content was used to construct a domain of situations that married couples find problematic. These findings were used in the design of the subsequent study reported in Chapter 11.

After the play-by-play interviews, the husband and wife were asked to "come to a mutually satisfactory resolution" of the most troublesome of the three problems, and this interaction was videotaped. There was no time limit; taping stopped when the couple felt they were done. Videotapes were transcribed and coded according to the procedure described in Chapter 4.

One methodological point needs to be clarified, namely, the selection of criterion groups. Any conceptualization of successful communication should include the means whereby one may discriminate between groups of couples who are satisfied with their marriages and groups of couples who are not. In the remainder of this book, two distinctions are made. The first is called the *clinic–nonclinic distinction.* Clinic couples were those who were seeking marriage counseling, and nonclinic couples were those who had answered an advertisement for couples who experience their relationship as "mutually satisfying." In addition to this criterion, all couples were given the Locke–Williamson factor analyzed 22-item Marital Relationship Inventory (subsequently called the MRI in this book), which is a widely used measure of marital satisfaction, and cutoff scores were used as provided by Burgess *et al.* (1971, pp. 327–331).

The second distinction uses the MRI and is called the *distressed–nondistressed distinction.* Distressed couples were those clinic couples in which at least one spouse's MRI scores were below a criterion (MRI score of 85), and nondistressed couples were nonclinic couples in which *both* the husband's and the wife's MRI scores were above a criterion (an MRI score of 102).

The subjects were two groups of 14 married couples. Fourteen clinic couples were referred to the study by marital counseling agencies or responded to an advertisement asking for research subjects who felt their marriage to be unsatisfactory. Fourteen nonclinic couples responded to an advertisement asking for couples who felt their marriage was "mutually satisfying." All 28 couples took the Marital Relationship Inventory (MRI). The 5 clinic couples with the lowest MRI scores and the 5 nonclinic couples with the highest MRI scores were selected for analysis. The 5 couples in the distressed group had average MRI scores of 69.30 with a standard deviation of 3.44; the five couples in the nondistressed group had average MRI scores of 108.50 with a standard deviation of 1.46, $t(8) = 23.46$, $p < .001$. There were no differences between the two groups of couples for husband's age, $t(8) = .17$, n.s., with nondistressed husbands averaging 25.8 years and distressed husbands averaging 26.8 years; no differences for wife's age, $t(8) = .36$, n.s., with nondistressed wives averaging 24.6 years and distressed wives averaging 23.6 years; and no differences for number of years married, $t(8) = .36$, n.s., with nondistressed couples married an average of 3.55 years and distressed couples an average of 3.48 years.

RESULTS ON POSITIVENESS

Nonsequential analyses will be presented on the distressed and nondistressed couples because they are more homogeneous groups than clinic and nonclinic couples; couples seeking marriage counseling who score high on marital satisfaction and couples who answered the "mutually satisfying" portion of the advertisement one of whom scored low on marital satisfaction are thus excluded from these analyses.[1] However, nonsequential analyses on all clinic and all nonclinic couples in two studies produced essentially similar patterns of results as the analyses for distressed and nondistressed couples (see Markman, 1976; Notarius, 1976; and Rubin, 1977 for details).

The reader will recall from Chapter 3 that Riskin and Faunce (1972) concluded that the most consistent discriminator across studies between distressed and nondistressed families was the ratio of agreement to disagreement. This suggests that this variable is an important candidate for operationalizing positiveness using only content, and not nonverbal behavior, codes. In the study reported in this chapter, the proportion of agreements to agreements plus disagreements was calculated. This ratio never entails dividing by zero if there were no disagreements in a transcript. For husbands $t(8) = 2.07$, $p < .05$ with distressed husbands averaging .46 and nondistressed husbands averaging .66. For wives, $t(8) = 7.78$, $p < .0001$, with distressed wives averaging .39 and nondistressed wives averaging .76. Consistent with Riskin and Faunce (1972), this index of agreement to agreement plus disagreement successfully discriminated couples along a distress dimension. There was, therefore, evidence that, considering only verbal behavior, nondistressed couples were more positive than distressed couples. Subsequent analysis of the proportion of agreements and disagreements analyzed separately showed that the only significant difference between the two groups was for agreement for the wives, $F(1,8) = 23.89$, $p < .01$, with distressed wives averaging 5.93% and nondistressed wives averaging 25.76%.

It is possible to examine separately the nonverbal component of positiveness by summing positive, neutral, and negative affect over all content codes. Therefore, the proportions of positive, neutral, and negative affect summed over

[1] Some of the results of this chapter were presented in Gottman, Markman, and Notarius (1977).

all content codes were calculated. A multivariate analysis of variance on the proportion of the three affect codes after arcsine square root transformation found no interaction effect of the husband–wife by the distress factor, with multivariate $F(3,14) = .72$, nonsignificant husband–wife main effect, $F(3,14) = 3.11$, but significant distress main effect, $F(3,14) = 12.44, p < .001$. Table 6.1 presents the univariate F-ratios and the means for the three nonverbal codes. Both neutral and negative affect contribute to the multivariate effect, but positive affect does not. These analyses indicate that agreement to disagreement ratios and nonverbal behavior during message delivery both independently discriminated distressed from nondistressed couples, although the F-ratios were larger for nonverbal behavior. *The positive–negative dimension of nonverbal behavior thus discriminated distressed from nondistressed couples better than the positive–negative dimension of verbal behavior.*

The findings about negative and positive nonverbal behavior are in contrast to the Birchler *et al.* (1975) study that found that on a high conflict task (the IMC) both negative and positive codes discriminated between distressed and nondistressed couples. We did get these results on *positive content codes* such as agreement, but, when only the nonverbal behaviors of message delivery were analyzed, *positive nonverbal codes* did not discriminate distressed from nondistressed couples. Birchler *et al.* (1975) combined both content and nonverbal cues in their summary positive and negative codes, but it would appear that greater discriminative power is obtained by separately studying the nonverbal aspects of message exchange.

However, a more precise descriptive picture about positiveness is obtained by *combining* content and affect codes. After all, each content code is delivered with a specific affect code. Hence, the preceding analyses, although theoretically interesting with respect to the positive–negative dimension, are not satisfying descriptively. Therefore, for each couple the proportion of each of the eight content codes for each of the three affect codes (neutral, positive, and negative) was calculated. Since the analyses were performed on proportional data, all variables were again transformed according to proper statistical convention for proportional data, using an arcsine square root transformation (Myers, 1966).

TABLE 6.1

Nonverbal Delivery of Messages Independent of Their Content—Univariate F-ratios for Distress Main Effect

Variable	Univariate F-ratio	Distressed Mean	Nondistressed Mean
Neutral Affect	11.67**	.65	.85
Positive Affect	.09	.10	.12
Negative Affect	35.36***	.25	.03

**p < .01
***p < .001
df = (3, 14), univariate F-ratios calculated with arcsine $\sqrt{x}$ transformation

Three multivariate analyses of variance were performed, one analysis on the eight content codes with neutral affect, one with the eight content codes with positive, and one with negative speaker affect. The design was a 2 × 2 design with distressed–nondistressed as the between-subjects factor and husband–wife as the within-subjects factor.

There were no significant main effects for the husband–wife factor for any of the affect codes; for neutral affect, multivariate F-ratio with Wilks Lambda criterion, $F(8,9) = 2.66$; for the positive codes, $F(8,9) = 2.68$; for the negative codes, $F(8,9) = 2.54$. There were also no significant husband–wife by distress interactions for the neutral codes, $F(8,9) = .52$, for the positive codes, $F(8,9) = .72$, and for the negative codes, $F(8,9) = 1.44$. There was, however, a significant distress main effect for the neutral codes, $F(8,9) = 3.71$, $p < .05$, and for the negative codes, $F(8,9) = 4.36$, $p < .05$. There was not a significant multivariate distress main effect for the positive codes, $F(8,9) = 1.18$.

The specific univariate F-ratios will shed light on the descriptive issue of positiveness. Table 6.2 presents the univariate F-ratios for the two significant multivariate F-ratios, that is, for neutral and negative affect. Here we can see that, with accompanying neutral affect, nondistressed couples were significantly more likely to agree than distressed couples, but there were no significant

TABLE 6.2

Content-by-Affect Codes Univariate Analyses of Variance
(Means in percentages)

Code	Univariate F-ratio	Distressed Mean	Nondistressed Mean	Multiple R
Neutral Affect				
Prob Feeling (PF)	4.03	30.29	38.79	
Mindreading (MR)	.00	7.07	8.18	
Prob Solving (PS)	1.88	8.68	5.82	
Comm Talk (CT)	.24	4.03	3.91	
Agreement (AG)	9.65**	8.36	19.83	
Disagreement (DG)	1.98	6.21	8.29	
Summarize Other (SO)	.49	.22	.56	
Summarize Self (SS)	1.34	.61	.09	
				R = .88
Negative Affect				
Prob Feeling (PF)	36.06***	11.88	1.10	
Mindreading (MR)	27.85***	5.07	.19	
Prob Solving (PS)	3.25	1.25	.19	
Comm Talk (CT)	.12	.28	.77	
Agreement (AG)	8.23*	.36	.00	
Disagreement (DG)	14.05**	5.27	.48	
Summarizing Other (SO)	1.00	.15	.00	
Summarizing Self (SS)	1.00	.06	.00	
				R = .89

*p < .05
**p < .01
***p < .001

[a]F-ratios computed on arcsine $\sqrt{x}$ transformation customary for proportional data.

differences between the two groups on the proportion of disagreement. For negative affect, however, agreement has a different connotation. An agreement statement such as "Sure, anything you say." delivered with negative affect is either sarcasm or a defeated, depressed agreement, and here we see that distressed couples' mean was significantly greater than the mean for nondistressed couples. There was also significantly more disagreement with negative affect in distressed than in nondistressed couples.

We can conclude from Table 6.2 that distressed couples were more likely to express their feelings about a problem, to mindread, and to disagree, all with negative nonverbal behaviors. The size of the univariate F-ratios is particularly striking, especially in this literature; for example, the omega-square for expressing feelings about a problem with negative affect (PF-) is .778, which suggests that this coding variable alone is accounting for approximately 78% of the variance in this classification of couples as distressed or nondistressed.

There are also important negative results in these analyses. Distressed and nondistressed couples did not differ on the relative frequency of metacommunicative statements or on the relative frequency of feeling statements made independent of affect. The two groups of couples also did not differ on the relative frequency of mindreading statements, although here again the nonverbal mode of delivery strongly discriminated the two groups. Considering the nonverbal mode of delivery of feeling statements, therefore, adds a great deal of discriminative power.

These results thus support Hypothesis 2 of the Structural Model of Chapter 3 for marital interaction that distressed couples are considerably more negative and less positive than nondistressed couples and that these differences are greater for negative than for positive behavior. Furthermore, nonverbal behavior, analyzed separately, is a better discriminator than verbal behavior. We will now consider the results on the reciprocity dimension.

RESULTS ON RECIPROCITY

Detailed sequential analysis requires long chains of interaction, and, if the analysis is to go beyond first-order sequences, data of more than 10 couples discussed previously must be included to give us adequate confidence in estimates of conditional probabilities. Therefore, for the sequential analyses, the data for all 28 couples in the sample, that is, all 14 clinic couples and all 14 nonclinic couples, were included.

To combine a set of couples for a group lag-sequence analysis, I recommend the following procedure. Modify Bakeman's program Joint so that a sequence of dummy codes follows at the end of each couple's data set; the data set would be [(Couple 1 Data) (Dummy Codes) (Couple 2 Data) (Dummy Codes) (Couple 3 Data) (Dummy Codes) . . .]. The number of dummy codes should exceed the maximum lag used in the lag-sequence analysis. Transitions

TABLE 6.3
Probability of Negative Affect Cycles

Criterion: H-	LAG					
	1	2	3	4	5	6
Nonclinic						
H-	.00	.20*	.08	.14*	.08	.06
W-	.16*	.04	.14*	.14	.12	.06
Z-score	4.77	8.38	4.08	5.54	3.31	a
Clinic						
H-	.00	.38*	.13	.22*	.22*	.22*
W-	.34*	.13	.26*	.18	.20	.18
Z-score	7.49	12.89	5.44	5.53	5.53	5.79

Criterion: W-	LAG					
	1	2	3	4	5	6
Nonclinic						
H-	.19*	.01	.16*	.01	.12*	.01
W-	.00	.19*	.07	.10*	.05	.19*
Z-score	9.23	7.18	7.91	2.77	5.60	7.18
Clinic						
H-	.27*	.11	.21*	.16	.19*	.17
W-	.00	.46*	.15	.29*	.20	.23*
Z-score	7.87	15.18	6.01	7.38	4.68	4.65

*Represents the probabilities with the highest Z-score, which is given immediately below the respective probabilities.

a Denotes the fact that no Z-score was > 1.96.

to and from dummy codes, and the number of dummy codes are ignored in the computation of all probabilities and Z-scores.

Table 6.3 presents results on the probability of negative affect cycles (i.e., affect independent of content). Negative cycles have higher conditional probabilities and Z-scores for clinic couples than for nonclinic couples.

Table 6.4 shows that there may be a slightly greater reciprocity of positive affect at early lags for *clinic* couples. This is contrary to what might have been predicted by a quid pro quo model, but it is consistent with Hypothesis 1 of the Structural Model (Chapter 3), that there is greater patterning of interaction in clinic than in nonclinic couples. Taken together, the analyses on the reciprocity of affect suggest that the reciprocity on negative affect is more characteristic of clinic than of nonclinic couples and that reciprocity of negative affect is a better discriminator between groups than reciprocity of positive affect. This latter conclusion is reminiscent of the within-subject correlations of husband and wife records of pleasing and displeasing events over 14 days calculated by Wills et al. (1974), who concluded that "The tendency to reciprocate displeasurable behaviors was stronger than for pleasurable behaviors [p. 808]." It is also the pattern of results predicted by Hypothesis 3 of the Structural Model, which was based on our literature review of this dimension.

TABLE 6.4
Probability of Positive Affect Cycles

Criterion: H+	LAG					
	1	2	3	4	5	6
Nonclinic						
H+	.00	.24*	.08	.13*	.16*	.09
W+	.27*	.07	.14*	.15	.10	.12
Z-score	6.44	8.48	2.05	3.34	4.94	a
Clinic						
H+	.00	.19*	.11*	.09*	.09	.09*
W+	.37*	.12	.16	.13	.16*	.15
Z-score	8.69	6.34	2.86	2.76	2.87	2.76
Criterion: W+	LAG					
	1	2	3	4	5	6
Nonclinic						
H+	.19*	.03	.09	.05	.06	.11*
W+	.00	.23*	.09	.13	.14*	.11
Z-score	6.99	6.60	a	a	2.53	2.92
Clinic						
H+	.19*	.08	.07	.09	.09	.09*
W+	.00	.26*	.15*	.13	.16*	.15
Z-score	7.80	7.85	2.61	a	2.87	2.76

*Represents the probabilities with the highest Z-score, which is given immediately below the respective probabilities.

DESCRIPTIVE ANALYSES

Although it is theoretically interesting to discuss the results on positiveness and reciprocity, detailed sequential and nonsequential analyses are necessary in order to obtain a complete description of the differences between clinic and nonclinic couples. This detailed description is also necessary clinically because interventions with clinic couples that purport an empirical base must be constructed on a complete analysis of the differences between these two groups of couples in resolving conflict.

Because detailed sequential analyses must be organized for concise presentation, each marital discussion was divided into three equal phases, beginning, middle, and end, much as the moves in a game of chess. *As in chess, the objective was to identify in each phase the major tasks of the phase and the major differences in maneuvers for the two groups of couples.*

Table 6.5 summarizes the distribution of the codes across three equal phases of the discussions. The tabulated numbers were obtained from the frequencies of all eight content codes summed over all spouses and all couples separately for equal thirds (in terms of thought units) of each couple's discussion. Standard deviations for each code, for each third, are tabulated to give

TABLE 6.5

Codes with Local Peaks in Frequency over Phases of Discussion
(all couples; Z-scores are tabulated: $(x-\bar{x})/\sigma x$)

Codes	Phase of Discussion		
	Beginning Third Agenda Building	Middle Third Arguing	End Third Negotiating
Prob. Feeling (PF)	⌈.74⌉	.40	-1.14
Mindreading (MR)	⌊.99⌋	.01	-1.01
Disagreement (DG)	.32	⌈.80⌉	-1.12
Summarizing Self (SS)	-1.16	⌊.58⌋	.58
Problem Solving/Info. Exchange (PS)	.58	.58	⌈1.15⌉
Agreement (AG)	-.70	-.43	1.14
Comm. Talk (CT)	-.93	-.13	1.06
Summarizing Other (SO)	-.94	-.11	⌊1.05⌋

Brackets are placed around codes with highest Z-scores to indicate local peaks that characterize each phase of the discussion.

local peaks for each code. The beginning third is characterized by local peaks in expressing feelings (PF) and in mindreading (MR), and it is labeled the "agenda building" phase of the discussion, since feelings about problems are aired and explored in this phase. The task of this phase is getting problems out for subsequent discussion.

The second phase is characterized by local peaks in disagreement (DG) and summarizing self (SS), and it is labeled the "arguing phase" of the discussion. The task of this phase is airing disagreements and exploring common ground in opinion and feelings about a problem.

The third phase is characterized by local peaks in problem solving and information exchange (PS), agreement (AG), communication talk (CT), and summarizing the other's or both points of view (SO). It is labeled the "negotiation phase" of the discussion. The task of this phase is coming to a mutually satisfying agreement on how to solve the problem.

Sequential analyses will be presented separately for each of the codes with local peaks in the three phases, for clinic and nonclinic couples, with the peak behaviors of each phase playing the role of the criterion behavior. The length of the chain is determined by that point at which conditional probabilities return to unconditional base rate levels.[2]

Codes of the Agenda Building Phase

There needs to be an adequate number of behaviors for the normal distribution to approximate the binomial (see Chapter 2). Therefore, sequences and

[2] This is arbitrary (See Gottman and Notarius, 1978) since, for example, it is reasonable in the case of cyclicity for conditional probabilities to return to base-rate levels for several lags and then be either at excited or at inhibited levels.

Table 6.6
Sequences with Codes of the Agenda Building Phase as the Criterion

Clinic Couples	Nc	Nonclinic Couples	N

HPFo $\xrightarrow{.225}$ WPFo → HPFo → WPFo → HPFo   (3.86)   **356**

"Cross-Complaining"

HPFo $\xrightarrow{.270}$ WAGo → HPFo $\xrightarrow{.166}$ WAGo → HPFo 5 (4.68)
(9.49)

$\xrightarrow{.051}$ WDGo (2.08)

"Validation"

WPFo $\xrightarrow{.286}$ HPFo $\xrightarrow{.262}$ WPFo → HPFo → WPFo → HPFo → WPFo   **290**
(4.72)   (6.86)   "Cross-Complaining"

$\xrightarrow{.093}$ WAGo   "Validation"
(3.91)

WPFo $\xrightarrow{.311}$ HPFo → WAGo   4
(3.35)

"Validation"

(2.93)
WPF+ $\xrightarrow{.111}$ HAGo   "Validation"   **90**

$\xrightarrow{.100}$ HPF+
(5.13)

No sequence with p > .070

(4.35)
HMRo $\xrightarrow{.140}$ WAGo   **100**

"Feeling Probe"

(3.52)
HMRo $\xrightarrow{.216}$ WAGo   "Feeling Probe"

$\xrightarrow{.088}$ WDGo → WDG-
(2.87)

(3.05)
WMRo $\xrightarrow{.115}$ HAGo   "Feeling Probe"   **87**

$\xrightarrow{.115}$ HDGo
(3.46)

(5.41)
WMRo $\xrightarrow{.206}$ HAGo   "Feeling Probe"

$\xrightarrow{.088}$ HDGo
(3.15)

PF = Feelings about a Problem	Nc = Frequency of criterion behavior
AG = Agreement	Z-scores in parentheses
MR = Mindreading	
DG = Disagreement	

Z-scores based on few instances of a behavior chain are not likely to be stable, and, in the remaining sections of this chapter, sequences will not be presented unless they are based on approximately 85 instances of the criterion[3] in each group of couples. All tabled conditional probabilities refer to the criterion behavior, at respective lags.

Table 6.6 presents the most likely wife-to-husband and husband-to-wife sequences for each group for criterion codes most prominent in the first phase of the discussion.

We can see that, for nonclinic couples, the most likely response to either spouse's neutral expression of feelings about a problem is a sequence that is interspersed by the wife's agreement: a sequence called "validation" in Table

[3] According to Siegel (1956), NPQ should be at least 9. Most of our P values are near .12, so that $N = 9/(.12)(.88) = 85$. This figure is, thus, a rough guide for reporting sequences.

6.6. For clinic couples, an expression of feelings about a problem is most likely to be met by an expression of feelings about a problem by the spouse: a sequence called "cross-complaining" in Table 6.6. There is an interesting low probability chain that begins with the clinic wife's expression of feelings about a problem, delivered with positive affect, that represents a low probability validation chain for clinic couples. Validation chains are thus possible for clinic couples with a particular antecedent (WPF+), but they are infrequent because WPF+ has a low base-rate among clinic couples ($p = .002$), and the conditional probability of a husband's agreement is also relatively low ($p = .111$).

Table 6.6 also shows that essentially the same cycles follow mindreading for both groups of couples. These cycles are sequences consisting of two steps that involve agreement by the wife when the chain is initiated by the husband and either agreement or disagreement when the chain is initiated by the wife. Note that disagreement by the husband is less likely for nonclinic ($p = .088$) than for clinic couples ($p = .115$) and that agreement by the husband is more likely than disagreement for nonclinic couples, but that agreement and disagreement are equally likely for clinic couples.

The wife's agreement plays an important role during the agenda building phase of problem discussion; she provides validation and draws out her husband.

Since both mindreading (MR) and feelings about problems (PF), when delivered with negative affect, discriminated distressed from nondistressed couples, we can obtain some insight on the function of these codes by investigating their consequences. These codes did not occur frequently enough for sequential analysis in nonclinic couples. For clinic couples, Table 6.7 presents the sequences that follow a PF-. For the wife, mindreading with negative affect is taken as a criticism and leads to a "negative exchange" in clinic couples (see Gottman et al., 1977, p. 472). This is one of the few analyses that also produced significant Z-scores for the AG- code; agreement with negative affect is sarcasm. This code is usually not indicated in the table because its conditional prob-

TABLE 6.7
Sequences Beginning with Expressing Feelings about a Problem with Negative Affect (for Clinic Couples Only), a Code that Discriminated the Two Groups in Nonsequential Analyses

$$\text{HPF-} \xrightarrow[(3.21)]{.141} \text{WPF-} \rightarrow \text{HPF-} \rightarrow \text{HMR-} \rightarrow \text{WAG-}$$

$$\text{WPF-} \xrightarrow[(10.00)]{.194} \text{WMR-} \rightarrow \text{WPF-} \rightarrow \text{WMR-} \rightarrow \text{HPF-} \rightarrow \text{WPF-} \rightarrow \text{WMR-}$$
$$\searrow \underset{(4.91)}{\overset{.124}{\longrightarrow}} \text{HPF-} \nearrow$$

PF = Feelings about a Problem
MR = Mindreading
AG = Agreement

TABLE 6.8
Sequences of the Arguing Phase

Clinic Couples	Nc	Nonclinic Couples	Nc
		(2.38)	
		.275	
HDGo → WDGo	90	HDGo → WPFo → HDGo	80
.114			
(6.25)		↳ WDGo → WDG-	
		.137	
		(4.96)	
(2.71)		(3.73)	
.284		.103	
WDGo → HPFo	67	WDGo → HDGo	87
↳ HCTo			
.075			
(2.15)			

DG = Disagreement	CT = Communication Talk
PF = Feelings about a Problem	Nc = Frequency of Criterion Behavior

abilities were always less than .07, and our decision rule excludes these codes from the chain diagrams. Nonetheless, the facts that sarcasm does occur and that it is more likely in these chains help describe the nature of the sequences as extremely negative exchanges that are difficult to exit (impermeable to other codes) for clinic couples.

Codes of the Arguing Phase

Table 6.8 presents the most likely husband-to-wife and wife-to-husband sequences for the arguing phase. In general, the disagreement sequences are short, and they are not dramatically different for the two groups: Disagreement by one spouse leads to disagreement by the other. For clinic couples, there is a small probability that the wife's disagreement will lead to the husband's communication talk, which leads to the next phase. Summarizing self occurs too infrequently for proper sequential analysis. However, to assess whether distressed couples are more likely than nondistressed couples to summarize themselves rather than their spouses (an index of "listening" to their partner), we calculated the proportion of summary statements that were summarizing self. For husbands, we found $t(8) = 1.92, p < .05$, with distressed husbands averaging .60 and nondistressed husbands averaging .10. For wives, we found $t(8) = 2.11, p < .05$, with distressed wives averaging .40 and nondistressed wives averaging .00. Therefore, the ratio of summarizing self to total summary statements discriminates distressed from nondistressed couples and lends support to the conclusion that distressed couples' communication is more likely to be characterized by a "summarizing self" syndrome rather than by summarizing the spouse or summarizing both positions.

TABLE 6.9

Sequences of Negotiation Phase with Problem Solving and Information Exchange as the Criterion

Clinic		Nc	Nonclinic		Nc

```
      (2.43)                              (2.76)
       .111                                .289
HPSo  →  WAGo  "Contract"    63    HPSo  →  WPFo  →  HAGo        83
     \                                   |(2.18)
      \                                  |.181
       ↘  WDG·  →  WSO+                  ↳  WAGo "Contract"
      .079                                          .157
      (3.51)                             ↳  WPSo ——→ HAGo "Contract"
                                       .181    (3.28)
                                     (6.89)  \
                                              ↘ HPSo "Counterproposal"
                                             .145
                                             (5.47)
```

```
                                              (2.21)
      (4.20)                       (2.01)      .076
       .139                         .293    ↗ WDGo
WPSo  →  HDGo  →  WDGo    72   WPSo  →  HPFo           92
     \                            |||      ↘ WAG+
      \                           |||     .065
       ↘  HPSo "Counterproposal"  |||    (3.82)
      .097                        ||↳ .141
      (3.49)                      || (2.72)
                                  ||   HAGo "Contract"
                                  ||
                                  |↳ .130
                                  | (5.13)
                                  |   HPSo→WPSo "Counterproposal"
                                  |
                                  ↳ .076
                                    (2.62)
                                     HCTo  →  WAG+
                                   .076
                                   (2.35)
                                     HDGo  →  WDGo
```

PS = Prob. Solving and Info. Exchange	SO = Summarizing Other
AG = Agreement	PF = Feelings about a Problem
DG = Disagreement	CT = Communication Talk

Codes of the Negotiation Phase

Table 6.9 shows sequences that begin with problem solving and information exchange (PS) as the criterion behavior. Agreement is less likely for clinic couples, particularly following the wife's PS codes. The clinic couples' PS codes are as likely to take them back to the arguing phase of the discussion as they are to move them forward to a negotiated agreement. It is important to notice that "counterproposal" strings, that is, strings where a PSo is followed by a spouse's PSo, are common for both groups. Contract strings are those that are terminated by an agreement, and these strings are more likely for nonclinic than they are for clinic couples.

Table 6.10 shows that agreement leads to more agreement at later lags in the sequence, particularly by the person who started the agreement chain. These results differ from those in the arguing phase, where disagreement led to disagreement by *the partner;* it seems that agreement makes the person who

TABLE 6.10
Sequences of Negotiation Phase with Agreement as the Criterion

Clinic	Nc	Nonclinic	Nc

Clinic:

(2.58)
.079
HAGo → WPSo → HAG+   101

Nonclinic:

(5.05)
.329
HAGo → WPFo → HAGo

WPF+ → WMR+ → WMRo → HAGo
.076
(2.16)

170

Clinic:

(2.21)
.245
WAGo → HPFo → WAGo   103

WPFo
.245
(3.30)

Nonclinic:

(8.27)
(8.45)   .259
.441   WAGo → HPFo → WAGo
WAGo → HPFo

WDGo
.061
(2.38)

263

AG = Agreement   PF = Feelings about a Problem
DG = Disagreement   PS = Prob. Solving and Info. Exchange
MR = Mindreading

agrees more agreeable, whereas disagreement makes the other person more disagreeable.

Table 6.11 shows that for clinic couples communication talk leads primarily only to more of the same; there is a low probability of exiting the chain. However, this is not the case for nonclinic couples for whom sequences of

TABLE 6.11
Sequences of Negotiation Phase with Communication Talk as the Criterion

Clinic	Nc	Nonclinic	Nc

Clinic:

(2.00)
.062
(5.08)   WCTo
.121
HCTo → WCTo → HCTo → HCT-

WCT+
.046
(3.34)

66

Nonclinic:

(4.27)
.260
HCTo → WAGo

73

Clinic:

(6.72)
.185
WCTo → HCTo → HCT- → WCTo   54

(5.59)
.074
WCT- → HCTo → HCT- → WCTo

.074
HPF+
(2.70)

Nonclinic:

No sequence with p > .070

45

AG = Agreement   PF = Feelings about a Problem
CT = Communication Talk

communication talk are quite short and easily exited. These results shed light on an old issue in the literature about whether metacommunication is functional (Goodrich & Boomer, 1963) or dysfunctional (Jackson, 1965). It would seem that metacommunication is dysfunctional if it becomes an absorbing state and functional if it is brief and permeable to other codes. It is not used more frequently by one group, but clinic couples enter long chains of it occasionally, whereas nonclinic couples enter short chains of it more frequently; the nonclinic chains contain the spouse's agreement. Hence, it may be that metacommunication is not indicative of good relationships or of poor relationships, but useful if utilized in some ways and dysfunctional if utilized in other ways.

The frequency of summary statements of the other (SO) was inadequate for a sequential analysis.

Context Effects

To analyze the effects of the nonverbal behavior of the listener, two kinds of analyses were performed: (a) contingency table analyses to determine the extent to which the listener's nonverbal behavior was negative concurrent with the speaker's neutral or positive nonverbal behavior; and (b) one analysis of the ability of the listener's nonverbal behavior to predict that person's subsequent lag-1 nonverbal speaker affect. Table 6.12 presents the contingency analyses. The clinic wife was more likely to be a negative listener than the nonclinic wife ($\chi^2(1) = 87.69$, $p < .001$), and the clinic husband was more likely to be a negative listener than the nonclinic husband ($\chi^2(1) = 334.91$, $p < .001$). The nonclinic wife was a negative listener 3.87% of the time, whereas the clinic wife was a negative listener 18.01% of the time. The nonclinic husband was a negative listener 6.21% of the time, whereas the clinic husband was a negative listener 30.06% of the time. Clinic husbands were more likely to be negative listeners than were their wives ($\chi^2(1) = 30.97$, $p < .001$).

The probability that the husband's negative behavior as a listener would transfer to his immediately consequent negative speaker affect was equally high for both nonclinic ($p = .20$, $Z = 3.30$) and clinic husbands ($p = .27$, $Z = 3.93$). However, clinic wives were far more likely ($p = .35$, $Z = 4.04$)

TABLE 6.12
Negative Context Effects

Husband Speaker Affect	Wife Listener Nonverbal Behavior	
Neutral or Positive	Neutral or Positive	Negative
Nonclinic	1512	195
Clinic	1194	375

Wife Speaker Affect	Husband Listener Nonverbal Behavior	
Neutral or Positive	Neutral or Positive	Negative
Nonclinic	1577	101
Clinic	1154	507

than nonclinic wives ($p = .03$, $Z = .06$) to become negative speakers after they had been negative listeners. If there is a cognitive editing process that moderates between listening and speaking, it is the nonclinic wife who performs this editing role and not the nonclinic husband.

Summary of Specific Nonsequential Results

1. Agreement to disagreement ratios discriminated between distressed and nondistressed couples, with higher ratios characteristic of nondistressed couples.

2. However, nonverbal behavior codes (affect) were more powerful discriminators than any of the verbal codes, including agreement and disagreement.

3. Distressed and nondistressed couples did not differ on the proportion of positive affect, but nondistressed couples displayed more neutral and less negative affect than distressed couples.

4. Nondistressed couples were less sarcastic (agreement with negative nonverbal behavior) than distressed couples.

5. Distressed and nondistressed couples did not differ on the frequency of expressing direct feelings, but distressed couples were more likely to express their feelings with accompanying negative affect than were nondistressed couples.

6. Couples did not usually directly ask their spouses about their feelings; instead, they mindread.

7. Distressed and nondistressed couples did not differ on the frequency of mindreading. However, distressed couples were more likely than nondistressed couples to mindread with negative affect, a code that, we have seen, in the sequential analyses functions as criticism (whereas mindreading with neutral affect functions as a sensitive feeling probe, much like a question about feelings).

8. Disagreement was not more common among distressed couples, but distressed couples were more likely than nondistressed couples to disagree with accompanying negative affect.

9. Distressed and nondistressed couples did not differ in the frequency of metacommunication.

10. In their summary statements, distressed couples were more likely than nondistressed couples to summarize themselves than their spouse. This was called the "summarizing self" syndrome.

Summary of Major Sequential Results

1. Interaction to resolve a marital issue can conveniently be divided into three phases: An *agenda building phase* (with local peaks in expressing feelings about a problem and in mindreading), an *arguing phase* (with local peaks in disagreement and summarizing self), and a *negotiation phase* (with local peaks

in problem solving and information exchange, agreement, communication talk, and summarizing the other).

2. *Agenda Building:* Nonclinic couples are more likely to enter validation sequences (PF → AG → PF) and less likely to enter cross-complaining sequences (PF → PF → PF) than clinic couples.

3. *Agenda Building:* Both groups explore feelings with the feeling probe sequence (MR → AG), but these sequences are more likely for nonclinic than for clinic couples.

4. *Arguing:* Disagreement is reciprocated by the partner, and this pattern is not dramatically different across groups.

5. *Negotiation:* Contract sequences (PS → AG) are more likely for nonclinic couples than for clinic couples following the husband's proposed solution (PS) ($p = .181$ and $p = .111$, respectively); contract sequences are also more likely for nonclinic than for clinic couples following the wife's proposed solution (PS) ($p = .141$, and $p = .056$, respectively, with the latter probability's Z-score less than 1.96).

6. *Negotiation:* Agreement makes subsequent agreement by the same person more likely later in the chain, and this pattern is not dramatically different across groups.

7. *Negotiation:* Communication talk is an absorbing state with long chains for clinic couples, which is a state impermeable to the codes, whereas communication talk is brief and easily exited for nonclinic couples, and it is usually followed by agreement. Communication talk is, thus, used differently in terms of pattern (but not frequency) by the two groups.

8. Clinic couples are more likely to reciprocate negative affect than are nonclinic couples.

9. Clinic couples are initially *more* likely to reciprocate positive affect, but at later lags they are *less* likely to reciprocate positive affect than are nonclinic couples.

10. Clinic spouses are more likely to be negative listeners when their partners are speaking nonnegatively than are their nonclinic counterparts.

11. There is a high probability that a person will be a negative speaker (nonverbally) if he or she has been a negative listener. The exception is the nonclinic wife, which suggests an editing function on her part that breaks negative affect cycles.

12. For clinic couples, expressing feelings with negative affect leads to negative exchanges that involve mindreading with negative affect, and these sequences are difficult to exit because they are relatively impermeable to other codes.

Summary of Phases and Basic Conclusion

To summarize the detailed results, we can return to the analogy of the chess game. In the agenda-building phase of the discussion, the nonclinic couple avoids expressing feelings with negative affect that lead to a "negative exchange" and sarcasm in clinic couples; the nonclinic couple uses a validation loop to get problems out for discussion, rather than cross-complaining, which is characteristic of clinic couples. Also, mindreading with negative affect, which is taken as criticism and blaming, is avoided by nonclinic couples, in favor of mindreading with neutral affect, which is taken as a feeling probe. With regard to mindreading, it is interesting that a neutral affect mindreading statement has the same consequences in both groups; it is only the case that negative affect mindreading is more common for clinic than for nonclinic couples.

In the arguing phase, the sequences are quite similar, and, if only this phase were analyzed, except for negative affect, the two groups of couples would look quite similar, with the exception that, of all the summary statements (which are quite rare), clinic couples would display a higher proportion of self-summary. However, this result on summary statements was not a strong effect.

In the negotiation phase, nonclinic couples are more likely to engage in contracting than in counterproposal strings. In both the beginning and the end phases of the discussion, we can see the crucial role played by agreement and negative affect codes. Whereas clinic couples are likely to *mirror* one another's codes, for example, with PF → PF and PS → PS sequences, nonclinic couples intersperse agreement and break negative affect chains by some editing process that intercedes between nonverbal behaviors while listening and nonverbal behaviors during message delivery. Whereas the behavior of clinic couples is more linked and contingent, nonclinic couples operate well at each stage of the discussion by *unlatching* their interaction patterns. This is consistent with Hypothesis 1 of the Structural Model (Chapter 3), on the degree of patterning in interaction. An important strategy for unlatching interaction is agreement.[4]

These results, therefore, strongly support the specific hypotheses presented in Chapter 3 on the differential degree of patterning in distressed and nondistressed marriages and the dimensions of positiveness and reciprocity. Of course, the results presented here must be replicated and extended if we are to have any confidence in the Structural Model presented in Chapter 3, and that is the function of the next several chapters.

The specificity of the findings presented in this chapter has important implications in reviewing the contributions of current theory. Many of the results would not have been predicted by current clinical folklore, or by general systems theory, or by social learning theory. For example, clinical folklore stresses

---

[4] The original paper by Jackson (1965) on family rules, which proposed the *quid pro quo* concept, did not actually describe it as a hypothesis of positive reciprocity. In fact, the specific clinical example Jackson presented in his paper emphasized *the fundamental importance of the proposal–agreement sequence in the initial definition of the quid pro quo* (see Chapter 1). As a contrast to the quid pro quo interaction, Jackson gave the following example:

H: I wish you would fix yourself up. Take $50 and get a permanent, a facial—the works!
W: I'm sorry, dear, but I don't think we ought to spend the money on me.
H: *!!ae*" I want to spend it on you!
W: I know, dear, but there's all the bills and things.   [p. 1539]

The contrast Jackson suggested to the quid pro quo is thus the proposal–counter-proposal sequence.

the importance of self-disclosure and the direct examination of feelings. Instead, the results show that couples in nondistressed marriages are indirect; they mindread rather than directly asked about feelings. Although mindreading is considered dysfunctional by clinical folklore and clients are asked to check out feelings with their spouses, the results suggest that it depends: Mindreading with neutral affect is taken as a feeling probe, whereas mindreading with negative affect is taken as hostile criticism.

Consider another example. General systems theory stresses the importance of metacommunication. On the contrary, it is an absorbing state with long chains for clinic couples, a state that is impermeable to other codes. For nonclinic couples, metacommunication is brief, it is easily exited, and it is usually followed by agreement. Metacommunication is, thus, used differently in terms of pattern (but not frequency) by the two groups. Once again, it depends.

A social learning theory would not be able to explain parsimoniously the inability of positive affect to discriminate distressed from nondistressed couples. Nor would it be able to explain why, since agreement follows an expression of feelings about a problem (PF) for nonclinic couples in the first third of the discussion, the frequency of PF does not increase but *decreases* in relative frequency later in the discussion. This would not be predicted from a simple reinforcement model. It is simply not useful to view listening in a validation loop as a reinforcement of a PF. It is more useful to view a validation loop as playing an important role in a longer chain of behaviors that naturally cluster into units *determined by the tasks and objectives of the discussion.*

The problem is not one of the size of the unit of analysis. If the entire discussion were to be considered more reinforcing for nondistressed couples, then one would predict that such discussions would be more frequent and, thus, more characteristic of nondistressed couples than of distressed couples. Yet, the opposite is true (see, for example, Phillips, 1975), which is logical if viewed from the perspective that conflict on an issue is more likely to continue and perhaps even to escalate if it remains unresolved.

The results of the present investigation, thus, have implications for the amount of precision one should require in data as a prologue to the construction of theory. Although *post hoc* understanding of a set of results in psychology is often possible from any perspective, in this case neither general systems theory nor social learning theory have been precise in their predictions, and their continued use as metaphors for understanding how marriages function is reminiscent of adding epicycles to Ptolemy's theory, which maintained that the Earth is at the center of the universe. Bateson was probably right when he said that the ability of a theory to survive depends on its ability to be vague and shrouded in a mystery that defies precise measurement and prediction. However, with respect to the two theories reviewed in this volume as well as with respect to clinical folklore, we must conclude with a shrug that simpler conceptions of the data are possible.

CHAPTER 7

The Generality of the Topography Results: A Recoding Study

THE RAUSH *ET AL.* STUDY

It would be useful to compare the results reported in this book with a major study in the field. Raush et al. (1974) have presented the most complete sequential analysis study on the interaction of couples in conflict situations. In their pioneering longitudinal study, they obtained newlywed couples from marriage licenses issued in the Washington, D.C. area and recruited forty-six couples for their sample. These couples were followed through pregnancy, after the birth of the first child, and again later. Audiotapes of their interaction at these stages were collected.

To standardize the conflict situations across couples, Raush et al. (1974) created a series of improvised conflict situations that were intended to be:

> . . . quasi-experimental, quasi-naturalistic situations of interactions where because of the separate instructions given to each partner a conflict of interest was created. . . . In each, efforts were made to get the couples personally involved in the situations so that they would be themselves as much as possible, rather than play stylized roles. To attain this end, no standardized set of instructions was read to each person. Instead, the general form was the same, but the instructor was free to vary the instructions to make them maximally relevant to the individual [pp. 56–57].

Four improvisations were designed. In each improvisation, one experimenter talked privately to the husband and one to the wife and created a situation

125

much as a method-acting director might set the scene for an improvised drama. The exception is that couples were asked to play through the improvisation as they normally would act, rather than to play idealized roles. Two of the improvisations were "issue oriented," a conflict of plans for celebrating an anniversary and a conflict between two television programs; two improvisations were "relationship oriented," in which one spouse was instructed to try to get close and the other was instructed to maintain interpersonal (i.e., psychological) distance.

Raush *et al.* (1974) found that the relationship-oriented improvisations posed a greater threat and greater difficulty to the couples than did the issue-oriented ones. Through a complex factor-analytic study (see Raush *et al.*, 1974, p. 156), six discordant and seven harmonious couples were identified, and results were reported for these couples for data collected at the newlywed stage of the relationship.

Differences between the interaction of the two groups of couples included harmonious couples' greater likelihood of keeping their interaction in the cognitive realm and lesser likelihood of using rejecting and coercive statements than was to be expected of discordant couples.

RECODING THE RAUSH *ET AL.* DATA

With Harold Raush's assistance, our laboratory undertook the project of recoding the Raush *et al.* audiotapes with the CISS. The recoding study was undertaken partly because the Raush *et al.* coding system lumped data into six summary codes—Cognitive, Resolving, Reconciling, Appealing, Rejecting, and Coercive—that were too general to compare with our own findings. Additionally, the coding unit in the Raush *et al.* study was the floor switch, not the thought unit.

Unfortunately, specific information on marital satisfaction scales for each couple was unavailable, so it was not possible to compare the sample Raush *et al.* obtained from marriage license records with the methods we used to recruit couples. The best comparison of the couples in our research with Raush *et al.*'s is probably to be obtained from agreement-to-disagreement ratios (Riskin and Faunce, 1972); therefore, the results of recoding the Raush tapes permit a location of the harmonious and discordant subsamples on the general continuum of marital satisfaction discussed in Chapter 1 of this book.

Coding affect from the Raush *et al.* audiotapes proved to be considerably more difficult than our usual experience of coding affect from videotapes. To obtain acceptable levels of reliability, two affect coders worked on each tape independently, and the reliability checker coded all the tapes. The decision rule was that a thought unit was coded as positive or negative only if the two coders agreed; otherwise, it was coded as neutral. Cohen's kappas for the affect codes were .892, .847, and .899 for neutral, positive, and negative affect, respectively. It was impossible to code listener behavior except in those instances in which a spouse was laughing or crying audibly, so these designations were abandoned for the recoding study. For the content codes, the following kappas were obtained: .852, Problem Feeling (PF); .820, Mindreading (MR); .812, Communication Talk (CT); .801, Agreement (AG); .822, Disagreement (DG); .812, Summarizing Self (SS); and .620, Summarizing Other (SO). Summarizing Other occurred very infrequently on the Raush et al. tapes. Hence, reasonably acceptable levels of reliability were obtained for the recoding study.

COMPARING THE RESULTS OF THE TWO STUDIES

Two sets of variables—agreement and disagreement—and the affect codes had been among the best discriminators of distressed and nondistressed couples in our data (see Chapter 6). A tabulation of these data for the Raush et al. tapes is given in Table 7.1. These results, when compared with the results of the Gottman, Markman, and Notarius (1977) study, suggest that on most variables *both discordant and harmonious couples in the Raush* et al. *(1974) study are in the distressed range of the Gottman* et al. *(1977) study.*

This was an entirely surprising result, but the comparison between the two studies is further strengthened by the fact that discordant and harmonious couples differ in the same directions as distressed and nondistressed couples in the Gottman et al. (1977) study. Subsequent sequential analyses also lend support to this conclusion. It is, thus, likely that the variables of the Structural Model distinguish among levels of distress as well as between distressed and nondistressed couples. To continue the comparison, affect cycles may be examined.

Affect Cycles

In comparing Table 7.2 to Table 6.3, it is clear that harmonious and discordant couples differ in essentially the same ways that nonclinic and clinic couples differ in the Gottman et al. study. Discordant couples were generally more likely to enter a negative-affect cycle than were harmonious couples. As in Table 6.3, Z-scores and conditional probabilities are generally higher for discordant couples than for harmonious couples.

TABLE 7.1
Agreement, Disagreement, and Affect for Raush et al.
(1974) Data and Gottman et al. (1977) Data

Variable	Raush et al. (1974) Study		Gottman et al. (1977) Study	
	Discordant	Harmonious	Distressed	Nondistressed
AG/(AG + DG)	.26	.38	.43	.71
Neutral Affect	.69	.74	.65	.85
Positive Affect	.04	.11	.10	.12
Negative Affect	.27	.15	.25	.03

TABLE 7.2
Probability of Negative Affect Cycles — Raush et al. (1974)

Criterion: H-	LAG					
	1	2	3	4	5	6
Harmonious						
H-	.00	.15*	.15*	.10	.15	.02
W-	.20	.10	.25	.05	.35*	.12
Z-score	—	2.66	2.66	—	3.33	—
Discordant						
H-	.00	.39*	.19	.30*	.20	.34*
W-	.18	.10	.14	.08	.13	.06
Z-score	—	6.58	—	3.69	—	4.90

Criterion: W-	LAG					
	1	2	3	4	5	6
Harmonious						
H-	.10	.08	.05	.05	.02	.05
W-	.00	.44*	.16	.39*	.13	.34*
Z-score	—	8.09	—	6.88	—	5.67
Discordant						
H-	.37*	.12	.21	.16	.16	.19
W-	.00	.44*	.10	.41*	.14	.30*
Z-score	3.95	9.53	—	8.75	—	5.65

*Represents the probabilities with the highest Z-score, which is given immediately below the respective probabilities.

Table 7.3 repeats the results of analyses identical to those presented in Table 6.4. Again, the pattern of differences (Z-scores and conditional probabilities) between harmonious and discordant couples is strikingly similar to differences between nonclinic and clinic couples. Discordant couples show higher Z-scores for positive affect at earlier (but not at later) lags than do harmonious couples.

A further test of the conclusion that both harmonious and discordant couples in the Raush et al. (1974) study fall into the distressed range of the Gottman et al. (1977) study is provided by an analysis of specific sequences.

Sequential Patterns

There are considerably less data for detailed sequential analysis in the Raush et al. (1974) data than in the Gottman et al. (1977) data. There are 1454 units and 4817 units in the two studies, respectively. Perhaps the best sequential discriminator in the Gottman et al. study was the finding that distressed couples engage in cross-complaining cycles and that nondistressed couples engage in validation cycles.[1] If the conclusion that Raush et al.'s couples are all

[1] There was an inadequate number of occurrences of the problem-solving and information-exchange code to test the counterproposal versus contracting patterns.

TABLE 7.3
Probability of Positive Affect Cycles — Raush et al. (1974)

Criterion: H+	LAG					
	1	2	3	4	5	6
Harmonious						
H+	.00	.38*	.17*	.17*	.25*	.04
W+	.21*	.08	.13	.17*	.13	.17*
Z-score	2.87	7.82	2.89	2.89	4.86	2.14
Discordant						
H+	.00	.29*	.00	.21*	.07	.07
W+	.29*	.07	.14*	.14*	.07	.07
Z-score	6.86	7.21	3.19	5.28	—	—

Criterion: W+	LAG					
	1	2	3	4	5	6
Harmonious						
H+	.28*	.03	.09	.03	.10	.10
W+	.00	.34*	.06	.23*	.13	.19*
Z-score	6.20	6.64	—	3.80	—	3.06
Discordant						
H+	.27*	.00	.40*	.07	.27*	.00
W+	.00	.27*	.00	.20*	.07	.20*
Z-score	6.85	6.66	10.67	4.85	6.93	4.85

*Represents the probabilities with the highest Z-score, which is given immediately below the respective probabilities.

in the distressed range is correct, then the same pattern of cross-complaining should be evident for both harmonious and discordant couples. Table 7.4 demonstrates that this is, indeed, the case. Table 7.4 lists conditional probabilities at each lag from the two criteria (expressing feelings about a problem with neutral affect) for the four key behaviors that would be involved in either cross-complaining or validation sequences. The results demonstrate that both groups engage in the cross-complaining cycles (PFO → PFO) characteristic of distressed couples in the Gottman et al. (1977) study. Furthermore, the conditional probabilities and Z-scores, on the whole, are a bit larger for the discordant than for the harmonious couples.

There are, of course, vast procedural differences between the two studies. Gottman et al.'s couples were married an average of 3 years, whereas Raush et al.'s couples were married an average of 4 months. Gottman et al. asked couples to come to a mutually satisfactory resolution of a real marital issue, and each issue was different in content for each couple. Raush et al. used a standard improvised conflict scene. Gottman et al.'s data were videotaped, whereas Raush et al.'s data were audiotaped. In both cases, however, coders used verbatim transcripts and the tapes for coding. Also, Gottman et al.'s subjects had identified themselves as clinic (seeking marriage counseling) or nonclinic (having a "mutually satisfying" relationship) in 1973, whereas Raush et al.'s

TABLE 7.4

Test of Patterns Following Expression of Feelings about a Problem with Neutral Affect (Raush et al., 1974)

Criterion: HPFO	LAGS					
	1	2	3	4	5	6
Harmonious						
HPFO	.00	.46*	.26	.30	.26	.35
HAGO	.02	.02	.01	.05	.01	.01
WPFO	.43*	.09	.38*	.13	.27	.19
WAGO	.03	.01	.02	.01	.02	.02
Z-score	3.85	5.09	5.43	—	—	—
Discordant						
HPFO	.00	.43*	.22	.34*	.23	.31*
HAGO	.00	.01	.01	.02	.00	.02
WPFO	.53*	.15	.43*	.17	.36*	.25
WAGO	.01	.01	.01	.02	.01	.00
Z-score	5.25	6.13	4.98	3.28	2.77	2.32

Criterion: WPFO	LAGS					
	1	2	3	4	5	6
Harmonious						
HPFO	.51*	.11	.37*	.27	.35	.27
HAGO	.02	.01	.05	.01	.03	.00
WPFO	.00	.52*	.14	.32*	.14	.33*
WAGO	.01	.01	.01	.02	.02	.03
Z-score	5.72	8.30	2.24	3.04	—	3.46
Discordant						
HPFO	.56*	.11	.32*	.20	.28	.22
HAGO	.03	.03	.01	.01	.02	.00
WPFO	.00	.47*	.17	.39*	.25	.32
WAGO	.01	.01	.01	.01	.01	.01
Z-score	4.93	7.23	2.86	3.92	—	—

PF = Feelings about Problems

AG = Agreement

*Represents the probabilities with the highest Z-score, which is given immediately below the respective probabilities.

couples were carefully selected from marriage license records in 1961. Although the age range in the two studies was similar, Raush et al. eliminated students in order to obtain a less transient population, whereas the Gottman et al. study consisted primarily of graduate students. Given the differences between the Gottman et al. (1977) and the Raush et al. (1974) studies, it is remarkable that similar patterns were obtained in the two studies and, furthermore, that the pattern of differences between distressed and nondistressed couples generally holds between discordant and harmonious couples even though these two groups are in the distressed range of the Gottman et al. study.

CHAPTER 8

The Issue Focus

INTRODUCTION

This chapter reports the results of a study designed to replicate and extend the results of the Raush et al. recoding study presented in Chapter 7. This study is intended to test the generalizability of the findings presented in Chapter 6 on positiveness and reciprocity; the objective is to test the generalizability of the two hypotheses about positiveness and reciprocity of the Structural Model of Marital Interaction across the range of conversations (both conflict and nonconflict) that couples may typically have in their everyday interaction. To extend the range of conversation studied, improvised conflict situations were empirically derived so that the conflict situations could be standardized across couples and be varied across a range of induced conflict. In addition to the empirically derived improvised conflicts, a non-decision-making task was designed to test the generality of the positiveness and reciprocity findings when couples were not engaged in resolving conflict.

IMPROVISATION AS A METHOD

Use by Raush et al.

Raush et al. (1974) commented on the objectives of their improvised conflict method. They wrote:

Research methods should be congruent with the nature of the problems under investigation. To examine communication and interpersonal conflict in marriage, we chose real married couples rather than madeup pairings. Rather than maintaining a laboratory atmosphere, we tried to make our stage settings real, even modifying the instructions for different couples to achieve maximum involvement. The aim was toward naturalizing the investigative approach. In one way, however, the Improvisations went counter to naturalism. For practical reasons, it would have been difficult to follow couples in their own homes, waiting for them to engage in different types of conflict in the presence of observers and recording equipment. The Improvisations method selects a limited range of conflict situations. Within the restrictions of these situations, however, the couples have considerable freedom. Unlike the usual laboratory situation, it is the subjects who produce, define, and extend the scale of events for one another. In terms of the two dimensions that Willems (1969) suggests for describing the range between laboratory experiments and naturalistic studies, the manipulations by the investigator of antecedent conditions is moderate and the imposition of units on the behavior studied is low [p. 6; emphasis removed].

The improvisations used in the Raush et al. study were not derived empirically; they were designed by Paul Blank and Wells Goodrich. In each scene, instructors spent time with each spouse "trying to establish personal involvement in the mood of the scene. Emphasis was placed not on role-playing but rather on the couple being themselves when they got together for the scene [Raush et al., 1974, pp. 56–57]." These improvisation scenes are, therefore, the experimenters' best armchair guesses about issues that typically induce conflict in marriage.

Empirically Derived Improvisations

The tasks that have been most successful in studying family and marital interaction are based on some good guesses about the conflict issues couples naturally discuss. For example, the Strodtbeck (1951) "revealed difference technique" obtained interactional differences in decision making consistent with anthropological investigations of three cultures in Southern Arizona (Navaho, Mormon, and Texan). In this technique,

Each couple was asked to pick three reference families with whom they were well acquainted. The husband and wife were then separated and requested to designate which of the three reference families most satisfactorily fulfilled a series of 26 conditions such as: Which family has the happiest children? Which family is the most religious? Which family is the most ambitious? After both husband and wife had individually marked their choices they were requested to reconcile their differences and indicate a final best choice from the standpoint of their family [p. 289].

Although there is currently no research that suggests what couples normally talk about, the Strodtbeck task falls under the realm of "gossip," which tends to be of universal interest. Thus, it is likely that the Strodtbeck task was not foreign to couples in any of the three cultures studied.

The Strodtbeck technique has been criticized by Olson and Ryder (1970) on the grounds that couples vary on the number of items they disagree on and that different couples disagree on different items. They suggested that this seriously complicates the data analysis. These authors suggested using the Color Matching Test (Goodrich and Boomer, 1963) to replace the revealed differences technique, but they subsequently developed the less costly and widely used Inventory of Marital Conflicts (IMC). The IMC is an 18-item inventory with 12 high-conflict and 6 low-conflict vignettes; it is similar to the Strodtbeck Revealed-Differences Technique. In the IMC, husband and wife are given two different versions of a marital event and are asked to come to consensus on who is most at fault. The level of conflict is manipulated by the discrepancy between the wife's version and the husband's version of the story. Since research on the complaints of married couples suggests that it is common for marital issues to be stated as an attribution of blame (a pattern that has been called "character assassination"; Stuart, 1969), the IMC is also probably tapping issues that are commonly discussed by married couples.

It is thus likely that both the Strodtbeck revealed-differences task and the Olson and Ryder IMC are successful tasks because they involve families in seminaturalistic activities. It therefore makes sense for the Raush et al. improvised conflict method to be extended by empirically deriving a domain of situations about which couples actually experience conflict.

In the area of social skills training, Goldfried and D'Zurilla (1969) suggested a method for empirically deriving social situations that college students found to be difficult to handle. The approach has been followed in areas such as assertion (McFall and Lillesand, 1971; McFall and Marston, 1970; McFall and Twentyman, 1973), the dating problems of shy college men (Twentyman and McFall, 1976), and the social problems of male psychiatric inpatients (Goldsmith and McFall, 1975). The basic approach is to obtain a domain of problematic situations from the populations of interest. Each situation is defined by its context (i.e., where it took place), the participants of the interaction, the interaction flow (who said what when), and the key time of difficulty for each participant. The key time represents the spot in the interaction flow when there is a clear task and a response demand defined by the situation. In assertion, for example, at a key time something may have to be said to refuse an unreasonable request.

EMPIRICALLY OBTAINED DOMAIN OF
PROBLEMATIC SITUATIONS

Conflict Tasks

To extend the Improvisation method, it thus seemed to be reasonable to obtain empirically a domain of situations that couples find problematic. Further evidence that this may be a profitable strategy was given by Mitchell, Bullard, and Mudd (1962), who, although they found significant differences between the intensity and frequency of problems confronting clinic and nonclinic marriages, also found that the rank-ordering of the severity of different problem areas was nearly identical between groups. In our own data with a standard problem inventory in the Gottman et al. (1976) study, the rank-order correlation coefficient of perceived severity between clinic and nonclinic couples was .94. It may, thus, be the case that all marriages need to deal with a consistent core of problematic situations.

To obtain empirically such a domain, we used the following procedure. Sixty couples served as subjects who participated in a play-by-play interview that was audiotaped. (This research will be more fully reported in Chapter 11.) After filling out a standard problem inventory used in our laboratory, these couples were asked to describe the context, interaction flow, and key times of difficulty for their three highest-rated problem areas. The interviewers tried to elicit as much descriptive detail as possible about a specific example of a discussion that examplified each problem area.

The audiotapes of the interviews were transcribed, and the 180 descriptions were summarized in short vignettes such as the following:

1. The wife would like her husband to talk to her more and to be more attentive. She does not know that he has been preoccupied the past several days with worries about the family finances. She senses his withdrawal and has been pouting for a few days to let him know she's upset, but he has paid no attention. He's come home from work, they've eaten supper, and the wife has decided to bring up her grievances. She says, "Why don't you treat me like a wife instead of a house-keeper?" The husband denies not treating her like a wife. The discussion continues with the husband trying to find out what is bothering his wife and listening to her complaints. She continues griping, and he is getting more fed up, since he is tired and just wants to relax. He finally says, "Oh shut up. You're so demanding all the time; why don't you just leave me alone?" She begins to cry and goes to the bedroom.

2. This couple is having sexual problems: They seldom have intercourse, and, when they do, neither of them finds it very satisfying. Recently, she has been dreaming that her husband is going out with other women. She had such a dream last night and woke up feeling rejected and hurt. Her husband was in the bathroom and, when he later entered the kitchen, she gave him a dirty, accusing look. She later let him know about the dream and said, "But I was just sure I wasn't satisfying you, so I thought there was bound to come along someone who would. I know you've never given me any reason to worry." He assured her that he wasn't interested in anyone else but added that he was getting discouraged by her insecurity and accusations and said, "When I wake up in the morning and have to face you after you've had one of those dreams, I feel what's the use, just what's the use?" She assured him that she knew he's been faithful and it's only been a dream. He said, "I'm trying to analyze these dreams. You've got some deep hostility toward sex."

The 180 situations were then reduced to 85 nonredundant situations that spanned issues of money, sharing events of the day, in-laws, sex, religion, recreation, friends, alcohol and drugs, two issues concerning children (whether to have children, or how to raise children), jealousy, household chores, and role definition. Six issues were most frequently identified as problematic for *both* the 30 clinic and the 30 nonclinic couples: sharing events of the day, money.

in-laws, sex, and children. On the basis of these six areas, six improvisations were written as a composite of the play-by-play summaries.

An example of the coach's instructions for preparing the husband and wife for an improvisation is given in Table 8.1 (the sex improvisation). There were two relationship-oriented improvisations: sex and sharing events of the day. In the sex improvisation, the wife is interested in having some time to make love with her husband, but he, unaware of his wife's intentions, has set priority on completing some task. In the improvisation on sharing events of the day, the husband wants to be close and to share some news, but the wife has decided she needs some time alone. The money, in-laws, and two children improvisations were similar to Raush et al.'s issue-oriented improvisations.

Nonconflict Task

Nearly all the research on marital interaction has involved conflict resolution and decision making. The only exception is a study by Birchler, Weiss, and Vincent (1975) that included a brief (4-minute) beginning period of "free conversation" during which "couples were instructed to talk about anything 'while we're setting up the equipment' [p. 352]." They found that *negative* behaviors discriminated distressed from nondistressed couples in both causal conversation and the Olson and Ryder (1970) IMC but that *positive* behaviors discrimi-

TABLE 8.1
Coach's Instructions for Sex Improvisation

Wife's side:

It's after dinner (the children are in bed, if you have children). You've finished what you have to get done for the day and are reading a book or watching T.V. (C_1). You are actually feeling a little restless and bored and would very much like to get close to your husband tonight, to spend some time alone together. He has seemed kind of preoccupied the past few days and just hasn't been very attentive or affectionate. And besides, it's been very hectic and you haven't had much of a sexual relationship recently. You decide tonight you'd really like to be close to him and to make love. You put aside what you are doing and go into the room where your husband is working on some things. Any questions?

C_1 — How might you be spending time alone in the evening?

Husband's side:

It's after dinner (the children are in bed, if you have children). You've been concerned the past few days about getting some project finished (C_1). You've decided tonight's the night to get it done. You go to your (study, cellar, garage, C_2) and get to working. You are quite involved in your work and feeling good about finally getting it done and having some time to yourself at last. It's been hectic lately and it seems like you have had so many demands on you recently—even from your wife. You just want to get this work done and you've finally managed to get some time alone.

Any questions?

C_1—Coach can find out what this might be—some project that would need some length of time—if husband is a student it might be a paper that's due, or perhaps a report or account for work—or maybe some major repair work that needs to be done.

C_2—Where would this be for you? Where do you like to work when you want to get something finished?

---

nated couples only on the IMC. To extend this body of research findings involving marital interaction on *nonconflict tasks,* we designed a "fun deck" exercise. It involves a deck of cards containing activities that couples had said they enjoyed doing (see Gottman, Notarius, Gonso, and Markman, 1976). Couples were instructed to "look through the deck, talk to each other, try to have a conversation about anything that comes to mind as you look through the deck. You could reminisce, or plan, or talk about anything you like. Try to have an enjoyable conversation [Rubin, 1977, p. 40]."

THE IMPROVISATION STUDY

Purposes of the Study

In a dissertation designed and conducted in our laboratory, Rubin (1977) used the improvisations and the fun deck in an empirical investigation. There were three purposes of the improvisation study. The first was to obtain a check on the generality of the results presented in Chapter 6. The second purpose was to assess how distressed and nondistressed couples' interaction varied as a function of the issue under discussion. The third purpose was to assess whether it was possible to discriminate distressed from nondistressed couples on a non-conflict, non-decision-making task.

Since the study presented in Chapter 6 used a different methodology, to assess the generality of our results it was necessary to design a criterion of comparability. The one improvisation was selected for which the *nonsequential* data most closely resembled the *nonsequential* data in Chapter 6, and then sequential results were compared across studies.

Design of the Study

Rubin (1977) used the improvisations and the fun deck with 38 married couples, 19 clinic and 19 nonclinic couples, recruited as described in Gottman *et al.* (1976, 1977; see Chapter 11). Sixteen clinic couples were referred by counseling agencies in the community and campus. Three clinic couples responded to a news release, identified themselves as experiencing marital conflict, and requested information on referral for marriage counseling. The 19 nonclinic couples responded to a news release and identified themselves as experiencing a mutually satisfying relationship. All couples were paid $20.00 for serving as subjects. As in previous studies, all couples took the Marital Relationship Inventory (MRI). The 19 clinic couples had an average score of 80.53, with a standard deviation of 12.20, and the 19 nonclinic couples had an average score of 103.16, with a standard deviation of 6.53 ($t[36] = 7.13$, $p < .001$). Nonetheless, the MRI scores for the total group of couples were not within cutoffs suggested by Burgess, Locke, and Thomes (1971), and, as in previous studies, a distressed subgroup and a nondistressed subgroup were identified. These groups were comparable to the subjects in previous studies in our laboratory: Ten distressed couples had a mean of 70.90 (SD = 7.59) and 10 nondistressed couples had a mean of 108.25 (SD = 2.55) on the MRI ($t[18] = 14.76$, $p < .001$). Neither the clinic and nonclinic nor the distressed and nondistressed groups differed significantly on any demographic variable (age, education, income, years married, and number of children). On the average, husbands were 34 years old and wives were 32 years old; the average couple had been married for 9 years, had one child, and earned $11,200.

The six improvisations came after the fun deck, in random order. The results of a generalizability study on the CISS coding of the videotapes in this study were presented in Chapter 5. A new generation of 10 coders was trained for this study, and the 55 hours of videotape were transcribed and coded in 1540 hours, that is, approximately 28 hours per hour of tape. The experiment was conducted in 6 months, and the tapes were coded in 18 months. The sample of data in this study was more than 8 times larger than the data sample reported in Chapter 6—there were 39,330 coded *behavior* units (and considerably more thought units).

The following list summarizes the improvised scenes that were the most conflictual for both clinic and nonclinic couples. They are presented in order of conflict (high to low), based on how many of the 60 couples in the previous interview study reported a problem with each issue, as in Mitchell, Bullard, and Mudd (1962).

(a) *Sharing Events of the Day* (Improvisation #5). The husband is excited about sharing with his wife something he experienced during the day. She, however, has been feeling harassed and is looking forward to some privacy and time to herself.

(b) *Money* (Improvisation #3). Both spouses are told that they have been on a tight budget because they have been saving for a major purchase. The wife has been feeling deprived and has managed to save some food money to purchase herself something small but special. She likes her purchase very much and is looking forward to sharing it with her husband. The husband has been feeling pretty short of pocket money because of the budget and wants to let his wife know he needs more money.

(c) *Sex* (Improvisation #2). The husband very much wants to complete some activity of his choosing "this evening" without being disrupted. The wife, however, wants to be close and to make love.

(d) *In-Laws* (Improvisation #4). The husband wants to visit his family for 4 days during Christmas and is looking forward to enjoying the special holiday festivities. The wife is reluctant to visit his parents because of specific grievances with her in-laws.

(e) *Decision to Have Children* (Improvisation #6). The wife wants to have children and wants a decision to be made about this. The husband is opposed to having children at this time for various reasons.

(f) and (g) *Discipline of Children* (Improvisation #7). In the improvisation for parents of younger children, the *wife* feels that the children need firmer discipline, whereas the husband advocates spontaneity and permissiveness as important for children. In the improvisation for parents of teenage children, the *husband* is concerned about his teenagers' irresponsibility and choice of friends, but the wife wants the children to develop independence and to feel free to confide in their parents. (We observed this role reversal in our interview data with the 60 couples.)

Procedure of the Study

Administration of the Tasks   Eight graduate students—seven male and one female—and two female undergraduate students were trained in a group setting to be coaches in administering the improvisations to the couples. In addition, Rubin also participated as the coach supervisor. A combination of didactic and role-playing approaches was used to train the coaches. Training took place in one 3-hour evening session. The coaches were observed and supervised throughout their participation in the project by Rubin. The importance of establishing rapport and of helping the couples to become personally involved in the situations was emphasized in the training procedures.

Instructions for administering the tasks for the entire procedure as well as the improvisations themselves were written for the coaches. Copies of the instruction sheets and of the improvisation booklets are available in Rubin (1977). The coaches became very familiar with the instructions and improvisations prior to beginning the project, but they were instructed to use the instruction sheets and improvisation booklets throughout the project.

Each improvisation contained designated points at which the coach was to elicit information from the spouse that would individualize and personalize the situation for the particular couple. The intent of using the improvisations was to have a set of standardized tasks but at the same time to increase the couples' potential for involvement and identification with the tasks by engaging them in providing details from their own lives in developing each situation.

Each couple was interviewed in one of two research rooms in the Indiana University Psychology Building. An attempt was made to make the rooms comfortable and pleasant. In one room, the video camera was placed on an upper shelf. For the other room, the camera was located visibly but unobtrusively behind a curtained glass window that separated the experimental room from an observation corridor. Each couple was interviewed by a team consisting of one female and one male coach. As earlier noted, the coaches followed a standardized set of instructions and procedures. After introducing themselves to the couple, one of the coaches said:

> As you may know, this project concerns how couples interact to solve problems. The project requires meeting two consecutive evenings, and you

will receive at the end of the second evening your $20 check for partici-
pating. Unless you have specific questions, we will begin and explain the
different tasks as we go along.

The consent form and the demographic information form were then completed. Next, each spouse was asked to complete the MRI. After this task was
done, the following instructions were read for administering the fun deck:

> Here is a deck of cards. We call this deck the "fun deck" because it contains
> things that some couples enjoy doing together. Look through the deck, talk
> to each other, try to have a conversation about anything that comes to mind
> as you look through the deck. You could reminisce, or plan, or talk about
> anything you like. Try to have an enjoyable conversation.

The coaches then left the couple in the interviewing room and went to the
observation corridor, where they videotaped the couple's interaction for 15
minutes.

Following the fun deck, the improvisations were administered in a random
order for each couple. The following general improvisation instructions were
read to the couple:

> We're going to stage a situation we call "improvising." We're going to
> coach you to imagine this situation, to help make it real for you, as it
> perhaps might actually happen. Now, this situation might be foreign to you.
> In that case, it's important for you to *pretend* that it is real.
>
> But, unlike acting, here it is important for you to be yourself, to behave *as*
> *you might normally do* in such a situation. Our concern is to find out how
> you will *actually* behave in this situation, not how you think you should act
> or how you think we want you to act.
>
> We won't be able to answer any questions after we get the two of you
> together. Just keep going until you feel that things have come to some
> conclusion, and then signal us. Try to stick to the situation and let it unfold
> as it actually would.

After answering any questions, the male coach and the husband met in one
room and the wife and female coach met in another room for details on the
improvisation. During coaching sessions, couples were encouraged to provide
information from their own lives at designated points in the development of the
improvisation in order to help them identify more closely with the situation.

As already noted, an example of the format for coaching an improvisation
is given in Table 8.1. At designated points in the improvisation (e.g., in Tables
8.1 C_1, C_2), the coach would elicit specific information from the spouse about
that particular part of the situation. For each of these designated points at which
time the spouse was asked to share information from his own life, the coaches
were provided with a standard set of questions to help in eliciting the information. The questions frequently began with open-ended inquiries. For example,
in the money improvisation, the coach at C_1 asked the spouse what might be

something for which he and his wife decided to budget. If the individual appeared to have difficulty with identifying a purchase, the coach could prompt the spouse by providing some suggestions or by asking the spouse to recall a similar event from the past. If the individual still had difficulty identifying something for which he decided to save, the coach could go on and emphasize that it would be a fairly expensive purchase and could provide some examples. If the spouse could absolutely not provide any information based on his own life events, he then would be asked to "pretend" but still to provide some specific detail about that point. Once the information was provided by the spouse, the coach would incorporate it into the improvisation and continue until the next point, at which the spouse is asked to contribute to the development of the situation (e.g., C_2). After completing the construction of the improvisation, the coach would summarize the situation, including the information provided by the spouse.

The spouses were then brought together and instructed to let the discussion unfold as it might at home. They were asked to signal the coaches when they felt they had reached a resolution. The coaches again left the interviewing room and went to the observation corridor to tape the couple's interaction.

The improvisation pertaining to the discipline of children was not administered to couples who did not have children. The rationale for this decision was that it would generally be too difficult for couples without children to identify with such a situation and that they would have had no shared experience from which to draw upon in developing the improvisation. Depending on the information obtained on the demographic sheet, couples were administered the improvisation concerning child discipline either for young children or for teenagers, not for both. After all improvisations had been administered, the couple was debriefed and thanked for participating.

POSITIVENESS RESULTS

The presentation of results will parallel the format used in Chapter 6. Using the same 2 × 2 repeated-measures design as in Chapter 6, with distress–nondistress as one factor and husband–wife as the repeated-measures factor, there were significant multivariate F-ratios for the content codes, independent of affect, for the fun-deck task and sex improvisations: $F(8,11) = 7.438, p < .01$ and $F(8,11) = 3.332, p < .05$, respectively. There were no significant spouse or distress-by-spouse interactions.

The ratio of agreement to agreement-plus-disagreement discriminated between distressed and nondistressed husbands on the fun deck ($t[18] = 3.07$, $p < .01$, with distressed husbands averaging .660 and nondistressed .837). The ratio also discriminated the two groups of wives on the fun deck ($t[18] = 1.81$, $p < .05$; distressed wives = .668, nondistressed wives = .796). The ratio also discriminated the two groups of wives on the sex improvisation ($t[18] = 3.48$,

$p < .01$, distressed wives = .501, nondistressed wives = .787) and on the sharing-events-of-the-day improvisation (t[18] = 1.84, distressed wives = .596, nondistressed wives = .783). *These results are consistent with results presented in Chapter 6.*

An analysis of the F-ratios for the two tasks for which the multivariate Fs were significant showed significant differences on agreement and disagreement, both on the fun deck task and on the sex improvisation. Nondistressed couples agreed more and disagreed less than did distressed couples on both tasks (see Table 8.2). Distressed couples were also more likely than were nondistressed couples to express their feelings about problems on the fun desk task (which was not a problem-solving task) and to provide metacommunication on the sex improvisation. *These results are consistent with the content-positiveness results of Chapter 6.*

An analysis of effect codes independent of content shows that on the sex improvisation (multivariate F[3,16] = 4.22, $p < .05$), in-laws improvisation (F[3, 16] = 4.80, $p < .05$), sharing-events-of-the-day improvisation (F[3, 16] = 6.58, $p < .01$), decision-to-have-children improvisation (F[3, 16] = 4.76, $p < .05$), and child-rearing improvisation (F[3, 4] = 5.57, $p < .05$), the affect codes alone were able to discriminate between distressed and nondistressed couples. Once again, the conclusion stands that nonverbal behavior is gener-

TABLE 8.2
Content Codes Independent of Affect

Variable	Univariate F-Ratio [a]	Distressed Mean	Nondistressed Mean
Fun Deck Task			
PF (Feelings about a Problem)	4.411*	0.421	0.349
MR (Mindreading)	1.803	0.065	0.047
PS (Problem Solving and Information Exchange	3.248	0.336	0.405
CT (Communication Talk)	2.075	0.017	0.008
AG (Agreement)	8.228**	0.108	0.158
DG (Disagreement)	4.875*	0.053	0.033
SO (Summarizing Other)	2.174	0.001	0.000
SS (Summarizing Self)	0.016	0.001	0.001
Sex Improvisation			
PF (Expressing Feelings about a Problem)	0.063	0.487	0.495
MR (Mindreading)	2.325	0.074	0.045
PS (Problem Solving and Information Exchange)	1.048	0.204	0.250
CT (Communication Talk)	4.848*	0.031	0.006
AG (Agreement)	5.575*	0.101	0.158
DG (Disagreement)	7.954*	0.096	0.046
SO (Summarizes Other)	2.826	0.004	0.000
SS (Summarizes Self)	1.000	0.003	0.000

*p < .05, **p < .01
[a] df = (1,18)

ally the best discriminator between distressed and nondistressed couples. For five of the six improvisations, the distress factor was significant at the .05 level, and, in every case, the nondistressed couples were more positive and less negative than were the distressed couples (see Table 8.3). *These results are consistent with those presented in Chapter 6, except for the fact that positive affect discriminated the groups as well as did negative affect.*

Once again, content-by-affect analyses were performed: one 2×2 multivariate analysis for each improvisation. Data were again transformed according to the statistical convention for proportional data, using the arcsine square root transformation (Myers, 1966). There was a significant difference between distressed and nondistressed couples for neutral affect for the fun deck (multivariate F-ratio with Wilks Lambda Criterion $F[8,11] = 5.02$, $p < .01$), for positive affect on the decision-to-have-children improvisation ($F[6, 13] = 5.02$, $p < .05$), and for negative affect on the sex improvisation ($F[6, 13] = 3.49$, $p < .05$). There were no significant spouse main effects or spouse-by-distress-interaction effects. Table 8.4 presents the univariate F-ratios for each of the four significant multivariate Fs. Nondistressed couples displayed a significantly higher proportion of neutral agreement codes (on the fun deck) and a significantly lower proportion of negative affect disagreement codes and negative affect codes in the expression of feelings about a problem (on the sex improvisation) than did distressed couples. *These results are consistent with the results in Table 6.2.*

On the fun deck, the distressed couples brought in their feelings about

TABLE 8.3
Affect Codes Independent of Content Codes: Univariate F-ratios for Distress Main Effect

Task	Variable	Univariate F-Ratio [a]	Distressed Mean	Nondistressed Mean
Sex [a]	Neutral affect	.092	0.673	0.606
	Positive affect	4.983*	0.197	0.375
	Negative affect	7.117*	0.130	0.002
In-Laws [a]	Neutral affect	0.337	0.822	0.786
	Positive affect	9.611**	0.056	0.186
	Negative affect	4.837*	0.121	0.031
Sharing [a] Events of the Day	Neutral affect	1.168	0.799	0.830
	Positive affect	5.533*	0.072	0.139
	Negative affect	8.659**	0.130	0.031
Decision [a] to Have Children	Neutral affect	0.299	0.853	0.846
	Positive affect	6.690*	0.058	0.148
	Negative affect	6.155*	0.089	0.007
Child [b] Rearing	Neutral affect	2.026	0.798	0.902
	Positive affect	10.199*	0.042	0.096
	Negative affect	5.617*	0.160	0.003

*$p < .05$
[a] $df = (1,18)$
[b] $df = (1,8)$

TABLE 8.4
Content-by-Affect Univariate Analyses of Variance for Tasks that Showed
a Significant Multivariate F-ratio

Task	Variable	Univariate F-Ratio	Distressed Mean	Nondistressed Mean
Fun Deck				
df = (1,18)	PF° (Feelings about a problem)	5.151*	0.342	0.272
	MR° (Mindreading)	2.288	0.051	0.035
	PS° (Problem Solving and Information Exchange)	1.651	0.290	0.340
	CT° (Communication Talk)	1.845	0.014	0.007
	AG° (Agreement)	7.370*	0.096	0.138
	DG° (Disagreement)	3.524	0.043	0.027
	SO° (Summarizing Other)	2.174	0.001	0.000
	SS° (Summarizing Self)	0.016	0.001	0.001
Decision to Have Children				
df = (1,18)	PF+ (Feelings about a Problem)	13.494**	0.019	0.082
	MR+(Mindreading)	0.034	0.016	0.014
	PS+ (Problem Solving and Information Exchange)	13.203**	0.001	0.023
	CT+ (Communication Talk)	0.625	0.002	0.004
	AG+(Agreement)	0.093	0.017	0.013
	DG+(Disagreement)	2.563	0.002	0.010
	SO+ (Summarizing Other)	b	0.000	0.000
	SS+ (Summarizing Self)	b	0.000	0.000
Child Rearing				
df = (1,8)	PF+ (Feelings about a Problem)	16.181**	0.018	0.063
	MR+ (Mindreading)	0.897	0.002	0.004
	PS+ (Problem Solving and Information Exchange)	5.092*	0.009	0.016
	CT+ (Communication Talk)	b	0.000	0.000
	AG+ (Agreement)	0.312	0.009	0.012
	DG+ (Disagreement)	1.590	0.003	0.000
	SO+ (Summarizing Other)	b	0.000	0.000
	SS+ (Summarizing Self)	b	0.000	0.000
Sex				
df = (1,18)	PF- (Feelings about a Problem)	8.556**	0.070	0.006
	MR- (Mindreading)	2.665	0.009	0.002
	PS- (Problem Solving and Information Exchange)	4.215	0.020	0.002
	CT- (Communication Talk)	1.000	0.001	0.000
	AG- (Agreement)	0.314	0.010	0.006
	DG- (Disagreement)	6.076*	0.019	0.003
	SO- (Summarizing Other)	b	0.000	0.000
	SS- (Summarizing Self)	b	0.000	0.000

*$p < .05$
**$p < .01$
b no variance

problems more than did the nondistressed couples. Therefore, even on a task designed specifically *not* to be problem oriented, the distressed couples discussed problems. For example, one distressed spouse said, "Here's a nice idea—have friends over for dinner," and the partner said, "Yeah, and then I'd be stuck with all the work," whereas agreement was more likely for nondistressed couples on this task.

To summarize: On the positiveness dimension, even across decision-making tasks and even for a non-decision-making task, the hypothesis that nondistressed couples are more positive and less negative was supported once again and generally replicated the results of Chapters 6 and 7.

Evaluation of the Discriminative Power of the Tasks

Based on the nonsequential analyses, the fun deck, the two child-oriented improvisations, and the sex improvisation gave the most consistent differences between distressed and nondistressed couples, considering both content-by-affect codes and affect codes independent of content.

Of all the improvisations, the content-by-affect codes for the sex improvisation are most similar to the analyses in Table 6.2, since negative affect for both feelings about problems and disagreement codes were significantly different in the same way in both tables; therefore, the remainder of this chapter will present sequential analyses for the sex improvisation.

RECIPROCITY RESULTS: SEX IMPROVISATION

Table 8.5 presents the probability of negative affect cycles. Once again, *negative affect cycles in clinic couples have higher conditional probabilities and greater reduction of uncertainty over base-rate probabilities than they do in nonclinic couples* (cf. Table 6.3). Table 8.6 presents the probability of positive affect cycles (cf. Table 6.4). Once again, Z-scores are higher for clinic couples at lag 1, but positive affect cycles at later lags show higher Z-scores for nonclinic couples. *Nonclinic couples in both studies show greater delayed reciprocity of positive affect and less immediate reciprocity of positive affect than do clinic couples.*

DESCRIPTIVE ANALYSES: SEX IMPROVISATION

To the extent possible, the presentation of the sequential analysis results will parallel the presentation given in Chapter 6. Unfortunately, some codes occurred too infrequently in the sex improvisation for sequential analysis to be made.

TABLE 8.5
Probability of Negative Affect Cycles—Sex

Criterion H-	LAG					
	1	2	3	4	5	6
Nonclinic						
H-	.00	.37*	.05	.26*	.00	.16*
W-	.00	.05	.00	.00	.11	.00
Z-score	—	10.77	—	7.52	—	4.26
Clinic						
H-	.07	.24*	.07	.15*	.05	.13*
W-	.17*	.07	.12*	.04	.09*	.13**
Z-score	5.57	7.88	3.46	4.07	2.29	4.04

Criterion W-	LAG					
	1	2	3	4	5	6
Nonclinic						
H-	.10	.00	.17**	.00	.10**	.07
W-	.00	.37*	.10*	.23*	.10*	.10*
Z-score	3.03	10.42	5.69	6.27	3.10	2.12
Clinic						
H-	.20*	.00	.26*	.05	.18*	.02
W-	.00	.39*	.03	.29*	.06	.17*
Z-score	5.62	14.59	8.14	10.21	5.22	5.21

*Represents the probabilities with the highest Z-score, which is given immediately below the respective probabilities.
**Refers to largest Z-score when both asterisks had Z > 1.96.

TABLE 8.6
Probability of Positive Affect Cycles—Sex

Criterion: H+	LAG					
	1	2	3	4	5	6
Nonclinic						
H+	.00	.40*	.10	.26*	.13	.25*
W+	.54*	.03	.37*	.01	.33*	.02
Z-score	9.95	8.76	6.01	4.27	4.83	3.69
Clinic						
H+	.00	.24*	.12	.17*	.12	.18*
W+	.31	.02	.17*	.01	.04	.01
Z-score	8.74	6.34	3.22	3.66	—	3.97

Criterion: W+	LAG					
	1	2	3	4	5	6
Nonclinic						
H+	.39*	.09	.26*	.12	.25*	.13
W+	.00	.49*	.01	.39*	.16	.35*
Z-score	7.47	10.78	4.25	7.21	4.08	6.14
Clinic						
H+	.34*	.06	.20*	.10	.17*	.10
W+	.00	.30*	.09	.21*	.11	.21*
Z-score	10.13	8.91	4.96	5.09	3.77	5.09

*Represents the probabilities with the highest Z-score, which is given immediately below the respective probabilities.

Table 8.7 presents the sequences obtained for expressing feelings about a problem. Table 8.7 should be compared to Table 6.6. For the husband's expression of feeling about a problem with neutral affect, the chains are similar in the two tables, and *the general conclusion holds: Clinic couples are more likely to engage in cross-complaining loops, and nonclinic couples are more likely to engage in validation loops.* A similar result is obtained for sequences that begin with the wife's expression of feelings about a problem with neutral affect: Cross-complaining is more likely for clinic than for nonclinic couples, and validation is more likely for nonclinic than for clinic couples. However, in this case, the husband's agreement enters into the validation chain for both groups of couples, whereas in Table 6.6 it was only the wife's agreement. Once again, the clinic wife's positive affect expression of feelings about a problem (WPF+) contained a low-probability validation loop, low because the base-rate probability is .036 and the conditional agreement by the husband is .071. On the whole, the strings obtained in Table 8.7 are quite consistent with those in Table 6.6.

Unfortunately, there were not enough instances of mindreading for sequential analysis (Clinic HMRo = 48, WMRo = 43; Nonclinic HMRo = 17, WMRo = 22), since at least 85 occurrences are necessary at P-values close to .10 for the normal distribution to be a good approximation to the binomial. A rough test that the feeling-probe sequence is common for both groups is provided by the lag 1 conditional probabilities and Z-scores for agreement following mindreading. For clinic couples, the conditional probability of the wife's neutral agreement (WAGo) following the husband's neutral mindreading (HMRo) was .271 ($Z = 7.60$), and for nonclinic couples this probability was .059 ($Z = .42$). For clinic couples, the conditional probability of the husband's neutral agreement (HAGo) following the wife's neutral mindreading (WMRo) was .140 ($Z = 2.86$), and for nonclinic couples it was .36 ($Z = 2.12$). However, with such small instances of these codes, Z-scores and conditional probabilities are difficult to interpret.

There was an adequate number of cases of disagreement for sequential analysis only for clinic couples, but Table 8.8 presents the obtained sequences. Again, conclusions must be tentative for nonclinic couples, but it is likely that the overall conclusion holds: Disagreement by one spouse leads to disagreement by the partner, and the pattern is not dramatically different across groups.

Clinic and nonclinic couples differed significantly on the proportion of summary statements that were Summarizing Self only for wives on this task: $t(36) = 1.84, p < .05$, clinic wives = .16, nonclinic wives = .00; this finding provides some support for the "summarizing self" syndrome found to be more characteristic of distressed than nondistressed couples in Chapter 6. In this study, summary codes were so rare on the sex improvisation that the total sample (all improvisations) had to be used.

Table 8.9 presents the sequence analyses with problem solving and information exchange (PSo) as the criterion. In Chapter 6, the agreement of clinic

TABLE 8.7
Sequences Beginning with Feelings about a Problem

Clinic Couples	Nc	Nonclinic Couples	Nc

Cross-Complaining

Clinic Couples:
HPFo $\xrightarrow{.302}$ WPFo → $\xrightarrow{.224}$ WPFo → HPFo → WDGo
WPFo $\xrightarrow{.121}$ WPSo
$\xrightarrow{.138}$ WPSo
Nc = 349

Nonclinic Couples:
HPFo $\xrightarrow{.161}$ WPSo
$\xrightarrow{.094}$ WAGo (Validation)
Nc = 180

Cross-Complaining

Clinic Couples:
WPFo → HPFo → WPFo → HPFo
WPFo $\xrightarrow{.145}$ HPFo $\xrightarrow{.335}$ WPSo
$\xrightarrow{.136}$ WPSo
$\xrightarrow{.088}$ HAGo
Nc = 272

Nonclinic Couples:
WPFo $\xrightarrow{.385}$ HPFo
$\xrightarrow{.105}$ HAGo → WPFo
Nc = 143

Clinic Couples:
WPF+ $\xrightarrow{.229}$ HPF+ → WPF+ → HPF+ → WPF+ → HPF+ → WPF+
$\xrightarrow{.071}$ HAG+
$\xrightarrow{.071}$ WPS+
Nc = 70

Nonclinic Couples:
WPF+ $\xrightarrow{.302}$ HPFo → WDG- → HCTo
$\xrightarrow{.235}$ WPF+ — HPF+
$\xrightarrow{.163}$ HPF+ $\xrightarrow{.094}$ WPS+ → HAG+
$\xrightarrow{.071}$ WAG+
Nc = 86

AG = Agreement
DG = Disagreement
PF = Feelings about a Problem
PS = Problem Solving and Information Exchange
Nc = Number of Criterion Behaviors

TABLE 8.8
Disagreement Sequences — Sex

Clinic Couples	Nc	Nonclinic Couples	Nc
HDGo $\xrightarrow{.233}$ WPFo	73	HDGo $\xrightarrow{.314}$ WPFo $\searrow^{.086}$ WDGo	35
WDGo $\xrightarrow{.131}$ HDGo	61	————————————	23

DG = Disagreement
PF = Feelings about a Problem
Nc = Number of Criterion Behaviors

wives entered into the chain for the husband's PSo, but the converse was not true. In this study, however, both husband and wife agreement entered into the chains for clinic couples. Nonetheless, they were always followed by a counterproposal sequence, rather than a contract sequence. In fact, there was only one contract sequence in which a PSo *ended* with an agreement rather than a counterproposal string (PSo → PSo), and this occurred when the PSo was given by the nonclinic husband. In all other cases, the strings were counterproposals. The sequence for the nonclinic wife's PSo is not a contracting sequence, and this result contradicts the results presented in Chapter 6. These results are partially but not completely consistent with the results in Table 6.9.

Table 8.10 presents the sequences for agreement as the criterion code. Once again, the conclusion holds that agreement by one spouse generally makes agreement by that person more likely later in the chain (cf. Table 6.10). For the nonclinic husband, however, the wife's agreement (with positive affect) did enter the chain. There were an inadequate number of communication talk codes for all groups to permit sequence analysis or for any lag 1 conditional Z-scores to be valid (clinic HCTo = 21, WCTo = 21; nonclinic HCTo = 13, WCTo = 7).

There were an inadequate number of occurrences of negative context codes for the sex improvisation for parallel context analyses to be carried out. Therefore, context analyses were conducted across all improvisations. Nonclinic husbands were negative listeners when their wives were nonnegative speakers 0.40% of the time, and clinic husbands were negative listeners 2.30% of the time, χ^2 (1) = 59.91, p < .01; for wives as listeners these percentages were 2.33% and 2.70% for nonclinic and clinic couples, respectively, χ^2 (1) = 1.82, n.s. Wives thus did not differ, but the nonclinic husband was far less likely to be a negative listener than the clinic husband. As in Chapter 6, an analysis was performed of the ability of the listener's negative nonverbal behavior to predict that person's subsequent lag-1 negative nonverbal speaker affect. The probability that the husband's negative behavior as a listener would transfer to his immediately consequent negative speaker affect was higher for clinic ($p = .458$; $z = 14.69$) than for nonclinic couples ($p = .170$; $z = 4.03$). For wives, both nonclinic and clinic wives had high conditional probabilities and z-scores (nonclinic: $p = .509$, $z = 35.00$; clinic: $p = .337$, $z = 9.40$). It thus appears that in this study it is the nonclinic *husband* who performs the cognitive editing function we noted for nonclinic wives in Chapter 6. Since the tasks in the Rubin study, taken together, were lower conflict tasks than the task in Chapter 6, one hypothesis we can generate is that nonclinic husbands perform a cognitive editing function that moderates between listening and speaking in lower conflict situations, while nonclinic wives perform this function on higher conflict tasks. Unfortunately, this hypothesis cannot be tested in the Rubin study because there is an insufficient frequency of the criterion codes to separately analyze context for high and low conflict improvisations.

RECIPROCITY RESULTS ACROSS IMPROVISATIONS

On five of the six improvisations, the nonverbal behaviors of distressed couples were more negative and less positive than those of nondistressed

TABLE 8.9
Sequences with Problem Solving and Information Exchange as the Criterion — Sex

Clinic Couples	Nc	Nonclinic Couples	Nc
	211		93
	165		89

AG = Agreement
PF = Feelings about a Problem
PS = Problem Solving and Information Exchange

TABLE 8.10
Sequences with Agreement as the Criterion — Sex

Clinic	Nc	Nonclinic	Nc
$HAG_o \xrightarrow{.169} WPS_o \rightarrow HAG_o \rightarrow WSO_o$	89	$HAG_o \xrightarrow{.304} WPF_o \rightarrow HPF_o$ $\xrightarrow{.109} WAG+ \rightarrow HAG_o \rightarrow WPF_o \rightarrow HPF_o$	89
$WAG_o \xrightarrow{.274} HPF_o \rightarrow WPS_o \rightarrow HPS_o$ $\xrightarrow{.262} HPS_o \xrightarrow{.167} \quad \xrightarrow{.107} WAG_o$	84	No Lag-1 Z-score > 1.96	42

AG = Agreement
PF = Feelings about a Problem
PS = Problem Solving and Information Exchange
SO = Summarizing Other

couples. The two groups of couples did not differ *nonsequentially* in nonverbal behavior on the fun deck and the money improvisation; however, it is possible for the two groups to differ in the reciprocity of positive or negative affect but not differ in relative frequency, since the two analyses are independent. Therefore, the *first set* of analyses presented in this section will be affect cycles over all tasks, and then affect cycles as a function of the seven tasks of the improvisation study.

The tasks induced different levels of conflict. Rank ordered by total agreement to total disagreement ratios for both groups of couples, the tasks induced conflict (from greatest to least) in the following order: Sex (AG/DG = 1.27), Having Children (AG/DG = 1.32), Money (AG/DG = 1.54), In-Laws (AG/DG = 1.56), Sharing Events of the Day (AG/DG = 1.58), Disciplining Children (AG/DG = 2.12), and the Fun Deck (AG/DG = 3.72). The rank-order correlation between clinic and nonclinic couples of conflict induced, as assessed by the AG/DG ratio, was .82 (t[5] = 3.20, *p* < .05), which compares favorably with the rank-order correlation of .94 in perceived severity of problems on the problem inventory.

The reciprocity of both positive and negative affect will be presented over all tasks and then separately for each of the tasks, with the exception of the sex improvisation. The two child-oriented tasks were combined.

Positive and Negative Reciprocity over All Tasks

Figure 8.1 shows the average Z-scores for positive reciprocity cross-lags (H + → W + averaged with W + → H +) over all tasks separately for nonclinic and clinic couples. From this figure, we can see that, over all tasks, positive reciprocity was not dramatically different for the two groups; at later lags (4, 5, and 6), clinic couples even exceeded nonclinic couples in positive reciprocity. Figure 8.1 also shows the cyclic property of positive affect that can only be understood with reference to the auto-lags drawn in Figure 8.2, which show peaks in positive affect by the spouse initiating the chain (average H + → W + and W + → H +). In brief, these graphs show positive affect cycles from husband to wife, and cross-lag and auto-lag positive affect chains were not appreciably different for the two groups.

Figure 8.3 illustrates the negative reciprocity cross-lags, and Figure 8.4 shows the negative affect auto-lags. Here, there were dramatic differences between the two groups. Clinic couples were far more likely to reciprocate negative affect than were nonclinic couples; these results are consistent with those presented in Chapter 7.

There was some evidence to suggest that the differences between nonclinic and clinic couples in positive (but not negative) reciprocity varied as a function of the level of conflict induced by the task. The lag 1 H + → W + Z-scores for the low-conflict fun deck task were 14.65 for nonclinic couples and 8.89 for clinic couples, whereas for the high-conflict sex improvisation these Z-scores

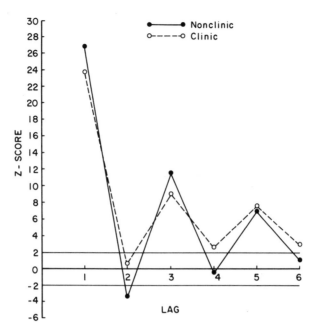

Figure 8.1 *Averaged Z-scores for positive reciprocity cross-lags over all tasks.*

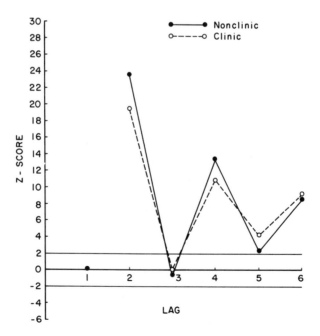

Figure 8.2 *Averaged Z-scores for positive reciprocity auto-lags over all tasks.*

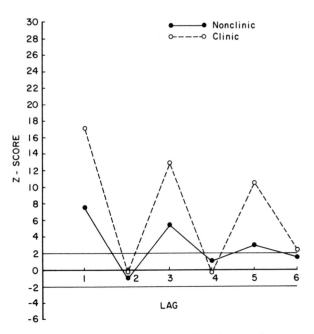

Figure 8.3 *Averaged Z-scores for negative reciprocity cross-lags over all tasks.*

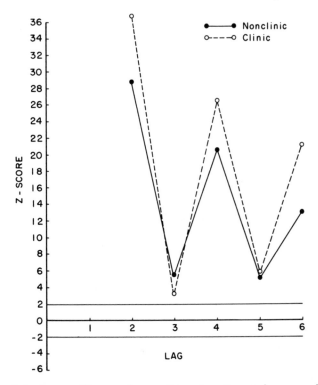

Figure 8.4 *Averaged Z-scores for negative reciprocity auto-lags over all tasks.*

were 9.95 for nonclinic and 8.74 for clinic couples. These Z-scores suggest that, although clinic couples have not changed their positive reciprocity Z-scores from the lowest- to the highest- conflict task, nonclinic couples showed considerably more positive reciprocity on the low-conflict task than they did on the high-conflict task. These differences did not exist for the lag 1 negative reciprocity Z-scores as a function of the conflict induced by the task. To continue investigating reciprocity differences between groups as a function of task, we will present positive and negative affect cycles separately by task.

Reciprocity on a Low-Conflict Task—The Fun Deck

Table 8.11 presents the results of the sequential analyses of negative affect cycles. Remember that on this task the two groups of couples did not differ significantly in the *nonsequential* analyses of positive or negative affect. Table 8.11 shows that there was no evidence of reciprocity of negative affect from husband to wife for nonclinic couples. Although nonclinic wives did show

TABLE 8.11
Reciprocity of Negative Affect Cycles — Fun Deck

	Lag					
Criterion H-	1	2	3	4	5	6
Nonclinic						
H-						
W-	Not enough instances of H- for sequential analysis.					
Z-Score						
Clinic						
H-	.00	.07**	.07*	.07*	.07*	.10**
W-	.10*	.07*	.10**	.00	.14**	.07*
Z-Score	5.30	4.19	5.32	4.19	7.27	6.50

	Lag					
Criterion W-	1	2	3	4	5	6
Nonclinic						
H-	.00	.00	.00	.00	.00	.00
W-	.00	.08*	.00	.00	.08*	.08*
Z-Score	—	5.92	—	—	5.92	5.92
Clinic						
H-	.10*	.07*	.07**	.05*	.05*	.07*
W-	.00	.12**	.05*	.07	.00	.02
Z-Score	7.22	7.57	5.31	4.30	3.37	5.31

*Represents the probabilities with the highest Z-score, which is given immediately below the respective probabilities.

**Refers to largest Z-score when both asterisks had Z > 1.96.

some cycling of negative affect at lags 2, 5, and 6, this did not affect the nonclinic husband. However, clinic husbands and wives are both continually affected by their negative affect, and the double asterisks show the greater tendency (evidenced by higher Z-scores and conditional probabilities) for a husband-to-wife-to-husband reciprocal pattern of negative affect. Therefore, *even on the lowest-conflict task, the fun deck, clinic couples were far more likely to reciprocate negative affect than were nonclinic couples.*

Table 8.12 shows the probability of positive affect cycles, and these data show that positive affect cycles are about equally likely for both groups.

Reciprocity on High-Conflict Tasks

Money. Table 8.13 shows a dramatic difference between the two groups of couples on the extent to which they reciprocate negative affect. The extremely high conditional probabilities and Z-scores demonstrate that even at lag 6 the probabilities are very high that the clinic couples will remain in a negative affect exchange. This is not the case for nonclinic couples, where the conditional probabilities reach a crest at lag 4 and decline thereafter: They have been

TABLE 8.12
Positive Affect Cycles — Fun Deck

			Lag			
Criterion H+	1	2	3	4	5	6
Nonclinic						
H+	.00	.16*	.07	.13*	.07	.09
W+	.33*	.07	.13	.09	.13*	.07
Z-Score	14.65	6.94	—	4.16	2.45	—
Clinic						
H+	.00	.21*	.06	.12*	.06	.10
W+	.22*	.07	.13*	.06	.09	.08
Z-Score	8.98	9.43	3.68	2.97	—	—
			Lag			
Criterion W+	1	2	3	4	5	6
Nonclinic						
H+	.25*	.05	.10*	.06	.09	.09
W+	.00	.23*	.08	.14*	.11	.12
Z-Score	14.39	10.41	2.25	3.27	—	—
Clinic						
H+	.27*	.03	.11*	.05	.09	.07
W+	.00	.19*	.07	.19*	.09	.13*
Z-Score	13.46	7.87	2.84	7.67	—	3.31

*Represents the probabilities with the highest Z-score, which is given immediately below the respective probabilities.

TABLE 8.13
Reciprocity of Negative Affect — Money

	Lag					
Criterion H-	1	2	3	4	5	6
Nonclinic						
H-	.00	.00	.10*	.25*	.05	.10*
W-	.05	.00	.05	.10	.05	.05
Z-Score	—	—	4.19	11.13	—	4.19
Clinic						
H-	.00	.61*	.07	.53*	.08	.50*
W-	.28*	.01	.23*	.01	.23*	.03
Z-Score	15.79	26.75	13.36	22.83	13.36	21.20

	Lag					
Criterion W-	1	2	3	4	5	6
Nonclinic						
H-	.02	.02	.05*	.00	.00	.05*
W-	.00	.05	.08**	.22**	.05	.12**
Z-Score	—	—	3.25	8.80	—	4.13
Clinic						
H-	.48*	.07	.46*	.04	.46*	.04
W-	.00	.51*	.04	.50*	.04	.43*
Z-Score	14.19	22.72	13.59	22.26	13.71	19.12

*Represents the probabilities with the highest Z-score, which is given immediately below the respective probabilities.
**Refers to largest Z-score when both asterisks had Z > 1.96.

more able than clinic couples to become unlatched from one another's initial negative affect.

Table 8.14 demonstrates nearly as dramatically that, whereas positive affect is reciprocated by both groups of couples, positive reciprocity is more probable for nonclinic than for clinic couples. On the money improvisation it was, thus, possible to discriminate the two groups of couples on both positive and negative *reciprocity,* but not nonsequentially on positive and negative affect. Because this difference in positive reciprocity between groups was not obtained in the overall analysis of the reciprocity of positive affect, we can expect different group patterns on other high-conflict tasks; this is the case for the next two improvisations.

In-Laws. Table 8.15 contains the extremely surprising finding that, on the in-law improvisation, nonclinic couples were consistently *more* likely to reciprocate negative affect than were clinic couples. The in-law improvisation was also the only task on which there was both a significant spouse main effect (multivariate $F[3,32] = 6.16$, $p < .01$) and a significant distress main effect

TABLE 8.14
Reciprocity of Positive Affect — Money

Criterion H+	Lag					
	1	2	3	4	5	6
Nonclinic						
H+	.00	.27*	.05	.19*	.08	.16*
W+	.36*	.05	.26*	.08	.21*	.11
Z-Score	12.80	9.63	8.61	5.82	6.13	4.23
Clinic						
H+	.00	.27*	.06	.15*	.10	.14**
W+	.26*	.05	.10*	.09	.13*	.10*
Z-Score	9.19	10.40	2.08	4.60	3.21	4.21

Criterion W+	Lag					
	1	2	3	4	5	6
Nonclinic						
H+	.47*	.02	.25*	.06	.18*	.08
W+	.00	.40*	.06	.27*	.11	.20*
Z-Score	18.38	15.39	8.59	9.42	5.94	6.09
Clinic						
H+	.32*	.06	.14*	.06	.41*	.07
W+	.00	.20	.10	.14*	.06	.17*
Z-Score	12.44	6.63	3.95	3.70	4.33	5.21

*Represents the probabilities with the highest Z-score, which is given immediately below
the respective probabilities.
**Refers to largest Z-score when both asterisks had Z > 1.96.

(multivariate $F[3,32] = 3.16, p < .05$). The in-law relationship was presented
as a problem situation in our interviews slightly more often by nonclinic than by
clinic couples. In our interviews, a typical situation was:

> Wife feels that her mother-in-law puts her down, particularly with respect to
> her housekeeping, her handling of the children, and the way she takes care
> of her son's needs. She expects her husband to defend her, and, when he
> does not, she feels rejected and wonders which family he is in—whether he
> is her husband or his mother's son. The husband feels put in a bind by these
> two women and tries to act as the neutral problem-solving mediator. He
> wants both women to get along, and he thinks that, in general, his wife is
> less fragile than his mother. He takes into account that they see his mother
> infrequently and wishes that his wife would try to be more understanding of
> his mother's little faults. She is reluctant to visit his parents. He feels they do
> not see enough of them.

On the in-law improvisation, the husbands' affect was significantly more likely
to be neutral than was their wives' ($F[1, 34] = 7.10, p < .05$, Hneutral = .836,
Wneutral = .783), and the wives were significantly more negative than were

TABLE 8.15
Reciprocity of Negative Affect — In-Laws

Criterion H-	Lag					
	1	2	3	4	5	6
Nonclinic						
H-	.00	.43*	.05	.24*	.14*	.19*
W-	.43*	.00	.33*	.10	.19**	.05
Z-Score	8.71	18.33	6.61	9.97	5.79	7.88
Clinic						
H-	.00	.26*	.07	.22*	.09*	.11**
W-	.17*	.11	.13	.11	.15	.17*
Z-Score	2.06	9.75	—	7.94	2.49	3.40

Criterion W-	Lag					
	1	2	3	4	5	6
Nonclinic						
H-	.15*	.00	.09*	.03	.05*	.05*
W-	.00	.32*	.09	.21*	.16**	.17**
Z-Score	11.53	12.43	6.50	7.47	5.26	5.82
Clinic						
H-	.09*	.03	.06	.03	.06**	.07*
W-	.00	.33*	.10	.23*	.14*	.21**
Z-Score	4.25	10.56	—	6.40	2.58	5.50

*Represents the probabilities with the highest Z-score, which is given immediately below
the respective probabilities.
**Refers to largest Z-score when both asterisks had Z > 1.96.

their husbands (F[1, 34] = 15.33, $p < .001$, Hnegative = .035, Wnegative =
.120). This was the largest difference between spouses on any improvisation
(see later section, this chapter, on spouse differences).

These results suggest that the in-law issue was particularly difficult for the
nonclinic wife. As further evidence, her conditional probabilities of reciprocating negative affect averaged .259 on those lags for which her Z-scores were
significant, whereas her husband's conditional probabilities averaged .168 on
those lags for which his Z-scores were significant. The equivalent conditional
probabilities were .208 for the clinic wife and .129 for the clinic husband.[1]

Nonetheless, our overall patterns hold for positive affect. Table 8.16 shows
that positive reciprocity was far more likely for the nonclinic than for the clinic
couple on this improvisation. In the sequential sense, for both positive and
negative affect, nonclinic couples on this improvisation can be described as

[1] Additional evidence on the in-law issue comes from another source. Bell (1975) wrote:

The most common in-law trouble is between the wife and the husband's mother. In part this is because in both
spouse and kin conflicts the husband's side of the family is most involved. . . . This is further supported by
Komarovsky (1962), who found that one third of the wives revealed serious dissatisfactions with their in-laws,
whereas the husbands enjoyed fairly satisfactory in-law relationships [p. 317].

TABLE 8.16
Reciprocity of Positive Affect—In-Laws

Criterion H+	LAG					
	1	2	3	4	5	6
Nonclinic						
H+	.00	.33*	.07	.19*	.08	.15*
W+	.36*	.06	.20*	.08	.12*	.09
Z-score	14.01	10.76	6.73	4.59	2.62	2.54
Clinic						
H+	.00	.19*	.07	.14*	.05	.14*
W+	.18*	.05	.09*	.03	.07	.05
Z-score	6.18	6.16	2.35	4.05	—	4.05

Criterion W+	LAG					
	1	2	3	4	5	6
Nonclinic						
H+	.49*	.03	.21*	.08	.17**	.09
W+	.00	.32*	.08	.18*	.12*	.13*
Z-score	15.05	11.26	4.77	4.79	2.96	2.73
Clinic						
H+	.24*	.05	.08	.06	.08	.03
W+	.00	.19*	.08	.08	.08	.05
Z-score	7.40	6.07	—	—	—	—

*Represents the probabilities with the highest Z-score, which is given immediately below the respective probabilities.
**Refers to largest Z-score when both asterisks had Z > 1.96.

affectively more connected with one another. The nonclinic wife could also be described as somewhat defensive, since the probability of a W− following an H+ was .090 (Z = 2.74) for nonclinic couples and .128 (Z = 11.19) for clinic couples; yet, this was not the case for an H− following a W+, which had probability .015 for clinic couples (Z = −.64) and .000 for nonclinic couples (Z = −2.51). The following excerpt illustrates nonclinic couples' interaction on the in-law improvisation:

W: But, ah, your parents seem like they, I don't know, doesn't seem like they don't really want me, you know, to have, they haven't accepted me as part of the family anyway. I mean, you know, in all their festivities and stuff whenever we've been there Xmas before, they just kind of leave me out.

H: They give you presents and stuff.

W: Oh, I know they give me presents and stuff, but it's not that . . .

H: Well, maybe they're not . . .

W: . . . it's just their attitude. I mean you can tell when you're sitting around and stuff with a group if you're being accepted or whether they're just being polite to you. And that's always the impression that your family has given to me. Because I happen to be married to you. And I just don't like that feeling of being an outsider. I mean it seems like if my parents did that to you at first.

H: *But I don't, that . . . it's gonna take time for you to be accepted.*

W: *A lot of times they'll be criticizing me and I'll look at you, and give you a kind of look you know, and you'll look back at me like, "Well, why are you looking at me like that for?"*

H: *Well, how in the . . .*

W: *You don't even know what's going on.*

H: *Oh yes I do. It's just that my family is . . .*

W: *Well, why don't you ever stand up for me then?*

H: *Because my family, they're all individuals but they're close. And so you stand up for yourself. If you don't stand up for yourself, they're not going to accept you. They're going to keep on criticizing you, because you . . .*

W: *I do stand up for myself.*

H: *. . . you stand up for yourself and present your reasons, and make shown, and show them that you're intelligent. I mean . . .*

W: *I let them know. I mean I stand up for myself. I don't just stand there and take the criticism and say, "Oh well, that's nice to know." But it just gets to the point where you after so long a time . . .*

H: *The main thing I could do is to be a mediator. I couldn't take your side or their side, I don't feel . . .*

W: *It seems like they just try to pick things out. And . . .*

H: *Well, why don't you come back at them and say, "Why did you pick that? What's wrong with it, I don't see anything wrong with it."*

W: *I know, but after you do that for so long, you know, 4 days and 4 nights and 5 days is a lotta time to be on the defensive.*

H: *Well, we don't have to stay that long.*

W: *Well, you want to stay 4 nights.*

H: *Yeah, well it's a long drive back so we could leave the next morning. So we'll get there one night and stay you know . . .*

W: *Well, that's still a long time.*

H: *. . . 4 days and then the fourth night that we stayed we'd leave the next morning. It wouldn't be that long. It's a long drive through between here and there and back.*

W: *I know but well put yourself in my position. How would you like to . . .*

This excerpt is fairly typical of the kind of conflict expressed by both husbands and wives and shows that the improvisations usually produced very personal conversations.

Sharing Events of the Day. Table 8.17 indicates that on this task the two groups were not very different in the extent to which they reciprocated negative affect, and Table 8.18 shows that the two groups were not very different in the extent to which they reciprocated positive affect; on the sharing events of the day improvisation, *clinic* husbands and nonclinic wives were somewhat more

TABLE 8.17
Reciprocity of Negative Affect—Sharing Events of the Day

Criterion H-	LAG					
	1	2	3	4	5	6
Nonclinic						
H-						
W-	Not enough instances of H- for sequential analysis.					
Z-score						
Clinic						
H-	.00	.36*	.11*	.31*	.12*	.25*
W-	.22*	.05	.19**	.07	.13**	.08
Z-score	7.11	15.63	5.87	12.63	2.97	9.63

Criterion W-	LAG					
	1	2	3	4	5	6
Nonclinic						
H-	.01*	.00	.00	.00	.00	.00
W-	.00	.51*	.05	.33*	.09	.27*
Z-score	2.05	20.13	—	12.35	—	9.60
Clinic						
H-	.20*	.06	.15*	.02	.14**	.06
W-	.00	.35*	.10	.27*	.13*	.23*
Z-score	6.49	14.93	4.41	10.16	4.12	8.20

*Represents the probabilities with the highest Z-score, which is given immediately below the respective probabilities

**Refers to largest Z-score when both asterisks had Z > 1.96.

TABLE 8.18
Reciprocity of Positive Affect—Sharing Events of the Day

Criterion H+	LAG					
	1	2	3	4	5	6
Nonclinic						
H+	.00	.36*	.09	.25*	.09	.21*
W+	.25*	.02	.09	.05	.07	.05
Z-score	10.12	11.84	—	6.46	—	4.75
Clinic						
H+	.00	.25*	.09	.20*	.12**	.12*
W+	.21*	.06	.12*	.04	.10*	.03
Z-score	9.54	10.26	4.47	7.85	3.57	3.82

Criterion W+	LAG					
	1	2	3	4	5	6
Nonclinic						
H+	.28*	.08	.14	.05	.11	.13
W+	.00	.17*	.09	.12*	.09	.07
Z-score	5.84	4.88	—	2.49	—	—
Clinic						
H+	.34*	.06	.15**	.09	.12*	.15*
W+	.00	.16*	.10*	.06	.05	.06
Z-score	13.24	6.12	4.50	—	3.14	4.50

*Represents the probabilities with the highest Z-score, which is given immediately below the respective probabilities.

**Refers to largest Z-score when both asterisks had Z > 1.96.

likely to reciprocate positive affect initiated by their spouses than were their counterparts.

For the remaining two child-oriented improvisations, there were an inadequate number of positive and negative events in nonclinic couples to do comparative sequential analyses.

SPOUSE DIFFERENCES

Obtained differences between husband and wife must be cautiously interpreted, since specific roles were assigned to each partner by the structure of the improvisations. Rubin (1977) discussed this problem. She wrote:

> . . . the multivariate F-ratio for the spouse main effect was significant at the .05 level of probability for the total sample of couples in the analyses of content codes by negative affect for the in-laws improvisation. . . . The univariate F-ratios revealed that in discussing this task wives used a greater proportion of codes for expressing feelings about a problem, mindreading, problem solving, agreement, and disagreement all accompanied by negative affect than did the husbands. However, in coaching wives for this improvisation, they were asked to play a role in which they did not want to visit their in-laws for the holiday and are prepared to identify specific grievances concerning their in-laws. Thus, it is difficult to ascertain specifically how much the results are biased by the wives portraying a particular role in this situation and how much influence can be attributed to their status as wives. (Appendix J, p. 1)

However, since wives used more negative affect than did husbands on three tasks—fun deck, sex, and in-laws—and since the fun deck contains no role-specific instructions, the patterns obtained on the improvisations may not be entirely a function of the improvisation roles. Spouse differences in affect are presented in Table 8.19.

On the whole, these results are consistent with Raush et al.'s (1974) finding that sex differences accounted for a small but significant portion of the reduction of uncertainty in couples' responses. They wrote:

> Furthermore, the data yield no evidence for the theory offered by Parsons and Bales (1955) about sex-role differentiation in marriage—that men are more instrumental (concerned with tasks) and women are more expressive (concerned with emotions). These husbands and wives appear to share responsibility for both instrumental and expressive acts. The findings are consistent with those of Heiss (1962), Leik (1963) and Levinger (1964), who found no real sex-role differentiation in interaction in intimate dyads [p. 141].

Raush et al. (1974) obtained results consistent with the Rubin improvisation study with respect to husbands' emotional expression. We found that on the sex and in-law improvisation, husbands were significantly more neutral than were their wives. In a similar vein, Raush et al. wrote:

TABLE 8.19
Spouse Differences in Affect

Task	Variable	Univariate F-ratio [a]	Husbands'	Wives'
Fun Deck	Neutral affect	0.336	0.870	0.832
	Positive affect	0.018	0.125	0.159
	Negative affect	4.730*	.005	.009
Sex	Neutral affect	18.809***	0.746	0.688
	Positive affect	10.559**	0.195	0.237
	Negative affect	4.602*	0.065	0.075
In-Laws b	Neutral affect	7.100*	0.836	0.783
	Positive affect	3.360	0.129	0.097
	Negative affect	15.334***	0.035	0.120

a df = (1,36)
b df = (1,34)
*p < .05
**p < .01
***p < .001

Moreover, certain trends in the data are surprising. It is generally assumed that wives are the more supportive members within families, but out results contradict this assumption. Husbands made more attempts to resolve the conflict and to restore the harmony to the relationship. Furthermore, wives used more of the negatively toned categories, rejection and coercion or personal attack, than did husbands [p. 141].

These conclusions held for the issue-oriented scenes in which role differences had not been induced as part of the improvisation instructions. This was the case in the fun-deck task of the Rubin study.

However, it may be the case that the husband's neutral problem-solving behavior is at times viewed as negative by the wife. Table 7.6 showed that there was an important sequence for clinic couples in which the husband's neutral problem solving (PSo) and information exchange statement led to a disagreement with negative affect by the wife significantly often ($p = .079, Z = 3.51$). For nonclinic couples in this study, there was a significant but low-probability relationship between the husband's PSo and the wife's counterproposal with negative affect ($p = .012, Z = 2.03$). The reverse, that is, the wife's neutral proposals in either group leading to negative affect codes by the husband, was not true. Also, in our laboratory Phillips (1975) found that a fight style couples low in marital satisfaction reported as characteristic was the Emotional Wife and the Problem Solver Husband; thus, the husband's neutral nonverbal behavior may be invalidating to the wife in the context of her strong negative nonverbal behavior. Nonverbal husband behaviors that seem neutral to two observers may not seem that way at all to clinic wives (see Chapter 12). Some light was shed on the husband's point of view in a recent unpublished study in my laboratory. Using Phillips' fight style questionnaire, Toler found two factors of the questionnaire that did not correlate with MRI scores; these two factors did, however, have clear interpretations as: (1) constructive fighting, and (2) withdrawing or walking out of an argument if it gets heated. These two factors

TABLE 8.20
Sequences of Validation and Cross-Complaining—Fun Deck

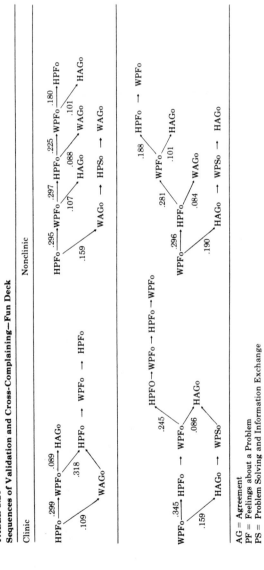

AG = Agreement
PF = Feelings about a Problem
PS = Problem Solving and Information Exchange

164

TABLE 8.21
Sequences of Contracting and Counterproposal—Fun Deck

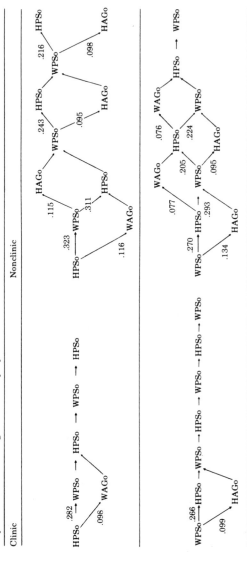

AG = Agreement
PS = Problem Solving and Information Exchange

TABLE 8.22

Comparison of Data from Chapters 6 and 8 on the Distribution of the Codes

		Phase of Discussion		
Code		Beginning 1/3	Middle 1/3	End 1/3
Mindreading	I	X	X	
	II	X	X	
Problem Feeling	I	X	X	
	II	X	X	
Problem Solving	I	X	X	
and Information Exchange	II	X	X	
Communication Talk	I		X	
	II	X		
Disagreement	I	X	X	
	II	X	X	
Agreement	I			X
	II			X
Summarizing Self	I		X	X
	II		X	X
Summarizing Other	I			X
	II			X

I = Research reported in Chapter 6
II = Research reported in Chapter 8

also predicted the husband's negative affect coded from videotapes of couples resolving a marital issue (as in Chapter 6), multiple $R = .68$. These results of the Toler study can be interpreted as suggesting that husbands high in negative affect are those that describe themselves as constructive but likely to walk out if the argument becomes heated. The problem-solver husband may be the one who finds his wife's negative affect intolerable.

DETAILED DESCRIPTIVE ANALYSES—FUN DECK

This chapter presented detailed sequential analyses of the highest-conflict task (the sex improvisation) and concluded that the obtained sequences generally paralleled those reported in previous chapters.

TABLE 8.23

Codes with Local Peaks over Phases of Discussion—Improvisation Study
(all couples, all tasks, Z-scores are tabulated $(X-\overline{X})/\sigma_X$)

	Phase of Discussion		
Codes	Beginning 1/3	Middle 1/3	End 1/3
Mindreading (MR)	.86	.22	- 1.09
Disagreement (DG)	.78	.35	- 1.13
Communication Talk (CT)	- .03	1.01	- .99
Problem Feeling (PF)	.45	.69	- 1.15
Summarizing Self (SS)	- 1.15	.69	.46
Prob. Solving and Info. Exchange (PS)	.52	.64	- 1.15
Agreement	- .88	- .20	1.09
Summarizing Other	- 1.03	.06	.97

This section is an investigation of whether the specific sequences that discriminated nonclinic from clinic couples on the high-conflict tasks, namely validation versus cross-complaining and contract versus counterproposal, would also discriminate nonclinic from clinic couples on a low-conflict task that did not involve decision making.

Table 8.20 presents the results of these sequential analyses and shows that, in general, these differences hold even for the fun-deck task. Agreement by both spouses is more likely to enter into the most probable sequences for nonclinic couples following an expression of feelings about a problem than it is for clinic couples.

Table 8.21 presents the detailed sequential analyses that demonstrate an equivalent result regarding the greater likelihood of contracting sequences for nonclinic couples than for clinic couples. The distribution of the codes across the phases of the discussion was also similar across the two studies[2] (see Tables 8.22 and 8.23).

SUMMARY

The results presented in this chapter have been remarkably consistent with the results presented in previous chapters. Earlier findings have been extended across a range of salient decision-making tasks and a non-decision-making task.

Findings on the positiveness dimension held; in this study, they were extended to positive affect. Perhaps this extension is a function of the experimental task. Birchler et al.'s (1975) results on positive MICS codes were also obtained on an improvised task, the Inventory of Marital Conflict (Olson and Ryder, 1970). The results on positive affect may not generalize beyond improvised conflict tasks, or they may be limited to relatively low conflict tasks.

Reciprocity findings were again remarkably consistent with those presented in previous chapters. This was also generally the case for the detailed descriptive analyses.

This chapter also reported results relevant to two questions: whether clinic and nonclinic interaction differences vary as a function of the issue under discussion and whether the two groups can be discriminated on the fun-deck improvisation, which is a non-decision-making task.

Positiveness and the reciprocity of positive and negative affect were used to answer the first question. Over all tasks, the consistent result was that clinic couples were less positive, more negative, and more likely to reciprocate negative affect and that the two groups did not differ significantly in the reciprocation of positive affect. However, on the in-law improvisation, this pattern did not hold. Nonclinic wives were more likely to reciprocate both positive and negative

---

[2] A comparison of the local peaks of all the codes over the two studies is given in Table 8.22. (Study I is the study reported in Chapter 6 and Study II is the study reported in Chapter 8, with X's referring to positive Z-scores in each third of the discussion.) Also, see Table 8.23.

affect, that is, to be more affectively connected than the clinic wives. The anatomy of this effect was investigated in this chapter.

Spouse effects were investigated, and on three improvisations there was a significant effect, with wives more likely to be negative than their husbands. These effects were interpreted with caution, and evidence was presented that the husband's "neutral" affect, as perceived by observers, may at times be negative as perceived by the wife (in terms of its impact on her subsequent behavior). The hypothesis was proposed in this chapter that the nonclinic husband plays an important role in creating a climate of agreement and in the editing function on low conflict issues, while the nonclinic wife plays this role on high conflict issues.

With respect to the second question, sequential analyses on the fun-deck task once again demonstrated their power to discriminate the two groups of couples. Whereas there was no difference between clinic and nonclinic couples in the nonsequential analyses of affect, negative-affect reciprocity was more likely for clinic couples even on this non-decision-making task. It was, thus, possible to discriminate the two groups on the fun deck by using several variables. Clinic couples were more likely than were nonclinic couples to express feelings about problems on this non-conflict task; clinic couples were less likely to agree with their spouses on this task than were nonclinic couples, and clinic couples were more likely than were nonclinic couples to reciprocate (but not exhibit) negative affect on the fun-deck task.

Detailed sequential analyses on the fun-deck task showed that the general patterns obtained on the sex improvisation and in other studies held for the fun-deck task. Cross-complaining was more likely and validation less likely for clinic than for nonclinic couples, and the same patterns held for counterproposal and for contractng loops. Thus, the detailed sequential code differences presented in Chapter 6 have a great deal of stability; they generally held for high- as well as for low-conflict tasks, and they held in the recoding of the Raush et al. (1974) data. We can begin to have some confidence in the positiveness and reciprocity hypotheses of the Structural Model.

Thus far we have considered clinic couples as a homogeneous group, except that in the recodings of the Raush study similar patterns of differences held between high and low clinic groups, as assessed by agreement to disagreement ratios. The following chapter presents a classification of clinic couples' interaction styles, both for the purpose of more precise description and for differential prediction of the outcomes of interventions with clinic couples.

CHAPTER 9

Styles of Marital Interaction in Clinic Couples

Classifications of marriages are ubiquitous. For example, Cuber and Harroff (1965) described five types: *conflict-habituated, devitalized, passive–congenial, vital,* and *total*; Bell (1975) described four types: *patriarchal, matriarchal, companionship,* and *colleague*. Most classifications are not based on the observation of marital interaction; they are global attempts to organize a vast array of variables concerning self-reports about belief systems, life styles, and cross-situational interaction patterns. In general, there has been scant investigation of the extent to which such consistent patterns exist in marriages.

CLASSIFICATION ON BASIS OF OBSERVATIONAL DATA

There have been three attempts at classifying marital interaction on the basis of observational data. Raush *et al.* (1974) defined two types of couples: *conflict-avoiding* and *conflict-engaging*. They noted that the avoidance of conflict on their tasks was usually accompanied by disqualifications, hedging, and denial. However, even though they noted that conflict-avoiding marriages are "so far as we can see, no less compatible, no less comfortable than other marriages [p. 82]," they nonetheless described the conflict-avoiding style as more constricted and as less capable of solving problems.

Recently, Hawkins, Weisberg, and Ray (1977) studied communication in couples' style as a function of social class. They defined four styles: *conven-*

tional, controlling, speculative, and *contactful.* The conventional style is low in disclosure and is defensive; the controlling style is high in disclosure and is defensive; the speculative style is low in disclosure but is supportive; and the contactful style is high in disclosure and is supportive. Couples interacted in several 5-minute tasks that were audiotaped. The tasks were: six incomplete sentences to complete jointly, the identification of a marital issue, and a discussion of what they liked about one another. Coders rated each couple directly on the extent to which their interaction fit each style. Although there was no code manual that grounded the four styles in specific kinds of behavior, assessments of interobserver agreement indicated that coders were probably rating the same basic dimensions. Hawkins *et al.* (1977) found that the higher the social class of couples, the more likely they were to be judged as contactful rather than controlling.

Perhaps the most ambitious attempt at classification of marital interaction is a recent unpublished study by Miller and Olson (1976). They recruited 396 couples from marriage license records in Washington, D.C. Couples were audiotaped using the Inventory of Marital Conflict (IMC), in which couples must agree, for a series of vignettes, who was most at fault in each vignette, the husband or the wife; the tapes were coded using the Marital and Family Interaction Coding System (MFICS) designed by Olson and Ryder (1970). Eighteen of the codes were selected from 29 for each spouse (36 variables), and relative frequencies of the codes were factor analyzed. The factor analysis produced three factors: (a) The Husband Task Leadership factor indicated husband initiation and leadership (high scores) or wife initiation or leadership (low scores); (b) High scores on the Opinionated Struggle factor indicated a deadlocked and highly personalized argument, with reiterated positions and disagreement; and (c) The Affective Coping factor; this included husband and wife laughter, both spouses' disapproval of each other, and husband self-doubt.

Using these factors, Miller and Olson performed a cluster analysis, selecting a generalized distance approach rather than a covariance method (see Gottman, 1978, for a review of empirical clustering techniques). Nine types of couples were identified from this analysis: (a) wife-led disengaged; (b) wife-led congenial; (c) wife-led confrontative; (d) husband-led disengaged; (e) cooperative; (f) husband-led expressive; (g) husband-led confrontive; (h) husband-led conflicted; and (i) husband-led conventional. Each of the nine types had specific profiles on the three factors.

THE NEED FOR CLASSIFICATION FOR CLINICAL INTERVENTION

Despite these important attempts at classifying interaction on the basis of observational data, there remains a need for categories that are more descriptive, particularly if such a classification system is to be useful to clinicians. The classification of interaction patterns based on an analysis of communication skill deficits is especially important for the design and improvement of intervention programs. It would, thus, be useful to devise a classification system that discriminates clinic from nonclinic couples. Furthermore, for the design of interventions for marriages seeking counseling, it would be important to have a classification system specific to clinic couples. More importantly, the clinician makes a unique demand of any classification system, namely, that it have specific implications for differential intervention. Because of this requirement, the less global and stylistic and the more specific and prescriptive the classification system, the better.

The most common form of clinical classification is in terms of symptoms of the identified patient in the family or marriage (see Gurman and Kniskern, 1978) using classical psychiatric categories. This system makes no attempt to classify the marital interaction patterns. Other clinical writing has described specific patterns rather than attempt to provide a complete classification system. Examples are the "united front couple" who present a false pretense of marital harmony (Schmidt, 1968), the "over adequate–under adequate" marriage in which the overadequate partner plays a martyr role as caretaker of the underadequate partner (Bowen, 1960), and the "conflictual" couple, who are engaged in "overt fighting much of the time [Kramer, 1968]." None of these clinical attempts at describing interactional patterns is based upon empirical data.

A PROPOSED CLASSIFICATION SYSTEM

An ideal classification system of clinic couples would, thus, be based on specific observable behaviors, would have specific implications for intervention, and would also simultaneously be intuitively appealing and conceptually simple. Toward these ends, based on clinical experience, Gottman et al. (1977) designed an intuitive univariate scaling of the CISS content and affect codes. Summing across all behavior units within one floor switch, each spouse's codes were scaled according to the following system: (a) Each positive listener or speaker nonverbal behavior = +1; (b) Each negative listener or speaker nonverbal behavior = -1; (c) Negative mindreading (MR-) = -2; (d) Problem solving = +1 if it is followed by an agreement within the floor switch; and (e) Agreement = +1 and disagreement = -1. For example, the following set of codes would be tallied and used to plot one point on the graph for the husband and one point for the wife:

Speaker H:	AG/H0,W0 PF/H+,W+	
Speaker W:		PF/H0,W+ DG/H-,W+

(AG = Agreement; PF = Feelings about problem; DG = Disagreement; H = Husband; W = Wife; 0 = Neutral; + = Positive; − = Negative)

The husband would have received a score of 2 while he was the speaker (one for the agreement [AG] and one for the H+); the wife would have received a score of 1 (for the listener behavior). When the wife was the speaker, she would have received a score of 1 (W+ = 1; DG = −1; W+ = 1; total = 1), and the husband would have received −1. Therefore, the husband's total is 2 − 1 = 1, and the wife's total is 1 + 1 = 2. These numbers (1,2) are then plotted as two points in a graph, a 1 for the husband's graph and a 2 for the wife's.

Figure 9.1 presents the *cumulative* point graphs for five nonclinic couples with the highest marital satisfaction scores. The data are from the study reported in Chapter 6. The cumulative curve can be cyclic, stay level, or move up or down, since codes are neutral, positive, or negative when scored during any floor switch. The trend in these nonclinic graphs is generally up. In contrast, Figure 9.2 presents the *cumulative* point graphs for the five clinic couples in the same study with the lowest marital satisfaction scores. These curves are more diverse, but they are not characterized by positive slopes for both husband and wife. *More importantly, the shape of the cumulative curves fit the intuitions we had as we watched the videotapes.* It was as if our own reactions were based upon some kind of affective cumulator. We found that we were also sensitive to slope changes. When watching the videotape, we often would note that something important had just occurred to change the interaction. Later, we would discover that our intuition was consistent with the point system, since at that juncture the cumulative point graph had usually changed slope (for example, around floor switch unit #5 in couple 19's graph).

Although it would make sense to perform sequential analyses couple by couple and then classify couples based on obtained likely sequences, there is usually not enough data for each couple to permit these analyses. The point graphs in Figures 9.1 and 9.2 provide a method for classifying couples that could circumvent the shortcomings of insufficient data for a couple-by-couple sequence analysis. *If the shapes of these curves relate to specific differences in sequences obtained by subgrouping couples, a classification of different sequential patterns could be obtained.*

Toward this end, graphs identical to those in Figures 9.1 and 9.2 were drawn for the data in the Rubin (1977) study. Since the sex improvisation of the Rubin study (see Chapter 8) was most similar to the data presented in Chapter 6 (which was the data used to draw Figures 9.1 and 9.2), point graphs on this improvisation were drawn to classify the interaction of clinic couples. The shapes of the curves were used to classify the couples. The graphs were divided into four groups. In the first group, both husband and wife curves were increasing throughout the interaction, much like a slanted figure J (see Figure 9.3); this curve is monotonically increasing, but it is concave in shape, that is, positively accelerated. Based on our results with the first set of point graphs (Figure 9.1 and 9.2), this group of clinic couples would seem to be having the most positive interaction.

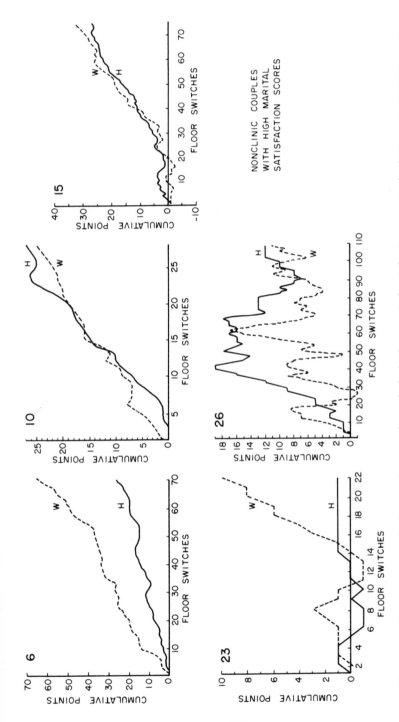

Figure 9.1 *Point graphs for the five nonclinic couples with the highest marital satisfaction scores in the Gottman et al. (1977) study.*

173

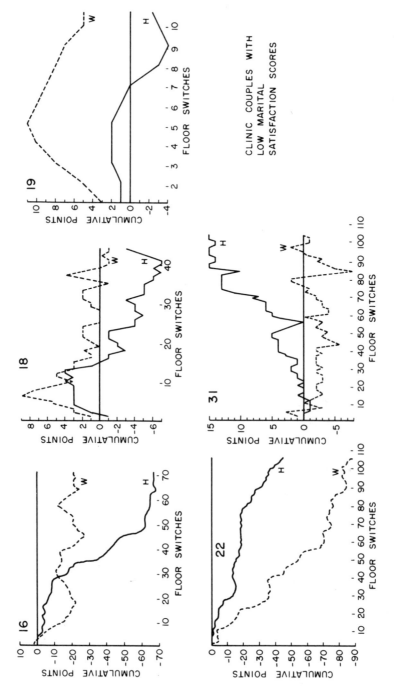

Figure 9.2 *Point graphs for the five clinic couples with the lowest marital satisfaction scores in the Gottman et al. (1977) study.*

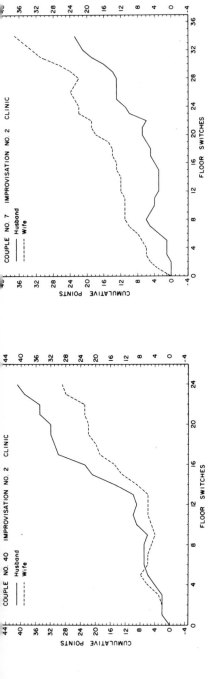

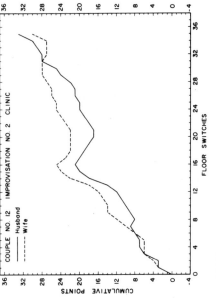

Figure 9.3 *Point graphs for the J-curve clinic group.*

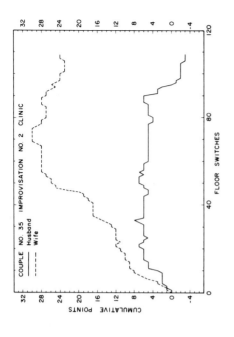

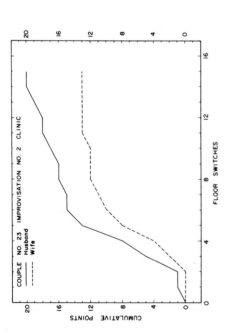

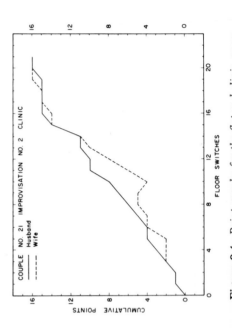

176

The next group of curves begin positively but have flat ends. This group of curves is presented in Figure 9.4. It seems logical that, for this group, there are lots of agreements and positive nonverbal behaviors in the beginning and middle of the interaction, but not at the end. Considering what we know about local peaks and sequences in the beginning, middle, and end of a discussion, we might infer that a flat end suggests more counterproposal than contracting sequences at the end of the discussion for this group of couples. In other words, *the flat end may be diagnostic of a contracting-skill deficit.*

The third group of curves was characterized by a flat beginning but positive slopes toward the latter phases of the discussion (see Figure 9.5). By similar reasoning, *the flat beginning may be diagnostic of a validation-skill deficit.*

The fourth group of couples had curves in which one spouse's curve went up and the other's went down. Figure 9.6 presents these graphs. The pattern holds for Couple 14 only for the last part of the discussion. In these discussions, one spouse seems to be doing most of the agreeing and the expressing of positive nonverbal behavior, whereas the other spouse is generally negative and disagreeable. These asymmetrical patterns most resemble clinical folklore describing the nagging-wife–problem-solving-husband or the warm, needy wife–cold, negative husband types.

The important check on this classification is the test of the hypothesis that the groups differ in specific social skills. Table 9.1 presents the conditional probabilities and Z-scores for cross-complaining, validation, counterproposal,

TABLE 9.1
Sequential Analyses for Four Clinic Interaction Categories

Sequence	J-curve	Flat Beginning	Flat End	Asymmetrical
Cross-complaining				
$p(H \rightarrow W)$	.13	.34	.22	.34
$z(H \rightarrow W)$	.45	3.09*	1.59	5.27*
$p(W \rightarrow H)$	.22	.50	.61	.40
$z(H \rightarrow W)$	.68	5.15*	6.00*	4.41*
Validation				
$p(H \rightarrow W)$	.04	.09	.06	.04
$z(H \rightarrow W)$	.84	1.48	-.26	-.41
$p(W \rightarrow H)$	.07	.12	.12	.04
$z(W \rightarrow H)$	.89	1.73	1.93	.02
Counterproposal				
$p(H \rightarrow W)$	.16	.21	.25	.17
$z(H \rightarrow W)$	1.84	1.80	1.61	2.32*
$p(W \rightarrow H)$	.15	.33	.35	.26
$z(W \rightarrow H)$	.55	3.72*	2.80*	3.43*
Contracting				
$p(H \rightarrow W)$	.10	.14	.12	.10
$z(H \rightarrow W)$	2.80*	2.99*	1.88	1.53
$p(W \rightarrow H)$	.05	.13	.06	.07
$z(W \rightarrow H)$	.24	1.68	.20	.90

*Represents the probabilities with the highest Z-score, which is given immediately below the respective probabilities.

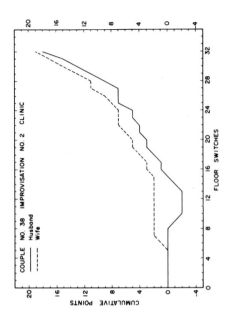

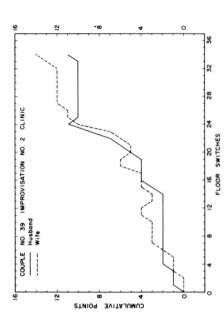

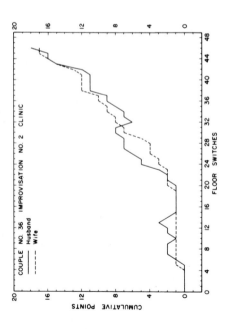

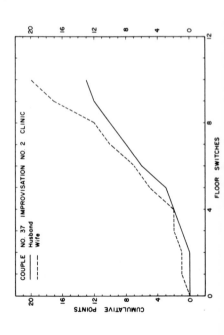

178

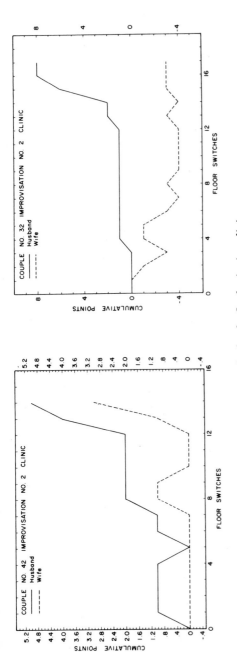

Figure 9.5 *Point graphs for the flat-beginning clinic group.*

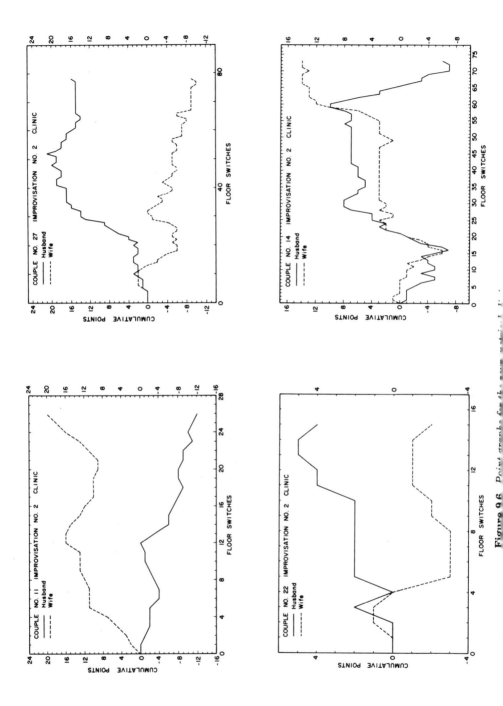

Figure 9.6. *Point graphs for the same material* ...

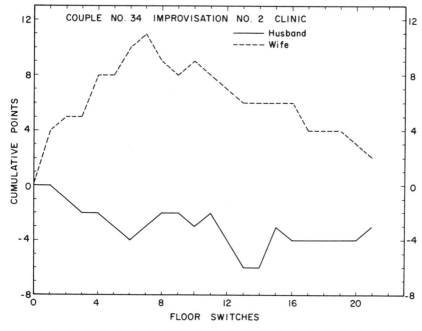

Figure 9.6 *Continued*

and contracting sequences for the four groups of clinic couples. There is an insufficient number of data to perform these sequential analyses couple by couple, and Table 9.1 presents only lag 1 conditional probabilities and Z-scores for each of the four groups.

The four groups do not differ in their likelihoods of engaging in validation sequences. However, flat-beginning couples are more likely to engage in cross-complaining sequences than are flat-end couples. Also, flat-end couples are less likely to engage in contracting sequences than are flat-beginning couples. These differences between the two groups are subtle: Flat-beginning couples are not quite as good as flat-end couples at initial exploration of the problem, but they are somewhat better at resolving the problem. These were precisely the differences hypothesized by the shapes of the curves. Furthermore, the two groups did not differ significantly in marital satisfaction scores; flat-beginning couples averaged 83.75 and flat-end couples averaged 90.00.

J-curve couples are the most skillful: They are not likely to engage in cross-complaining sequences, and they are likely to engage in contracting sequences. They also seem to be opposite in pattern to the asymmetrical couples, both partners of which are likely to engage in cross-complaining and counter-proposal sequences. Also, the marital satisfaction scores of these two groups are

TABLE 9.2

Investigation of Social Skill Differences in Classification of Marital Interaction Patterns by Point Graphs—Clinic Couples

Variable	J-Curve	Flat End	Flat Beginning	Asymmetrical
Cross Complaining Conditional Probability	.34	.60	.53	.67
Validation Conditional Probability	.14	.16	.12	.10
Ratio: p(validation) / p(cross comp)	.41	.27	.23	.15
Counterproposal Conditional Probability	.38	.41	.36	.43
Contracting Conditional Probability	.28	.17	.21	.16
Ratio: p(contracting) / p(counterproposal)	.74	.41	.58	.37

significantly different, with J-couples' average marital satisfaction equal to 87.83 and asymmetrical couples' average marital satisfaction equal to 66.20 (t[9] = 3.26, p < .01). Asymmetrical curve couples thus seem to have skill deficits in both the beginning and the final stages of the discussion of a marital issue.

A rapid summary index of the differences among these four groups would involve the *relative* likelihood of validation to cross-complaining and the *relative* likelihood of contracting to counterproposals. Table 9.2 presents these ratios, summing over spouses. Using these indices, we see that the four groups are in the rank orders suggested by our discussion of their social skills deficits.

Thus far, this chapter has presented a method for classifying the interaction of clinic couples that is related to differential deficits in problem-solving skills. Other sequential indices of interaction can be examined that also are indepen-

TABLE 9.3

Positive and Negative Affect Cycles (Lag-One) for Four Groups of Clinic Couples

Group, Variable	Lag-One Positive Reciprocity		Lag-One Negative Reciprocity		Unconditional Probability			
	H+→W+	W+→H+	H-→W-	W-→H-	H+	H-	W+	W-
Clinic J-Curve								
p	.28	.47	.00	.00	.20	.02	.18	.01
z	.82	3.33*	-.23	-.23				
Clinic Flat Beginning								
p	.53	.43	.00	.00	.09	.01	.11	.02
z	6.75*	6.54*	-.26	-.26				
Clinic Flat End								
p	.42	.21	.00	.00	.06	.01	.08	.00
z	5.38*	4.65*	.00	.00				
Asymmetrical								
p	.17	.18	.20	.30	.06	.11	.07	.09
z	1.94	2.61*	2.33*	3.84*				

*Represents the probabilities with the highest Z-score, which is given immediately below the respective probabilities.

dent of the point graphs (which are based on frequencies), such as the probabilities of positive and negative affect cycles. Table 9.3 presents these lag 1 conditional and unconditional probabilities and Z-scores. The asymmetrical group was the only one with significant negative affect cycles. This is consistent with the overall picture of low marital satisfaction and social-skill deficits in both problem exploration and resolution for asymmetrical couples. It was somewhat surprising that couples with flat-beginning and flat-ending curves had larger Z-scores for positive reciprocity than did the J-curve couples. J-curve couples are, thus, less likely to enter into either positive or negative cycles than are the flat-beginning and flat-end groups, who are very similar in affect cycles; these three groups did not differ in affect or in the reciprocity of affect, but they

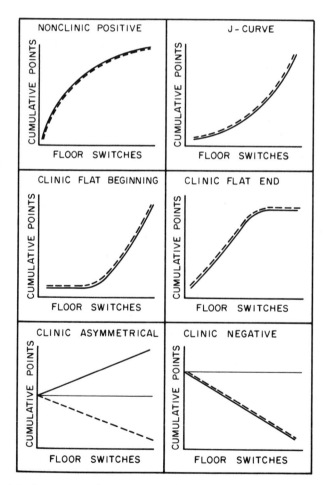

Figure 9.7 *Summary schematic diagram of hypothesized classification scheme showing six types of marital interaction.*

TABLE 9.4
Probabilities of Negative Listeners Becoming Negative Speakers in the Next Lag

Spouse	J-Curve	Flat Beginning	Flat End	Asymmetrical
Husband				
p	.00	.00	.00	.32
z	-.19	.00	.00	4.67*
Wife				
p	.00	.00	.25	.22
z	-.19	-.24	8.72*	2.94*

*Represents the probabilities with the highest Z-score, which is given immediately below the respective probabilities.

did differ in specific codes representing validation, cross-complaining, contracting, and counterproposals.

Another index that we can examine is the cognitive editing function discussed in Chapter 6. The reader will recall that the variable discussed was the probability that negative *listening* behavior by one person would become negative *speaking* behavior by the same person in the next lag. The probabilities that this will occur when the spouse's speaking affect was neutral are given in Table 9.4. The sequence that represents the *absence* of this editing process is most likely for asymmetrical couples, is next most likely for flat-end wives, and does not occur at all for flat-beginning and J-curve couples.

Figure 9.7 is a summary schematic diagram that combines patterns obtained to date for both clinic and nonclinic couples. There are six patterns represented, each representing a different interactional style. The two additional patterns come from Figure 9.2, namely, the nonclinic positive and the clinic negative patterns.

SUMMARY OF RESULTS AND CONCLUSION

To summarize, there seem to be consistent differences between the four groups of couples. J-curve couples have highest marital satisfaction scores and do not seem to have deficits as great as the other three groups in cross-complaining during the initial stages of a discussion or in counterproposals in the final stages. Asymmetrical couples, in contrast, have the lower marital satisfaction scores and have deficits in all dimensions of interaction—with cross-complaining, with counterproposals, with negative affect cycles, and with the editing function. Flat-end and flat-beginning couples are generally quite similar. They differ primarily (a) in the superiority of flat-beginning over flat-end couples in avoiding cross-complaining loops and in the editing function; and (b) in the superiority of flat-end over flat-beginning couples in avoiding counterproposals. In general, then, the inferences made from the point graphs are quite consistent with the sequential analyses.

The point graphs also provide the necessary data base for developing a mathematical model necessary to discuss dominance as an asymmetry in predictability. The following chapter will present this model and present results testing it.

CHAPTER 10

Dominance in Marital Interaction

The review in Chapter 3 suggested that defining *dominance* as asymmetry in predictability is sensible and consistent with diverse findings related to this dimension. At the end of this chapter I will discuss the precise sense in which the dominance concept is best interpreted in the research presented in this book. We now turn to the problem of how the definition is to be operationalized as a mathematical model. This chapter will propose a mathematical model for examining lead and lag relationships through spectral analysis of time series. Spectral analysis is currently employed in many fields. For example, in economics wholesale price indices are lead indicators of retail price indices, which implies that the wholesale market dominates the retail market.

Whereas measures of the rate or relative proportion of a code collapse across time, time-series measures retain information about patterning over time. If X causes Y, then Y will lag behind X; that is, variations in X will produce subsequent variations in Y, and this relationship is, therefore, asymmetrical in predictability. This chapter will propose a particular model for applying time-series analysis. Because time-series methods are not widely known, the chapter will introduce time-series analysis methodology and the prerequisites necessary for understanding the phase spectrum.

INTRODUCTION TO BIVARIATE TIME-SERIES ANALYSIS

A time-series is a set of observations ordered in time, such as the Dow–Jones Industrial Average, or monthly wheat prices, or weekly ratings of presidential popularity before an election. One very general problem that can be addressed by time-series analysis is the study of the relationship between two time series X_t and Y_t. There are many variations of this problem.

In one variation, Y_t is the dependent variable (for example, the number of premature infants who die per month in a given hospital) and X_t is an intervention that equals zero (i.e., does not exist) for some set of points and equals one (i.e., exists) for another set. Figure 10.1 illustrates some variations of intervention curves. In (a) the intervention is on and stays on; in (b) the intervention is some impulse input (e.g., a tax rebate given once); in (c) the intervention is gradual; and in (d) it is gradual but ephemeral. An example of (d) was described in Gottman and Glass (1978) as conducted by Zimring (1975). Zimring evaluated a gun-buyback program, assuming that buying back guns should gradually reduce the number of murders per month and that, after the funds were cut off, the number of murders per month should gradually increase. In these cases, the problem of assessing the relationship between X_t and Y_t is the assessment of the intervention effect, and the problem is called an interrupted time-series experiment, whose solution is described in Glass, Willson, and Gottman (1975) and in Hibbs (1977).

Another variation of the bivariate time-series problem is the black box

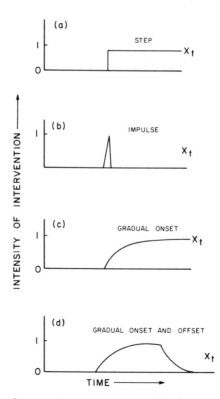

Figure 10.1 *Types of interventions; one variation of the bivariate time-series problem.*

Figure 10.2 *The bivariate time-series problem conceptualized as the black box problem.*

problem in engineering (see Figure 10.2). The problem is to describe the system, that is, how it works to transform input into output (see Box and Jenkins, 1970, on transfer functions).

A form of the bivariate time-series problem can also be employed to study the lead–lag relationship indicating dominance between persons. In this case, X_t represents the behavior of one person of a dyad, and Y_t represents the behavior of the other. Using this type of time-series problem, we will analyze the point graphs introduced in Chapter 9. In the bivariate problem, many questions are possible, such as "How connected are the two people?" and "Is one person in some sense driving the interaction?" We are concerned with these two questions in this chapter, but, to discuss this variation of the bivariate problem, we must first be able to conceptualize the fluctuations of *one* time series.

UNIVARIATE TIME-SERIES ANALYSIS

The first concept we need to introduce is the notion that any observed time series is considered to be one example that has been sampled from a population of similar processes. Each sample from a basic process is called a *realization* of the process. The failure to recognize this fundamental distinction between a realization and its process may cause confusion in the interpretation of results. The second concept is *stationarity*. A stationary time-series varies about a fixed mean and has the same "probability structure" throughout.

To grasp the meaning of *probability structure*, we need to understand the concepts of *autocovariance* and *autocorrelation*. Just as we can calculate the correlation between two sets of data $(X_1, X_2, \ldots, X_N)$, $(Y_1, Y_2, \ldots, Y_N)$ and pair them $(X_1, Y_1), (X_2, Y_2), \ldots, (X_N, Y_N)$, so we can apply the same method to a single time-series. To calculate the first-order autocorrelation coefficient, we pair points lagged 1 time unit:

X_t	X_{t+1}	
X_1	X_2	
X_2	X_3	
.	.	Used in calculating r_1
.	.	
.	.	
X_{N-1}	X_N	

Lag One

Similarly, to calculate the second-order autocorrelation coefficient, we pair points lagged two time units:

Lag Two	
X_t	X_{t+2}
X_1	X_3
X_2	X_4
.	.
.	.
.	.
X_{N-2}	X_N

Used in calculating r_2

These calculations can be continued to produce a set of autocorrelations as a function of lag, namely, $r_1, r_2, \ldots, r_K, \ldots$. When r_K is plotted as a function of the lag k, the resulting function is called the *correlogram* (see Figure 10.3).

Just as the covariance is the numerator of the correlation coefficient, the autocovariance is the numerator of the autocorrelation coefficient (see Equation 10.2).

By the term *same probability structure*, we mean that the plot of the autocovariance of points (as a function of lag) calculated from points early in the series is like the autocovariances of a set of contiguous points anywhere else in

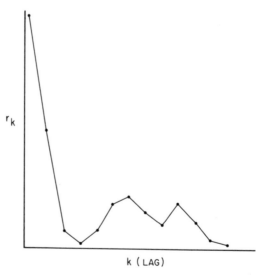

Figure 10.3 *The correlogram, a plot of the autocorrelation coefficient as a function of the lag.*

the series. Confidence limits on the autocorrelation were derived by Bartlett (1946) and are roughly given by:

$$\text{var}[r_k] \simeq \frac{1}{N}, \tag{1}$$

where N is the number of points in the time series (see Box and Jenkins, 1970, p. 35).

The autocorrelation is calculated as:

$$r_k = \frac{\sum_{t=1}^{N-k} (Z_t - \bar{Z})(Z_{t+k} - \bar{Z})}{\sum_{t=1}^{N} (Z_t - \bar{Z})^2} \tag{2}$$

where $\bar{Z}$ is the mean level of the series.

Note the following example: Compute r_1 for the following series.

t	1	2	3	4	5	6	
Z_t	47	64	20	51	17	13,	$\bar{Z} = 35$
$Z_t - \bar{Z}$	12	29	-15	16	-18	-22	

$$\sum_{t=1}^{5} (Z_t - \bar{Z})(Z_{t+1} - \bar{Z}) = (12)(29) + (29)(-15) + (-15)(16) + (16)(-18)$$
$$+ (-18)(-22) = -219$$

$$\sum_{t=1}^{6} (Z_t - \bar{Z})^2 = (12)^2 + (29)^2 + \ldots + (-22)^2 = 2274$$

$$r_1 = \frac{-219}{2274} = -.10, \text{ the first-order}$$
$$\text{autocorrelation coefficient.}$$

The second concept, *stationarity,* is related to the concepts of autocorrelation and autocovariance in a simple way: Correlograms of most stationary time series die out rapidly (exponentially, in fact) with increasing lag, whereas those of most nonstationary series do not. It is important to note that a series with a linear trend will have a correlogram that dies out; but it does so along a straight line, not exponentially. The fact that the correlogram dies out with increasing lag simply means that one's ability to *predict* a set of points from the past becomes worse as one recedes into the past.

There are two procedures for the analysis of univariate time series. One procedure is called *time-domain analysis* and the other is called *frequency-domain analysis.* In both kinds of procedures, the goal is to construct models to estimate the parameters of the time-series process. Recall that the observed series is but one sample of a process, so we are attempting to construct the model from sample data. In time-domain analysis, the basic question of the models can be stated (autoregressively) as "How predictable is the series from its past?" The model is written as an autoregressive equation:

$$X_t = a_1X_{t-1} + a_2X_{t-2} + \ldots + e_t, \tag{3}$$

where e_t is the residual. Time-domain models are sought such that $(X_t - \text{MODEL}) = $ random uncorrelated white noise (Equation 4); that is, the residual is not autocorrelated, has a mean of zero, and has some fixed variance σ_e^2 independent of time.

An advantage of time-domain analysis is that fewer points are required than for frequency-domain analysis. Granger and Hughes (1968) have reported encouraging spectral results with short series, but their results are not widely accepted. Although we mentioned the importance of the concept of stationarity, Box and Jenkins' (1970) contribution was to extend models proposed in the 1920s by Yule (1927) for a wide class of nonstationary time series. Nonetheless, there are many interesting kinds of nonstationary time series not covered by the Box and Jenkins extension. Thus, the mathematics discussed here can be gener-alized to some kinds of nonstationary time series.

In frequency-domain analysis, the basic question in modeling the series is "What are the component oscillations in the series?" Figure 10.4 depicts the general idea. X_t is composed of two superimposed components, a slow sine wave of large amplitude and a fast wave of small amplitude. Whittaker and

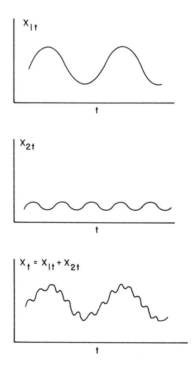

Figure 10.4 *Schematic illustration of the superposition of two sine waves of different frequencies, the reverse of decomposition of a complex wave.* (**Note:** *This illustration ignores the concept of phase.*)

Robinson (1924) were able to show that the brightness of a variable star was the sum of two periodic terms and were able to conclude that they were observing a binary star. Unfortunately, such orderly data are extremely rare. Nonetheless, the basic model in the frequency domain involves a superposition of sine and cosine frunctions of frequency bands that contribute to the overall variance of the series such that:

$$(X_t - \Sigma \text{ components}) = \text{white noise.} \qquad (5)$$

The goal is, therefore, the same in model building in time or frequency domains. An advantage of frequency-domain analysis is that each component of X_t (which must oscillate at a different frequency) is statistically independent and, thus, accounts for separate parts of the variance of X_t. This is true because a particular set of the cosine and sine functions form an orthogonal set, making the mathematics of frequency-domain estimation quite elegant. For a discussion of model building using Box–Jenkins models and the interrupted time-series experiment, the reader is referred to Glass, Willson, and Gottman (1975) and to Gottman and Glass (1978).

Our discussion will continue with frequency-domain models. Briefly, each time series generates a function called the *spectral density,* which has peaks at frequencies (or, more correctly, at frequency bands) that make major contributions to the overall variance of the time series. Thus, in Figure 10.4 the spectral density of the top graph would have a spike at a low frequency and would be zero everywhere else; the spectral density of the middle graph would have a spike at a high frequency and be zero elsewhere; and the spectral density of the bottom graph would have two spikes, one at the high and one at the low frequency. The spectral density is a function of the original series autocovariances that is called the *weighted Fourier transform* (see, for example, Chatfield, 1975).

An intuitive understanding of the relationship between the autocovariances and the spectral density function can be obtained by considering a perfectly seasonal series, such as vegetable prices (see Figure 10.5). The top graph is the raw data, wholesale prices plotted each month. The middle graph is the autocorrelation plotted as a function of lag, in other words, the correlogram. Note that it dies out, but it also oscillates positively and negatively as it dies out; this is true because, for example, summer prices are negatively correlated with winter prices (a lag of about 5 months), but summer prices are positively correlated with next year's summer prices. The bottom graph is the spectral density function, and it should show one major peak, corresponding to an annual cycle. The curves in Figure 10.5 make good intuitive sense, since seasonal series are more predictable at appropriate lags than at other lags. June prices will, of course, be most highly correlated with prices in neighboring months of the same year and will decline in correlation with prices in other seasons. Then, the June-to-June correlations across years will be high (though not as high as for neighboring months in the same year), and this June-to-June correlation will

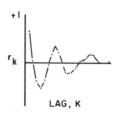

Figure 10.5 *Simulation of a seasonal time-series. The top graph comprises the raw data; the middle graph is the sample correlogram; the bottom graph is the spectral density function.*

decline with increasing lag between years. This description is a summary of Figure 10.5. It follows that such a correlogram should characterize series of one major cycle, and, therefore, the spectral density function should show one peak, as it does in Figure 10.5.

BIVARIATE TIME-SERIES ANALYSIS

Just as the autocorrelation was defined within one time series, the *cross-correlation* function is defined between two time series. The cross-covariance can be defined as:

$$C_{XY}(k) = \frac{1}{n} \sum_{t=1}^{n-k} (X_t - \bar{X})(Y_{t-k} - \bar{Y}). \tag{6}$$

This estimate is not unbiased (it would be if we divided by [n − k] instead of n), but it has less mean square error than the unbiased estimate. The cross-correlation is:

$$r_{XY}(k) = \frac{C_{XY}(k)}{\sqrt{C_{XX}(0)} \ \sqrt{C_{YY}(0)}} = \frac{C_{XY}(k)}{S_X S_Y}. \tag{7}$$

The cross-correlation computes a series of correlations between two time series. When the lag, k, is zero, the time series are perfectly lined up and the correlation is computed from the pairs (X_1, Y_1), (X_2, Y_2), ... When the lag, k, is one, the correlation is computed from pairs (X_1, Y_0), (X_2, Y_1), (X_3, Y_2), . . . , and so on. It is important to notice that $C_{XY}(k)$ is not equal to $C_{YX}(k)$, since different points are used in the computation of these two statistics.

The concept of a spectral density function (which peaked at frequency bands that contributed to the variance of the series) can be generalized for the bivariate case. A function called the *sample cross spectrum* is defined. Just as the spectral density was the Fourier transform of the autocovariance, the weighted Fourier transform of the cross-covariance is the cross-spectrum (see Jenkins and Watts, 1968, p. 342). However, the cross spectrum is a bit more complicated. It has two parts, the *cross-amplitude spectrum,*[1] which shows whether the same frequency components are associated with large or small amplitudes in the two series, and the *phase spectrum,* which shows whether frequency components in one series lead or lag the same frequency in the other series. The phase spectrum in what we are interested in.

Unfortunately, the phase spectrum is somewhat difficult to explain, but it is important in our discussion of dominance. Sander (1977) used the phase spectrum in discussing the interaction of physiological systems. He suggested that "both *adaptation* and *integration* of biologic systems can be resolved as features of phase synchronization . . . [p. 139]." The phase relationships between different physiological systems within one individual are analagous to the relationships of two people in an interacting dyad. The phase relationship determines the lead or lag, or synchrony, between two time series. In the next section, I will discuss the interpretation of the phase spectrum, since it relates directly to the issue of which series leads or lags.

Interpreting the Phase Spectrum

If one series has a fixed time lag with respect to the other, that is, $Y_t = X_{t-k}$, then the phase spectrum is a straight line of slope k (see Appendix 10.1 for a proof). Intuitively, what a fixed time-lag means is that, regardless of how slowly or rapidly one spouse is changing, the other spouse follows those changes at a fixed lag. It should be noted that using the slope of the phase spectrum as a

---

[1] A measure of the square of the correlation of frequency components in the two series is given by a function called the *coherence*. The coherence is somewhat easier to interpret than the amplitude spectrum, and it is recommended by Granger and Hatanaka (1964). The coherence is defined as:

$$k^2 = \frac{[\text{cross spectrum of Y with X}]^2}{(\text{spectrum of Y}) \times (\text{Spectrum of X})}.$$

Granger and Hatanaka (1964) wrote: "[The coherence] is analogous to the square of the correlation coefficient between two samples and is interpreted in a similar way, i.e., the larger [the coherence] the more closely related are the two components [p. 77; material in brackets added]." For more discussion of the coherence, see Gottman (1978).

measure of lead and lag might leave out valuable information, since the method averages across all frequencies. Two series may be periodic in a certain frequency band and have a particular phase relationship in that band but some other phase relationship at another frequency band. This would be obscured by the slope method of analysis. For example, a zero slope between husband and wife could mean that there is no lead or lag relationship, or it could mean that sometimes the wife leads and sometimes the husband leads. This problem can be partly addressed by separately examining different pieces of the phase spectrum.

A two-component model was suggested by Granger and Hatanaka (1964) (see Figure 10.6). In this model, the frequency range is divided into two parts, a slow and rapid oscillation component, which is an extension of the model that fits the Whittaker and Robinson data (see Figure 10.4). This model is interpreted as follows: Lead–lag relationships vary as a function of how rapidly the series is changing; components that change slowly may have a different lead–lag relationship than components that change rapidly. The two-component model complicates the concept of dominance. For example, it is possible for the wife's series to lag behind the husband's only for slow oscillations or to lag for slow but not for fast oscillations. Dominance, then, can refer to the slope of the phase spectrum in each of the two halves of the frequency range. If the two-component model is to be applied, each component must have a theoretical referent.

If the two time-series plotted are indices of affect (as they are in the point

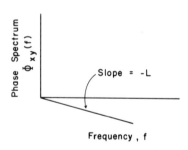

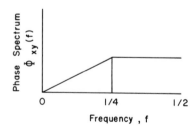

Figure 10.6 *Models of the lead–lag relationship, using the phase spectrum. The top graph shows a one-component model, the bottom a two-component model.*

TABLE 10.1
Patterns of Marital Dominance in the Two-Component Model

	Slopes of the Phase Spectrum	
	Mood (Slow) Component	Expressive (Fast) Component
1. Equalitarian	Zero	Zero
2. Wife Expressive Dominance	Zero	Positive
3. Husband Expressive Dominanace	Zero	Negative
4. Wife Mood Dominance	Positive	Zero
5. Wife Dominant	Positive	Positive
6. Wife Mood/Husband Expressive Dominance	Positive	Negative
7. Husband Mood Dominance	Negative	Zero
8. Huband Mood/Wife Expressive Dominance	Negative	Positive
9. Husband Dominant	Negative	Negative

graphs of Chapter 9), the slow component may be interpreted as slow variations in affect, such as those in mood states, and the fast component may be interpreted as more immediate variations in affect, such as those in rapid emotional expressions. We refer to these components as *mood fluctuations* for the slow component and *expression fluctuations* for the rapid component. A similar distinction, using the rapidity of changes, was made by Ekman and Friesen (1975) for facial expressions; they distinguished "moods" as slower changes and "expressions" as faster changes in facial displays (see Chapter 3). A mood is related to an emotional expression, but only part of the expression is displayed in the longer lasting mood, although the full facial expression may occasionally flash on and off. In mood, synchrony implies a linkage in slowly moving affective expression. Synchrony in the rapid expressive component implies a tighter linkage of affect.

Table 10.1 represents the nine dominance patterns possible with the two-component model. Note that it is conceptually possible for one pattern of dominance to exist in the more immediate, mercurial, expressive component and another to exist in the mood component. For example, dominance pattern 6 would imply that a wife can get her husband to respond only with more long-lasting fluctuations in her affect, whereas, if the husband wishes to get his wife to respond, he must use more immediate fluctuations in affect.

DOMINANCE IN MARITAL INTERACTION

This section will present results testing the hypothesis that a clearly defined dominance pattern is characteristic of clinic couples, whereas an equalitarian pattern is characteristic of nonclinic couples. The data base is the Rubin Improvisation Study, and the time series are the point graphs introduced in Chapter 9.

Spectral analysis usually requires long series ($N = 200$), so that one can be confident of the stability of spectral statistics (Jenkins and Watts, 1968); however, Granger and Hughes (1968) worked with series of 65 points. This chapter will present results of spectral analysis with those series that have 65 or more points. First, the three highest conflict improviṣations will be combined and the results presented for the two-component model of the phase spectrum. Next, the four lowest conflict improvisation results will be presented for these couples in order to test the hypothesis that dominance patterns are consistent across tasks with varying degrees of conflict.

The analytic procedure was as follows. First, the frequency range was arbitrarily divided into 20 parts. The number of points is arbitrary, but it should usually not exceed $N/3$; since our shortest series are $N = 65$, 20 is a reasonable number of parts. Because the phase spectrum, by definition, is always zero at the endpoints of the frequency range ($0 \leq f \leq 1/2$), the slopes should be calculated by omitting these endpoints. For the mood component linear regression, points 1–10 are used, and, for the expressive component points, 11–19 are used.

Table 10.2 presents the results of the *high-conflict* improvisation analyses. Over these three improvisations, nonclinic mood component slopes were not significantly different from clinic slopes; nonclinic expressive component slopes averaged $-.006$ and clinic expressive component slopes averaged $-.128$, $t(18) = 1.77$, $p < .05$. These results can be summarized by calculating the proportion of couples that had zero (nonsignificant at $p < .10$), positive significant, or negative significant slopes in each component. These calculations

TABLE 10.2
Application of the Two-Component Model to Test the Dominance Hypothesis on High-Conflict Tasks

Group, Couple No.	Impro-visation	Mood Component		Expressive Component	
		Slope	t-ratio	Slope	t-ratio
Clinic					
14	2	.393	6.20****	−.260	−7.06****
27	2	.004	.04	−.213	−1.53*
35	2	−.009	−.43	−.234	−1.34
07	3	.048	.51	−.132	−1.50*
22	3	.060	3.22***	−.135	.86
27	3	.061	2.45**	.139	.88
29	3	−.311	−1.35	−.508	−5.47****
39	3	−.098	−2.30**	−.025	−.66
11	6	.077	.36	.083	.57
12	6	−.203	−2.49**	−.130	−2.60**
14	6	.129	1.50*	.252	5.64****
27	6	.100	.48	−.199	−2.18**
35	6	−.015	−.19	−.306	.340***
Nonclinic					
01	3	−.056	−1.04	−.092	−1.45
02	3	−.247	−2.85**	.086	1.07
20	3	.018	.14	.146	2.23**
25	3	−.340	−2.15**	−.061	−.36
01	6	.001	−.01	−.139	−5.82****
10	6	.306	5.31****	−.077	−.53
25	6	.104	1.51*	.098	.86

*p < 10; **p < .05; ***p < .01; ****p < .001.

are summarized in Table 10.3. For the mood component, these proportions were not significantly different across clinic and nonclinic couples: Slope (clinic) = .020, slope (nonclinic) = .031, $t(18) = .81$. As for the expressive component, however, for clinic couples a negative slope was far more likely than any other, whereas for nonclinic couples a neutral slope was far more likely than any other. For nonclinic couples, there is an equal and low probability that slopes will be significantly positive or negative in both mood and expressive components. For clinic couples, the pattern is different. If a dominance pattern (significant slope) is present, it is more likely to be positive (husband lags) in the mood component and negative (wife lags) in the expressive component.

By far the most common clinic pattern is the zero–negative (No. 3 in Table 10.1) Husband Expressive Dominance pattern. By far the most common nonclinic pattern is the zero–zero (No. 1 in Table 10.1) Equalitarian pattern. *These results provide evidence for the hypothesis that nonclinic couples are characterized by equalitarian dominance patterns, whereas husbands are dominant in clinic couples.* Furthermore, the dominance is of a particular type, characterized by lead–lag relationships in which the wife lags, *but only for rapid changes in affect expression by the husband.*

Table 10.4 presents the dominance analyses for these couples for the four low-conflict tasks. Once again, only series for which $N \geq 65$ were considered. For the mood component, the mean slope for clinic couples was $-.016$, not significantly different from the mood component's slope on high-conflict tasks $t(11) = .38$. For the mood component, the mean slope for nonclinic couples was .56, which was not significantly different from the nonclinic slope for high-conflict tasks $t(5) = 1.01$.

For the expressive component, the nonclinic mean slope was $-.097$, not significantly different from the mean slope for high-conflict tasks, $t(5) - 1.25$. For the expressive component, the clinic mean slope was .001, which was significantly different from the high-conflict mean slope, $t(11) = 2.05, p < .05$. *Hence, both nonclinic and clinic couples displayed an equalitarian dominance pattern on low-conflict tasks.* These results are summarized in Table 10.5, which shows the increased probabilities for both groups that the slope will be zero for both components.

The results are consistent with Hypothesis 1 of Chapter 3, which predicted a greater degree of patterning for clinic than for nonclinic couples. These results also show that dominance patterning is a function of situational aspects of the

TABLE 10.3

Summary Probabilities of Dominance Patterns in the Two-Component Model—High-Conflict Tasks

Group	Mood Component				Expressive Component		
	Zero	Positive	Negative		Zero	Positive	Negative
Clinic	.54	.31	.15		.39	.08	.54
Nonclinic	.43	.29	.29		.71	.14	.14

TABLE 10.4

Application of the Two-Component Model to Test the Dominance Hypothesis on Low-Conflict Tasks

Group, Couple No.	Improvisation	Mood Component		Expressive Component	
		Slope	t-ratio	Slope	t-ratio
Clinic					
12	1	-.025	-.40	-.126	-.84
14	1	.030	.89	-.113	-.77
27	1	.097	1.96**	-.090	-.81
35	1	.018	.57	.074	1.47*
39	1	.018	.58	-.011	-.54
07	4	.032	.21	.070	.72
14	4	-.107	-1.46*	.033	.30
27	4	.183	4.22***	.183	.83
07	5	-.127	-1.33	.219	3.35***
27	5	-.071	-.30	-.050	-.57
35	5	-.128	-1.56*	.168	2.61**
39	5	-.076	-2.38**	.050	1.19
11	7	.087	.86	-.090	-.87
22	7	-.122	-5.97****	-.228	-1.18
27	7	-.055	-.28	-.070	-.82
Nonclinic					
01	1	.198	2.45**	-.350	-2.17**
02	1	.035	.99	.012	.61
10	1	-.048	-1.55*	.020	.26
20	1	.029	.47	.045	.96
25	1	.042	1.02	-.087	-1.76*
01	4	.039	2.57**	-.293	-1.40*
02	4	.095	.75	-.045	-.79
10	7	.059	1.11	-.076	-1.57*

*$p < .10$; **$p < .05$; ***$p < .01$; ****$p < .001$.

interaction and that it may not appear on all experimental tasks. Furthermore, dominance as defined in this chapter is a complex construct once the dimension of time is considered. It is only in the rapid oscillation component and only for high conflict tasks that dominance patterns were observed. As a check on this conflict effect, all time series with $N \geq 40$ were analyzed for the highest-conflict task—sex improvisation. The discrimination between groups was stronger for this high-conflict task. The mean slope for clinic couples' expressive component was $-.257$, and $.061$ for nonclinic couples, $t(5) = 2.13, p < .05$. All four clinic slopes were negative; two nonclinic slopes were positive, and one was negative (see Figure 10.7).

TABLE 10.5

Summary of Probabilities of Dominance Patterns in the Two-Component Model—Low-Conflict Tasks

Group	Mood Component			Expressive Component		
	Zero	Positive	Negative	Zero	Positive	Negative
Clinic	.64	.14	.21	.80	.20	.00
Nonclinic	.71	.29	.00	.63	.13	.25

Further elaboration on the structural model hypothesis concerning degree of patterning is provided by Sander's (1977) discussion of biorhythmicity. His discussion explored the relationship of *organization* to *integration* between physiological systems and the *differentiation* between systems that is a part of developmental conceptualizations. He referred to this relationship as a paradox of "contrasting tendencies of synchronization and differentiation [p. 141]." He wrote:

> Although rhythm entrainment and phase synchronization help us to visualize mutual participation, simultaneity, and bonding between subsystems, they do not account for a concurrent tendency in development, namely, that of separation, differentiation, and individuation [p. 141].

A looser organization, he argued, would result in a system that was more adaptive in response to perturbation. He wrote that:

> *perturbation* of the "disjoined" or partially independent subsystem as a consequence of its adaptive encounter with the surround does not spread to the rest of the system. The subsystem is, in effect, insulated from the rest of the system. . . . On the other hand, when the system is tightly coupled and relatively poor in such states of equilibrium, perturbation of one subsystem preempts the function of the rest of the component subsystems to restore variables to their region of stability [pp. 141–142].

Applied to the marital dyad, this discussion implies that the expressive affect dominance we have found to be characteristic of clinic couples in high-conflict situations produces a dyadic linkage that is not adaptive to environmental perturbations of affective expression. In short, the system is not differentiated or resilient. For example, events that increase negative affect in the husband should produce delayed reciprocal negative affect in the wife, a situation we

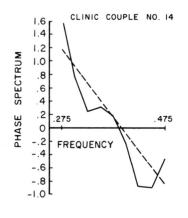 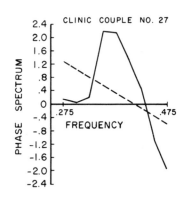

Figure 10.7 *Illustration of the expressive component of the phase spectra for clinic and nonclinic couples for the sex improvisation task (with* **N** ≥ *40).*

Figure 10.7 (*continued*)

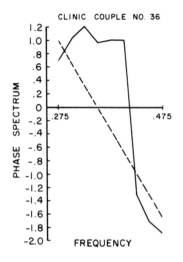

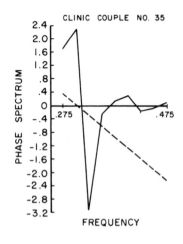

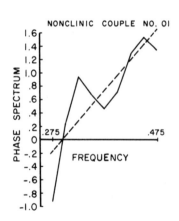

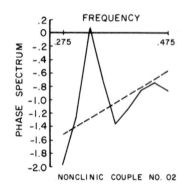

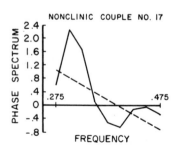

consistently found in the negative affect cycle analyses. This discussion implies that it will be more difficult to change nonclinic marriages and easy to change clinic marriages in the direction of increasing *negative* affect cycles. The patterning detected thus relates to stability in nonclinic marriages and instability in clinic marriages.

A PRECISE INTERPRETATION OF DOMINANCE

Asymmetry in predictability is not always best interpreted as dominance. For example, in mother–infant caretaking interactions, the fact that the mother's behavior is more predictable from her baby's behavior than conversely may be purely a function of the caretaking context; in play interactions, the same asymmetry may be indicative of the social/cognitive developmental level of the infant. If a mother waits for her baby to be interested in play and her behavior is thus highly predictable from her baby's, but not vice versa, it does not make much sense to refer to the baby's behavior as "dominant" in the same sense as a alpha male monkey's aggressive behavior toward a beta male may be called dominant. Another example may strengthen this point. Vaughn and Waters (1978) found that, among preschool children, visual gaze data taken during free play indoors did not correlate significantly with data on aggressive social encounters, although the gaze data was highly correlated with peer picture sociometric data on liking, which measures a child's preferences in affiliation with peers in that social group; in other words, children tended to look most at those children with whom they would *prefer* to play but with whom they usually do not play. In short, asymmetry in predictability need not always imply dominance. Dominance is a function of the interactants and the situational context of the interaction. The conceptual label given to asymmetry in predictability should vary as a function of the dependent measures, the situational context (e.g., the goals and tasks of the interaction), and the nature of the interactants.

The dependent measure that forms the point graphs is best interpreted as affective, or emotional expression, and this interpretation is strengthened when we focus on asymmetry in the rapidly changing components of the variable in the cross-spectral time-series analyses. The asymmetry we discovered in clinic couples can be interpreted in two equivalent ways: (a) the husband tends to drive the wife's affective expression more than vice versa; and (b) *the husband is less emotionally responsive to the wife than she is to him.*

An alternative interpretation of the dominance dimension that stems from the point graphs is, thus, that among clinic couples *there is an asymmetry in emotional responsiveness.* This interpretation illuminates the sense in which the dominance should be interpreted in the research reported in this book. This is a very precise meaning of the term dominance, and this interpretation completes the development of the Structural Model.

APPENDIX 10.1

If Y(t) = X(t − k), then the Fourier transform of Y(t) is

$$F(Y(t)) = \int_{-\pi}^{\pi} e^{iwt}\, Y(t)\, dt = \int_{-\pi}^{\pi} e^{iwt}\, X(t - k)\, dt.$$

Let u = t − k. Then:

$$F(Y(t)) = \int_{-\pi}^{\pi} e^{iw(u+k)}\, x(u)\, du = e^{iwk} \int_{-\pi}^{\pi} e^{iwu}\, x(u)\, du$$
$$F(Y(t)) = e^{iwk}\, F(X(t)).$$

Therefore, the phase spectrum ϕ = wk, and, hence, its slope is the time-lag k. For more discussion and an extension to categorical data, see Gottman (1979).

CHAPTER 11

The Individual Social Competence Hypothesis

In this book, the behavior of each spouse is observed in the context of social interaction with the partner. Therefore, differences obtained between clinic and nonclinic couples might not be a function of the *individual's* social ability, but of the dyad's. In an important paper, Birchler, Weiss, and Vincent (1975) addressed this issue when they wrote, "The question is whether marital "distress" is limited to the specific relationship or whether it is confined to the person who carries it from situation to situation [p. 349]." There are two possible interpretations of this statement, which I refer to as the *individual social competence* hypothesis. One interpretation, as stated by Birchler *et al.* (1975), is a trait interpretation. In this sense, social skillfulness is an ability an individual carries into any social situation, and, therefore, competence ought to be detectable in any relationship. A second interpretation views social competence as a characteristic of the individual, but one specific to a set of situations or specific to one relationship.

One method of testing the trait interpretation is to observe the interaction of married people with strangers as well as with their spouses. Both Ryder (1968) and Winter, Ferreira, and Bowers (1973) reported that married people are far more polite to strangers on a decision-making task than they are to spouses. Birchler *et al.* (1975) studied the interaction of distressed or nondistressed couples with their spouses or with married, opposite-sex strangers in conversation or on the Olson and Ryder (1970) Inventory of Marital Conflict (IMC) task. Subjects in the Bircher *et al.* study interacted with two strangers, one from a distressed and one from a nondistressed marriage. Using their Marital Interaction Coding System (MICS), they replicated the Ryder (1968) and Winter et al. (1973) results, that married people were far more negative and far less positive to their spouses than they were to strangers, particularly on the IMC task.

Birchler et al.'s findings were quite complex. Two kinds of correlations were reported: (a) the degree of consistency of persons in positive and negative behaviors with their spouses and strangers (averaged over distressed and nondistressed strangers); and (b) the amount of consistency between the two strangers. Let us reexamine their results. First, consider correlations between spouses and strangers. There were no significant correlations in the conversation task between spouse and stranger in either positive or negative behavior; this was true for both husbands and wives and for both distressed and nondistressed couples. On the IMC task, only the distressed husband's positive behaviors were consistent from wife to stranger. This is very weak evidence of consistency.

Correlations were also calculated between the two strangers, who came either from a distressed or from a nondistressed marriage. Here the data showed some evidence of consistency, but only *positive* behavior showed consistencies for subjects in the group of nondistressed couples. That is to say, nondistressed couples' positive behavior was consistent across the two strangers, but their negative behavior was not. In conversation, again examining consistency across strangers, for nondistressed couples, both husbands' and wives' correlations were significant; on the IMC task, only the husbands' correlation was significant. Both positive and negative behavior showed consistencies for distressed couples. For positive behavior in conversations, only the husbands' correlation across the two strangers was significant; for positive behavior on the IMC, both spouses' correlations across the two strangers were significant. For negative behavior in conversation, both spouses' correlations across the two strangers were significant; for negative behavior on the IMC, only the wives' correlation across the two strangers was significant. *There is, thus, evidence for consistency in interaction with strangers, particularly for distressed husbands. However, there is not evidence for consistency from spouse to stranger.* There is a way to behave with strangers, but it is not predictable from the way a person behaves with his or her spouse. Similar results were reported by Birchler (1972) on the same sample for consistency in looking.

An important comparison in the Birchler et al. (1975) study was not presented in their paper, namely, the assessment of whether distressed and nondistressed couples differed when they interacted with strangers. However, a calculation of the t-ratios is possible from their tables and the following results were obtained: Combined over settings, the two groups did not differ in positive interaction with strangers [$t(22) = .53$, n.s.; $\overline{X}_{DIS} = 3.03$; $X_{NONDIS} = 3.34$] or in negative interaction [$t(22) = .68$, n.s.; $\overline{X}_{DIS} = .51$, $\overline{X}_{NONDIS} = .41$]. Therefore, although the groups differ when interacting with spouses, *they do not differ when interacting with strangers.* Overall, then, the Birchler et al. (1975) results do not support the hypothesis that distressed couples carry their distress from the marital relationship to other relationships. In fact, they seem more consistently positive to strangers than do the nondistressed couples.

The comparison of interactions with spouse with interactions with strangers makes the assumption that social skillfulness is a trait. However, the central question addressed by an individual social competence hypothesis is one of whether a distressed spouse carries dysfunctional behaviors into an interaction *with the partner* or whether this dysfunctional behavior is merely a *response to* the spouse's dysfunctional behavior. Hence, although the evidence suggests that individual social competence is not a trait, the concept may still make sense within a specific relationship or within a specific set of issues within a relationship. If social skill is specific to particular situations and in interaction with particular individuals, the interactions of people with strangers is interesting but, perhaps, is not germane to the individual social competence hypothesis. The question, then, becomes one of whether an individual's behavior is in some sense "carried into" a relationship or is a response to the partner's behavior.

The question may be logically unanswerable by examining data taken from social interaction. This point was made by Watzlawick, Beavin, and Jackson (1967), who noted that "causality" in a negative interaction cycle is simply a matter of how one chooses to punctuate the cycle. They also suggested that the husband is likely to perceive his withdrawal as *caused* by the wife's nagging and that she is likely to perceive her nagging as *caused* by the husband's withdrawal. Thus, it may be difficult to disentangle causality or perceived causality from a study of the stream of interaction.

Another way to approach the individual social competence hypothesis is to use the methods of the social-skill training literature (e.g., see McFall & Twentyman, 1973), which has relied heavily on role-play assessments of social skill. In this assessment procedure, a domain of problematic situations is generated empirically (see Goldfried & D'Zurilla, 1969), and the subject role-plays responding to a set of situations, each of which contains a response demand. The situations can be presented in standardized format on audiotape, and the subject's responses can be audiotaped and coded. This procedure was followed in the following study.

PROCEDURES AND SUBJECTS

Using the 85 nonredundant situations obtained in interviewing 60 couples (see Chapter 12), two tapes were constructed, one for the husband (83 situations selected) and one for the wife (82 situations selected). Each situation described a marital problem and then presented a simulated spouse's statement prior to the response demand made of the subject. Husbands and wives heard the identical simulated spouse statement in each problem situation. For example, one situation the subjects responded to was

> (Wife, Item No. 10) You and your husband are planning a weekend trip. He asks you to take the car in for a tune-up because the spark plugs are misfiring. You are very busy, but you will try. On the trip your husband

hears the plugs misfire. He asks if you took the car in for a tune-up and you say no because you were too busy. He says, "I was busy too, but you took responsibility for the car and you didn't fulfill that responsibility." You say:

Situations were sorted into five content areas depending on the type of problem posed. The five areas were: *communication, sex, jealousy, in-laws,* and *chores.* *Communication* included problem situations of spending time together, conversations, sharing feelings, recreation, and life style. *Sex* involved only problem situations relating to physical affection, including manner, style, and frequency of sexual intercourse. *Jealousy* included situations in which one spouse felt jealous of the partner's attentions to other people (of either sex). *In-laws* problem situations always involved spouse differences in relating to in-laws. *Chores* problem situations included household maintenance, errands, management of children, decisions to have children, and budget and finance situations. The wife situations were read by a female narrator, but the husband's comment was acted by a male (and conversely for the husband situations). Husband and wife responded in separate rooms to taped situations. The following instructions on an audiotape were used to introduce the role-playing sessions:

> Okay. Just relax. I am going to explain what we will be doing here. Just try to make yourself as comfortable as possible while I tell you what to expect.
>
> You will be responding to situations which we have obtained from previous research. These situations are ones which married people most commonly find problematic. That does not mean that every couple has problems with these situations. But they are taken from the real life experiences of couples. According to our research, most marriages need to cope with the same kinds of issues.
>
> We are going to start by presenting you with a number of imaginary or simulated situations in which people have trouble. We want you to respond in each situation as you normally would. Just be yourself. We would like to see how you would actually behave in these situations. Remember it is important that you respond naturally, not as you think you *ought to* respond, but as you actually might respond.
>
> In each situation listen carefully and try to imagine, or visualize, that the episode as it is being described is actually happening to you. The more vividly you imagine yourself really being involved in each situation and the more naturally you act, the better. Imagine those settings familiar to you, like the car or the living room of your home, in as much detail as possible.
>
> After the essential details of a situation have been described, a bell will sound (bell sounds). When you hear this bell, I want you to respond out loud, using the words you would actually use in that situation if it were really happening to you. Don't talk to me or describe to me what you would say. Respond as if you were talking directly to your spouse. You will get only one opportunity to respond to each situation. Don't take too much time thinking about your answers. It is best to respond as honestly and spontaneously as you can.
>
> Okay. Now just relax. In a few seconds we'll begin with the first of these situations.

When the subject had finished a response, he or she signalled an experimenter in an observation corridor by pressing a button placed on a comfortable armchair. The button lit a small signal lamp in the corridor. Corridors and experimental rooms were also connected by two-way intercoms. A female experimenter was in the corridor adjoining the wife's experimental room, and a male experimenter was in the corridor adjoining the husband's experimental room. Situations were presented through a speaker in the experimental rooms, and a lavaliere microphone worn by the subject recorded his or her responses.

Subjects in this study were recruited by contacting local ministers, offering each couple a $20 subject fee and suggesting that $8 of the fee be donated to the church. The recruiting procedure was quite effective in drawing a wide range of couples with considerable variation in age and income.

There were 36 couples in the study, 15 below the mean in marital satisfaction and 21 above the mean in marital satisfaction. These two groups of couples did not differ significantly on any demographic variable: the husband's age $[\bar{X}(low) = 32.00, \bar{X}(high) = 31.76, F(8,27) = .003]$; the wife's age $[\bar{X}(low) = 30.73, \bar{X}(high) = 31.48, F(8,27) = .032]$; the number of years they were married $[\bar{X}(low) = 8.27, \bar{X}(high) = 9.05, F(8,27) = .046]$; the husband's education $[\bar{X}(low) = 17.2$ years, $\bar{X}(high) = 17.71$ years, $F(8,27 = .413]$; the wife's education $[\bar{X}(low) = 15.73$ years, $\bar{X}(high) = 15.90$ years, $F(8,27) = .054]$; the number of children $[\bar{X}(low) = .93, \bar{X}(high) = 1.24, F(8,27) = .813]$; or the husband's income $[\bar{X}(low) = 7.67, \bar{X}(high) = 8.19, F(8,27) = 2.401$, n.s.].

The tape-recorded situations were designed so that the simulated spouse statements before the response demands ranged across a set of CISS content codes and were delivered either with positive or with negative affect. Two independent coders checked the content and affect codes for each situation. There were, thus, 10 scales, the five types of problems—Communication, Sex, Jealousy, In-Laws, and Chores—with a positive- or negative-affect simulated spouse statement.

The first thought-unit of each subject was coded by using the CISS, and coded data were summarized by using the decision rule shown in Table 11.1.

TABLE 11.1
Decision Rule for Scoring a Response as Either Positive or Negative

	Affect Code		
	0	+	–
Content Code	Code Received		
Problem Feelings (PF)	+	+	–
Mindreading (MR)	+	+	–
Prob. Solving and Info. Exchange (PS)	+	+	–
Communication Talk (CT)	–	–	–
Agreement (AG)	+	+	–
Disagreement (DG)	–	–	–
Summarizing Other (SO)	+	+	–
Summarizing Self (SS)	–	–	–

RESULTS AND DISCUSSION

Table 11.2 presents the results of the 2 × 2 repeated measures analysis of variance. Couples were split on their average marital satisfaction scores (at the mean), which was the between-subjects factor, and husband–wife was the within-subjects factor. Couples high and low in marital satisfaction could be discriminated on the communication-negative scale, the sex-positive and sex-negative scales, the in-laws-positive scale, the chores-positive scale, and the chores-negative scale. In each case, *high-satisfaction couples were more positive than low-satisfaction couples.* There were no significant interactions on any scale. However, there were main effects for the spouse factor, and these effects had a consistent pattern. Husbands were more positive than wives on the positive scales, whereas wives were more positive than husbands on the negative scales. This cross-over effect suggests complementarity of roles: *Wives were more likely than their husbands to be agreeable and to express positive affect in response to complaints, even when the complaints were negatively stated.* This is consistent with the cognitive editing function of the nonclinic wife, which was described in Chapters 6 and 8. In our culture it appears to be the wife's responsibility to keep negative affect from escalating in high conflict situations.

The results of this study demonstrate that, even when individuals *imagine* themselves responding to their spouses, the behavior of low- and high-marital satisfaction subjects can be discriminated across several content domains of problem situations. This provides support for the individual social competence hypothesis in the marital interaction, rather than as a trait.

TABLE 11.2

Positivity of Responses on Each Scale for Couples High and Low in Marital Satisfaction and for Wives Compared to Husbands

Scale	Low Satis.	High Satis.	F	Wives	Husbands	F
Communication						
Positive	11.07	13.50	1.76	7.62	17.23	50.72***
Negative	14.40	19.74	5.58*	20.15	14.62	16.74***
Sex						
Positive	3.57	5.08	8.01**	4.23	4.59	.49
Negative	4.30	5.66	4.19*	4.71	5.41	1.51
Jealousy						
Positive	6.00	7.21	1.55	5.68	7.68	5.45*
Negative	5.33	7.26	3.34	7.12	5.71	3.91
In-Laws						
Positive	3.27	4.58	5.99*	2.76	5.24	24.35***
Negative	3.20	3.92	2.82	4.79	2.41	25.79***
Chores						
Positive	20.33	25.11	4.31*	21.94	24.06	1.39
Negative	13.20	16.63	4.60*	15.53	14.71	.31

*p < .05
**p < .01
***p < .001

Taken together, the literature review and the results of this study point to differences in individual modes of responding as a function of marital satisfaction even in problematic marital situations where the spouse is not present, but merely imagined. However, in interaction with strangers, distressed and nondistressed spouses cannot be distinguished. This suggests that individual social competence should not be conceptualized as a trait, but, rather, as a relationship-specific construct. Furthermore, not all issues are equally effective in discriminating high- from low-satisfaction couples. Sex items gave the highest F-ratios, which is consistent with the results presented in Chapter 8.

The appendix of this chapter presents item analysis results that could be useful in selecting the best items in the husband and wife inventories toward employing the method of this investigation as an assessment device that is considerably less expensive than coding videotapes of marital interaction.

APPENDIX 11.1

Item Analysis

An additional purpose of the study presented in this chapter is to conduct an item analysis to improve the discrimination of subjects on a dimension of marital satisfaction. The best items would, then, constitute a shorter marital-interaction role-play assessment measure. In general, a good item will have an item characteristic curve such that subjects low on a criterion dimension differ from subjects high on the criterion in the probability of some response (usually called "response alpha"). Items that behave in the inverse manner are also

TABLE 11.3
Item Analysis for Husbands' Role-Play Assessment Measure

Positive Items		Weight	Negative Items		Weight
* 7[a]	Chores	1	2	Sex	1
10	Chores	1	3	Chores	1
23	Chores	-2	* 4	Chores	1
*25	Chores	2	21	Communication	-1
*33	Jealousy	-2	22	Communication	1
40	Communication	2	26	Chores	-1
46	Chores	1	35	Jealousy	1
47	Chores	3	36	Sex	2
52	Communication	3	38	Communication	-2
58	Sex	2	42	In-Laws	-3
59	Sex	1	43	Communication	2
*65	In-Laws	1	*49	Communication	2
66	Chores	2	56	Jealousy	2
*78	Chores	2	*73	Sex	1
			75	Communication	3
			77	Sex	-1
			79	Communication	-3
			80	Chores	1
			*86	Chores	2

*Items that overlap with wives' set of items.

[a] Numbers are item numbers in complete list of items.

TABLE 11.4
Item Analysis for Wives' Role-Play Assessment Measure

Positive Items	Weight	Negative Items	Weight
1[a] Jealousy	1	4 Chores	1
5 Chores	-1	13 Jealousy	2
7 Chores	1	17 Communication	1
8 Chores	-2	18 Chores	1
11 In-Laws	2	24 Communication	2
12 Chores	2	28 Chores	2
16 Communication	2	34 Communication	1
20 Jealousy	-1	41 Communication	3
22 Communication	-2	44 Chores	-2
25 Chores	1	45 In-Laws	2
32 In-Laws	-1	49 Communication	2
33 Jealousy	-2	50 Communication	2
39 Chores	1	51 Sex	3
55 Communication	1	54 Chores	2
56 Jealousy	1	57 Communication	3
60 Chores	-1	67 Communicatio	1
61 Jealousy	2	70 Jealousy	2
65 In-Laws	2	72 Communication	2
75 Communication	2	73 Sex	2
76 Chores	3	74 Chores	2
77 Sex	2		
78 Chores	1	86 Chores	1

[a] Numbers are item numbers in complete list of items.

good items, but they are negatively keyed. In the present investigation, subjects were divided into two groups by splitting at the median on marital satisfaction scores, and, for each item, the probability of response alpha was thus calculated as the proportion of subjects who responded positively in each group. Items were selected as good only if the probabilities of response alpha differed by at least .10, in which case the weight suggested for the item is +1. Weights are differences in the probabilities in response alpha multiplied by 10 and rounded off to the nearest integer. For husbands, these items, their content area, and weights are presented in Table 11.3.

For wives, these items, their content area, and weights are presented in Table 11.4.

There were 43 items for wives and 33 items for husbands: 22 items on the wives' inventory are responses to positive affect items, and 21 are responses to negative affect items; for husbands, 14 items are positive items and 19 are

TABLE 11.5
Weighted Positive and Negative Scores for Good Items on Each Inventory

Variable	Low Satisfaction Mean	High Satisfaction Mean	t[a]
Husband Positive	14.87	25.05	3.44**
Husband Negative	4.07	12.32	3.36**
Wife Positive	10.20	24.53	3.73**
Wife Negative	27.47	46.26	3.01**

[a] $df = 32$
** $p < .01$

negative. It is interesting that only 9 items overlap in the two sets (see asterisks in Table 11.3). From only these items, a weighted positive-item score and a weighted negative-item score was calculated for each subject. Table 11.5 presents the means and the t-tests for these variables, with couples split at the group mean on average marital satisfaction.

Therefore, another result of this study is two shorter inventories. The complete inventories are available on request; item numbers correspond to Tables 11.3 and 11.4. Also, beside each item number the CISS code for the simulated spouse statement is given.

CHAPTER 12

The Couple's Perception of Their Interaction

The Structural Model has demonstrated its ability across studies to discriminate distressed from nondistressed couples. A test of the validity of a model derived from observational data coded by trained observers would be for such a model to emerge from the couple's perception of their own interaction as they interact, and the ability of such a model to also discriminate distressed from nondistressed couples. In this chapter I will report the results of these tests.

One of Raush et al.'s (1974) major theoretical objectives was to mitigate "the controversy between intrapersonal and interpersonal theories of personality . . . [p. 49]." To accomplish this goal, they suggested that it is necessary to study the meaning that people assign to interpersonal events. Borrowing from Piaget, they defined a *schema* as "a structure for organizing experience. A schema gives meaning to events. The meanings need not be conscious, but they define the thoughts, feelings, and behaviors that are probabilistically contingent on particular events and their contexts [p. 42]." It was difficult for Raush et al. to do more than generate hypotheses about couples' perceptions (or schema) of interpersonal events, since they only gathered observational data. Even by analyzing sequences of behaviors, we can only guess at how these events are viewed cognitively by the participants in the interaction.

THE NEED FOR A COGNITIVE SYSTEM

What is needed is some system for conceptualizing, or approximating, the couple's perception of their own behavior during social interaction. We know from the wook of Osgood (see, for example, Osgood, Suci, & Tannenbaum, 1957) that a major factor in people's perception and judgment of events is an evaluative, positiveness component. This dimension is basic to sociological investigations of marital satisfaction. Research on marital satisfaction from a sociological tradition produced questionnaire measures with adequate psychometric properties and pointed to the importance of the couple's perception of their relationship and the process of resolving differences. However, research from this tradition did not provide a system for constructing models of relationship satisfaction that are grounded in cognitions about social interaction.

Behavior Exchange Theory

A compelling system for constructing models of cognitions about social interaction that may correlate with relationship satisfaction is behavior exchange theory (Thibaut & Kelley, 1959). Thibaut and Kelley suggested that a relationship can be viewed as a marketplace in which two people exchange a set of behaviors from their repertoires and that these behaviors are exchanged with certain rewards and costs to each of the interactants. For example, when person A produces behavior No. 76 from his repertoire and receives behavior No. 35 from B's repertoire, the exchange has reward R_A and cost C_A to person A and reward R_B and cost C_B to person B (Thibaut & Kelley, 1959, p. 14).

Difficulties in Application. Despite the conceptual appeal of behavior exchange theory, it is difficult to apply the theory to the study of complex behavioral systems. There are several methodological problems that must be solved. First, there is the problem of operationalizing the notion of "behavioral repertoire," and, second, there is the problem of obtaining a measure of the degree of satisfaction (reward and cost) that results from a behavior exchange. Gergen's (1969) review summarized this difficulty in applying behavior exchange theory. He wrote, "Working with the entire behavioral repertoire of two persons and gauging the satisfactions for each behavior for each of the parties would not only be cumbersome, but at present the measurement problems would also be insurmountable [p. 39]." In attempts to overcome these problems, investigators have experimentally constrained the behavioral repertoire available to the dyad and have also *experimentally* manipulated the rewards and costs to each person for each behavioral alternative. This solution was also reviewed by Gergen (1969), who wrote, "A most promising way to proceed might thus be to collapse the spectrum of behaviors available to the two persons and to arrange the situation in such a way that the satisfaction engendered by each behavioral alternative is specified by the experimental situation [p. 30]."

Even though this approach may have considerable promise in studying fundamental processes of group interaction, it must satisfy an additional criterion to be useful to the study of marital interaction. This requirement is that process variables obtained from operationalizing behavior exchange theory must be able to discriminate marriages high in satisfaction from those low in satisfaction. To date, the decision to restrict the response alternative available to the dyad and to determine experimentally the payoff matrix has not met this criterion. Speer's (1972) study utilizing an extension of the Prisoner's Dilemma game was conducted in the spirit of the suggestion to reduce the couples' behavioral repertoire and experimentally determine the payoff matrix, but Speer, studying 60 clinic and 60 nonclinic couples, found that none of the response variables discriminated the two groups on four forms of the game. There are several reasons why the Speer study yielded negative results. First, perhaps the problem was that rewards and costs were manipulated by the experimenter (as they are in the Prisoner's Dilemma game), not assigned by the couple. It would seem to be more consistent with Thibaut and Kelley's original formulation of the theory for each person subjectively to evaluate rewards and costs for each exchange. This approach would, then, be a first approximation of the couple's own perception of their own interaction on an evaluative dimension. Second, perhaps interaction must be studied with a paradigm that allows the couple access to a wider behavior repertoire than is provided by the two choices (cooperate or compete buttons) of the Prisoner's Dilemma game; or, third, perhaps there is a sampling problem—dysfunctional communication may be specific to some tasks or situations (such as discussion of an unresolved marital issue) and may not occur on just any task.[1]

OPERATIONALIZING BEHAVIOR EXCHANGE: THE TALK TABLE

The Procedure

To pursue these possibilities, it would be necessary to design a paradigm (a) that makes it possible for each spouse to rate the satisfaction of a particular exchange; (b) that minimally constrains the couple's behavior repertoire; and (c) that makes it possible for the couple to rate the satisfaction of exchanges on a wide range of possible tasks.

Toward these ends, a "talk table" was constructed. It is a double sloping box with a toggle switch that lights a button on the side of the spouse who has the floor to speak. Only one spouse may speak at a time. On each side of the table, there are two rows of five buttons, one row on the left and one on the right. The five buttons on the left are used by a speaker to code the "intended

---

[1] Recently, Revenstorf found that, if the Prisoner's Dilemma game is preceded by couples' discussion of items on the high conflict Inventory of Marital Communication Task (Olson & Ryder, 1970), nontherapy couples will increase their cooperation on the PD task, whereas therapy couples will increase their competitive behavior, compared to the situation in which the PD game was played first (Revenstorf, 1978, personal communication).

impact" of his or her message before yielding the floor to the partner. The five buttons on the right are used to code the "impact" of the message received by the partner. The five buttons are labeled "super negative," "negative," "neutral," "positive," and "super positive." Although the partners can see one another perfectly and are seated facing one another across a typing table, metal shields block the buttons from the view of the other person so that neither spouse can see the codes assigned by her or his partner. The procedure for using the talk table is summarized in Table 12.1. The coding unit here is different from the thought unit; it is the floor switch, the unit used in studies reported in Chapters 9 and 10, and also the unit used by Rausch et al. (1974).

Each button press activates a light on an array on the side of the talk table that faces the video camera, and, as an added precaution, an experimenter records the lights as they are activated. A record of the couple's ongoing ratings of impact and intended impact is obtained, and their interaction is simultaneously videotaped for subsequent analysis.

Once the talk table was constructed, the power of behavior exchange theory became clear as a system for generating alternative phenomenological models to discriminate satisfied from dissatisfied relationships. These models may provide a first approximation to the schema that Rausch et al. proposed. In no sense does the original behavior exchange theory suggest a unique set of process variables for operationalizing relationship satisfaction; the discussion that follows will explore equally plausible alternatives derived from the theory.

Alternative Schemata of Relationship Satisfaction

The talk table variables may be used to test several alternative schemata that couples use in their perception of relationship satisfaction; once again, the test is that the variables derived from these models should be able to discriminate between distressed and nondistressed marriages.

Figure 12.1 illustrates the variables derivable from the talk table. A speaker has an intended impact (Intent) for a particular message and then sends a message that has a particular impact (Impact) on the listener. There are several

TABLE 12.1
The Talk Table's Procedure

Husband	Wife
1. Speaks, rates "Intended Impact," yields the floor.	
	2. Rates "Impact" of spouse's message, speaks, rates "Intended Impact" of own message, yields the floor.
3. Rates "Impact" of spouse's message, speaks, rates "Intended Impact" of own message, yields the floor.	
(And so on)	

INTENT   [SPEAKER]   MESSAGE   [LISTENER]   IMPACT

Figure 12.1 *Diagram illustrating the use of the terms intent and impact used to generate alternate models of the couple's perception of their interaction.*

possibilities for variables that could be used to test schemata that might discriminate between distressed and nondistressed couples. In the discussion that follows, I will use the words "model" and "schema" interchangeably. By model and schema, we recognize a way of organizing the couple's perception of their ongoing interaction.

It may be that, regardless of the speaker's intended impact, the messages of nondistressed couples will have a more positive impact than the messages of their distressed counterparts. This is the *impact model.* On the other hand, it could be that the intent of messages, not impact, discriminates the two groups. This is the *intent model.* Alternatively, it could be that the relationship between intent and impact might discriminate the two groups. For example, it could be the case that there is less discrepancy between the intended impact and the actual impact of messages exchanged in nondistressed marriages. This is a *communication model,* in which "good communication" would be defined as *low discrepancy between intent and impact* and hypothesized as more characteristic of high satisfaction marriages. The communication model is independent of the previous two models, since, if distressed couples *intend* their messages to be more negatively received than do the nondistressed couples, the intent–impact discrepancy of the two groups would not differ even if the impacts of their messages were more negative.

As I have discussed previously with respect to observational data, another model of the differences between the two groups of marriages is that there is a greater *reciprocity* of positive exchanges in nondistressed than in distressed marriages. Recall that *by reciprocity of positive exchange we mean here that one partner's positive response makes subsequent positive responses of the other partner more likely.* It is important to remind the reader that reciprocity of positive exchange as defined in this way differs from the *quid pro quo* that has become an influential conception in the behavioral literature on marriage counseling (Azrin, Naster, & Jones, 1973; Lederer & Jackson, 1968; Rappaport & Harrell, 1972; Stuart, 1969; Weiss, Hops, & Patterson, 1973). The *quid pro quo* is also called a "reciprocity contract," but reciprocity is used somewhat differently in the marriage counseling literature.

To summarize my arguments from a sequential analytic perspective, in a reciprocal interaction we reduce uncertainty in our knowledge of one spouse's positive behavior just by knowing something about the partner's antecedent behavior. The test for my use of the term *reciprocity* is that the conditional probability of the consequent code must be significantly greater than the unconditional probability of the consequent code (for example, see Patterson, 1974). For the talk table, this means that the conditional probability (p) of a consequent positive wife code (W+), given an antecedent positive husband code (H+), must be significantly greater than the unconditional probability of occurrence of W+. Symbolically, what must be demonstrated is that $p(W+/H+) > p(W+)$. (See also Raush, Barry, Hertel, & Swain, 1974.) In the talk table studies, these analyses can be performed to assess the ability of reciprocity variables to discriminate distressed from nondistressed marriages. Although this discussion may be belaboring a point, the distinction between high rates of positive codes and (my definition of) reciprocity has not been made in the clinical literature on family interaction. For example, what Alexander (1973b) meant by reciprocity was the correlation across families between parent-to-child supportive behavior and child-to-parent supportive behavior, which he found to be significantly different from zero (father–son $r = .69$, $p < .05$; mother–son $r = .59$, $p < .05$). If these correlations are used, Alexander's definition is not equivalent to reciprocity as I have used it. A family with high rates of supportiveness could be distributing these behaviors noncontingently throughout a discussion. In this case, the correlations obtained would be high due to different base rates *across* families, but there would still be no evidence of reciprocity *within* a family.

The reader will recall that one further advantage of the talk table is that the models generated are not limited to the task; that is, couples may interact on different tasks. We cannot rule out the possibility that couples' interaction will vary as a function of the level of conflict induced by a task and that distressed and nondistressed couples might not differ on relatively trivial tasks that do not induce high levels of conflict. The effect of situational context on marital and family interaction has been either ignored or minimized (Riskin & Faunce, 1972). For example, Haley (1964, 1967) placed no importance on the tasks he chose for families to work on. Jacob and Davis (1973) reported considerable stability across experimental tasks to the structure of talk and interruptions in father–mother–child interactions, but all of their situations were low-conflict tasks. Therefore, one dimension of contextual variation that has been ignored is the degree to which the decision-making task induces conflict. It is, theoretically, important to ascertain whether the variables derived from behavior exchange theory can discriminate nondistressed couples from distressed couples in low-conflict as well as high-conflict tasks.

TWO STUDIES ON THE TALK TABLE

To test these hypotheses, two studies with the talk table were conducted, with the second study designed to test the replicability and generality of the findings from the first study. The results of these studies were reported recently (Gottman, Notarius, Markman, Bank, Yoppi, & Rubin, 1976) and will be briefly summarized here.

Study 1

Subjects and Procedure.   Thirty couples responded to an advertisement asking for couples who classified their relationship either as "mutually satisfying" or as "experiencing marital difficulties." All couples were paid $10 for participating, and it was made clear that no therapy would be offered. In addition, other clinic couples were recruited from campus and community mental health centers in Bloomington, Indiana. Of the 15 clinic couples, 11 were referred from clinical sources and 4 responded to the advertisement. The two groups of couples did not differ significantly in age, educational level, or the number of years married. Couples were, on the average, 24.95 years old and had been married an average of 3.22 years.

Couples interacted on the talk table, after a brief interview (see Gottman et al., 1976, p. 17), on three low-conflict tasks and two high-conflict tasks. The tasks were described by Gottman et al. (1976) as follows:

> Each couple then completed three low-conflict tasks: (a) The choice questionnaire (Haley, 1964) is a consensus decision-making task that requires an agreed-upon ranking of personal preferences using lists such as new cars or breeds of dogs. (b) Three Thematic Apperception Test cards (Locke, 1951) required the couple to create jointly one story for each set of cards. (c) One of two tasks was administered first individually and then again for consensual ranking; one task (called NASA) involved rank ordering 15 items for their survival value for a life-and-death trip to the moon. Correct answers had been supplied by the National Aeronautics and Space Administration (Hall, 1971). The other task designed for this study (called the food task) involved rank ordering 10 items according to their nutritional value. Correct answers had been supplied by a nutrition specialist at Indiana University. A pilot study with 147 undergraduates, conducted to determine whether there was a sex bias to the tasks, revealed no significant sex differences in knowledge on either the food or the NASA task. (a) The Inventory of Marital Conflict (IMC) (Olson & Ryder, 1970) has been frequently used in marital research. The IMC is a high-conflict consensus decision-making task, in which the couple is presented with three short vignettes of marital conflict and required to agree on which spouse in the vignette is primarily responsible for the problem. (b) The couple was also asked to discuss a current problem that they had agreed in the interview was most salient and asked to try to come to a mutually satisfactory resolution of this problem. Within each session the five tasks were randomly ordered [p. 17].

Results.   The first question about the talk table is the extent to which it taps the same dimension as questionnaire measures of marital satisfaction. To answer this question, analyses, for both husband and wife, of two principal components were conducted on the talk table variables with the MRI scores included in the analyses.

Table 12.2 indicates that in each case both the talk table impact variables and the MRI loaded highly on the first component, which accounted for a large

TABLE 12.2

Principal Components Analyses of Talk Table Impact Variables and the
Questionnaire Measure of Marital Satisfactions (for all couples)

Variables [a]	First Component Loadings	
	Husband	Wife
Super Negative	-.73	-.64
Negative	-.85	-.63
Positive	.70	.72
Super Positive	.31	.41
MRI	.83	.83
Percent of Variance Accounted for by the First Component	54.19	49.77

[a] Neutral is not included in the analysis because talk table impact variables are proportions, and all five talk table impact variables form a linearly dependent set, since they sum to 1.0.

proportion of the total variance. Hence, in married couples the talk table impact variables do, to a large extent, tap the same dimension measured by the MRI, namely, marital satisfaction.

The major findings were that, across all tasks, regardless of the level of conflict induced by the task, the impact of messages was more positive for nondistressed than for distressed couples. The multivariate Wilks-Lambda was $F(4,25) = 4.54$, $p < .01$, with significant univariate differences on negative impact ($F[1,28] = 10.66$, $p < .01$) and positive impact ($F[1,28] = 7.36$, $p < .05$). Once again, on a positiveness dimension, distressed and nondistressed couples could be discriminated in the direction that was predicted by Hypothesis 2 of the Structural Model of Marital and Family Interaction (Chapter 3). Hypothesis 2 was the prediction that nondistressed couples would be more positive and less negative than distressed couples and furthermore, that these differences would be greater for negative than for positive behaviors. Perceptions by the couple thus follow the same patterns as observers' coding, in which interobserver reliability can be checked. About 24% of distressed couples' messages received a negative impact code, compared to 11% of nondistressed couples' messages. About 34% of distressed couples' messages received a positive impact, compared to 50% of nondistressed couples' messages. About 2% of distressed couples' messages received a super positive impact code, compared to 17% of nondistressed couples' messages. There were no significant differences between husbands and wives and no significant distress-by-spouse interactions. Thus, the impact model received support.

Gottman et al. (1976) have tested alternative models that may suggest the nature of the schemata that Raush et al. (1974) proposed. There were no significant differences in the intended impact of messages sent. This set of results suggested that distressed couples send messages that they intend to be received more positively than they actually are. Both groups of couples have highly positive intent, but only nondistressed couples have positive impact. Thus, in an average sense, that is, when intent and impact are averaged across messages, *an intent–impact or communication model was supported.* Furthermore, results showed that *this model and the impact model were equally able to be used to discriminate distressed from nondistressed couples in this study, regardless of the level of conflict induced by the decision-making task.* A check on the high–low conflict manipulation showed that, based on coding videotapes, agreement-to-disagreement ratios were much higher for all couples for the low-conflict tasks (1.49) than for the high-conflict tasks (.67).

Gottman et al. (1976) used a different statistical procedure for testing the reciprocity dimension than the Z-scores used in this book. They used an analysis of covariance on conditional probabilities, with unconditional probabilities as the covariate. With a sufficiently large amount of interactional data for each couple, this is a superior procedure to the Z-score methods used in this book, because it controls for ceiling and floor effects. However, Gottman et al.'s (1976) data were extremely variable in the number of floor switches per couple, and, in this case, for many couples estimates of conditional probabilities may not be stable. In that event, a Z-score analysis is preferable because the analysis of covariance method is likely to be extremely conservative in making Type II error. Therefore, the reciprocity analyses presented by Gottman et al. (1976) may have been too hasty in concluding that there is no evidence for reciprocity effects in the talk-table data. It is unfortunate that these authors did not understand the problems inherent in their statistical methods at the time their paper was written, but perhaps they can be excused if we remember that the lag-sequential methods used in this book were developed subsequent to the publication of their paper (see Bakeman & Dabbs, 1976; Gottman & Bakeman, 1979; Sackett, 1977).

Sequential reanalyses of Gottman et al. (1976) are presented for clinic and nonclinic couples in Tables 12.3 and 12.4. Table 12.3 presents the negative reciprocity results. There were insufficient data to go beyond lag 3. These results show that both Z-scores and conditional probabilities are higher for clinic than for nonclinic data, a result consistent with the nonverbal interaction data reciprocity analyses presented earlier in this book. Table 12.4 presents the positive reciprocity results; these findings also parallel the nonverbal interaction analyses. Neither Z-scores nor conditional probabilities are dramatically different across groups.

To compare these results with those presented in Gottman et al. (1976), lag 1 Z-scores were computed from Tables 3 and 6 of Gottman et al. (1976). They are presented in Table 12.5. These analyses are for low marital satisfaction clinic couples (distressed) and high marital satisfaction nonclinic couples (nondistressed). In these results, Z-scores are larger in distressed couples than in nondistressed couples, and negative reciprocity Z-scores are larger than positive reciprocity Z-scores for distressed couples. Once again, these results are completely consistent with those presented in Chapters 6, 7, and 8. It thus appears that the data derived from the evaluative dimension of the couples'

TABLE 12.3
Negative Reciprocity Schema: Study 1

Criterion: H-	LAG		
	1	2	3
Nonclinic			
H-	.00	.15	.05
W-	.25	.10	.10
Z-score	1.72	.80	.71
Clinic			
H-	.00	.38*	.00
W-	.33*	.00	.24
Z-score	2.92	4.37	1.84

Criterion: W-	LAG		
	1	2	3
Nonclinic			
H-	.17	.00	.17
W-	.00	.26*	.00
Z-score	.99	2.27	1.24
Clinic			
H-	.28*	.00	.22
W-	.00	.29*	.00
Z-score	2.85	2.80	1.93

*Represents the probabilities with the highest Z-score, which is given immediately below the respective probabilities.

TABLE 12.4
Positive Reciprocity Schema: Study 1

Criterion: H+	LAG		
	1	2	3
Nonclinic			
H+	.00	.64*	.04
W+	.57*	.05	.46*
Z-score	4.03	6.24	4.09
Clinic			
H+	.00	.62*	.04
W+	.52*	.00	.46*
Z-score	4.31	6.04	4.85

Criterion: W+	LAG		
	1	2	3
Nonclinic			
H+	.63*	.00	.55*
W+	.00	.56*	.04
Z-score	3.92	5.40	4.34
Clinic			
H+	.62*	.02	.52*
W+	.00	.43*	.00
Z-score	4.09	3.81	3.89

*Represents the probabilities with the highest Z-score, which is given immediately below the respective probabilities.

TABLE 12.5
Reciprocity Analyses on Talk Table Impact Data—Study 1

	Group	
Variable	Distressed	Nondistressed
Positive Reciprocity		
p(W+)	.34	.54
p(W+/H+)	.43	.56
Z-score	2.52	.48
p(H+)	.39	.64
p(H+/W+)	.35	.69
Z-score	.98	1.25
Negative Reciprocity		
p(W-)	.30	.16
p(W-/H-)	.45	.17
Z-score	4.00	.19
p(H-)	.29	.06
p(H-/W-)	.40	.08
Z-score	2.93	1.00

perception of their own interaction are consistent with those obtained from the observational coding system. To test the generality of these results, a second study was undertaken and reported in Gottman et al. (1976).

Study 2

Subjects and Procedure. A second sample of 30 couples, 14 clinic, and 16 nonclinic, was recruited from the geographical areas served by two community mental health centers, with an identical procedure to that used in Study 1. Again, clinic and nonclinic groups did not differ on demographic variables. However, they had been married an average of 9.44 years and were an average of 32.50 years old.

One high-conflict task (the IMC) and one low-conflict task (the food task) were selected from Study 1. The procedure was changed slightly because it is possible that the lack of differences on the intent variables in Study 1 could have resulted from the couples' not understanding how they were to code the intent of their messages. Hence, more explanation and a specific example were provided for the intent codes in Study 2.

Results. Again, there were no significant intent differences between the two groups, but differences in impact were again significant. The multivariate Wilks-Lambda was $F(4,33) = 7.01, p < .001$, with significant univariate differences on positive impact, $F(1,36) = 19.87, p < .001$. This result replicated the positiveness finding of Study 1 on the talk table. About 30% of the distressed couples' messages were coded as positive, compared to 55% of the nondistressed couples' messages. *This pattern, therefore, again lends support to an impact and to an intent—impact discrepancy model of communication.*

However, in the second study, Gottman et al. (1976) reported a conflict by distress interaction effect; that is, "It was easier to discriminate distressed from nondistressed couples on the high-conflict than on the low-conflict task [p. 20]." The presence of a conflict-by-distress interaction in the second study and its absence in the first study could be due to differences in couples' length of time married between the two studies, or it could be due to differences in procedure between the two studies.

A differential test of these hypotheses is provided by an unpublished study (reported separately in two masters theses by Bank [1974] and Yoppi [1974]) designed to replicate the procedures of Study 2 with a population similar to that used in Study 1. Subjects were 30 couples. Fifteen nonclinic couples responded to an advertisement and classified their marriages as "mutually satisfying"; of 15 clinic couples, 6 responded to the advertisement and classified their marriages as "experiencing marital difficulties," and the 9 other clinic couples were referred from mental health agencies in Bloomington, Indiana. Yoppi and Bank included in their final nonclinic group only those nonclinic marriages whose average MRI scores was ≥100 and in their final clinic group couples who average MRI score was <100. Two of the clinic couples were eliminated from the sample by these cutoffs. Six additional clinic couples were eliminated because they did not fall within the age range of the clinic couples in Study 1. The average age of the remaining 22 couples (7 clinic and 15 nonclinic) was 25.40 years, and they had been married an average of 2.70 years, figures comparable to those of the sample in Study 1. Again, there were no significant demographic differences between groups. The procedure of this study was identical to that of Study 2.

Despite the small sample size of the remaining clinic couples, the results provided a replication of most of the major findings of Study 1: Again, there were no significant intent differences between groups; there was a significant impact difference between groups that reached significance only for husbands; and a significant task effect was again obtained for the impact ratings, with ratings more positive on low-conflict tasks. Again (as in Study 1), there was a significant group-by-conflict interaction, so *it was possible to discriminate clinic from nonclinic couples as easily on low- as on high-conflict tasks.* Again, there were significant discrepancies between intent and impact between groups in the predicted direction, on both high- and low-conflict tasks. There was an inadequate sample size for reciprocity analyses. These results suggest that the conflict-by-group interaction on Study 2 was probably due to the fact that these couples were married longer than were the couples in Study 1. (Gottman et al. (1976) suggested that the significant conflict-by-distress interaction for couples who are married longer could be accounted for by a hypothesis that

> couples who have been married longer (Study 2) have learned to exchange
> more positive messages in low-conflict situations and to avoid situations of
> high conflict. This is consistent with the clinical picture of the "stable–

unsatisfactory" marriage (Lederer and Jackson, 1968), or the "united-front" couple (Kramer, 1968), who can present a satisfactory image of themselves to the public in social situations but are unable to hide behind this image when discussing real marital issues [p. 21].

Tables 12.6 and 12.7 present reanalyses of reciprocity for Study 2. Table 12.6 presents the negative reciprocity results. There was an insufficient number of negative impact codes to go beyond lag 3 for nonclinic couples. These results show that Z-scores and conditional probabilities are, once again, higher for clinic than for nonclinic couples. Table 12.7 presents the results for the positive reciprocity analyses. Once again, there are no dramatic consistent differences between groups. These results thus replicate those of Study 1.

Table 12.8 represents a reanalyses of the lag 1 Z-scores from Gottman et al.'s (1976) tables for distressed and nondistressed couples. Once again, negative, and not positive reciprocity, discriminates the two groups of couples.

In discussing the positiveness results of these two studies, Gottman et al. (1976) wrote that

The data from the present investigation support a "bank account" model of nondistressed marriage rather than a reciprocity model. In a bank account

TABLE 12.6
Negative Reciprocity Schema: Study 2

Criterion: H-	LAG			
	1	2	3	4
Nonclinic				
H-	.00	.15	.00	a
W-	.27*	.00	.06	a
Z-score	6.49	1.96	.59	
Clinic				
H-	.00	.41*	.00	.38*
W-	.39*	.00	.30*	.00
Z-score	6.56	7.55	4.82	6.90

Criterion: W-	LAG			
	1	2	3	4
Nonclinic				
H-	.10	.00	.05	a
W-	.00	.20*	.00	a
Z-score	.54	3.63	-.30	
Clinic				
H-	.36*	.00	.28*	.00
W-	.00	.36*	.00	.28*
Z-score	5.36	6.38	4.17	4.36

[a] Insufficient number of instances to continue.

*Represents the probabilities with the highest Z-score, which is given immediately below the respective probabilities.

TABLE 12.7
Positive Reciprocity Schema: Study 2

Criterion: H+	LAG					
	1	2	3	4	5	6
Nonclinic						
H+	.00	.70*	.00	.64*	.00	.65*
W+	.80*	.00	.70*	.00	.68*	.00
Z-score	7.50	10.12	9.43	8.67	8.84	8.75
Clinic						
H+	.00	.68*	.00	.62*	.01	.58*
W+	.57*	.01	.51*	.01	.42*	.01
Z-score	8.82	13.50	9.49	11.71	6.89	10.46

Criterion: W+	LAG					
	1	2	3	4	5	6
Nonclinic						
H+	.70*	.00	.56*	.00	.60*	.00
W+	.00	.72*	.00	.73*	.00	.69*
Z-score	5.45	10.38	9.36	10.63	7.61	9.41
Clinic						
H+	.56*	.00	.54*	.01	.49*	.02
W+	.00	.55	.02	.49*	.01	.49*
Z-score	7.58	10.23	8.88	8.41	7.56	8.41

*Represents the probabilities with the highest Z-score, which is given immediately below the respective probabilities.

TABLE 12.8
Reciprocity Analyses on the Talk Table Impact Data: Study 2

	Group	
Variable	Distressed	Nondistressed
Positive Reciprocity		
p(W+)	.45	70
p(W+/H+)	.54	.79
Z-score	2.16	2.34
p(H+)	.41	.70
p(H+/W+)	.51	.76
Z-score	2.45	1.57
Negative Reciprocity		
p(W-)	.22	.14
p(W-/H-)	.35	.20
Z-score	3.80	2.06
p(H-)	.24	.08
p(H-/W-)	.33	.12
Z-score	2.51	1.78

> model, a nondistressed marriage differs from a distressed marriage in that there are more positive "deposits" than negative "withdrawals." In a non-distressed marriage the consequent positive impact codes are not contingent upon the spouse's antecedent coding. Perhaps it is precisely this *lack* of reciprocity in a context of high positive exchange that characterizes stable positive interaction in nondistressed couples [p. 21].

My reanalyses of the reciprocity data must qualify the bank account model by adding that, in nonclinic marriages, a withdrawal from the account is not followed by another withdrawal as readily as it is in clinic marriages. This, then, provides some stability for the account.

These results show that, on the dimensions of positiveness and reciprocity, there is a remarkable parallel between the couples' perception of their interaction and patterns obtained from the coding of verbal and nonverbal behavior. They also suggest the value of an intent–impact schema and of a bank-account schema for describing the couples' perception of their interaction.

The two studies demonstrate the usefulness of the talk table as a way of tapping the couple's perception of their interaction. Subsequent research has shown that the talk table is not differentially obtrusive for clinic and nonclinic couples. Results obtained from observers' coding of videotapes of couples both with and without the talk table (using the Couples Interaction Scoring System described in Chapter 4) show that, although the talk table constrains interaction—for example, only one person has the floor at a time—it constrains the interaction of clinic and nonclinic couples in the same way.

PREDICTIVE VALIDITY OF THE TALK TABLE: THE MARKMAN STUDY

Subjects and Procedure

An additional criterion for testing models derived from the talk table is their ability to *predict* relationship satisfaction. In a dissertation conducted in my laboratory, Markman (1977) assessed the predictive capability of talk table measures in a 2½-year longitudinal study of 26 couples planning to marry. In the initial assessment, couples had known one another an average of 32.2 months, with a range of 2–72 months. Couples completed questionnaires to assess their confidence that they would marry, their satisfaction with the relationship (a version of the MRI), their sexual adjustment, communication (the Navran Primary Communication Inventory; Navran, 1967), their emotional adjustment, the severity of relationship issues (the Problem Inventory), value dissimilarity, personality dissimilarity, perceived similarity, differences in what they expected from the marriage on a marriage contract revealed-differences task, and value expectations discrepancy. Influence patterns in decision making were assessed by comparing individual rankings with a group-consensus ranking, and intent and impact were assessed using the talk table on a range of decision-making tasks, which included a marriage contract task, the food task, the Inventory of Marital Conflict, and a task in which couples resolved a relationship issue, as described in Study 1 (preceding). Markman's first follow-up was taken 1 year later, and it again included questionnaire and laboratory assessment. His second follow-up occurred 2½ years after the first assessment.

Results

Figure 12.2 presents the talk-table impact ratings for couples high and low at each assessment on relationship satisfaction (MRI or a rewording of the MRI for unmarried couples). Subjects in the low group had average scores below 100, and subjects in the high group had scores above 100. These data show a linear trend: Impact differences for males and for females were signficant by Time 3, so the initial differences were predictive of differences 2½ years later [F(males) = 5.5, $p < .05$; F(females) = 10.5, $p < .01$]. Thus, the impact model has demonstrated predictive validity with respect to relationship satisfaction. Markman's findings on the predictive power of initial impact ratings were also supported in a cross-lagged panel correlational analysis conducted on male and female impact ratings on the relationship issue problem-solving task. Impact

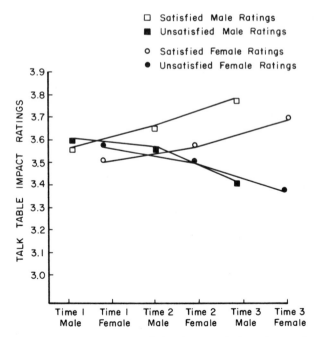

Figure 12.2 *Impact ratings from satisfied and unsatisfied couples as a function of time. (From Markman, 1977, p. 56. Reproduced with permission.)*

ratings at Time 1 significantly predicted relationship satisfaction $2\frac{1}{2}$ years later ($r = .88$, $p < .01$ for males; $r = .64$, $p < .01$ for females), whereas the correlations between relationship satisfaction at Time 1 and impact ratings $2\frac{1}{2}$ years later were negative or not significant. *Correlations between talk-table impact variables across all tasks and relationship satisfaction $2\frac{1}{2}$ years later were in the .60s, whereas the highest correlations previously obtained in the mate selection field were in the .40s (Terman & Wallin, 1949), and these previously obtained correlations contained common method variance in the two measures, which was not the case for the Markman study.*

In one analysis, Markman correlated all measures taken at Time 1 to discover if the talk-table measures were tapping the same dimension as the marital satisfaction measures, a result portrayed in Table 12.2 of this chapter for married couples. Markman discovered that, for couples planning to marry, male impact scores correlated significantly only with male perceived similarity ($r = .403$, $p < .05$), and female impact scores also correlated significantly only with male perceived similarity ($r = .388$, $p < .05$). It is interesting that talk-table impact scores did not correlate with actual personality similarity, with value similarity, or with a combination of these two variables, especially since perceived similarity, and not actual similarity, during engagement has been known to be a predictor of later marital satisfaction (Burgess et al., 1971). Correlations between talk-table impact scores for couples later in the longitudinal study provided a replication of Table 12.1. For married couples in Markman's longitudinal study, the talk table tapped marital satisfaction, whereas for couples planning to marry, the talk table tapped perceived similarity.

In a stringent test of the *communication deficit model* of relationship satisfaction, Markman found that initial intent–impact discrepancy, assessed at each message exchanged, was a poor predictor of later relationship or marital satisfaction but that impact ratings were excellent predictors. Therefore, as a longitudinal model, more weight should be placed on the bank account model, which stresses the importance of positively perceived exchanges, than on the communication deficit model, which stresses intent–impact match. This is probably true because of the initial importance of *perceived* similarity in creating satisfying relationships in unmarried couples. Intent–impact match may become more important in predicting marital satisfaction the longer the couple is married.

Although our major criterion tests for variables obtained from behavior exchange theory are related to relationship satisfaction, Markman also addressed the literature on mate selection in his dissertation. He found the initial talk-table measures not as good at predicting later marital *status* as the unmarried couples' own initial confidence that they would marry. Self-predictions of later marital status accounted for 49.6% of the variance in marital status $2\frac{1}{2}$ years later. However, initial talk-table measures did as well at predicting later marital status as mate selection measures; they accounted for 23.3% and 27.6% of the variance in later marital status, respectively. Markman also found that the initial decision-making style of couples who were more likely to be married at each follow-up assessment was characterized at Time 1 by mutual give and take rather than by either male or female dominance. This pattern was determined by Markman's measure of power in the revealed differences tasks, that is, the difference between individual and group consensus rankings. Couples who were more likely to be married at follow-up were also characterized by more positive female intent and impact ratings than were couples who were likely to be still unmarried upon follow-up. This finding was supported by Bank (1974) and by Yoppi (1974), who reported that clinic wives had significantly less power in the decision-making process than did nonclinic wives (F = 8.30, $p < .01$), with power assessed as in Markman's study.

The Markman study is the first longitudinal test of the predictive power of the operational definitions derived from behavior exchange theory, and it is a dramatic demonstration of the usefulness of talk-table measures in providing causal explanations of the functioning of marital relationships.

The research reviewed in this chapter suggested that the talk table is successful in operationalizing behavior exchange theory and tapping the couple's perception of their interaction. An intent model and a positive reciprocity model failed to receive support as schema for the couple's perception of their interaction. A communication model (intent–impact discrepancy) received consistent support as a discriminator between distressed and nondistressed couples, but not as a predictor of relationship satisfaction in a longitudinal study of couples planning to marry. Perhaps the most powerful discriminator in the cross-sectional studies and predictor in the longitudinal study was impact. The results also provided support for the bank account model of relationship satisfaction discussed in this chapter.

RELATIONSHIPS BETWEEN PERCEPTION AND BEHAVIOR

Gurman and Knudson (1978) recently criticized behavioral conceptualizations of marital therapy. They noted that behavioral approaches assume that changing behavior so that the couple's interaction is more positively reciprocal will change the couple's perception of their relationship, as measured by increased marital satisfaction. They disagreed with this assumption:

> This premise is not "wrong." It is simply incomplete, even from a social-learning point of view. An "impression" is based on the other's behavior *as interpreted* through the individual's *perceptual* system which has developed out of his experiences with previous significant others. If, however, behavior is, in fact, interpreted (perceived), then a change in husband's behavior *may* or *may not* change his wife's impressions and expectations [p. 129].

It would, thus, be important to investigate the relationship between behavioral and perceptual models of clinic and nonclinic marriages.

Murstein et al.'s (1977) study using questionnaires reported that the *perception* of marital interaction as positively reciprocal (the *quid pro quo* belief) was *negatively* related to marital satisfaction. This is consistent with the failure of positive reciprocity of the talk table data to discriminate clinic from nonclinic couples. The *quid pro quo* belief is reminiscent of the patterning of specific codes in clinic couples. Clinic couples are most likely to engage in sequences in which complaint is met with cross-complaint, in which a proposed solution of a problem is met with a counterproposal, and in which negative affect is met with negative affect. On the dimensions of reciprocity of positive and negative impact on the talk table, the results obtained were consistent with patterns found from the coding of videotapes with the nonverbal codes of the CISS.

Nonclinic couples, on the other hand, are more likely than clinic couples to engage in sequences in which a complaint is first met with agreement, assent, or validation, in which a proposed solution is met with accepting modification of one's own position and a contracting sequence, and in which negative affect is not as likely to be met with negative affect.

The negative relationship between a *quid pro quo* belief and marital satisfaction in the Murstein et al. (1977) study may be related to the clinic couples' mirroring of behaviors; that is, for clinic couples, complaint is met with cross-complaint, proposal with counterproposal, and negative affect by one spouse with subsequent negative affect by the partner. Agreement is not interspersed. This mirroring of behavior (particularly negative nonverbal behavior) is characteristic of territorial disputes in other species (see Wilson, 1975). It is not unreasonable that some form of interpersonal "territorality" is a basic issue in clinic couples. The mirroring in the behavior sequences is a vying for symmetry during territorial disputes in other species. The generalization of space in human relationships may be related to intimacy, in the sense that a territorial dispute is an attempt to increase interpersonal distance. This would suggest that a *quid pro quo* arrangement could be functional in relationships with greater interpersonal distance. In fact, Murstein et al. (1977) found that a *quid pro quo* belief was positively correlated with indices of relationship satisfaction among college roommates.

The argument implies that, to the extent that couples are concerned with territoriality (inferred from the mirroring of behavior), they will maintain interpersonal distance. This concept can be tested indirectly by examining the consequences of increased interpersonal distance in communication. In close relationships that are functioning well, couples may develop an efficient, fairly private system of communicating, and the concept of interpersonal distance may be assessed to some extent by the "privateness" of this communication system.

Any investigator who trains observers to code the nonverbal behavior of married couples will soon come upon questions such as, "When is a smile actually a smirk?" Observers must use the decision rules of our culture to arrive at agreement in their reading of faces, voices, and bodies. However, in a close relationship, a system of message exchange may develop that is idiosyncratic and, perhaps, at times discrepant from cultural rules for reading meaning from nonverbal behavior. If this is the case, the discrepancy between observers' coding and spouses' coding will be an index of interpersonal closeness. If the discrepancy exists only for nonclinic couples, this would support the hypothesis that the mirroring of behaviors in the sequences of clinic couples is related to the "interpersonal territoriality" involved in clinic couples' disputes.

There is evidence that couples with higher marital satisfaction scores claim to be better at reading their spouse's nonverbal behavior than do couples with lower marital satisfaction scores (Navran, 1967). There is also some evidence that they are, in fact, better at this task (Kahn, 1970). In Kahn's study, each couple was given a 16-item communication test. For 8 of the items, the wife was the sender. An example of an item is the following:

> You and your husband are sitting alone in your living room on a winter evening. You feel cold. [Verbal message: "I'm cold. Aren't you?"]
> —a. You wonder if he is also cold or it is only you who are cold.
> —b. You want him to warm you with physical affection.
> —c. You want him to turn up the heat. [pp. 450–451]

The wife in this situation was given one of the three meanings to communicate using only the given verbal message and any additional accompanying nonverbal behavior. The maximum score a couple could receive on this test was 16. The mean score for couples in the high-satisfaction group was 9.05 and for couples in the low-satisfaction group 7.33; $t(40) = 1.93, p < .05$. Kahn (1970) concluded that dissatisfied husbands consistently distorted their wives messages "to attribute negative connotations to their wives' attempts to communicate affection, happiness, and playfulness [p. 455]." Apparently, couples in satisfied marriages have a nonverbal signal–response system that is relatively free of this kind of distortion. We are currently extending Kahn's work in my laboratory.

If couples with higher marital satisfaction are indeed better at reading their spouses' nonverbal behavior, these couples would tend to develop a private message system. If couples have *not* developed a private message system, then observers and spouses should tend to code behavior in similar ways. Therefore, to the extent that either group of couples differs in their own coding from observers' coding of the same messages, there may be a private message-system involved. If the private message-system exists only for nonclinic couples, this provides some evidence that the mirroring of behavior may be related to territoriality and interpersonal distance.

A test was provided by using the Couples Interaction Scoring System (CISS) to code the videotapes of couples *interacting on the talk table* to resolve a marital issue. The CISS nonverbal codes were then compared to the talk-table impact codes.

To compare the CISS nonverbal affect codes with the talk-table impact codes, the nonverbal behavior of the speaker immediately before a floor switch (when the spouse would code impact) was tabulated in one of three rows of a contingency table (0, +, −) whose columns were one of three talk-table impact codes (0, +, −), as shown in Table 12.9. If a significant chi-square is obtained, it would suggest that the two dimensions are not independent and that there is no evidence for a private message system; the couples' coding and the observers' coding would be similar. These tables were calculated separately for clinic and nonclinic couples resolving a marital issue, once for wives as speakers and once for husbands as speakers.

For wives as speakers, the chi-square for clinic couples was 8.24, $p < .05$, but, for nonclinic couples, the chi-square was 1.89, $p > .05$. The two dimensions were, thus, not independent for clinic couples, but they were independent for nonclinic couples. There is, thus, evidence for a private message system only for nonclinic couples. Another index of these results is the ratio of on-diagonal elements to off-diagonal elements in Table 12.9. This ratio gives an index of the hit rate of observers at predicting talk-table impact scores. The hit rate is lower for nonclinic couples (.509) than for clinic couples (.671).

For husbands as speakers, the chi-square for clinic couples was 5.07, $p > .05$, and, for nonclinic couples, the chi-square was 3.15, $p > .05$. Although these chi-squares show the same pattern as for wives as speakers, the two dimensions are independent for both groups of couples.

These results suggest that, whereas clinic husbands are reading their wives as observers do, nonclinic husbands are reading their wives differently from observers. This discrepancy between spouses and observers was distributed in the chi-square matrix as displayed in Table 12.10. Observers' hit rates were highest for positive nonverbal behavior; they tended to differ from husbands most in coding behavior neutral that the husbands coded as positive and in coding behavior negative that the husbands coded as neutral or positive.

The issue of the extent to which couples' interaction on the talk table differed from their interaction off the talk table was addressed in a brief methodological study. In general, although the talk table was reactive, the interaction of the two groups of couples differed in the same ways both on and off the talk table. For example, on the talk table the average ratio of agreement to disagreement was 1.33 for clinic couples and 2.02 for nonclinic couples (cf.

TABLE 12.9
Comparison of Talk Table Codes with C.I.S.S. Affect Codes

		Speaker's Impact on Spouse (Talk Table Code)	
		0	+	−
Speaker's Nonverbal Behavior	0			
as Coded by	+			
Observer (C.I.S.S. Code)	−			

TABLE 12.10
Distribution of the Discrepancy between Observers and Spouses Coding
of Nonclinic Wives

Wives' Nonverbal Behavior as Coded by Observers	Wives' Impact on Husbands			
	0	+	-	Total
Neutral (0)	.285	.510	.204	1.000
Positive (+)	.367	.400	.233	1.000
Negative (-)	.444	.333	.222	1.000

Table 6.1). The talk table, thus, generally improved communication, that is, increased these ratios for both groups but maintained their differences. Similarly, differences in nonverbal behavior were maintained between groups: The proportion of neutral affect on the talk table was .708 for nonclinic and .662 for clinic couples; the proportion of positive affect, .212 for nonclinic and .108 for clinic couples; and the proportion of negative affect was .079 for nonclinic and .230 for clinic couples. Except for the differences obtained in positive affect, these results compare well with results obtained from the CISS (see Table 6.1).

SUMMARY

This chapter has investigated couples' perception of their interaction and has tested alternative schema of that perception through use of the talk table. Results indicate a remarkable degree of consistency with positiveness and reciprocity analyses obtained from observational data. Furthermore, in two discriminant studies and in one predictive study, a bank account schema, rather than a *quid pro quo* schema of satisfying marital interaction, received support.

From a study of the relationship between behavior and perception, it appears that couples who are not satisfied with their relationship and who mirror behaviors rather than intersperse agreement exhibit the following behaviors: They (a) maintain interpersonal distance (as in territorial disputes); (b) do not develop a private message-system; and (c) are not as effective at reading their partners' nonverbal behavior.

CHAPTER 13

Couples' Interaction at Home

THE ISSUE OF GENERALIZABILITY ACROSS SETTINGS

To what extent is it possible to generalize from interaction sequences in a group of couples observed in the laboratory to their interaction when they are alone at home? There is currently no research addressed to the important question of the generalizability of marital interaction across settings.

There is some evidence to suggest that differences in setting affect family interaction, although the evidence is scant. The only systematic comparison is a study by O'Rourke (1963). He used a shortened form of the Bales IPA to study the interaction of families on two tasks—making up a story about several Thematic Apperception Test cards and solving a set of standardized family problems. Unfortunately, the O'Rourke study has many serious methodological weaknesses, among which are the lack of attention to observer bias (since the author, who knew the hypotheses, was the only observer) and observer reactivity, no assessment of interobserver reliability, and no control of possible order effects (since this was a within-subject study). If these limitations are ignored, the results (although quite complex) generally suggest that family interaction tends to be more positive at home than in the laboratory.

However, in our laboratory we have often been thanked by couples who found the laboratory assessment procedures therapeutic, even though the procedures were not designed as therapy. This observation would lead to the formulation of a hypothesis precisely opposite to O'Rourke's, namely, that interactions in the laboratory are likely to be more positive than similar interactions at home, without the presence of strangers. The presence of strangers in a relatively public and unfamiliar setting such as the laboratory should, logically, have the effect of increasing politeness, decreasing negative interaction, and increasing the likelihood of a closing decision-making ritual. The last prediction is sensible when one considers the fact that, once people are in the laboratory in the evening, they want to get home at a decent hour, and so finishing the discussion in a reasonable length of time is both desirable and proper experimental subject etiquette.

PROCEDURE

To avoid problems of repeated assessment and possible order effects, a between-subjects design was selected. Nineteen couples responded to a newspaper advertisement announcing two weekend "couples communication workshops" that were to be held in a local church. The workshops and the experimental design evaluating these workshops are described in detail in Chapter 14. As usual, after completing the Demographic Information Form, the MRI, and the Problem Inventory, all couples were interviewed in the laboratory, using the play-by-play procedure described in Chapter 6, and the problem rated as the major marital issue for both husband and wife was identified. Ten couples were then randomly assigned to a condition in which they were asked to come to a mutually satisfactory resolution of the problem and were videotaped in the laboratory; this was the standard procedure used in Chapter 6. Eight of the 9 other couples were given a portable audio cassette recorder and a cassette and were asked to complete a tape at home when they were alone within the following week. One of the 9 couples canceled their appointment. All 10 couples completed the videotape, and 7 out of 8 completed the cassette tape.

The two groups of couples did not differ significantly on any demographic variable. The average ages of the couples in the laboratory group were 29.8 for husbands, 29.5 for wives; for the home group, these ages were 34.0 for the husbands and 33.0 for the wives. There were no significant differences in ages [t(husbands) = .47; t(wives) = .39]. The couples in the laboratory group had been married an average of 7.9 years, and the couples in the home group had been married an average of 11.8 years; this difference was not significant (t = .47). The couples in the laboratory group had an average of 1.3 children, and the couples in the home group had an average of 1.9 children; this difference was not significant (t = .60).

The MRI scores for the two groups averaged 89.30 for the laboratory group and 93.38 for the home group, and, once again, these differences were not significant: t = .73. However, it should be noted that both groups of couples in this study were intermediate in marital satisfaction to the distressed (average = 69.30) and nondistressed couples (average = 108.5) in the study reported in Chapter 6. The interaction patterns of the couples in the present study should also be intermediate to those of distressed and nondistressed couples, and, thus, the prediction of the present investigation is that these couples' interactions should resemble those of distressed couples at home and those of nondistressed couples in the laboratory.

CODING OF AFFECT FROM VOICE TONE

For the tapes of the present investigation, affect was coded solely from the speaker's voice tone, using the vocal nonverbal cues of the CISS affect coding system. The picture of the videotape was totally concealed by a screen that attached to the video monitor. One code was added to the voice tone coding system to include the research on non-ah disturbances (summarized in Chapter 3). Since non-ah disturbances are generally related to a speaker's tension, the negative affect code combined all non-ah codes with the voice negative code. Table 13.1 presents the results of the generalizability study of coding affect from voice tone. As is evident from this table, the affect codes based solely on voice tone have a considerable degree of reliability. Coders were unaware of the hypotheses, procedures, or purposes of this study. It was known to the coders as the "voice study," and the emphasis was placed on coding voice tone from all tapes.

TABLE 13.1
Generalizability Study* Results for Speaker Affect Coding from Voice Tone

Code	Frequency	Mean Square Transcripts	Mean Square Residual	Cronbach Alpha
Two Pages				
Voice Positive	78	53.086	1.943	.929
Voice Neutral	587	398.271	.548	.997
Voice Negative	139	187.729	1.176	.988
Non-Ah Positive	4	.352	.000	1.000
Non-Ah Neutral	88	15.976	2.205	.757
Non-Ah Negative	25	8.729	.348	.923
All Negative	256	71.561	1.143	.969
Four Pages				
Voice Positive	98	116.231	1.575	.974
Voice Neutral	1171	2394.598	19.948	.984
Voice Negative	141	241.331	2.548	.979
Non-Ah Positive	10	2.058	.058	.945
Non-Ah Neutral	296	162.615	1.748	.979
Non-Ah Negative	28	8.033	.433	.898
All Negative	475	190.857	1.554	.984

*This generalizability study includes the transcripts from the study reported in this chapter on the home interaction of clinic couples.

RESULTS

Table 13.2 presents the results on the variable of agreement to disagreement ratio for the two groups, and these results suggest that ratios less than one, characteristic of distressed couples, describe home interaction, whereas ratios greater than one, characteristic of nondistressed couples, describe interaction in the laboratory. Table 13.3 presents the results on positive and negative affect and on the reciprocity of positive and negative affect. Because there were low rates of positive affect, only lag-1 conditional probabilities are presented for both positive and negative affect. However, at home negative-affect cycles continued with highly significant Z-scores into the sixth lag [$p(H- \mid H-)_6 = .325$, $Z = 5.77; p(W- \mid W-)_6 = .387, Z = 6.25$). Note that a comparison of the conditional probabilities in Table 13.3 with those of Table 6.3 shows that the home interaction of these intermediate marital satisfaction couples showed greater negative-affect reciprocity than did that of the clinic couples in Chapter 6 (.50 versus .34; .39 versus .27), and their laboratory interaction showed levels of negative reciprocity comparable to nonclinic couples (.14 versus .16; .14 versus .19). The major affect differences between home and laboratory, both in unconditional probabilities and in conditional probabilities, occurred in negative affect. Both husbands and wives were more negative in the home than in the laboratory and were more likely, and more predictably likely, to reciprocate negative affect in the home than in the laboratory.

Table 13.4 presents conditional probabilities and Z-scores for the four specific sequences that discriminated clinic from nonclinic couples in Chapter 6.

The differences between home and laboratory are entirely consistent with those reported in Table 6.6. Couples' interaction at home was less likely to result in validation sequences than was interaction in the laboratory. A similar conclusion held for cross-complaining, namely, that it was more predictably obtainable at home than in the laboratory. This conclusion is difficult to see from Table 13.4, because there is an intermediate step for wives that involves a transition from neutral affect while speaking: WPFo→ WPF− → HPFo (see the footnote to Table 13.4). Contracting loops are also more likely in the laboratory, whereas cross-complaining loops are more likely at home.

The results of this study suggest that, on all important dimensions, the

TABLE 13.2
Positiveness Assessed Using Agreement-to-Disagreement Ratios

Ratios	Home	Laboratory
Husband Agreement to Husband Disagreement	.82	2.36
Wife Agreement to Wife Disagreement	.81	1.44

TABLE 13.3

Probabilities of Positive and Negative Affect and Lag-One Reciprocity of
Positive and Negative Affect at Home and in the Laboratory

	Home	Laboratory
P(W+)	.042	.034
p(W+|H+)	.125	.135
z-score	2.01	4.71
p(H+)	.017	.028
p(H+|W+)	.070	.080
z-score	2.93	2.78
p(H-)	.240	.142
p(W-|H-)	.200	.139
z-score	7.18	-.86
p(H-)	.184	.103
p(H-|W-)	.389	.139
z-score	6.20	1.12

TABLE 13.4

Cycles of Validation, Cross Complaining, Contracting, and Counterproposal at
Home and in the Laboratory

	Home	Laboratory
Validation		
p(WAG|HPF)	.07	.11
z	1.41	4.24
p(HAG|WPF)	.08	.28
z	1.94	8.69
Cross-Complaining		
p(WPF|HPF)	.14	.15
z	2.37	1.54
p(HPF|WPF)*	.06	.14
z	.45	2.16
Contracting		
p(WAG|HPS)	.12	.13
z	4.75	5.84
p(HAG|WPS)	.10	.30
z	3.43	9.35
Counterproposal		
p(WPS|HPS)	.13	.12
z	1.68	1.20
p(HPS|WPS)	.18	.13
z	3.20	1.65

*For this group of couples there was an unusual sequence WPFO→WPF- with conditional
probability .23 and z-score 5.02 followed by HPFo with lag-2 conditional probability .12
and z-score 3.92, suggesting an added link to the cross-complaining chain WPFo→WPF--
HPFo. There is also a chain WPFo→WPF-→HPF-; the lag-one conditional probability
between WPF- and HPF- is .10 with z-score 2.46.

PF = Feelings about Problem
PS = Problem Solving and Information Exchange
AG = Agreement

interaction of couples is more negative and more negatively reciprocal at home than in the laboratory. However, these results are limited because the couples represented in this study were not comparable in marital satisfaction scores to the distressed couples in the study reported in Chapter 6. Two additional comparisons would be useful. First, the cutoff scores used in the studies previously reported in this book could be used to create comparison groups within laboratory and home groups. Second, home tapes could be obtained from a group of clinic couples in marital therapy in order to provide a comparison group of home tapes from couples who identify their marriage as in need of change by a professional. This could not be assumed about the couples who were interested in the brief, educationally oriented communication workshop.

In the laboratory group, three couples were within the low satisfaction range of previous studies, with a mean MRI score of 74.67 (SD = 6.71), and two couples were within the high satisfaction range, and with a mean MRI score of 103.75 (SD = .35). In the home group, two couples were in the low range, with a mean MRI score of 72.25 (SD = 7.42), but, unfortunately, only one couple was within the high range, with an MRI score of 104.50. The results that will be presented for these four groups must be considered exploratory and highly tentative. The results are offered in the absence of any other available data on the subject, and the proper attitude of cautious interest is recommended. For the statistical comparisons possible within these four groups, there were no significant differences on demographic variables.

Table 13.5 presents means for the four groups on the agreement-to-disagreement ratio, positive and negative affect. An examination of this table suggests that agreement-to-disagreement ratios discriminate high and low marital satisfaction couples better in the laboratory than at home but that affect assessed from voice tone is a better discriminator at home, particularly of negative affect; low satisfaction couples display much more negative affect at home than in the laboratory, but this is not the case for high satisfaction couples. There is also a potential for greater discrimination between high and low marital

TABLE 13.5
Positive and Negative Affect and Agreement to Disagreement Ratios

Variable	Home		Laboratory	
	Low Satisfaction	High Satisfaction	Low Satisfaction	High Satisfaction
Husband AG/DG	3.60	1.00	1.67	6.67
Wife AG/DG	.43	2.00	.80	4.22
p(W+)	.030	.122	.024	.015
p(H+)	.002	.012	.029	.029
p(W-)	.272	.171	.176	.124
p(H-)	.248	.049	.144	.116

AG = Agreement
DG = Disagreement

satisfaction couples at home on the dimension of positive affect than there is in the laboratory.

Table 13.6 presents the affect reciprocity results for two lags; there is insufficient data to go beyond lag 2. Once again, the conclusion holds that high and low satisfaction groups can be discriminated more powerfully at home than in the laboratory. The conditional probabilities of negative affect cycles in lag 2 are enormous; $p(H- \mid H-$ two lags ago$) = .708$, $Z = 10.95$ and $p(W- \mid W-$ two lags ago$) = .565$, $Z = 7.08$. In the laboratory, these probabilities and Z-scores are much smaller: $.306$, $Z = 3.24$ and $.300$, $Z = 2.52$, respectively. Furthermore, they are closer to the same conditional probabilities of high satisfaction couples in the laboratory than at home.

For these four groups, there is an inadequate number of instances of many of the neutral affect codes that have served as the criterion codes for the validation, cross-complaining, contracting, and counterproposal sequences. There are several problems with presenting these sequential data. An examination of the frequencies of the codes shows that one problem is that a great proportion of the problem feeling (PF) and problem solution and information exchange (PS) codes were delivered with negative rather than with neutral affect, which was not the case in previous laboratory-based studies reported in this book. For example, for the low satisfaction home group, 80.4% of the husbands' PF statements were delivered with negative affect; 50.8% of the PS statements were negative. Another problem is that, since there is only one couple in one of the groups, there is a sufficient number of observations in this case only to examine problem solving and information exchange (PS) sequences, and these must be examined with great caution. Because of these facts, it appears that, to some extent, *there are entirely different most likely sequences in the low satisfaction at-home group than we obtained previously in laboratory investigations.*

Table 13.7 shows that the familiar sequences are common and work in famil-

TABLE 13.6

Negative Affect Reciprocity as a Function of Marital Satisfaction and Home versus Lab Setting

	Home				Laboratory			
	Low Satisfaction		High Satisfaction		Low Satisfaction		High Satisfaction	
	LAG		LAG		LAG		LAG	
	1	2	1	2	1	2	1	2
Criterion: H-								
H-	.000	.708*	.000	.333*	.000	.306*	.000	.237*
W-	.528*	.085	.000	.333	.143	.184	.051	.102
Z	3.58	10.95	-.81	2.29	-1.08	3.24	-1.97	2.91
Criterion: W-								
H-	.422	.113	.000	.000	.233	.000	.111	.048
W-	.000	.565*	.000	.286	.000	.300*	.000	.175
Z	1.85	7.08	-.94	1.14	1.20	2.52	-.50	1.23

TABLE 13.7
Sequences Exploring Feelings about Problems

Low Satisfaction at Home

HPF- → WCTo → HPSo → WDG-
.222   .216   .129
(2.45) (4.42) (3.09)

WPFO → WCT- → HPSo
.160   .161
(2.30) (2.31)

WPF- → WMR-
.091
(2.35)

High Satisfaction at Home: Insufficient N for Sequential Analysis

Low Satisfaction in Lab

HPFo → HPF-   Cross-Complaining
.167
(4.75)

→ WPF-
.097
(2.22)

HPF- → HPFo
.320
(2.89)

→ WPFo   Cross-Complaining
.240
(2.17)

→ WAGo
.160
(3.29)

WPFO → HPFo   Cross-Complaining
.213
(1.77)

→ HAGo   Validation
.180
(2.08)

→ HCTo
.131
(2.90)

High Satisfaction in Lab

HPFo → HPF-
.219
(3.47)

→ WAGo   Validation
.156
(1.51)

HPF- → WAGo
.208
(2.29)

→ HPFo
.208
(2.13)

WPFo → HAGo   Validation
.353
(3.39)

WPF- → HAGo
.391
(4.48)

→ HCT-
.087
(3.54)

PF = Feelings about Problem   AG = Agreement
CT = Communication Talk   DG = Disagreement

244

iar ways to discriminate high from low marital satisfaction couples. However, at home, new sequences are common in low satisfaction couples. These sequences involve mindreading with negative affect, which is casting blame (for example, "You don't care about the way we live.") and which discriminated distressed from nondistressed couples in Chapter 6 and was connected to PF statements with negative affect. Disagreement (DG) and communication talk (CT) with negative affect are also involved in these sequences. To summarize, in the tapes of low satisfaction couples at home, new sequences with highly negative affect arise that were not observed in a similar group in the laboratory. This is further evidence that the laboratory-based differences between couples as a function of marital satisfaction actually underestimate differences at home.

Table 13.8 presents the common sequences involving problem solving and information exchange (PS). In the laboratory, counterproposal sequences are more likely for low satisfaction than for high satisfaction couples, but contracting is more likely for low than for high satisfaction couples. This only partially replicates earlier findings. At home, once again the low satisfaction sequences are new and involve cycles of negative affect, disagreement, communication talk, and problem solving and information exchange.

Two conclusions can be drawn from this subsequent analysis of the data. First, the general conclusion holds that the interaction of couples is more negative at home than in the laboratory, particularly on negative affect and negative affect reciprocity. Second, it is easier to discriminate low from high satisfaction couples at home than it is in the laboratory, and, thus, differences between these two groups obtained in the laboratory may *underestimate* these differences at home.

To have confidence in the generality of this conclusion, it is important to determine if the home tapes of couples who volunteered for the brief, educationally-based weekend workshop were comparable to the distressed couples who sought marital therapy who served as the subjects of other studies reported in this book. It would thus be useful to study a group of couples who seek therapy for marital problems as a group with which to compare the home tapes obtained from couples who signed up for the communication workshop.

A comparison group of seven couples in marital therapy was thus recruited using the same procedures described in Chapter 6; the procedures described in this chapter for obtaining and coding the tapes were also again used. These seven tapes were intermixed for coding purposes with the tapes discussed earlier in this chapter and were coded by the same group of coders during the same period; coders were thus unaware of the source of these tapes. The demographic characteristics of this group were not significantly different from those of the overall home group previously discussed. Mean ages were 36.2 for husbands and 35.3 for wives; t(husbands) = 1.20, t(wives) = .96. Couples in this group were married an average of 13.1 years; t = 1.06. The couples in this group had an average of 2.1 children; t = .72. The marital satisfaction scores for this therapy group averaged 97.89, and the difference between this and the overall home workshop group (mean = 93.38) was not significant; t = 1.62.

TABLE 13.8

Sequences Involving Problem Solving and Information Exchange

Low Satisfaction at Home

HPSo ——→ WDG-
.129
(3.09)

HPS- ——→ WCT-
.219
(3.70)
——→ WDG-
.094
(2.00)

WPSo ——→ WPS-
.294
(3.69)

WPS- ——→ WPSo
.317
(5.24)

WPSo ——→ HPSo   Counterproposal
.316
(2.97)
——→ HAGo   Contracting
.298
(3.56)

High Satisfaction in Lab

HPSo ——→ HPS-
.148
(4.94)

HPS- ——→ HPSo
.471
(5.37)

WPSo ——→ HPSo   Counterproposal
.196
(2.43)
——→ HAGo   Contracting
.179
(1.98)
——→ WPS-
.161
(4.74)

High Satisfaction at Home

HPSo ——→ WPS+   Counterproposal
.231
(2.04)

Low Satisfaction in Lab

HPSo ——→ WPSo   Counterproposal
.192
(1.87)

HPS- ——→ HPSo
.429
(3.83)

WPS- ——→ HPSo
.429
(5.14)
——→ HDG-
.095
(4.28)

PS = Problem Solving and Information Exchange
CT = Communication Talk

AG = Agreement
DG = Disagreement

246

TABLE 13.9

Positiveness Comparisons in the Home Interaction of Clinic and Workshop Couples

Variable	Home Clinic	Home Workshop
HAG/DG	1.69	.82
WAG/DG	1.65	.81
p(W+)	.054	.042
p(W+ǀH+)	.179	.125
z	2.87	2.01
p(H+)	.017	.017
p(H+ ǀW+)	.046	.070
z	1.91	2.93
p(W-)	.203	.240
p(W-ǀH-)	.449	.500
z	7.93	7.18
p(H-)	.178	.184
p(H-ǀW-)	.425	.389
z	8.72	6.20

AG = Agreement
DG = Disagreement

TABLE 13.10

Cycles of Validation, Cross-Complaining, Contracting, and Counterproposal in Clinic and Workshop Couples at Home

Variable	Home Clinic	Home Workshop
Validation		
p(WAGoǀHPFo)	.19	.07
z	6.66	1.41
p(HAGoǀWPFo)	.11	.08
z	2.66	1.94
Cross Complaining		
p(WPFoǀHPFo)	.09	.14
z	2.18	2.37
p(HPFoǀWPFo)	.13	.06*
z	3.13	1.45
Contracting		
p(WAGoǀHPSo)	.13	.12
z	4.29	4.75
p(HAGoǀWPSo)	.10	.10
z	2.64	3.43
Counterproposal		
p(WPSoǀHPSo)	.16	.13
z	2.53	1.68
p(HPSoǀWPSo)	.13	.18
z	2.13	3.20

*See footnote, Table 13.4

PF = Feelings about Problem
PS = Problem Solving and Information Exchange
AG = Agreement

Table 13.9 presents data on positiveness and reciprocity of affect variables for the home clinic group and repeats the same data for the home workshop group. The clinic group has higher agreement-to-disagreement ratios than the workshop group. However, on nonverbal positive affect, negative affect, and positive and negative reciprocity the two groups are quite comparable.

Table 13.10 presents data on cycles of validation, cross-complaining, contracting, and counterproposal for the home clinic group and repeats the same data for the home workshop group. Except for the greater likelihood of the wives' validating the husbands' expression of feelings about the problem (PF) in the clinic group, the two groups are quite comparable in conditional probabilities and Z-scores. To summarize, the home tapes obtained from the workshop couples are not markedly different from those that were obtained from clinic couples recruited from mental health agencies.

SUMMARY

The results presented in this chapter provide support for the conclusion that, in general, the interaction of couples at home alone contains far more negative affect, more negative affect reciprocity, less agreement compared to disagreement, lower probabilities of finding validation and contracting loops, and high probabilities of finding cross-complaining and counterproposal loops than does the interaction of comparable couples in the laboratory. Furthermore, the results suggest that *differences* between high and low marital satisfaction couples obtained in the laboratory are, in fact, likely to be an underestimate of these differences at home. Taken together as a generalizability study, these results suggest that one can place confidence in the differences previously reported in this book as holding true for the interaction of couples at home alone.

CHAPTER 14

Clinical Intervention: Applied and Theoretical Implications

HISTORICAL INTRODUCTION

In 1942, the American Association of Marriage Counselors was organized. Forty-two percent of its membership were educators, ministers, and sociologists; 18% were social workers; 12% were clinical psychologists; 9% were psychiatrists; and 21% were other physicians, mostly gynecologists and urologists (Mudd, 1955). These are probably representative of the professionals who did marriage counseling in the 1950s. Therapy with distressed marriages has undergone considerable change since World War II.

One aspect of marriage counseling that has changed dramatically since 1942 is the relatively recent involvement of both spouses in the same therapy session. Therapy sessions with both husband and wife were extremely rare in the 1940s and 1950s, and usually the wife and husband saw separate counselors. In 1955, Mudd wrote that the Marriage Council of Philadelphia (established in 1932) made "every effort to work with both husband and wife" but that "each partner is seen separately at weekly interviews of approximately 50 minutes each [p. 71]." With respect to conjoint interviews, she expressed the great caution of her time: "As part of the intake process and at intervals, *when deemed appropriate by the counselor and each partner,* a joint interview with husband and wife is held [p. 71]." Why was there such a reluctance to conduct joint interviews? The answer concerns the prevailing view of clinical ethics.

Maurice Karpf, who in 1951 was invited to address the National Council of Family Relations and to present some guiding principles in marriage counseling, had this to say about joint interviews:

> Joint conferences with both partners can be helpful but are difficult and extremely dangerous and should be resorted to only after careful consideration and planning [p. 51, emphasis deleted]. . . . Husband and wife may make the wildest accusations and say the most cutting things to each other without necessarily bearing a permanent grudge. *Once these things are said in the presence of a third party, they tend to become fixed* and take on a totally different significance and value . . . the joint conference can, therefore, become the means of further separating the spouses instead of bringing them together. . . . Hence it should be used sparingly and with the utmost care [p. 51, emphasis added].

This is one example of assumptions that underlie the ethics of an era and that are so powerful in determining what is then considered acceptable clinical practice. There were other ethical issues that concerned marriage counselors in the 1950s, including the therapist's invasion of the couples' privacy (see Lane, 1955) and issues believed to surround transference and countertransference. Many of these ethical concerns were inherited from psychoanalysis, which also affected conceptions of etiology and diagnosis and of the analysis of the goals of marriage counseling.

CONCEPTIONS OF MARITAL DISTRESS
PROMINENT IN THE 1950s

Because of the influence of psychoanalysis, it was even revolutionary for the same counselor to see both husband and wife. Vincent (1957) wrote, "a general principle of psychoanalysis advises against such simultaneous treatment of spouses by the same analyst . . ." [p. 331]. However, the great difficulty of scheduling sessions and coordinating treatment led Mudd (1955) to write, "We also, on the basis of experience, felt it was often confusing and even separating in effect upon the husband and wife [to see separate counselors] [p. 71]."

Psychoanalytic practices also made it difficult for marriage counselors to focus on the marital relationship. Instead of a distressed marriage, they saw two inadequate, neurotic people. For example, Berkowitz (1948) wrote, "Inevitably we see that people who come to us because of marriage difficulty have carried over unresolved childhood problems into marriage to an extensive degree [p. 1]." The focus on the individual was due to the current emphasis of personality theory, and, in the 1950s, a personality theory's focus on the *individual* had a profound influence on marriage counseling. For example, Sacks (1949) defined diagnosis as follows: "Diagnosis involved appraising each individual's behavior and personality in terms of his current functioning [p. 215]." What were the implications of this focus on the individual personality? Given the complexity of understanding *one* individual's personality, the possibility of understanding a marriage as the vector sum of several personalities, with each person having separate primary families and defense mechanisms of their own, must have seemed mind boggling. In fact, as late as 1965, in an important paper Gerald Handel stated his view of the central question of studying whole families in a way that demonstrated the enormous intellectual encumbrance inherited by individual personality theory. Handel's basic question was, "How do the several personalities in a family cohere in an ongoing structure that is both sustained and altered through interaction [p. 21, emphasis deleted]?" The conception of *interaction* as the major focus of counseling was a conceptual leap away from prevailing psychological theories.

Another important feature of marriage counseling in the 1950s was the view of women that was inherited from psychoanalysis as well as from the postwar cultural pressures to bring women back from the factories and into the kitchen.

BAD MARRIAGES AND "IMMATURE" WIVES

An artifact of the emphasis on individual personality combined with the fact that two-thirds of the individuals who sought treatment for marital problems were women was an orientation to marital therapy that would correctly be called sexist today. The woman became the focus of treatment. For example, in 1949, Sacks, who is a woman, presented her marital cases with the headings "Mrs. R." and "Mrs. C.," rather than "Mr. and Mrs." The description of one case illustrates the bias that operated to label the woman as the identified patient. Sacks wrote that Mrs. C. felt tied down by her child and had violent thoughts about it. She resented her husband's freedom, his ability to work and spend money on himself at will (which she could not do), and his lack of interest in the home or in the child. Sacks wrote that "arguments about budget and home management pointed up Mr. C.'s resentment of giving up so much of his earning to her [p. 220]." The case report also noted that "Mr. C.'s chief device for handling his wife was to walk out during an argument and refuse to speak for days. Occasionally he responded to her taunting by a sudden expression of aggression and would strike her [p. 222]." However, the summary of the case was that Mrs. C. required treatment because "Mrs. C.'s inability to assume a wife and mother role, her striking immaturity, made it impossible for Mr. C. to integrate his positive feelings and strivings into a mature relationship with his wife [p. 227]." Despite Mrs. C.'s request that one social worker see both her and her husband, "In view of the diagnostic formulation," Sacks wrote, "the assignment of separate workers was considered desirable [p. 223]." Perhaps the client's request was viewed by the case worker as simply another trick of an immature woman.

As willing clients, women were also willing targets for the label of immaturity. In one report of successful psychoanalysis with both husbands and wives, Mittleman (1948), a female analyst, worked with a woman who "felt worthless because she had experienced clitoral but not vaginal orgasm [p. 331]," which was interpreted as relating to her immaturity. Unfortunately, the myth of the vaginal orgasm was not criticized until 1971 by Masters and Johnson's research. The analyst also pointed out to the wife that her "aggressive" arguing with her husband was an indication of her desire to escape feelings of worthlessness by being superior to him and was seen as an indication of her penis envy.

Even though psychoanalysis exerted a great influence on counselors' conceptions of human sexuality, marriage counseling in the 1950s was also influenced by the Kinsey report. This important study led counselors directly to educate their clients about normal sexual behavior and physiology. Contrasted with this directive influence, which was so contrary to psychoanalysis, marriage counseling in the 1950s also had to contend with the growing influence of client-centered, nondirective therapy. In 1952 Carl Rogers addressed the National Council on Family Relations (Rogers, 1952), and it is clear from the text of the discussion that, despite the fact that at the time Rogers worked only with individuals and not at all on marital problems, prominent marriage counselors reported that, in response to Rogers' writing, they were becoming more nondirective in their own work. Over 10 years later, Shapiro and Budman (1965) were to identify nondirective methods as a major reason given by clients for their premature termination and defection from family and marital therapy. Therefore, the influence of nondirective therapy turned out to be unfortunate in marital and family therapy.

CHANGING CONCEPTIONS OF DIAGNOSIS AND TREATMENT

I have summarized the predominant mode of marriage counseling after World War II and in the 1950s. However, the thinking of one maverick, Nathan Ackerman, was to gain force during the late 1950s and to take form as "systems theory," and it is important to examine his point of view.

Ackerman was a pioneer. As early as 1937, he had written a paper on the unity of the family. In 1950, Ackerman and Sobel presented a model of family diagnosis that suggested that the family's *interaction patterns* and also marital interaction patterns ought to be the targets of diagnosis, rather than the identified patient's personality. Ackerman (1954) wrote, "of particular importance is the need to evaluate pathology of individual personality not in isolation, but within the frame or the psychosocial structure of the family . . . a central aspect of this study is the development of criteria for the diagnosis of *marital interaction* [p. 379, emphasis added]." This was a radical departure from diagnosis as the analysis of personality. Ackerman (1954) wrote:

> In undertaking to diagnose marital relationships, we are not concerned with the autonomous functions and pathology of individual personalities, but rather with the dynamics of the relationship, that is, with the reciprocal role functions that define the relations of husband and wife. A relationship represents more than the sum of the personalities that make it up. The whole is greater than the sum of its parts [p. 380].

Ackerman's analysis led him to reconceptualize both the diagnosis of marital dysfunction and the goals of psychotherapy.

First, calling for a major modification of psychoanalysis, Ackerman (1954) argued that the principles that govern relationships are not the same as those that govern the behavior of an individual. Next, he argued that the goal of psychotherapy with couples was to create "healthy" marital *interaction;* he even suggested that some marriages between neurotic individuals could be healthy even if the personalities of the partners remained neurotic. The major problem encountered by neurotics, he proposed, was when the "increased health and strength of one partner became an added menace to the other [p. 384]." He thus anticipated Jackson's (1957) concept of family homeostasis.

To analyze interaction, Ackerman employed the language of social psychology. In a family, the breakdown of healthy relationships results in what he called "prejudicial scapegoating." He suggested that scapegoating may be organized in a family around any of a set of issues, such as life-style issues (spontaneity versus control, for example) or obedience versus defiance. He proposed that diagnosis proceeds by the search for competing emotional alliances and for the "adaptive value of the secondary gains of illness [Ackerman, 1966, p. 87]."

Ackerman also suggested the transformation of the role of the family therapist from a passive to an active role. The therapist, he wrote, first discovers "the idiosyncratic language of the family," how the family talks and avoids talking about issues. Next,

> as the therapist strips away denials, displacements, rationalizations, and other disguises, the essential conflicts between and within family members come into clearer perspective. Acting as a catalyst, the therapist provokes increasingly candid disclosures of underlying currents of interpersonal conflict. . . . A further function of the family therapist is to neutralize prejudicial assault and scapegoating [1966, p. 96].

The family therapist's major techniques, Ackerman proposed, are confrontation, calling attention to "pathogenic" ways of interaction, and fostering the substitution of "healthier" ones. Ackerman called one of his techniques "tickling the defenses," which he described (Ackerman, 1966) as "a tactic of catching the family members by surprise, by exposing dramatic discrepancies between their self-justifying rationalizations and their subverbal attitudes [p. 97]." Ackerman's brand of family therapy thus implied an active, directive, confronting and dramatic therapist. The therapist, he suggested, also dramatizes the family's dysfunctional interaction patterns by focusing on nonverbal as well as verbal behavior. He wrote, "In the service of this effort he may make effective use of certain forms of "body talk." He confronts the members forthrightly with the meaning of certain units of nonverbal communication as reflected in mood, expression, posture, gesture, and movement [1966, p. 97]."

The family therapist, in Ackerman's view, was, therefore, not, as Ackerman described the psychoanalyst, "anonymous, a mirror for the patient's inner mental life [p. 101]." In fact, the therapist was described by Ackerman as the captain of a ship whose "calm, firm presence must offer the needed assurance against family catastrophe [p. 98]" and who "steers a path between the extremes of a rigid avoidance of the dangers of closeness and uncontrolled explosion of rage . . . [p. 98]." Like Odysseus steering between Skylla and Charybdis, the family therapist's activities were given the proportions of an epic adventure.

THE RISE OF SYSTEMS THEORY

Ackerman's viewpoints represented a major shift in orientation from the fixed personality of the individual to the more mercurial social interaction of the dyad. Although he deserves the role of founder, by the mid 1950s, in this shift Ackerman was not alone. He was part of a growing movement toward viewing the family as a social system and in confrontation as the tool of an active, directive therapist. Geurin's (1976) history of family therapy depicted the years between 1950 and 1954 as the period when family therapy "was more or less underground [p. 4]." During this period, the dramatic and strange confrontation therapy methods of John Rosen with schizophrenics attracted the interest of the Bateson group in California and the Bowen group at the Menninger Clinic.

The last half of the 1950s marked the public emergence of family therapy. Bateson, Haley, Jackson, and Weakland developed many of the basic concepts of family diagnosis and treatment. Jackson's 1957 paper on homeostasis presented examples of the upset in balance caused by any change in family conditions, particularly by the *improved* mental health of the identified patient in the family. Much of this early work was based on logical argument rather than on extensive clinical experience. Haley (1973) described the development of the double-bind theory of schizophrenia. He wrote, "In 1954 Bateson coined the term "double bind" and argued that it was etiologic to schizophrenia. This was deduced, not observed. Given the ways a schizophrenic confuses his levels of message, he must have been raised in a learning situation where his parents imposed conflicting messages [p. 114]." Later, the group began to observe schizophrenics and their families, and they subsequently modified the double-bind hypothesis to consider schizophrenia as a *response* to a current family process, rather than as purely etiologic. This shift had implications for family therapy. As Haley (1973) wrote, "To think of his behavior as *responsive,* so that change in his family was necessary if he was not to be schizophrenic, was a new way of thinking [p. 115]." In the last half of the 1950s, family therapists became more aware of one another. Haley (1973) wrote, "I believe it was in 1957 that we discovered other people who were doing family therapy [p. 115]." Family therapists were amazed by the similarity of their conceptualizations, and an active period of the development of therapeutic technique followed.

Public interest in family therapy was also facilitated by an error in reading comprehension. Olson (1970) wrote that John Bell misunderstood a report by John Bowlby and interpreted Bowlby's procedure as treating the whole family. Olson (1970) wrote that "after John Bell's report, others then began to speak more openly about their experiences with families in treatment [p. 504]."

THE NEXT TWENTY-FIVE YEARS OF SYSTEMS THEORY

Olson's (1970) review of the historical development of the fields of marital and family therapy made the following point about research methodology, that "both fields have much needed an empirical and theoretical base and neither group has had adequate training in research methodology or theory development. . . . Neither group has attempted much in terms of empirical investigations [p. 505]." Despite the truth of Olson's conclusions, it is nonetheless also true that "a body of principles have become widely accepted without these principles having been subjected to empirical test [Leslie, 1964, p. 67]."

A body of research literature, much of it of questionable methodological quality, has developed in the past 25 years. Since 1970, there have been two excellent reviews of research on marital therapy, by Gurman and Kniskern (1978) and Jacobson and Martin (1976). Gurman and Kniskern separately reviewed nonbehavioral and behavioral approaches to marital therapy, whereas Jacobson and Martin focused exclusively on behavioral therapy. Gurman and Kniskern reported that the typical nonbehavioral study used only one evaluative perspective of change (the therapist's or the client's), as well as a global measure of change or marital satisfaction. In an earlier review, Gurman (1973) also found that, in 75% of the studies on marital therapy, the therapist and the principal investigator were the same person, a criterion he used for negatively judging the design adequacy of the studies reviewed.

Gurman and Kniskern concluded that individual therapy for marital problems produced far lower rates of improvement than did other forms of therapy. Despite their confidence in this conclusion, it would be wise to avoid drawing any conclusions, since most of the outcome measures are based solely on therapist or client reports, which are highly subject to bias, and have not demonstrated that they have adequate psychometric properties. In a methodological comment, Gurman and Kniskern (1978) criticized behavioral therapy studies of marital and family therapy because they did not use the therapist's judgments of outcome. They wrote, "It is as if the implicit message were that despite the therapist's assumed expertise as a change-agent, he/she offers no uniquely valuable perspective in assessing clinical change! [p. 852; emphasis deleted]" This criticism misses the major contribution of a behavioral approach to therapy, which is epistemological, and intends to avoid the bias and self-protective congratulations that have characterized most other forms of marital and family therapy. Therapist ratings are notoriously subject to this bias.

Unfortunately, as we discussed in Chapter 1, systems approaches to family and marital therapy have not been subjected to systematic and rigorous investigation. Despite this fact, the approach has flourished and has become the predominant mode of therapy with couples and families. Clinical folklore appears to be a more powerful vehicle for establishing the consensual validity of ideas than is scientific method. A most remarkable accomplishment of family and marital therapists who call themselves systems theorists is that the same family therapists who were identified as impressive therapists 25 years ago are still considered impressive therapists without a shred of convincing evidence. This group still presents itself as courageous and revolutionary, when it has actually become insular and ingrown. The courage to subject one's hypothesis to potential disconfirmation is probably behavior therapy's major contribution. Without this courage, family therapy has remained essentially unchanged in a quarter of a century, and hypotheses continue to be accepted by repetition, in the same spirit in which American advertising sells its products. The clients are the major victims of this advertising campaign. It is fair to say that, by far, the best research on therapy outcome with couples has been behavioral, and I will now review that literature.

BEHAVIORAL MARITAL THERAPY

Behavioral approaches to therapy with couples were initially inspired by two sources, Lederer and Jackson's (1968) *Mirages of Marriage* and Patterson and Reid's (1970) paper on reciprocity and coercion in families. Lederer and Jackson developed Jackson's (1965) idea of the *quid pro quo* (something for something) as the implicit rule of successfully functioning relationships. The rule was similar in some respects to Thibaut and Kelley's (1959) behavior exchange theory, which led Patterson and Reid to test the hypothesis that couples match their rates of positive behaviors. These notions and the research methods used to test them have been critically reviewed in Chapter 3 of this book.

The first investigation of the marital behavior therapy literature was a paper by Stuart (1969). Stuart used the method of reciprocal *quid pro quo* contracts with four couples. In each case, "the couples sought treatment as a last-ditch effort prior to obtaining a divorce," and "In each instance, the wife listed as her first wish that her husband converse with her more fully [p. 678]." Tokens earned by husbands for conversation were "redeemable at the husband's request from a menu stressing physical affection [p. 679]." Couples also wished to increase the frequency of sexual intercourse. Stuart reported increases in conversation, sex, and marital satisfaction that persisted after 48 weeks. Stuart's approach may be criticized as an overly simplistic approach to marital distress (talk exchanged for sex), but its contribution lay in its specificity. Contracting was launched as a therapeutic procedure.

Azrin, Naster, and Jones (1973) assigned a set of contracts with 12 couples in a 4-week educational course that followed 3 weeks of what was poorly described as "an undirected 'catharsis-type' control procedure [p. 368]." They reported increases in marital satisfaction on their marital happiness items over and above those collected in the 3-week period, as well as increases in areas not directly counseled.

There were obvious methodological limitations to these first two investigations. First, the authors were the therapists, and this introduced a host of problems, including the impossibility of disentangling the stated procedures of therapy from the therapist. Second, in both studies, there was no control group. Third, the operations used to assess outcome were extremely limited, and their psychometric properties are unknown. Azrin *et al.* (1973) designed their own few items to measure marital happiness, oblivious to over 40 years of sociological research.

A major methodological breakthrough was made by the Oregon group (which included Patterson, Weiss, and their associates) in the development of measures such as the Marital Interaction Coding System (MICS), in their use of the Locke–Wallace marital adjustment scale, and in the development of the Spouse Observation Checklist (SOC). We have discussed the importance of these measures in this book. Using their experience in training parents of aggressive boys, the Oregon group also demonstrated that their measures met standards of reliability, and they used these measures in ways to minimize experimental bias (for example, by having MICS coders blind as to whether the tapes were pre- or posttherapy tapes).

The Oregon group also developed a complex multicomponent treatment package that was based on their clinical experience. The treatment package contained six modules:

1. Pinpointing contingencies for use in contracts using the pleases and displeases checklist (SOC), particularly those behaviors relating to relationship satisfaction
2. Teaching communication skills such as paraphrasing and reflecting spouse statements, a module that used modeling, behavior rehearsal,

and videotape, "depending on how readily clients proceed [Margolin, Christensen, & Weiss, 1975]

3. Teaching conflict resolution skills such as learning to decide whether the couple is in an "Emotional Expressiveness" modality or a "Problem Solving" modality

4. Using "utility matrices" for potential rewards (pleases) when drawing up contracts

5. Negotiating and contracting that are not *quid pro quo,* but "good faith" contracts. These contracts were intended to avoid mistrust and the "you go first" syndrome allegedly incurred by *quid pro quo* contracts

6. Terminating the treatment so that the therapist's activity is gradually faded and couples are required to become more active in negotiating their own contracts.

Jacobson and Martin (1976) pointed out that, although the results of the Oregon group with this treatment package are promising, "Nevertheless, conclusions regarding the effectiveness of the Oregon treatment package remain tentative due to the absence of control groups [p. 548]." Subsequently, in the two best studies in this area, Jacobson (1977, 1978) tested the effectiveness of a treatment package that he derived from the Oregon group's treatment package just described.

Jacobson (1977) randomly assigned 5 couples to an experimental group and 5 to a waiting-list control group. Using the MICS, he found that the treatment group decreased from pre- to posttest in the mean proportion of negative and increased in the mean proportion of positive MICS codes; there was no change for the waiting-list group. A similar pattern was obtained for the Locke–Wallace scale. A 1-year follow-up of the Locke–Wallace scores showed that marital satisfaction scores remained high. Jacobson was the only therapist for the couples, and, unfortunately, there was no follow-up MICS data.

Jacobson's initial study was the first report of a controlled investigation of a systematic, structured marital therapy procedure that used data beyond self-report measures. The results were especially interesting because of a methodological innovation Jacobson introduced. In addition to the group design, for four of the five experimental couples, a multiple-baseline design was used in which the individualized presenting complaints of each couple were monitored over the course of the treatment. In a multiple baseline design, both the bahaviors that are targeted for change and other behaviors are monitored over time; usually, specific effects are predicted only for targeted behaviors. If this occurs, and marital satisfaction also changes, then change on the targeted behavior is strongly implicated as relating to changes in marital satisfaction. A visual scan of the two graphs presented by Jacobson led him to conclude that the treatment interventions were responsible for the observed changes.

In a subsequent study, Jacobson (1978) compared a *quid pro quo* and good faith contract to a waiting-list control group and a nonspecific control group.

This control group was designed to resemble the therapy group in all ways except in the active ingredients of the therapy. The two forms of contracting were not different on any of the measures (frequency of positive and negative behaviors, Locke–Wallace score, and a marital happiness scale), but both groups were significantly different from the waiting-list group on all measures and from a nonspecific control group on three of the four measures (all except the marital happiness scale).

In this study, there were three therapists, none of whom were the author, and there were no significant therapist or therapist-by-treatment interactions. This is an important result, because it suggests that a replicable treatment method was developed. Furthermore, it reduces the therapist's role as the central charismatic change agent and mysterious artist. The two contracting groups decreased significantly in negative MICS behaviors, whereas the waiting-list group and the nonspecific control group did not change significantly; only good faith couples improved significantly more than did the nonspecific control group. Both experimental groups also showed similar patterns in Locke–Wallace scores, and these differences held upon follow-up. Jacobson's research is, clearly, the single most important contribution in marital therapy to date.

ASSESSMENT OF BEHAVIORAL MARITAL THERAPY TO DATE

There are two criteria we can apply to evaluate these experiments. The first is the criterion of effectiveness, and we must conclude that, for the first time since 1942, with a set of psychometrically sound outcome measurements and appropriately controlled experimental designs, there is now an approach to therapy that may prove effective for distressed couples. This is no small accomplishment, and it is due to the work of the Oregon group and Neil Jacobson. We must add that, even though the results are promising, all of these studies are based upon very small samples, and we must be cautious about these conclusions.

The second criterion for evaluating these experiments is an increased understanding of marital interaction and the processes of change, and on this criterion the research reviewed leaves two questions unanswered.

The first unanswered question concerns the empirical basis of the interventions. Any marital therapy intervention makes some assumptions about what is wrong with the marriage and what it must be like for it to be a better marriage. The assumptions of this work have evolved and developed their own brand of clinical folklore, in much the same way as systems family therapy evolved.

The first empirical investigation reviewed as a study by Stuart (1969). The assumption of this study was that couples in distress needed to negotiate reciprocal agreements so that an equitable exchange of positive behaviors characterize the marriage, rather than the mechanism Patterson and Reid (1970) called "coercion." In a coercive marriage, each person exercises control by initiating a sequence of escalating aversive behaviors that are terminated only by the spouse's complaince. This hypothesis of a distressed marriage was extrapolated from Patterson's work with families with problem children. The children exercised control by escalating their aversive behaviors until their parents eventually gave in. Coercive control, thus, hypothesizes a sequence of escalating demands delivered with negative affect by one spouse that is eventually terminated by agreement or compliance by the partner.

There is no evidence that such a sequence characterizes distressed marital interaction. In fact, we have reported in this book that distressed marital interaction is not characterized by the *termination* of negative affect cycles, but rather by their continuation. However, Stuart's therapy procedure assumed *both* that coercive control was indeed the problem of his four couples *and* that a reciprocal exchange of positive behaviors would replace the coercive sequence. The *quid pro quo* was, thus, a technological invention designed to replace coercive interaction. Note that this does not follow directly from a coercive control assumption. To change the coercive control sequence, it might be sufficient to modify the consequences of an aversive control attempt. The assumption behind Stuart's intervention is that coercive control is the *only* means of obtaining agreement or compliance in the distressed marriage, and if another mechanism (the *quid pro quo*) is substituted, then aversive control tactics should extinguish. This is a hope more than a logical argument, since one would expect aversive control tactics to extinguish partly as an inverse function of how reinforcing their consequences remain.

A second unanswered question concerns the ingredients of the intervention. Historically, *quid pro quo* contracting had to be supplemented by other therapeutic methods. Therapists who used contracting methods to establish the *quid pro quo* as the new interaction pattern of the distressed couple reported that they also had to include some reeducation of the couple's perception of their marriage. This point was made in Stuart's (1969) early paper. In subsequent studies, this reeducation developed into a full-blown component of therapy that was added to the contracting intervention; it became known as "communication skill training."

At this time, it is difficult to disentangle the communication skill component from the contracting component, since they tend to be so closely entwined in this research. In a recent paper, Witkin (1977) compared the Weiss therapy program to the Minnesota Couples Communication Program (Nunnally, Miller, & Wackman, 1975). The comparison is interesting because, to the extent that one can judge from published descriptions (see Miller, Nunnally, & Wackman, 1976), by a fortunate historical accident the Minnesota Couples Communication Program, which appears to have been influenced by sensitivity training concepts as represented by the National Training Laboratory, does not seem to include *quid pro quo* contracting. Using the MICS, Witkin found that couples in the Minnesota program were less negative nonverbally and more positive nonverbally on follow-up than were the couples in the Weiss program. It may, therefore, be the case that contracting is not the only essential active ingredient in the Jacobson and Weiss experiments.

Further evidence that aspects of the intervention other than contracting or skill training may be important is provided by a study by McLean, Ogston, and Graver (1973), who evaluated a multicomponent skill training program for married couples in which one spouse was depressed. Eighty percent of the identified patients were women. The comparison group received a variety of treatments for depression, none of which included marital therapy. The experimental group received (a) "training in social learning principles [p. 325]," by which they meant increasing the frequency of positive statements and decreasing the frequency of negative statements; (b) "immediate feedback as to the perception of verbal interactions between patient and spouse [p. 325]," a component that used a device called "cue boxes" that were very similar to the talk table (Chapter 12); using the cue boxes, couples activated a green light "whenever they felt their spouse was being supportive, constructive, complimentary or otherwise positive in reaction to their discussion [p. 325]"; and (c) "training in the construction and use of reciprocal behavioral contracts."

Patients in the experimental group reported significant improvement in their original symptoms related to depression, in depression adjective checklist scores, and the experimenters found a decrease in the proportion of negative statements on half-hour recordings of home interactions. No such changes occurred in the comparison group.

The "talk-table" component of the treatment was interesting for several reasons. First, these authors reported that, "After approximately 6 hours of spaced home practice with cue boxes, couples in a pilot study reported little advantage in continuing with cue boxes, inasmuch as increased sensitivity to interpersonal social cues rendered them unnecessary [p. 326]." Second, the proportion of negative feedback cues declined from 61% to 45% for the depressed patient and from 44% to 39% for the spouse from the first to the last therapy session. Third, the authors felt that this component was an active ingredient of the observed changes. They wrote:

> Patients in the experimental group responded positively to the application of feedback techniques and to the specificity involved in reciprocal behavior contracts. Many had been unaware of the aspects of their verbal behavior the spouse considered as either positive or negative. What was intended as a constructive comment (i.e., "you'd feel better if you didn't weep so much") was perceived by the spouse as criticism.

Important aspects of contracting may be its use in changing the couple's perception of the problem from global to specific and in teaching each spouse what the partner considers positive.

To summarize, behavioral marital therapy research to date meets the criterion of effectiveness but not the criterion of understanding process, and the research is, thus, in the somewhat embarrassing position of having to explain the effectiveness of a complex, multicomponent program the design of which was not based on a sound empirical footing.

An alternative to the method by which the behavioral marital therapy programs have evolved is to build the intervention program empirically, basing its design on a knowledge of what interactional and cognitive processes discriminate distressed from nondistressed couples. I will now discuss this approach to clinical intervention.

EMPIRICAL PROGRAM DEVELOPMENT

The concept of empirical program development is not new; its roots lie in the study of intellectual functioning. It was implicit in the charge made to Binet and Simon in 1908 by the French Ministry of Education. They were to find a method for understanding children with learning problems that would lead to the identification of processes that discriminated problem from nonproblem learners, such that these processes could be used for the design of remedial programs. In the original plan, assessment, process, and intervention were closely linked. This concept was, unfortunately, later modified by Terman in the United States and Spearman in England.

The concept of empirical program development has also been described in the important work of Butterfield and his colleagues. Butterfield (1978) outlined the steps for using instruction to understand the processes that differentiate a target from a nontarget population. He suggested four steps following the identification of two groups as "proficient" and "deficient."

The first step is to *analyze the processes of the task* on which the discrimination of people into proficient and deficient groups is based. The second step is to use measures of process to show that such a differentiation of groups is possible. The third step is to teach deficient people to process as proficient ones and then to demonstrate that this raises their performance to the level of similarly instructed proficient people. The fourth step is the reverse of the third, that is, to show that, if proficient people are taught to process as deficient people, their performance will show a decrement. The two groups Butterfield studied were normal and retarded people. The task was a serial memory task on which practice was permitted, and the process measure involved rehearsal; that is, the process of importance was based on the observation that retarded people did not rehearse on this task, whereas normal people did.

It is interesting that, in the area of social skill training, the same basic strategy for empirical program development was independently proposed by Goldfried and D'Zurrilla (1969). They suggested three steps for program development following identification of two groups, called "competent" and "incompetent." The first step is *situational analysis,* in which a domain of social situations is identified that is problematic to the target (incompetent) group. The second step is *response enumeration,* which is a construction of a domain of possible alternative responses to each problematic situation. The third step is *response evaluation,* to judge each alternative response on some criterion (see Goldfried & Linehan, 1977).

An example of the application of the Goldfried and D'Zurrilla model is the work of McFall and his associates on assertion training (see Goldsmith & McFall, 1975; McFall & Lillesand, 1971, McFall & Marston, 1970, and McFall & Twentyman, 1973).

Gottman and Markman (1978) reviewed these approaches to program development and evaluation and suggested a general procedure that could be applied to psychotherapy research. Applied to marital therapy, the procedure is, first, to find process dimensions that distinguish marriages that are believed by the spouses to be functioning well from marriages that are believed by the spouses to be functioning badly. In this book, the process measures identified in the Structural Model complete this step of program development. Based on these process differences, the second step is to design an intervention program that teaches couples who believe their marriages are functioning badly to interact (according to the Structural Model) as do couples who believe their marriages are functioning well. The third step is to classify couples according to the social skills taught in the program and to discover what kinds of gains are made by what kinds of couples. This knowledge could then lead to modification of the program based on an understanding of deficits of specific types of couples (with respect to the social skills taught by the program) and how these interact with the program.

The Relationship between Effectiveness and Process Issues

The issues of the effectiveness of the program and an understanding of process are separate, but these issues have not been separately addressed in the literatures on social skill training or behavioral marital therapy. An important indication of the separateness of these two issues is that what must be demonstrated for an understanding of process is that *to the extent that people in the target population master the skills taught by the program, they will become like the people in the nontarget population.* This is a claim far different from the simple effectiveness claim, which is that people in the target population will become like people in the nontarget population after they complete the program.

A simple example may help to clarify the distinction. Suppose that a tennis player develops a new system for playing tennis that involves a new kind of serve and backhand. Suppose further that this program was derived empirically, for example, by comparing the videotapes of winners with those of losers. To test the program's understanding of process, we only need to demonstrate that people who master the new backhand and serve are more likely to win tennis matches than are people who do not master the new backhand and serve.

This is a different claim from the effectiveness claim, which states that people who take the new tennis course will be better players. Many factors can intervene to limit the effectiveness claim, including the starting ability of the students, how poor their previous training was, how ingrained their poor habits are, how motivated they are to improve their game, how good a teacher they have in the course, how well-designed the program of instruction is, and so on. None of these factors is related to the basic validity of the new tennis program. Of course, both questions are of interest to a potential student who is deciding on whether or not to take the tennis course or whether to take this course or some other course of comparable expense. Nonetheless, the interests of the consumer are not the same as the interests of the theoretician of the game of tennis.

This distinction is crucial in the analysis of the empirically derived therapy program for couples that will be discussed in this chapter.

Of course, there are some basic conceptual differences between a marital therapy program and a tennis program. It would be very difficult, for example, simply to instruct a distressed couple to be less negative nonverbally if they feel negative, even though negative affect is a central process dimension of the Structural Model related to marital satisfaction. Only some dimensions will make sense to couples as ingredients of an intervention program. Hence, the ingredients of the intervention program may have to be designed to influence the process variables rather than to modify them directly. It may, therefore, become necessary to hope that what is taught by the intervention program affects the basic process dimensions that cannot be taught directly but that are presumed to affect marital satisfaction.

Alexander and his associates (see Alexander & Barton, 1976) followed this approach with families with a delinquent member. The process distinction was based on a defensive versus supportive code, assessed from the interaction of families with a delinquent or nondelinguent member. However, the intervention consisted of a complex package including contracting, "clear communication of substance and feeling, . . . clear presentation of 'demands' and alternatives, . . . negotiations, wherein all family members receive payoff when they reciprocally compromise [Alexander & Barton, 1976, p. 178]," therapists' distinguishing "requests" from "rules," training in social reinforcement, and token economies. The therapy was, thus, not directly related to the process variables. Only the experimental group changed significantly from pretest to posttest on process measures. The outcome measures were recidivism of delinquent behavior in the target child after 3–15 months and the number of nontargeted siblings referred. This research program illustrates the methodological point that it is possible to assess the extent to which improvement on process measures relates to improvement on outcome measures even when the intervention does not appear to affect *directly* the process measures. The problem introduced by a complex intervention program is that it is difficult to assess what aspects of the program were responsible for changes in the criterion. However, the problem can be circumvented if the research question concerns only the relationship between process and criterion variables.

The common statistical procedure of computing a multiple correlation between process and outcome measures can be used to assess how changes on process variables contribute differentially to changes on the outcome measures. Both control and experimental subjects can be combined for this analysis, since it may be that some control-group subjects also serendipitously change on the process variables, and one would wish to include all natural variability into the regression equation. Thus, the process question about an intervention program can be addressed by a single regression equation. The equation would also give information on the differential usefulness of several process dimensions in predicting change on the outcome measures, which might affect the design of the therapy procedures.

We have considered two criteria to evaluate a therapy program, process understanding, which used the regression equation between process and outcome, and effectiveness. An integrated evaluation of an intervention program that addresses both questions can be divided into three phases. The first phase involves a demonstration of the process equation. As the intervention program becomes more effective, there will be a restriction of range in process and outcome measures, and the size of the regression coefficients should decrease. The regression equation would, thus, be most useful in the early phase of program development. If the process test supports our claims but the program is not effective, we proceed to a second phase of the evaluation, in which the effectiveness of a modified program is tested.

The second phase of the program's development and evaluation may consist of a replication of phase one (perhaps with a modified program), possibly with an extension of the effectiveness claim to test transfer of therapeutic gains outside the laboratory. Transfer of training has been proposed as an important issue in behavior change research (see, for example, Nay, 1976).

The third phase consists of an exploration of the limits of the program's effectiveness. One type of phase three study is the classification study, in which the question is "What kinds of couples are helped most and helped least by the program?"

The three phases have both theoretical and practical import. Each phase results in the modification of the program and in the enhancement of its effectiveness. The theoretical aspect of the evaluation lies in perfecting the model that relates process variables to outcome variables. The three phases are summarized in Figure 14.1.

Choice of a Criterion Measure of Marital Satisfaction

A note should be added on the choice of a criterion variable. At the time of this writing, the most commonly used measure of marital satisfaction in therapy research is the Locke–Wallace (1959) inventory. However, when the research project reported in this book began in 1973, a modification of the Locke–Williamson Marital Relationship Inventory (MRI) was selected, based on a recommendation by Burgess, Locke, and Thomes (1971). Since the MRI was the

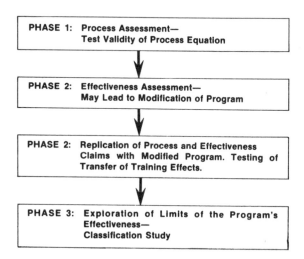

Figure 14.1 *Flowchart of the three phases in program development and evaluation.*

criterion variable for the research that was used to develop the intervention program, it continued to be the criterion for assessing therapeutic gains. To compare the two measures, in a recent study in my laboratory, 22 couples filled out both inventories, in counterbalanced order. For husbands, the Locke–Williamson and the Locke–Wallace correlated .886, and for wives they correlated .558. Thus, particularly considering the correlation for wives, it is possible that, although the two forms have a great deal of common variance, they are, to some extent, different. Furthermore, mean scores tend to be higher on the Locke–Wallace, although the standard recommended *cutoff* scores are the same. The husbands' mean and standard deviation was 102.500 and 8.954 for the Locke–Williamson and 120.136 and 17.902 for the Locke–Wallace. The wives' mean and standard deviation was 104.318 and 7.247 for the Locke–Williamson and 122.227 and 16.239 for the Locke–Wallace. A cutoff score of 100 is commonly used in *both* inventories for discriminating "highs" and "lows" in marital satisfaction, but these data show that a score of 100 on the Locke–Wallace is correlated with one about 18 points lower on the Locke–Williamson (MRI). Another salient difference between the two forms is that there are items on the Locke–Williamson MRI that are not likely to change from pre- to posttest because the items ask for factual historical information about the marriage, such as how many issues have actually been marital problems and because high weight is given to marital happiness ratings on the Locke–Wallace. Thus, the two measures are similar but not equivalent; readers should be cautious in generalizing from one measure to the other, and the MRI is probably not as sensitive a measure of change as the Locke–Wallace.

To continue this comparison between marital satisfaction scores obtained from the Locke–Williamson inventory with those obtained from the Locke–

Wallace inventory, I conducted a small validity study. Wills *et al.* (1974) had found that the Locke–Wallace inventory predicted home recording rates of pleases, displeases, and pleases-to-displeases ratios. To compare the Locke–Williamson inventory with the Locke–Wallace inventory, 6 clinic and 8 non-clinic couples (selected exactly as described in Chapter 6) recorded positive and negative interactional events ("pleases," P and "displeases," D) daily for 7 days using a golf counter with two cumulators. The record keeping procedure used was similar to that described by Wills, Weiss, and Patterson (1974), with the exception that there were no "love day" instructions. The mean proportion of husband-plus-wife pleases to pleases plus displeases (P/(P + D)) was .62 for clinic couples, and .87 for nonclinic couples, $t(12) = 1.92$, $p < .05$. The daily means of pleases and displeases were 71.2 and 40.5, respectively, for clinic couples, and 141.6 and 13.4, respectively, for non-clinic couples $\chi^2 (2) = 30.69$, $p < .001$. There was thus a tendency for nonclinic couples to report being more positive *and* less negative at home than clinic couples. These results demonstrate, above common method correlation, that the Locke–Williamson and Lock–Wallace inventories are tapping a similar dimension, despite the possibility that the MRI is not as sensitive a measure of change.

DESCRIPTION OF AN EMPIRICALLY DERIVED MARITAL THERAPY PROGRAM

An intervention program was derived from the research reported in Chapters 6 and 12 of this book, and it was published by Gottman, Notarius, Gonso, and Markman (1976) in a book designed for couples. There are five concepts, or social skills, that comprise the intervention program. Gottman *et al.* (1976), in a "preface for the professional," summarized these social skills as follows:

> 1. *Listening and Validation* deals with reducing the proportion of summary statements that are Summarizing Self (SS) and ending what we call the "SS Syndrome." The skill taught is check-out and paraphrasing; the cognitive organizer is the intent–impact model, which we get from our talk-table studies. *Validation* is a skill related to the higher frequency of "accepting" behaviors, such as assent and agreement (see Weiss *et al.*, 1973), when one's spouse is expressing feelings. Validating a spouse's position does not usually imply agreement with the position to non-distressed couples but, rather, communicates "I can see how you think and feel that way, even if I don't see it the way you do." The *objective of this chapter* is to enable couples to get feedback on intent–impact discrepancies, call a "Stop Action" when there is a discrepancy, and use the Interim Troubleshooting Guide to find an intervention (usually a listening and validation procedure) to improve communication. The chapter also begins to build a language of "marital games" that can be used as tags of specific behavior patterns so that the couple can monitor and intervene to change these patterns. Rather than teach couples directly to mindread with

positive nonverbal behavior, we do it indirectly. We make them aware of mindreading as a way of attributing blame. We do not expect to eliminate mindreading, but we do expect to affect its nonverbal delivery.

2. *Leveling* is a skill to reduce mindreading (attributing feelings, thoughts, motives, behaviors) of the spouse, which distressed couples usually do with negative, nonverbal cues. Leveling reduces blaming. It is well-known that distressed couples' complaints are general attacks on a spouse's character. The behavioral objective is to be able to transform such a general attack to a specific statement, such as "When you do X in situation Y, I feel Z," so that this statement can become an agenda item. To assist in this process, the feeling chart, assertion instructions, discussions of catastrophic expectations, and the suggestion box are methods based upon an analysis of the components of the leveling task from our knowledge of couples who have trouble leveling. These couples are the conflict avoiders who feel lonely, cut off, or who intellectualize feelings and issues. We also found that in nondistressed marriages the nonverbal behavior of the listener was more positive while the spouse was expressing feelings than it was in distressed marriages. This finding relates to our stress on being a good receiver of leveling statements (Chapter 2).

3. *Editing* is a skill designed for couples continually engaging in bickering or escalating quarrels. For the extreme case, we wrote Chapter 7, "Getting through a Crisis." For the nonextreme case, it is well-known that even highly distressed couples are capable of being nice to strangers. This has been found in research (Birchler, Weiss, & Vincent, 1975; Halverson & Waldrop, 1970; Ryder, 1968; Winter, Ferreira, & Bowers, 1973) and is also a part of many books on etiquette (such as Eleanor Roosevelt's (1962) book).

This chapter teaches couples to proofread their own behavior so that they can self-control escalating quarrels. They learn to "edit" the scripts of other couples, they learn nine rules of politeness, and then learn specific etiquette rules with one another (Chapter 7). Even for couples engaged in escalating quarrels, editing works as a renewal process so that they can back off, act like strangers, get in touch, and level within a climate of positive or considerate behavior.

4. *Negotiating agreements* has the objective of identifying three parts of a "Family Meeting"—gripe time, agenda-building time, and problem-solving time. At the end of this segment, couples may still begin a Family Meeting with negative nebulous complaints, but they learn to change them into specific negative complaints (Leveling) and then into positive suggestions.

To achieve closure of the Family Meeting, we have the couple use the "Up Deck," a deck of cards containing specific behaviors that they decide to increase in frequency. A contract is used to close the deal. This latter part of the Family Meeting using contracting is a common part of many behavior therapy approaches to couples and to family therapy (Alexander, 1973; Azrin, Naster, & Jones, 1973; Leaderer & Jackson, 1968; Stuart, 1969; Weiss, Hops, & Patterson, 1973). We find that nondistressed couples have more PL/AG sequences (where one person proposes a plan and the other agrees) and more AM (accepting modification of one's own position) and that these tend to occur in the last third of the discussion. In fact, the first third of a discussion for distressed couples is characterized by more communication about communication (meta communication) statements than is true for nondistressed couples. We describe this in Chapter 5, "Hidden Agendas" (Gottman, 1976).

5. *Hidden Agendas* deals with wheel-spinning in discussions and is related to an unstated issue of positiveness, responsiveness, or status (Mehrabian, 1972). It also begins to get at issues of closeness. We have found that some couples who learn the first four skills will say something like "The marriage is better, but it's still dull," or "I still feel cut off, lonely." Hidden agenda dimensions, when addressed, begin to get at these marital issues. (pp. xxi–xxiv)

Details of these skills, including materials and exercises for the couple, are included in the text and appendices of Gottman *et al.* (1976).

PHASE ONE ASSESSMENT

An advertisement was placed in the local newspaper announcing a "Couples Communication Program." Interested couples were asked to come to a public meeting in the local public library. There they were met by the author, who explained that there would be two formats of the program that would be tested, an "individual" and a "group" format. The individual format was a control group (described later). Couples were informed that they would have to sign up for the program and that they would be randomly assigned to one of the formats.

Couples who signed up for the program made appointments for preassessment in the laboratory, which consisted of signing a consent form describing the assessment procedures (pre- and post-) and both formats of the communication program and of being informed of their rights to confidentiality and to discontinue their participation at any time. This procedure was required by the University's Human Subjects Committee. Couples then filled out the Demographic Information Sheet, the Marital Relations Inventory (MRI), and the Problem Inventory. Following the standard play-by-play interview by one project staff member on the major marital issue, each couple was videotaped attempting to come to a mutually satisfying decision of this issue. These procedures are identical to those described previously in this book. The postassessment differed from the preassessment in only one way—a brief short answer and multiple-choice test of the concepts in the book (titled "What Do You Remember?") was also administered. This test was designed to check the control-group manipulation; couples in this group were expected to score lower on this test than couples in the "group" format.

Couples were informed about which format they had been assigned to after the preassessment was completed. The couples in the "individual" format were in a bibliotherapy control group. They received all the materials from the Gottman *et al.* (1976) book (then in manuscript form), and they were assigned a "consultant" (the interviewer), whom they could telephone for up to six half-hour individual sessions, at their discretion. It was predicted that few couples in this group would read the materials, practice the recommended exercises, or take advantage of the consultant's time. This was generally the case; only two couples of the six in this group called a consultant; one couple scheduled an appointment, and one couple asked questions on the telephone but did not schedule an individual meeting.

Couples in the group format (the experimental group) met for eight consecutive 3-hour sessions held in a local church on Monday evenings. Each session began with an examination on assigned readings, followed by a lecture and demonstration. After the lecture and demonstration, each couple worked with a "consultant" for the evening in exercises designed to teach each communication skill introduced in the lecture and to apply each skill to a real marital issue. Consultants rotated to a new couple each week, a procedure that was adopted to maximize learning by giving each consultant experience with as many couples as possible.

Consultants were either graduate students in counseling or staff members in our laboratory who had had extensive experience coding videotapes but no formal training in counseling or clinical psychology. All consultants were trained by a graduate student in clinical psychology in a group in seven 2-hour sessions. The sessions consisted of discussions on the Gottman et al. (1976) manuscript and of role-plays that were to be used in the experimental group. Consultants were instructed to be helpful to the couple and supportive of any gains they observed, to admit their limitations, to keep referring the couple back to the skills being learned, and to ask for help from a supervisor when in doubt. Consultants were supervised during the study by one of the authors of the Gottman et al. (1976) book.

Subjects

There were 23 couples who signed up for the preassessment. Half of these couples had been randomly assigned to a bibliotherapy control group and half to the experimental group, but only 17 of the 23 couples completed the preassessment; 11 had been assigned to the experimental group and 6 to the control group.

There were no significant demographic differences or marital satisfaction differences between these two groups. The average age of bibliotherapy control group (C) husbands were 33.33 years, and the average of experimental group (E) husbands was 32.91, $t(15) = .11$; for wives, the C group average age was 32.33, and the E group average age was 31.36, $t(15) = .26$. The average number of years married was 10.33 for the C group and 7.91 for the E group, $t(15) = .77$. The average number of children for the C group was 2.33 and 1.92 for the E group, $t(15) = .83$. The average husband MRI score was 89.33 for the C group and 89.91 for the E group, $t(15) = .12$; for wives, these marital satisfaction scores were 90.17 for the C group and 90.55 for the E group, $t(15) = .06$.

Of the 6 couples in the C group, within the 10-week period between pre- and postassessment, 3 separated and later divorced. One of these three couples could not be persuaded to return for a postassessment, but two of the separated couples did return for a postassessment. None of the couples in the E group separated during this period, nor did any of them separate or divorce within the next year.

Surprisingly, there were no significant differences in postknowledge test scores between the two groups. Two people scored the test independently, and their intercorrelation was .97 for husbands and .96 for wives. Control husbands averaged 18.9 and E husbands averaged 25.0, $t(15) = .91$; control wives averaged 15.9 and E wives averaged 23.1, $t(15) = .91$. The maximum score on the test was 67.0. There was a great deal of variability in scores within both C and E groups, which suggests that some couples in each group mastered or did not master the basic concepts in the materials. This was true despite the enormous difference in time the staff spent with the two groups of couples. This may suggest that couples can do as well learning the concepts from the materials without intensive guidance as they can with intensive guidance. Perhaps the major difference that will be observed between groups will be on the process measures derived from interaction data, as a function of the greater rehearsal time the E group had with the exercises.

Process Variables

The Structural Model provides the process variables. Changes on these process variables will be used to predict changes in the couple's MRI score. There are five process variables: Variable 1 is the change from pre to post in the proportion of husband affect that is negative, and Variable 2 is the same variable for the wife's negative affect; Variable 3 is the change from pre to post in Z-score for negative-affect reciprocity with the husband's negative affect as the criterion, and Variable 4 is the equivalent change in Z-score with the wife's negative affect as the criterion; Variable 5 is the change in dominance from pre to post, assessed as the slope of the phase spectrum. Recall that this measure is to be interpreted as asymmetry in emotional responsiveness, with the wife more responsive than the husband.

Because each of these variables must be calculated separately for each videotape, a minimum recording time of 1 hour was used for this study. Table 14.1 is a summary of the correlation matrix for changes in criterion and with changes in the process variables. The pattern of correlations indicates that changes in process measures within one dimension of the Structural Model are more highly correlated than are changes across dimensions. Furthermore, there is some evidence that changes in process measures are significantly correlated with changes in the couple's marital satisfaction. In particular, decreases in the wife's negative affect predict increases in the couple's marital satisfaction. Although nonsignificant, there is some possibility that changes in asymmetry in

TABLE 14.1
Summary of Phase One Assessment

	1	2	3	4	5
1. changes in couple's marital satisfaction	—				
2. changes in husband negative affect	-.161	—			
3. changes in wife negative affect	-.545*	.714**	—		
4. changes in reciprocity (husband criterion)	.054	.156	.192	—	
5. changes in reciprocity (wife criterion)	-.002	.448*	.319	.682**	—
6. changes in dominance	.323	-.109	-.254	-.462*	.121	—

*p<.05
**p<.01

emotional responsiveness away from a negative slope of the phase spectrum (husband less responsive) also predict increases in marital satisfaction.

The multiple correlation coefficient indicates the combined ability of changes in the process variables to predict changes in the criterion variable. The multiple correlation coefficient was .658, which is some, but not an impressive, increase over the .545 correlation magnitude for changes in negative wife-affect.

One problem with the asymmetry in emotional responsiveness measure (also called "dominance") as a change measure is that one cannot distinguish between changes toward an equalitarian pattern (from negative to zero slope) and changes toward the wife's being less emotionally responsive than her husband (from negative to positive slope). It would, thus, be interesting to compute changes in the *absolute value* of the amount of asymmetry. A reduction in this variable would be equivalent to a reduction in *any* asymmetry in emotional responsiveness, be it husband or wife. When changes in this variable (call it "absolute dominance patterning") are substituted for changes in the dominance variable, the multiple correlation coefficient becomes .757, which is a reasonable increase over .545. This is especially interesting because changes in absolute dominance patterning are not correlated with changes in marital satisfaction ($r = -.032$). Change in absolute dominance patterning is, thus, a suppressor variable (Wiggins, 1973); in fact, change in absolute dominance patterning is correlated with change in negative reciprocity [.517 with $Z(W-|H-)$ and .389 with $Z(H-|W-)$], so the change in absolute dominance patterning thus sharpens the regression by eliminating irrelevant variance between changes in the criterion and changes in negative reciprocity. This completes the process equation analyses.

An analysis of variance on changes in couples' marital satisfaction, performed to assess the effectiveness of the intervention, resulted in a significant change, $F(1,14) = 5.203, p < .05$. Most of this change came from changes in the husband's marital satisfaction, $F(1,14) = 4.996, p < .05$. The control group dropped from a mean of 92.6 to 86.2, and the experimental group increased from a mean of 89.9 to 92.3. Changes in wife's marital satisfaction were not significantly different across groups, $F(1,14) = 1.914$, n.s.; the control group dropped from a mean of 94.0 to 90.8, and the experimental group increased from a mean of 90.6 to 94.4. Although encouraging, these changes are not extremely impressive, but perhaps the divorce and separation rates can be added to the overall findings; recall that half of the control group divorced within a year of the study, whereas none of the experimental group did. To some extent, the bibliotherapy group was an intervention for two of the couples in this group, who increased in marital satisfaction, decreased in wife negative-affect, and had high posttest knowledge scores. The study did support the contention that the process variables were predictive of changes in the criterion, which was the objective of this study.

The intervention at this phase of the research cannot be judged as highly effective. Discussion of the program after the posttest with the couples in the experimental group gave us a consistent picture of their dissatisfactions. They found the weekly Monday meetings tedious; they often spent Mondays dreading an evening of marital conflict, and many times they debated or decided not to attend. They also felt that there was too much material to read, and usually they did not do the assigned homework. Several couples recommended that less material be presented in a briefer period, such as a weekend workshop, suggested that we not rotate consultants, suggested that a more pleasant atmosphere could be created by having a potluck lunch prepared by the participants, and stated that follow-up sessions in the home would be valuable in assisting them to apply the communication skills. This was precisely the format we tested in the second phase. Because so many separations occurred in the bibliotherapy group, it was considered unethical to repeat this control, and other designs for the experiment were considered.

PHASE TWO ASSESSMENT

Once again, an advertisement was placed in the local newspaper, this time announcing two weekend sessions of a "Couples Communication Workshop." Interested couples telephoned the laboratory, and, after preassessment, they were randomly assigned to the first workshop (held at the end of February) or to the second (held in April). The experimental design for this study is the time-lagged control design (see Gottman, McFall, & Barnett, 1969) portrayed in Table 14.2. The design has two halves. Couples in Group 2 constituted what I will call an "invited treatment" control group that was preassessed twice at times corresponding to the pre- and postassessments of the couples in Group 1. The logic of this design was to avoid the well-known problem of waiting-list

TABLE 14.2
Design of Phase Two Study

	Time Line				
Group 1	Pre Assessment (Mid February)	Workshop (End of February)	Post Assessment (End of March)	—	Followup (Mid May to Mid August)
Group 2	Pre Assessment No. 1 (Mid February)	—	Pre Assessment No. 2 (End of March)	Workshop (Mid April)	Post Assessment (Mid May)

control groups, namely, that people seek help elsewhere. Since the date of the second workshop was set and scheduled not too far from the first assessment, it would be less likely for couples to seek help elsewhere during the waiting period. The post assessment for Group 1 took place approximately 2 weeks after the last two sessions were held that followed the workshop. These follow-up sessions were conducted individually by the consultant who had worked with the couple during the weekend workshop. The second half of the design constitutes, in part, an independent replication of the effects of the workshop. It is only partly a replication, because Group 2 has experienced two assessments before the workshop instead of one, and there is some reason to believe that assessment in the laboratory is in itself therapeutic (see Chapter 13). Finally, the design included both a postassessment for Group 2 that also took place 2 weeks after the two sessions that followed the workshop were completed (about 4 weeks after the workshop) and a follow-up assessment for Group 1 that took place approximately 2 months (but in some cases as long as 5 months) after the last of the two sessions following the workshop.

Half of the couples in each group were randomly selected to complete their assessment tapes at home, as described in Chapter 13, and half of the couples in each group were selected to complete their tapes in the laboratory. All tapes were limited to a half-hour in length in order to reduce the amount of coding, since there were to be three assessments per group in this study, instead of two. Both video- and audiotapes were coded as described in Chapter 13, with affect coding based entirely on voice tone. Once again, coders were unaware that an intervention study had been performed, nor were they aware of the order in which the tapes were made. The home tapes had two purposes; one purpose was to use the preassessment tapes to determine the generalizability of interaction patterns from laboratory to home, and another purpose was to assess transfer of therapeutic change on interactional process variables to the home (see Figure 14.1).

A detailed description of this revised format, the workshop, and all the materials for lectures and scripts for role-plays and demonstrations is presented in Gottman (1976). The film shown on Sunday is distributed by Research Press. The schedule is:

SATURDAY
9:00   Coffee; each couple meets a consultant.
9:30   "What Is Communication?" lecturette, followed by a structured role-play by staff, a lecturette on feedback, and role-play by staff
10:00 The floor exercise—each couple works with a consultant
11:00 Constructive talking and constructive listening lecturette, and role-plays by staff
12:00 Potluck lunch and socializing
1:00   Politeness lecturette and role-play by staff
1:45   Getting in touch exercise—each couple works with a consultant
3:00   The "Family Meeting" lecturette
3:15   Family Meeting exercise using the Up-deck
5:00   Couples leave for day; staff meeting
SUNDAY
1:00   Coffee; each couple meets with consultant.
1:30   Hidden agenda lecturette and role-play by staff; show film *Three Styles of Marital Conflict*
2:00   Discuss film in group, pinpointing dysfunctional interaction patterns
2:30   Exercise in which couples use communication skills to work on one marital issue, this time, examining any hidden agendas
4:00   Consultants discuss homework, and couple lists all the ways that doing homework can be sabotaged and how to avoid the sabotage. (Lecturette on destructive fight-styles introduces this exercise.)
4:30   Consultant sets up first individual follow-up meeting with couple.
5:00   Couples leave; staff meeting (Gottman, 1976, p. 32)

Subjects

Eighteen couples signed up for the workshop. Nine of these couples were assigned to Group 1, and 9 were assigned to Group 2. In Group 1, 4 couples completed the at-home cassette preassessment, and 5 couples completed the in-lab video preassessment; in Group 2, these numbers were 3 and 5, respectively.

Demographic characteristics and marital satisfaction scores for home versus lab groups were given in Chapter 13. For husbands' age, Group 1 couples averaged 34.0 and Group 2 couples averaged 29.0, $t(15) = 1.10$, n.s. For wives' age, Group 1 couples averaged 33.4 and Group 2 couples averaged 28.0, $t(15) = 1.27$, n.s. For years married, Group 1 couples averaged 12.2 years and Group 2 couples averaged 5.9, $t(15) = 1.55$, n.s. For the number of children, Group 1 couples averaged 1.89 and Group 2 couples averaged 1.13, $t(15) = 1.47$, n.s. For the husbands' MRI score, Group 1 couples averaged 88.11 and Group 2 couples averaged 92.88, $t(15) = .82$, n.s. For the wives' MRI score, Group 1 couples averaged 87.56 and Group 2 couples averaged 94.75, $t(15) = 1.10$, n.s. To summarize, although Group 2 couples tended to be younger, married fewer years, with fewer children, and with higher marital satisfaction scores, these differences were not significant. The same pattern of no significant differences held when comparing home versus laboratory taping subgroups within each group.

There was considerable difficulty in obtaining tapes from the home cassette couples of both groups. Although all couples in the cassette groups completed the marital satisfaction inventories, only 4 out of 7 completed the second at-home tape, and only 2 out of 7 completed the third at-home tape. In the video groups, 8 out of 10 completed the second tape, and 7 out of 10 completed the third tape. Comparing couples who completed tapes with those who did not, there were no significant differences on any variables, demographic or marital satisfaction, nor were there differences in the amount of change in marital satisfaction. Since most of these couples did come for the laboratory phase of each assessment, the problem can probably be attributed to the aversiveness of discussing a marital issue at home (see Chapter 13).

Outcome Assessment

Figure 14.2 presents the results of the study for the criterion variable, average marital satisfaction. The study was analyzed in two parts. The first part of the analysis was a 2×2 repeated measures design, which produced a significant groups-by-assessment time interaction, $F(1, 13) = 8.72, p < .05$. A subsequent correlated t-test showed that the change in Group 2 between pre-assessments was not significant, $t(6) = 1.67$. The direction of the change is, nonetheless, interesting in the context of a recent finding by Jacobson (1978) that the marital satisfaction scores of a waiting-list group deteriorated. There may be something beneficial about the invited treatment control condition.

The second part of the analysis compared Group 2's marital satisfaction scores before and after the workshop and Group 1's marital satisfaction scores from posttest to follow-up. Group 2 also experienced a significant increase in marital satisfaction from before to after the workshop, $t(5) = 2.64, p < .05$. Group 1 decreased in marital satisfaction from posttest to follow-up, but the decrease was not significant, $t(7) = 1.51$.

The results suggest that the new format of the intervention program was effective in increasing marital satisfaction, which was the goal of Phase Two of the program evaluation.

Process Assessment

Because of the difficulty in obtaining completed home cassette tapes for couples in each group, there is an insufficient N for a meaningful analysis of variance. Furthermore, most of the half-hour tapes did not contain a sufficient number of floor switches necessary to compute the dominance statistic. Instead, an exploratory analysis of negative affect and negative affect reciprocity for grouped data will be presented in this section in order to determine if changes

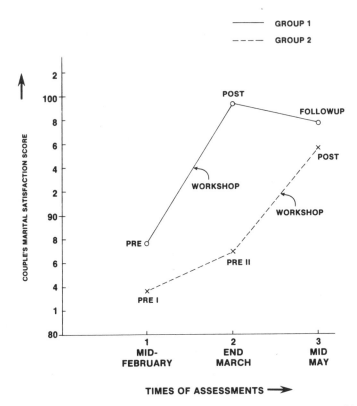

Figure 14.2 *Phase Two study results on the criterion variable, couple's marital satisfaction (MRI) scores.*

in these variables parallel changes in the couple's marital satisfaction and in order to assess transfer of training. Table 14.3 is a summary of these analyses. Negative husband affect in Group 1 showed a steady decrease, whereas it increased in Group 2 between preassessments and then decreased between the second preassessment and the postassessment of Group 2. This pattern held for cassette and video couples. Negative wife affect showed a similar pattern except for the increase in negative affect for Group 1's cassette couples from posttest to follow-up. This piece of data may be indicative of a problem in the long-term maintenance of some therapeutic gains, particularly when these gains are assessed at home. Perhaps these differences are related to the decrement, albeit nonsignificant, in marital satisfaction from posttest to follow-up. For negative affect reciprocity, Group 1 cassette couples decrease in Z-score from pre- to postassessment, but there is again a significant Z-score in the Group 1 video couples on follow-up. Changes in reciprocity of negative affect for Group 2 between preassessments are inconsistent; one decreases and the other increases.

TABLE 14.3
Affect and Reciprocity Changes in Phase Two Study

Variable: Husband Negative Affect (H–)				
Group 1		PRE	POST	FOLLOWUP
	Video	.116	.112	.093
	Cassette	.174	.110	.092
Group 2		PRE I	PRE II	POST
	Video	.090	.133	.087
	Cassette	.195	.230	—
Variable: Wife Negative Affect (W–)				
Group 1		PRE	POST	FOLLOWUP
	Video	.142	.153	.110
	Cassette	.299	.134	.189
Group 2		PRE I	PRE II	POST
	Video	.142	.208	.111
	Cassette	.180	.254	—
Variable: (W–│H–)				
Group 1		PRE	POST	FOLLOWUP
	Video	-1.02	.39	2.16
	Cassette	7.72	-.47	-.09
Group 2		PRE I	PRE II	POST
	Video	-.17	-.36	.18
	Cassette	2.61	3.55	—
Variable: (H–│W–)				
Group 1		PRE	POST	FOLLOWUP
	Video	-.27	.00	2.71
	Cassette	5.64	-.51	.00
Group 2		PRE I	PRE II	POST
	Video	.00	-.43	.00
	Cassette	2.71	1.84	—

Examining Table 14.3 for transfer of training effects (Group 1) shows that changes held on follow-up; the only exception is a slight increase in the wives' negative affect on follow-up. In Group 2, there was generally a large decrement from the pre-I to the pre-II assessment. There is, thus, some evidence that treatment effects were not limited to the laboratory. Taken as a whole, and with the caution that the small N makes confidence in interpretation difficult, the process variable results are consistent with the changes in the criterion variable. This completes the analysis of Phase Two of the evaluation.

PHASE THREE ASSESSMENT

The theoretical purpose of the Phase Three investigation was to test the predictive validity of the classification system proposed in Chapter 9 for predicting differential change. The applied question was, "What kinds of couples benefit most and least from this program?" The intervention program was modified for this study in only two ways. First, the training of the consultants was systematized and standardized. Twenty-three consultants were trained. There were four $2\frac{1}{2}$-hour training sessions and an 8-hour session that simulated the procedures of the workshop. (Training procedures and materials are available in a masters thesis by Toler [1979].) Second, to enhance the maintenance of change, there were four follow-up sessions after the workshop instead of two, and these four sessions were conducted by the consultant in the couple's home.

As a more conservative assessment procedure (and cheaper, in terms of coding time), posttesting was dropped, and only follow-up testing 1½ to 2 months after the last home session) was maintained. The posttesting was dropped to reduce the amount of material to code. The length of taping was maintained at one-half hour for the same reason.

For this study, 23 new consultants were trained, entirely by nonprofessional laboratory staff who had previously been trained by the author, Cliff Notarius, and Howard Markman. The project was formally supervised by a clinical psychologist who agreed to be available in the event of emergencies but who knew nothing about the program and who, in fact, never had to be called. The study was administered by the Psychiatric Division of the Student Health Services of Indiana University. This was, therefore, the first study in the series that the author did not supervise and in which the program was adopted by another agency. All pre- and follow-up videotape assessments were made in the video studio of the Student Health Services. In this laboratory, studio couples were seated so that a ¾ shot of each face could be obtained, in the hope that this arrangement would result in slightly higher Cronbach alphas for the affect codes than was possible in a profile shot.

There was no need for a control group in this study because the classification research question concerns the *differential* effectiveness of the program as a function of the classification of couple's interaction using preassessment tapes.

Subjects

Couples were recruited in a manner identical to that of the Phase Two study, using newspaper advertisements announcing a Couples Communication Workshop. Four workshops were held in 1977, one in February, one in April, one in June, and one in July. There were approximately 7 couples in each workshop (6 in February, 7 in April, 7 in June, and 7 in July). Husbands' ages averaged 28.3, with a standard deviation of 4.1; wives' ages averaged 27.4, with a standard deviation of 3.0. Couples had an average of .4 children, with a standard deviation of .6; the couples were married an average of 4.1 years, with a standard deviation of 3.2 years. Husbands' MRI scores averaged 90.33, with a standard deviation of 13.29; wives' MRI scores averaged 92.04, with a standard deviation of 10.14. Twenty-three couples completed both pre- and follow-up assessments.

Coding of Tapes

Videotapes in this study were coded using all affect codes, and not just the voice codes. Voice codes had been used in the Phase Two study to make the home cassette tapes comparable to the laboratory videotapes. Once again, coders were unaware that a therapy study had taken place, and they were blind to the order of the two assessments for each couple. Table 14.4 presents the Cronbach alphas for this coding. These alphas are based on the coding of 46 tapes, with reliability checking on two pages of each transcript. Cronbach alphas for affect were not higher than they had been using a profile shot, which lends additional support to the overall importance of voice-tone cues in coding affect. Cohen's kappas over all transcripts combined as one matrix were .897 for content and .833 for affect, computed for each transcript separately; Cohen's kappas for content averaged .89, with a standard deviation of .09 and for affect averaged .68, with a standard deviation of .22.

Assessments of Changes

Table 14.5 presents the results of the assessment of changes in criterion and process measures. The results indicate significant changes in marital satisfaction and in husbands' negative affect from pre- to follow-up assessments, with a marginally significant change in wives' negative affect. These results are not inconsistent with results previously obtained. Because the size of these pre-to-follow-up effects are smaller than the pre-to-post effects in the Phase Two study, the issue of maintenance of change still exists for this intervention.

To test the hypothesis that the intervention was differentially effective as a function of the couples' classification on the preassessment, couples were classified as described in Chapter 9. There were 10 asymmetric cases, 5 negative cases, 3 positive cases (includes J-curve and positive), 3 flat-end cases, and 2 flat-beginning cases. Unfortunately, cases were not uniformly distributed across categories: Asymmetrical and negative cases comprised 65% of the couples. Recall that asymmetrical couples were the least skillful at resolving

TABLE 14.4
Generalizability Study Results for Phase Three Study

code	fre-quency	mean square transcripts	mean square residual	cron-bach alpha
Content				
Problem Feeling (PF)	852	224.861	1.510	.987
Mindreading (MR)	176	28.696	.429	.971
Problem Solving (PS)	1108	246.319	2.338	.981
Communication Talk (CT)	89	7.368	.170	.955
Agreement (AG)	312	31.397	.143	.991
Disagreement (DG)	217	35.810	.686	.962
Summarizing Other (SO)	38	2.505	.140	.894
Summarizing Self (SS)	45	2.086	.219	.810
Question (Q)	227	22.930	.073	.994
Affect				
Positive (+)	195	17.239	1.155	.874
Neutral (o)	2179	359.137	1.611	.991
Negative (-)	231	66.369	3.160	.909

Cohen's Kappa for content codes was .897 and for affect codes was .883, with one matrix calculated for all transcripts.

TABLE 14.5
Analysis of Phase Three Study—Undifferentiated

Variable	Pre	Post	t-ratio
Couple Marital Satisfaction	91.696	94.478	2.19*
Husband Negative Affect	.063	.028	-2.10*
Wife Negative Affect	.100	.059	-1.81
Z(W-|H-)	.874	.536	- .80
Z(H-|W-)	.943	.646	- .82
Dominance	.118	.008	-1.48
Absolute Dominance	.211	.212	.03

*p<.05

conflict. Data were analyzed using seven 5 × 2 repeated measures analyses of variance. Table 14.6 presents the results of these analyses. For only one variable, husband negative affect, was there evidence of differential change as a function of the classification. Means for negative affect by group are presented in Table 14.7. An experiment-wise protection alpha of .01 and the mean square error term from the analysis of variance were used. Note that only husbands in flat-beginning marriages become *more* negative after therapy; negative couples improved most on this variable. Asymmetrical and negative groups improved significantly more than did the flat-beginning group [$t(18) = 2.61, p < .01$, and $t(18) = 3.82, p < .01$, respectively]. The intervention is thus most effective for couples initially lowest in social skill. The intervention, thus, increased negative affect only in husbands who are neutral in the agenda-building phase of the discussion and decreased negative affect most in husbands who are negative in this phase. We will see later that husband negative affect increased only when both husband and wife were neutral in the agenda building phase. The lack of expressiveness in the agenda building phase is a poor prognosis in terms of the process variables. In fact, it will turn out to be the case that the wife's *negative* affect is a positive prognostic indicator when the husband is neutral in the agenda building phase.

The classification system proposed in Chapter 9 is a failure in predicting differential change on the criterion measure of marital satisfaction. This is so because in terms of marital satisfaction the intervention is equally effective for

TABLE 14.6
Analysis of Phase Three Study Using Classification of Pre-Tapes

Variable	Time F-ratio	Time × Group F-ratio
Marital Satisfaction	4.07*	.18
Husband Negative Affect	5.90*	2.88*
Wife Negative Affect	3.72	1.75
Negative Reciprocity Z(W-|H-)	.64	1.01
Negative Reciprocity Z(H-|W-)	.64	.76
Dominance	1.84	.12
Absolute Dominance	.00	.59

*p<.05

TABLE 14.7
Means on Husband Negative Affect in Phase Three Study as a Function of Initial Classification

Group	Pre	Post
1. Negative	.126	.024
2. Positive	.022	.005
3. Flat Ending	.009	.011
4. Flat Beginning	.058	.142
5. Asymmetrical	.062	.019

all couples, regardless of their initial levels of social skill. In a sense this is unfortunate because it does not assist us in improving the intervention by learning who was helped most. An additional analysis was performed to assess whether *Structural Model variables* on the preassessment data are able to predict changes in marital satisfaction. Table 14.8 presents these correlations for both the Phase One and the Phase Three studies. Recall that, for these studies, tapes were coded with the same affect codes but that the Phase One study included only a postassessment, whereas the Phase Three study included only a follow-up assessment. Table 14.8 presents these correlations. The correlations are greater for the Phase One study than for the Phase Three study, probably partly due to the restriction of range in the Phase Three study. The patterns are reasonably consistent. *In general, couples improved most in a marital satisfaction score* (a) *when wives were initially high in negative affect but low in reciprocating their husband's negative affect;* (b) *when there were lower initial levels of the asymmetry of the husband's emotional responsiveness and* (c) *when husbands were initially low in negative affect.* This implies that a particular kind of couple can benefit most from the intervention. The correlations varied somewhat between the two studies. In the second study, the couples that increased most in a marital satisfaction score were those in which the wife's negative affect was high, but the husband's negative affect was not high. Reciprocity and dominance variables were no longer predictive of changes in marital satisfaction.[1]

The kind of marriage most helped by the intervention program is, therefore, one in which (a) *the husband* is not highly negative, does not reciprocate his wife's negative affect, and is not dominant (he is, thus, as influenced emotionally by her as she is by him), and in which (b) *the wife* expresses negative affect, but not in response to her husband's negative affect. Subsequent research is necessary in order to understand this configuration of variables. The surprising result is that the wife's negative affect, if it is not reciprocating the husband's negative affect, is an indicator of a *positive* prognosis. Except for this result, we would have concluded from these results that the better the preassessment indicators, the more positive the prognosis. However, these results suggest that it is important for the wife to express negative affect *if it is not reciprocating the*

---

[1] A multiple regression was performed for each study, using the change in the couple's marital satisfaction as a dependent variable and the Structural Model preassessment variables as the independent variables. For the Phase One study, the multiple correlation coefficient was .710, and, for the Phase Three study, the multiple correlation was .543.

TABLE 14.8
**Correlations across Two Studies between Preassessment Variables
and Changes in Marital Satisfaction**

Pre-Assessment Variable	Phase One Study			Phase Three Study		
	Change Couple Marital Satisf.	Change Husband Marital Satisf.	Change Wife Marital Satisf.	Change Couple Marital Satisf.	Change Husband Marital Satisf.	Change Wife Marital Satisf.
Husband Negative	.125	-.092	.266	-.326*	-.361*	-.204
Wife Negative	.485**	.141	.608**	.185	.346*	.011
Reciprocity Z(W–│H–)	-.155	-.533**	.217	.067	.155	-.018
Reciprocity Z(H–│W–)	-.168	-.437*	.117	-.193	-.157	-.164
Dominance	-.197	-.401*	.043	.005	.108	-.073
Absolute Dominance	.226	.042	.304	-.155	-.054	-.185

*p<.05
**p<.01

husband's negative affect, and if the husband is not less emotionally responsive than she is. The hypothesis that can organize these results is that it is helpful if the wife expresses negative affect and the husband in some sense facilitates this—he does not reciprocate her negative affect, is not very negative himself, and does not dominate and, hence, responds emotionally to his wife.

It would be useful to have more information about the couples who improved most and least from the interventions in the two studies. Although the point graphs did not do well in predicting differential change in marital satisfaction, because of the effectiveness of the intervention, they may have descriptive value. To the extent that the point graphs include sources of variation and information not captured by the variables of the Structural Model, variables such as content codes (i.e., agreement and disagreement) and information about patterns over time (such as skill deficits) in each third of the interaction, it will be interesting to examine the point graphs of couples with best and worst configurations on the preassessment variables.

For hypothesis-generating purposes, in the Phase One study two couples were selected with pure profile types on all the preassessment variables that correlated with changes in a marital satisfaction score. One couple, Couple #13, was in the control group, had a nonnegative dominance score of .162, high wife negative affect (.265), low husband negative affect (.084), and low reciprocity scores [Z(W–│H–) = .15, Z(H–│W–) = .72]. The other couple, Couple #8, was also in the control group, had dominance score −.459 (i.e., husband dominant, high wife negative affect (.279), high husband affect (.221), and high reciprocity scores [Z(W–│H–) = 3.55, Z(H–│W–) = 2.60]. Figure 14.3 presents the pre- and postgraphs for these couples. Note that the postassessment graph of Couple #13 is more positive than is that of Couple #8. The preassessment graphs are differentiated immediately by the wife in Couple #13, being far more negative than the wife in Couple #8; the husbands were initially quite similar, but, in the latter part of the interaction, the husband in Couple #8

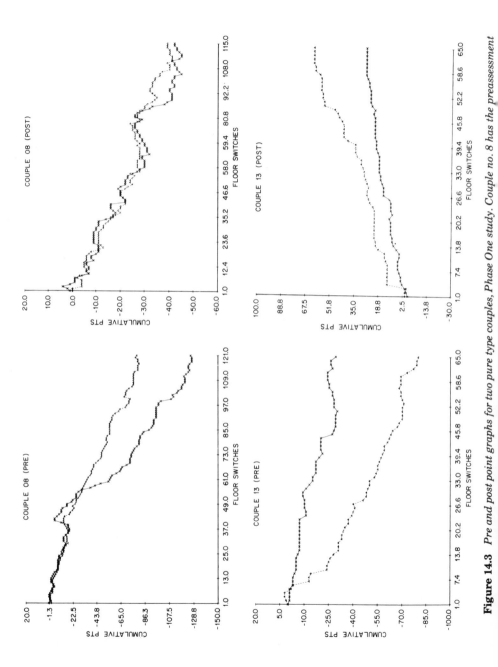

Figure 14.3 Pre and post point graphs for two pure type couples, Phase One study. Couple no. 8 has the preassessment

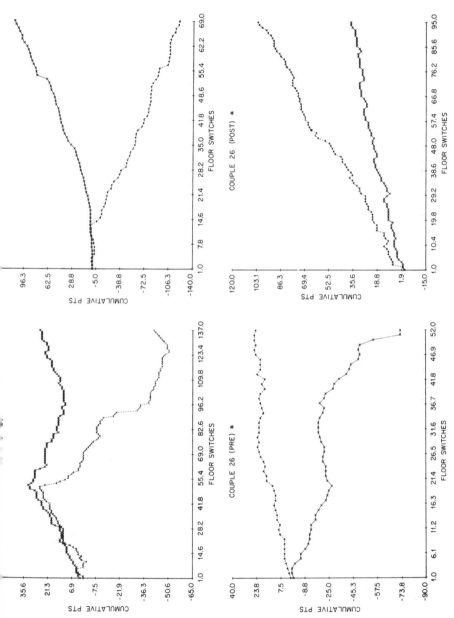

Figure 14.4 Pre and follow-up point graphs for two pure type couples, Phase Three study, who have the preassessment configuration for least improvement in marital satisfaction (MRI) scores.

285

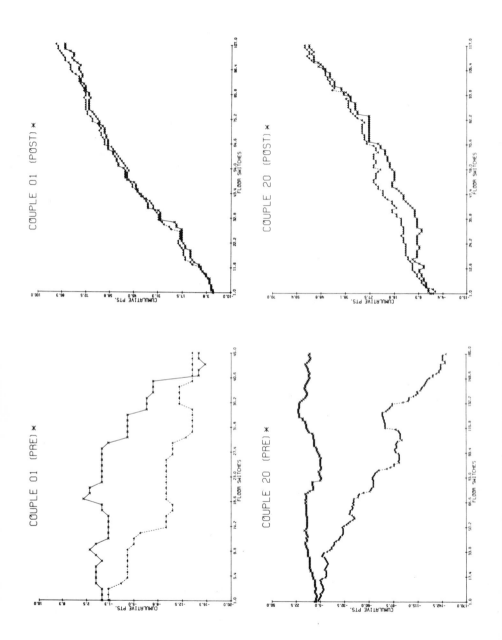

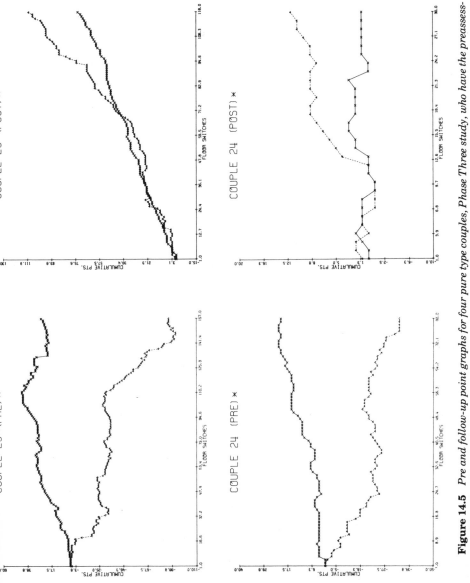

Figure 14.5 *Pre and follow-up point graphs for four pure type couples, Phase Three study, who have the preassessment configuration for most improvement in marital satisfaction (MRI) scores.*

becomes sharply negative: His graph changes slope, whereas his wife's does not. Two hypotheses are suggested: (a) an initial divergence of the graphs, with the wife's being more negative in the first part of the interaction an indicator of a good prognosis; and (b) a change in the husband's slope toward a more negative slope as an indicator of the poor prognosis. Data from the Phase Three study were then used to test these hypotheses.

For the Phase Three study, only preassessment husband and wife negative affect correlated with changes in marital satisfaction; two couples were selected as pure types of the low wife negative affect–high husband negative affect profile; the mean wife negative affect was .109, and the mean husband negative affect was .206 for these couples. Four couples were selected with the opposite profile, that is, high wife negative affect–low husband negative affect; the mean wife negative affect was .173, and the mean husband negative affect was .058 for these couples. Figures 14.4 and 14.5 present the pre- and follow-up point graphs for these two groups. The follow-up assessment curves of the second group of couples are more positive than are those of the first group. The only consistent difference in the preassessment curves is that, in the second group of couples, the wife was negative in the first third of the interaction and the husband was not negative, whereas, in the first group, in the first third the wife was positive instead of negative. The usefulness of a sudden shift downward in slope in the husband's graph as an indicator was not supported. Therefore, the initial divergence of the graphs, with the wife negative and husband relatively neutral is the indicator of good prognosis. *Thus, the first third of the interaction, that is, the agenda building phase, may be critical for a positive prognosis.*

SUMMARY

This chapter reviewed research on clinical intervention with couples, suggested that modern intervention programs are beginning to demonstrate promising results, and argued for research oriented more toward an understanding of the processes of change. A three-phase model for research was proposed and applied. Results suggested that (a) changes in the variables of the Structural Model could be used to predict changes in marital satisfaction; (b) an intervention program whose design was in part based on the Structural Model could produce significant changes in marital satisfaction; (c) these effects could be enhanced in the Phase Two study; (d) changes in interaction transferred to the home at posttest, and laboratory assessments indicated that these effects held on follow-up; and (e) variables of the Structural Model applied to the preassessment data were able to predict *differential* changes in the Phase Three study.

These steps are only a beginning toward a more informed understanding of marital interaction and clinical intervention for couples. It has been the major argument of this book that an attention to the descriptive phase of scientific investigation has a great deal to contribute toward that understanding.

CHAPTER 15

Epilogue: Structure Is Constraint

In 1939, in their pioneering work on marital satisfaction, Terman et al. began by noting that, at that time, a variety of strongly held beliefs existed about what creates and constitutes a successful marriage. Among these beliefs were a series of hypotheses about the importance of sex on the wedding night, which, in retrospect, seem charming and anachronistic. More important, even at that time, they were wrong. Terman's introduction was a call for empirical research that employed quantitative methods and statistics to challenge these cherished everyday assumptions about so important a cultural institution as marriage.

Terman's research launched a 40-year program of systematic investigation that this volume interpreted as pointing to the importance of studying the social interaction of married couples by observational methods, particularly how couples resolve conflict and reach consensus.

Our own time is not without its own set of strongly held beliefs and excess theoretical baggage. We have been remarkably reluctant to test and discard sensible hypotheses, and, over time, many of them have acquired a kind of truth of their own. We have also splintered into autonomous research traditions that have at times reached heights of intellectual isolation and self-protection.

The time has arrived for remembering the spirit of Terman's work, and in some senses this spirit is a call for hard, dust-bowl empiricism. The time has also come when this empiricism will make it possible for us to create in a new way, because we have new conceptual tools.

One set of conceptual tools are some dimensions that came from personality and child rearing research, which have variously been called: (a) positiveness, evaluation, warmth, inclusion; (b) status, control, dominance, potency; and (c) activity, tension, tempo. These dimensions also surfaced repeatedly in research on social interaction, in work on the expression and recognition of emotions, in ethological investigations, in the study of nonverbal behavior, attraction, person perception, and implicit personality theory.

Furthermore, these dimensions were capable of being sharpened by noting that: (a) hypotheses about their function in social interaction often involve sequences, and we can now study sequences directly using information theory, instead of having to infer them from rate measures; (b) we can now directly and reliably study nonverbal behavior as people interact; (c) we now know the importance of studying interaction as a function of contextual variables, such as what couples discuss and the settings of these conversations; (d) we can use marital satisfaction as a criterion with the knowledge that it is not an arbitrary variable, but has reasonably sound psychometric work behind it; and (e) we can apply a clinical social competence metaphor to attempt to discriminate well functioning from poorly functioning relationships.

Nonetheless, much as was the case when Terman began his work, the study of couples' interaction with these conceptual tools occurs in the context of hypotheses that we have inherited, and these hypotheses necessarily shape what we decide to look for. What is our heritage? General systems theory stressed the importance of "analogic communication," that is, nonverbal communication that modifies and contextualizes conversation ("digital communication"), and it stressed the importance of metacommunication. Social learning theory stressed the importance of social reinforcement and the quid pro quo. Behavior exchange theory stressed the importance of the interactants' social cognitions, particularly with respect to the rewards and costs of specific types of exchanges. In this book these hypotheses, together with sequential analytic techniques, formed the background for a reconceptualization of communication patterns in marital interaction. The first objective, then, is the search for pattern and structure in the stream of behavior. Unfortunately, the term "structure" as it has been applied to the study of social interaction has been little more than a metaphor implying some form of organization. However, the use of information theory in the analysis of sequence now makes it possible to define precisely the term "structure": Structure is constraint determined by the reduction of uncertainty in temporal patterns. This definition of the term leads to specific hypotheses about structure than can be summarized as a structural model. This reconceptualization led to two things: (a) a search for patterns of interaction that discriminate clinic from nonclinic couples, and (b) the Structural Model.

We can summarize the major patterns obtained from a series of observational studies reported in this volume as follows: The discussion of a marital issue by a couple can be divided into three phases. Each phase can be characterized by the inferred tasks and strategies employed to accomplish these tasks, much as the beginning, middle, and end games of chess can be characterized by observing the moves of the players. In the beginning phase the task is agenda building, characterized by the expression of feelings about the problems under discussion. During this phase nonclinic couples use validation sequences rather than the cross-complaining sequences that describe the interaction of clinic couples. In the last phase the task is negotiation, and contracting sequences characterize nonclinic couples while counter-proposal sequences characterize clinic couples.

In the middle phase it is difficult to discriminate the two groups of couples. Disagreement is characteristic in this middle "arguing" phase. However, the variables of the Structural Model discriminate the two groups during this phase as well as during other phases of the discussion.

The Structural Model involved an analysis of positive and negative affect, paying special attention to nonverbal behavior. Negative affect, assessed nonverbally, was the most consistent discriminator of clinic and nonclinic interaction. Also, positive and negative affect reciprocity was analyzed using information theory concepts that compare conditional with unconditional probabilities. Negative affect reciprocity consistently discriminated the two groups of couples while positive affect reciprocity was not a consistent discriminator. Dominance was reconceptualized as asymmetry in predictability in the behavior of husband and wife. Using the point graphs that tap affective expression, asymmetry was found to be characteristic in the rapid affect component of the emotional expression of clinic couples. This can be interpreted as an asymmetry in emotional responsiveness: The wife is more emotionally responsive to the husband than vice versa in clinic couples, while there is no such asymmetry in nonclinic couples.

The Structural Model and the specific patterns described above were robust discriminators, generalizing across studies, the issues the couples discussed, from conflict resolution to nonconflict resolution, and from the laboratory to the home.

The Structural Model also emerged when couples coded their own interaction using the talk-table; this result replicated, and the talk-table data predicted the relationship satisfaction of engaged couples over a $2\frac{1}{2}$ year period.

An intervention program based on these findings produced significant changes in the criterion variable (marital satisfaction); furthermore, the process equation was supported, and treatment effects replicated and extended outside the laboratory and on long-term follow-up.

The major *methodological* goal of this book was to establish the role of *description* in the study of social interaction. There is currently a confusing emphasis on the word "theory," which is used to mean a wide variety of things in psychology. For example, in a recent introductory psychology text, Mussen, Rosenzweig, and Geiwitz (1977) wrote, "A coherent, integrated set of interrelated hypotheses is called a theory [p. 14]." I believe that this is an inadequate use of the word "theory," and that a more useful meaning might improve the process of scientific investigation.

The behavioral sciences have suffered from premature theorizing and from the neglect of the descriptive phase of scientific investigation. Physics had its Tycho Brahe, who carefully charted and described the motions of heavenly bodies; its Johannes Kepler, who detected patterns in Brahe's data (such as the elliptical motion of the planets around the sun at a focus of the ellipse) long before Isaac Newton was able to generate theory to explain the observed pattern. The work of these three men suggests a meaning for the word "theory" that could be useful in the social sciences. *The word "theory" should mean explaining patterns in well-described phenomena.* The point is that, in effect, we have "theorized" without a well-described set of phenomena, and often the result resembles the theorizing of medieval alchemists. Therefore, this book is a call for detailed descriptive research in the study of social interaction. The call is a suggestion that investigation proceed in four phases:

1. Description and the discovery of pattern: Obtaining the phenomenon.
2. Parsimonious representation of the phenomenon: Model building.
3. Testing the model: Prediction and intervention studies.
4. Understanding the model (explaining pattern): Theory.

This book has presented research on the first three phases, and speculations throughout about the fourth phase. Theory that emerges from these three phases, that is constructed to explain a model of stable patterns, will have a new character and a solid empirical footing. At this stage of investigation of social interaction, we need our Brahes and Keplers. While it is fun to look at the stars and dream, this was not the only thing that produced the Universal Theory of Gravitation.

Appendix

MATERIALS AVAILABLE FROM THE AUTHOR ON REQUEST

1. QUESTIONNAIRES
    a. Demographic Information Sheet
    b. Problem Inventory
    c. MRI (Marital Satisfaction Measure)
2. SITUATIONS FOR INDIVIDUAL COMPETENCE ASSESSMENT
    a. Husband Items
    b. Wife Items
3. COUPLES INTERACTION SCORING SYSTEM (CISS) MANUALS
    a. CISS Content Codes
    b. CISS Affect Codes
    c. CISS Affect from Voice Tone
    d. Manual for Training Those Who Train Coders

COMPUTER PROGRAMS

1. Computer program JOINT for lag-sequence analysis is available from Dr. Roger Bakeman, Department of Psychology, Georgia State University, University Plaza, Atlanta, Georgia 30303.
2. Spectral time-series analysis program CROSSPA is available from the

Digital Computing Laboratory as part of soupac, University of Illinois, Champaign—Urbana, Illinois 61820. This program must serve as input for the slope calculations. For all data in this book, 20 lags were used, and the end points dropped (they are always zero). One line was computed for points 1–9, and another for points 11–19. The slope of the first line is the rapid dominance component; if it is negative, the husband leads assuming that the husband's data are the first series read by CROSSPA.

References

Ackerman, N. W. The family as a special and emotional unit. *Bulletin of the Kansas Mental Hygiene Society,* 1937, *12,* 1–8.

Ackerman, N. W. The diagnosis of neurotic marital interaction. *Social Casework,* 1954, *35,* 139–147.

Ackerman, N. W. *Treating the troubled family.* New York: Basic Books, 1966.

Ackerman, N. W., & Sobel, R. Family Diagnosis: An approach to the study of the pre-school child. *American Journal of Orthopsychiatry,* 1950, *20,* 744–752.

Adkins, D. A., & Johnson, S. M. What behaviors may be called deviant for children? A comparison of two approaches to behavior classification. Paper presented at the Western Psychological Association Convention, Portland, Oregon, April, 1972.

Alexander, J. F. Defensive and supportive communications in family systems. *Journal of Marriage and the Family,* 1973, *35,* 613–617. (a)

Alexander, J. F. Defensive and supportive communication in normal and deviant families. *Journal of Consulting and Clinical Psychology,* 1973, *40,* 223–231. (b)

Alexander, J. F., & Barton, C. Behavioral systems therapy for families. In D. H. Olson (Ed.), *Treating relationships.* Lake Mills, Iowa: Graphic, 1976.

Alexander, J. F., & Parsons, B. V. Short-term behavioral intervention with delinquent families: Impact on family process and recidivism. *Journal of Abnormal Psychology,* 1973, *51,* 219–233.

Altmann, S. A. Sociobiology of rhesus monkeys. II. Stochastics of social communication. *Journal of Theoretical Biology,* 1965, *8,* 490–522.

Argyle, M. *Social interaction.* Chicago: Aldine, 1969.

Attneave, F. *Applications of information theory to psychology.* New York: Holt, 1959.

Azrin, N. H., Naster, B. J., & Jones, R. Reciprocity counseling: A rapid learning based procedure for marital counseling. *Behavior Research and Therapy,* 1973, *11,* 365–382.

Bakeman, R., & Dabbs, J. M. Jr. Social interaction observed: Some approaches to the analysis of behavior streams. *Personality and Social Psychology Bulletin,* 1976, *2,* 335–345.

Bales, R. F. *Interaction process analysis.* Cambridge, Massachusetts: Addison-Wesley, 1950.

Bales, R. F., & Slater, P. E. Role differentiation in small decision-making groups. In Talcott Parsons & Robert Baler (Eds.), *Family, socialization, and interaction process.* New York: Free Press, 1955.

Bandura, A., Ross, O., & Ross, S. A. A comparative test of the status envy, social power, and secondary reinforcement theories of identification. *Journal of Abnormal Social Psychology,* 1963, *67,* 527–534.

Bank, S. Commodity behavior exchange models for assessing marital success. Unpublished masters thesis, Indiana University at Bloomington, 1974.

Barry, W. A. Marriage research and conflict: An integrative review. *Psychological Bulletin,* 1970, *73,* 41–54.

Bateson, G. Critical evaluations. *International Journal of Psychiatry,* 1966, *2,* 415–417.

Bateson, G. Information and codification. In J. Ruesch & G. Bateson (Eds.), *Communication: The social matrix of psychiatry.* New York: W. W. Norton, 1968.

Bateson, G. *Steps to an ecology of mind.* New York: Ballantine Books, 1972.

Bateson, G., Jackson, D. D., Haley, J., & Weakland, J. Toward a theory of schizophrenia. *Behavioral Science,* 1956, *1,* 251–264.

Becker, W. C. Consequences of different kinds of parental discipline. In M. L. Hoffman & L. M. Hoffman (Eds.), *Review of child development research, Vol. 1.* New York: Russell Sage, 1964.

Beels, C., & Ferber, A. Family therapy: A view. *Family Process,* 1969, *8,* 280–317.

Bell, R. Q. A reinterpretation of the direction of effects in studies of socialization. *Psychological Review,* 1968, *75,* 81–95.

Bell, R. Q. Contributions of human infants to caregiving and social interaction. In M. Lewis & L. A. Rosenblum (Eds.), *The effect of the infant on its caregiver.* New York: Wiley, 1974.

Bell, R. R. *Marriage and family interaction.* Homewood, Illinois: Dorsey Press, 1975.

Berkowitz, S. J. An approach to the treatment of marital discord. *Journal of Social Casework,* 1948, *29,* 1–6.

Bernard, J. Factors in the distribution of success in marriage. *American Journal of Sociology,* 1934, *40,* 49–60.

Birchler, G. R. *Differential patterns of instrumental affiliative behavior as a function of degree of marital distress and level of intimacy.* Doctoral thesis, University of Oregon, 1972.

Birchler, G., Weiss, R., & Vincent, J. Multimethod analysis of social reinforcement exchange between maritally distressed and nondistressed spouse and stranger dyads. *Journal of Personality and Social Psychology,* 1975, *31,* 349–360.

Birdwhistell, R. L. *Introduction to kinesics.* Louisville: University of Kentucky Press, 1952.

Bishop, Y. M. M., Fienberg, S. E., & Holland, P. W. *Discrete multivariate analysis: Theory and practice.* Cambridge, Massachusetts: M.I.T. Press, 1975.

Borke, H. A family over three generations: The transmission of interacting and relating patterns. *Journal of Marriage and the Family,* 1967, *29,* 638–655.

Bowen, M. A family concept of schizophrenia. In D. Jackson (Ed.), *The etiology of schizophrenia.* New York: Basic Books, 1960.

Box, G. E. P., & Jenkins, G. M. *Time-series analysis: Forecasting and control.* San Francisco: Holden-Day, 1970.

Brand, S. *Two cybernetic frontiers.* New York: Random House, 1974.

Brazelton, T. B., Koslowski, B., & Main, M. The origins of reciprocity: The early mother–infant interaction. In M. Lewis & L. A. Rosenblum (Eds.), *The effect of the infant on its caregiver.* New York: Wiley, 1974.

Brown, W. Some experimental results in the correlation of mental abilities. *British Journal of Psychology,* 1910, *3,* 296–322.

Bruner, J. S., & Tagiuri, R. The perception of people. In G. Lindzey (Ed.), *Handbook of social psychology, Vol. 2.* Reading, Massachusetts: Addison-Wesley, 1954.

Bugental, D. E., Kaswan, J. W., Love, L. W., & Fox, M. N. Child versus adult perception of evaluative messages in verbal, vocal, and visual channels. *Developmental Psychology,* 1970, *2,* 367–375.

Bugental, D. E., Love, L. R., & Kaswan, J. W. Videotaped family interaction: Differences reflecting presence and type of child disturbance. *Journal of Abnormal Psychology,* 1972, *79,* 285–290.

Bugental, D. E., Love, L. R., Kaswan, J. W., & April, S. Verbal–conflict in parental messages to normal and disturbed children. *Journal of Abnormal Psychology,* 1971, *77,* 6–10.

Burchinal, L. G., Hawkes, G. R., & Gardner, B. Marriage adjustment, personality characteristics of parents and the personality adjustment of their children. *Marriage and Family Living,* 1957, *17,* 366–372.

Burgess, E. W., & Cottrell, L. S. *Predicting success or failure in marriage.* New York: Prentice-Hall, 1939.

Burgess, E. W., Locke, H. J., & Thomes, M. M. *The family.* New York: Van Nostrand Reinhold, 1971.

Burgess, E. W., & Wallin, P. *Engagement and marriage.* Chicago: J. B. Lippincott, 1953.

Butterfield, E. C. Observing cognitive development. In G. P. Sackett (Ed.), *Observing behavior, Vol. 1.* Baltimore: University Park Press, 1978.

Caputo, D. V. The parents of schizophrenics. *Family Process,* 1963, *2,* 339–356.

Chance, M. R. A. Attention structure as the basis of primate rank orders. *Man,* 1967, *2,* 503–518.

Chance, M. R. A., & Jolly, C. *Social groups of monkeys, apes, and men.* New York: Dutton, 1970.

Chance, M. R. A., & Larsen, R. *The Structure of social attention.* London: Wiley, 1976.

Chatfield, C. *The analysis of time-series: Theory and practice.* New York: Wiley (Halsted), 1975.

Cheek, F. E. The "Schizophrenogenic" mother in word and deed. *Family Process,* 1964, *3,* 155–177.

Cheek, F. E., & Anthony, R. Personal pronoun usage in families of schizophrenics and social space utilization. *Family Process,* 1970, *9,* 431–448.

Christensen, H. T. Children in the family: Relationship of number and spacing to marital success. *Journal of Marriage and the Family,* 1968, *30,* 283–289.

Clausen, J. A., & Williams, J. R. Sociological correlates of child behavior. In H. Stevenson, J. Kagan, & C. Spiker (Eds.), *Child psychology: The 62nd yearbook of the National Society for the Study of Education.* Chicago: University of Chicago Press, 1963.

Clore, G. L., & Byrne, D. A reinforcement–affect model of attraction. In T. L. Huston (Ed.), *Foundations of inte:personal attraction.* New York: Academic Press, 1974.

Cohen, J. A coefficient of agreement for nominal scales. *Education and Psychological Measurement,* 1960, *20,* 37–46.

Corsini, R. J. Understanding and similarity in marriage. *Journal of Abnormal and Social Psychology,* 1956, *52,* 337–342.

Cronbach, L. J., Gleser, G. C., Nanda, H., & Rajaratnam, N. *The dependability of behavioral measurements: Theory of generalizability for scores and profiles.* New York: Wiley, 1972.

Cuber, J. F., & Harroff, P. B. *The significant Americans.* New York: Appleton-Century-Crofts, 1965.

Cutright, P. Income and family events: Marital stability. *Journal of Marriage and the Family,* 1971, *33,* 291–305.

David, G. *Patterns of social functioning in families with marital and parent–child problems.* Toronto: University of Toronto Press, 1967.

Davitz, J. R., & Davitz, L. J. The communication of feelings by content-free speech. *Journal of Communication,* 1959, *9,* 6–13.

Dean, D. G. Emotional maturity and marital adjustment. *Journal of Marriage and the Family,* 1966, *28*(4), 454–457.

Efron, D. *Gesture and environment.* New York: King's Crown, 1941.

Ekman, P., & Friesen, W. V. *Unmasking the face.* Englewood Cliffs, New Jersey: Prentice-Hall, 1975.

Ekman, P., Friesen, W. V., & Ellsworth, P. *Emotion in the human face.* New York: Pergamon Press, 1972.

Ekman, P., Friesen, W. V., & Tomkins, S. S. Facial affect scoring technique (FAST): A first validity study. *Semiotica,* 1971, *3,* 37–58.

Exline, R. V. Explorations in the process of person perception: Visual interaction in relation to competition, sex, and need for affiliation. *Journal of Personality,* 1963, *31,* 1–20.

Exline, R. V., Gray, D., & Schuette, D. Visual behavior in a dyad as affected by interview content and sex of respondent. *Journal of Personality and Social Psychology,* 1965, *1,* 201–209.

Exline, R. V., & Messick, D. The effects of dependency and social reinforcement upon visual behavior during an interview. *British Journal of Social and Clinical Psychology,* 1967, *6,* 256–266.

Ferber, A., Mendelsohn, M., & Napier, A. (Eds.). *The book of family therapy.* Boston: Houghton-Mifflin, 1973.

Ferreira, A. J., & Winter, W. D. Information exchange and silence in normal and abnormal families. *Family Process,* 1968, *7,* 251–276.

Fienberg, S. E. *The analysis of cross-classified categorical data.* Cambridge, Massachusetts: M.I.T. Press, 1978.

Fleiss, J. L. Measuring nominal scale agreement among many raters. *Psychological Bulletin,* 1971, *76,* 378–382.

Fleiss, J. L., Cohen, J., & Everitt, B. S. Large sample standard errors of kappa and weighted kappa. *Psychological Bulletin,* 1969, *77,* 323–327.

Frank, G. The role of the family in the development of psychopathology .*Psychological Bulletin,* 1965, *64,* 191–205.

Gergen, K. *The psychology of behavior exchange.* Reading, Massachusetts: Addison-Wesley, 1969.

Glass, G. V., Willson, V. L., & Gottman, J. M. *Design and analysis of time-series experiments.* Boulder: Colorado University Associated Press, 1975.

Gödel, K. *On formally undecidable propositions of Principia Mathematica and related systems.* Edinburgh, England: Oliver & Boyd, 1962.

Goldfried, M. R., & D'Zurilla, T. J. A behavioral-analytic model for assessing competence. In Spielberger, C. D. (Ed.), *Current topics in clinical and community psychology, Vol. 1.* New York: Academic Press, 1969.

Goldfried, M. R., & Linehan, M. M. Basic issues in behavioral assessment. In A. R. Ciminero, H. Adams, & K. Calhoun (Eds.), *Handbook of behavioral assessment.* New York: Wiley, 1977.

Goldsmith, J. B., & McFall, R. M. Development and evaluation of an interpersonal skill training program in assertion training. *Journal of Abnormal Psychology,* 1975, *84,* 51–58.

Goldstein, H. S. (Ed.) *Readings in family therapy.* New York: MSS Educational Publishing Co., 1969.

Goodman, N., & Ofshe, R. Empathy, communication efficiency, and marital status. *Journal of Marriage and the Family,* 1968, *30,* 597–603.

Goodrich, D. W., & Boomer, D. S. Experimental assessment of modes of conflict resolution. *Family Process,* 1963, *2,* 15–24.

Gottman, J. *Distressed marital interaction: Analysis and intervention.* Champaign, Illinois: Research Press, 1976.

Gottman, J. Nonsequential data analysis techniques in observational research. In G. P. Sackett (Ed.), *Observing behavior, Vol. II: Data collection and analysis methods.* Baltimore: University Park Press, 1978.

Gottman, J. Detecting cyclicity in social interaction. *Psychological Bulletin,* 1979, *86,* 338–348.

Gottman, J., & Bakeman, R. The sequential analysis of observational data. In M. Lamb, S. Soumi, & G. Stephenson (Eds.), *Social interaction methodology.* Madison: University of Wisconsin Press, 1979.

Gottman, J., & Glass, G. V. Analysis of interrupted time-series experiments. In T. Kratochwill (Ed.), *Strategies to evaluate change in single subject research.* New York: Academic Press, 1978.

Gottman, J., & Markman, H. Experimental designs in psychotherapy research. In S. Garfield & A. Bergin (Eds.), *Handbook of psychotherapy and behavior change, Second edition.* New York: John Wiley & Sons, 1978.

Gottman, J., Markman, H., & Notarius, C. The topography of marital conflict: A study of verbal and nonverbal behavior. *Journal of Marriage and the Family,* 1977, *39,* 461–477.

Gottman, J. M., McFall, R. M., & Barnett, J. T. Design and analysis of research using time-series. *Psychological Bulletin, 1969, 72,* 299–306.

Gottman, J., & Notarius, C. Sequential analysis of observational data using Markov chains. In T. Kratochwill (Ed.), *Strategies to evaluate change in single-subject research.* New York: Academic Press, 1978.

Gottman, J., Notarius, C., Gonso, J., & Markman, H. *A couple's guide to communication.* Champaign, Illinois: Research Press, 1976.

Gottman, J., Notarius, C., Markman, H., Bank, S., Yoppi, B., & Rubin, M. E. Behavior exchange theory and marital decision making. *Journal of Personality and Social Psychology, 1976, 34,* 14–23.

Granger, C. W. J., & Hatanaka, M. *Spectral analysis of economic time series.* Princeton, New Jersey: Princeton University Press, 1964.

Granger, C. W. J., & Hughes, A. O. Spectral analysis of short series—A simulation study. *Journal of the Royal Statistical Society (A), 1968, 131,* 83–99.

Guerin, P. J. Jr. Family therapy: The first twenty-five years. In P. J. Guerin, Jr. (Ed.), *Family therapy: Theory and practice.* New York: Gardner Press, 1976.

Guerin, P. J. (Ed.) *Family Therapy: Theory and practice.* New York: Gardner Press, 1976.

Gurman, A. S. The effects and effectiveness of marital therapy: A review of outcome research. *Family Process, 1973, 12,* 145–170.

Gurman, A. S., & Kniskern, D. P. Research on marital and family therapy. In S. L. Garfield & A. E. Bergin (Eds.), *Handbook of psychotherapy and behavior change, Second edition.* New York: Wiley, 1978.

Gurman, A. S., & Knudson, R. M. Behavioral marriage therapy: I. A psychodynamic-systems analysis and critique. *Family Process, 1978, 17,* 121–138.

Haley, J. Research on family patterns: An instrument measurement. *Family Process, 1964, 3,* 41–65.

Haley, J. Speech sequences of normal and abnormal families with two children present. *Family Process, 1967, 6,* 81–97.

Haley, J. Testing parental instructions to schizophrenic and normal children. *Journal of Abnormal Psychology, 1968, 73,* 559–565.

Haley, J. We became family therapists. In A. Ferber, M. Mendelsohn, & A. Napier (Eds.), *The book of family therapy.* Boston: Houghton-Mifflin, 1973.

Hall, E. T. *The hidden dimension.* New York: Doubleday, 1969.

Hall, E. T. *Handbook for prexemic research.* Washington, D.C.: Society for the Study of Visual Communication, 1974.

Hall, J. Decisions, decisions, decisions. *Psychology Today,* 1971, November, 51–88.

Hall, J., & Williams, M. S. A comparison of decision-making performances in established and ad hoc groups. *Journal of Personality and Social Psychology, 1966, 3,* 214–222.

Halverson, C. F., & Waldrop, M. R. Maternal behavior toward own and other preschool children: The problem of "ownness." *Child Development, 1970, 41,* 839–845.

Hamilton, G. V. *A research in marriage.* New York: Lear Publications, 1948.

Handel, G. Psychological study of whole families. *Psychological Bulletin, 1965, 63,* 19–41.

Hartup, W. W. Perspectives on child and family interaction: Past, present, and future. In R. M. Lerner & G. B. Spanier (Eds.), *Child influences on marital and family interaction.* New York: Academic Press, 1977.

Hawkins, J. L., & Johnson, D. Perception of behavioral conformity, imputation of consensus, and marital satisfaction. *Journal of Marriage and the Family, 1969, 31,* 507–511.

Hawkins, J. L., Weisberg, C., & Ray, D. L. Marital communication style and social class. *Journal of Marriage and the Family, 1977, 39,* 479–490.

Hazlett, B. A., & Estabrook, G. F. Examination of agonistic behavior by character analysis. I. The spider crab. (*Microphrys bicornutus*) . *Behaviour, 1974, 48,* 131–144.

Heiss, J. Degree of intimacy and male–female interaction. *Sociometry, 1962, 25,* 197–208.

Hetherington, E. M., & Martin, B. Family interaction and psychopathology in children. In H. C. Quay & J. S. Werry (Eds.), *Psychopathological disorders of childhood*. New York: John Wiley & Sons, 1972.

Hibbs, D. A. Jr. Problems of statistical estimation and causal inference in time-series regression models. In H. A. Costner (Ed.), *Sociological methodology 1973–1974*. San Francisco: Jossey-Bass, 1974.

Hibbs, D. A. Jr. On analyzing the effects of policy interventions: Box–Jenkins and Box–Tiao vs. structural equation models. In D. R. Heise (Ed.), *Sociological methodology 1977*. San Francisco: Jossey-Bass, 1977.

Hicks, M. W., & Platt, M. Marital happiness and stability: A review of the research in the sixties. *Journal of Marriage and the Family*, 1970, *32*, 553–574.

Hill, C. T., Rubin, Z., & Peplau, L. A. Breakups before marriage: The end of 103 affairs. *Journal of Social Issues*, 1976, *32*, 147–168.

Hollenbeck, A. R. Problems of reliability in observational research. In G. P. Sackett (Ed.), *Observing behavior, Vol. II.: Data collection and analysis methods*. Baltimore: University Park Press, 1978.

Hops, H., Wills, T. A., Patterson, G. R., & Weiss, R. L. The marital interaction coding system (MICS). Unpublished manuscript, University of Orgon, 1972.

Huston, T. L., & Levinger, G. Interpersonal attraction and relationships. In M. R. Rosenzweig & L. W. Porter (Eds.), *Annual review of psychology*. Vol. 29. Palo Alto, California: Annual Reviews, Inc. 1978.

Hutt, S. J., & Hutt, C. *Direct observation and measurement of behavior*. Springfield, Illinois: Charles C Thomas, 1970.

Izard, C. E. *The face of emotion*. New York: Appleton-Century-Crofts, 1971.

Jackson, D. D. The question of family homeostasis. *Psychiatric Quarterly (Supplement)*, 1957, *31*, 79–90.

Jackson, D. D. Family rules: Marital quid pro quo. *Archives of general psychiatry*, 1965, *12*, 1535–1541.

Jacob, T. Family interaction in disturbed and normal families: A methodological and substantive review. *Psychological Bulletin*, 1975, *82*, 33–65.

Jacob, T., & Davis, J. Family interaction as a function of experimental task. *Family Process*, 1973, *12*, 415–525.

Jacobson, N. S. Problem solving and contingency contracting in the treatment of marital discord. *Journal of Consulting and Clinical Psychology*, 1977, *45*, 92–100.

Jacobson, N. S. Specific and nonspecific factors in the effectiveness of a behavioral approach to the treatment of marital discord. *Journal of Consulting and Clinical Psychology*, 1978, *46*, 442–452.

Jacobson, N. S., & Martin, B. Behavioral marriage therapy: Current status. *Psychological Bulletin*, 1976, *83*(4), 540–556.

Jaffe, J., & Feldstein, S. *Rhythms of dialogue*. New York: Academic Press, 1970.

Jenkins, G. M., & Watts, D. G. *Spectral analysis and its applications*. San Francisco: Holden-Day, 1968.

Johnson, S. M., & Bolstad, O. D. Methodological issues in naturalistic observation: Some problems and solutions for field research. In L. A. Hamerlynck, L. C. Handy, & E. J. Mash (Eds.), *Behavior change: Methodology, concepts, and practice*. Champaign, Illinois: Research Press, 1973.

Jones, R. R. Intraindividual stability of behavioral observations: Implications for evaluating behavior modification treatment programs. Paper presented at the Western Psychological Association Convention, Portland, Oregon, April, 1972.

Jones, R. R., Reid, J. B., & Patterson, G. R. Naturalistic observations in clinical assessment. In P. McReynolds (Ed.), *Advances in psychological assessment, Vol. 3*. San Francisco: Josey-Bass, 1975.

Jones, S. J., & Moss, H. A. Age, state, and maternal behavior associated with infant vocalizations. *Child Development*, 1971, *42*, 1039–1051.

Kahn, M. Non-verbal communication and marital satisfaction. *Family Process*, 1970, *9*, 449–456.

Karpf, M. J. Some guiding principles in marriage counseling. *Marriage and Family Living*, 1951, *13*, 49–52.

Kendon, A. Some functions of gaze direction in social interaction. *Acta Psychologica*, 1967, *26*, 1–47.

Kerckhoff, A. C., & Davis, K. E. Value consensus and need complimentarity in mate selection. *American Sociological Review*, 1962, *27*, 295–303.

Kilbride, H., Johnson, D., & Streissguth, A. P. Early home experiences of newborns as a function of social class, infant sex, and birth order. Unpublished manuscript, University of Washington, 1971.

Kinsey, A. C., Pomeroy, W. B., & Martin, C. E. *Sexual behavior in the human male*. Philadelphia: W. B. Saunders, 1948.

Klein, N., Alexander, J. F., & Parsons, B. V. Impact of family systems intervention on recidivism and sibling delinquency: A study of primary prevention. Paper presented at the Annual Convention of the Western Psychological Association, Sacramento, California, April, 1975.

Knapp, M. *Nonverbal communication in human interaction*. New York: Holt, Rinehart, & Winston, 1972.

Komarovsky, M. Class differences in family decision making on expenditures. In N. N. Foote (Ed.), *Household decision-making*. New York: New York University Press, 1961.

Kramer, C. H. The theoretical position: Diagnostic and therapeutic implications. In C. Kramer, B. Liebowitz, R. Phillips, S. Schmidt, & J. Gibson (Eds.), *Beginning phase of family treatment*. Chicago: Family Institute of Chicago, 1968.

Landis, C. Studies of emotional reactions: II. General behavior and social expression. *Journal of Comparative Psychology*, 1924, *4*, 447–509.

Landis, C. The interpretation of facial expression in emotion. *Journal of General Psychology*, 1929, *2*, 59–72.

Lane, L. The entrance and exit of the marriage counselor. *Marriage and Family Living*, 1955, *17*, 58–61.

Lederer, W. J., & Jackson, D. D. *The mirages of marriage*. New York: W. W. Norton and Co., 1968.

Leik, R. K. Instrumentality and emotionality in family interaction. *Sociometry*, 1963, *26*, 131–145.

Lennard, H. L., & Bernstein, A. *Patterns in human interaction*. San Francisco: Jossey-Bass, 1969.

Leslie, G. R. Conjoint therapy in marriage counseling. *Journal of Marriage and the Family*, 1964, *26*, 65–71.

Levinger, G. Task and social behavior in marriage. *Sociometry*, 1964, *27*, 433–448.

Levinger, G. Marital cohesiveness and dissolution: An integrative review. *Journal of Marriage and the Family*, 1965, *27*(1), 19–28.

Levinger, G. Little sandbox and big quarry: Comment on Byrne's paradigmatic spade for research on interpersonal attraction. *Representative Research in Social Psychology*, 1972, *3*, 3–19.

Levinger, G., Senn, D. J., & Jorgensen, B. W. Progress toward permanence in courtship: A test of the Kerckhoff–Davis hypothesis. *Sociometry*, 1970, *33*, 427–443.

Lewis, M., & Rosenblum, L. A. (Eds.) *The effect of the infant on its caregiver*. New York: Wiley, 1974.

Lidz, T., Cornelison, A. Fleck, S., & Terry, D. The intrafamilial environment of schizophrenic patients: II. Marital schism and marital skew. *American Journal of Psychiatry*, 1957, *114*, 241–248.

Light, R. J. Measures of response agreement for qualitative data, some generalizations and alternatives. *Psychological Bulletin*, 1971, *76*, 365–377.

Lindsley, O. R. An experiment with parents handling behavior at home. *Johnstone Bulletin*, 1966, *9*, 27–36.

Locke, H. J. *Predicting adjustment in marriage: A comparison of a divorced and a happily married group*. New York: Henry Holt & Co., 1951.

Locke, H. J., & Wallace, K. M. Short marital-adjustment and prediction tests: Their reliability and validity. *Marriage and Family Living,* 1959, *21,* 251–255.

Locke, H. J., & Williamson, R. C. Marital adjustment: A factor analysis study. *American Sociological Review,* 1958, *23,* 562–569.

√Loeff, R. G. *Differential discrimination of conflicting emotional messages by normal, delinquent, and schizophrenic adolescents.* Unpublished doctoral dissertation, Indiana University, 1966.

√Love, L. R., Kaswan, J. W., & Bugental, D. B. *Troubled children: Their families, schools, and treatments.* New York: Wiley, 1974.

Luckey, E. B., & Bain, J. K. Children: A factor in marital satisfaction. *Journal of Marriage and the Family,* 1970, *32,* 43–44.

MacColl, L. A. *Fundamental theory of servomechanisms.* New York: Van Nostrand, 1946.

Margolin, G., Christensen, A., & Weiss, R. L. Contracts, cognition, and change: A behavioral approach to marriage therapy. *The Counseling Psychologist,* 1975, *5,* 15–26.

Mark, R. A. Coding communication at the relationship level. *Journal of Communication,* 1971, *21,* 221–232.

Markman, H. J. A description of verbal and non-verbal communication in distressed and nondistressed marital dyads. Unpublished masters thesis, Indiana University at Bloomington, 1976.

Markman, H. J. *A behavior exchange model applied to the longitudinal study of couples planning to marry.* Unpublished doctoral dissertation. Indiana University at Bloomington, 1977.

Maslow, A. H. The role of dominance in the social and sexual behavior of infra-human primates: I. Observation at Vilas Park Zoo. *Journal of Genetic Psychology,* 1936, *48,* 261–277.

Masters, W. H., & Johnson, V. *Human sexual inadequacy.* Boston: Little, Brown, & Co., 1971.

Mathews, V. D., & Milhanovitch, C. S. New orientations on marital maladjustment. *Marriage and Family Living,* 1963, *26*(3), 300–304.

McFall, R. M., & Lillesand, D. B. Behavior rehearsal with modeling and coaching in assertion training. *Journal of Abnormal Psychology,* 1971, *77,* 313–323.

McFall, R. M., & Marston, A. R. An experimental investigation of behavior rehearsal in assertive training. *Journal of Abnormal Psychology,* 1970, *76,* 295–303.

McFall, R. M., & Twentyman, C. Four experiments on the relative contributions of rehearsal, modeling, and coaching to assertion training. *Journal of Abnormal Psychology,* 1973, *81,* 199–218.

McLean, P. D., Ogston, K., & Graver, L. A behavioral approach to the treatment of depression. *Journal of Behavior Therapy and Experimental Psychiatry,* 1973, *4,* 323–330.

Mehrabian, A. *Nonverbal communication.* New York: Aldine-Atherton, 1972.

Mehrabian, A., & Wiener, M. Decoding of inconsistent communications. *Journal of Personality and Social Psychology,* 1967, *6,* 109–114.

Miller, B. C., & Olson, D. H. Cluster analysis as a method for defining types of marriage interaction. Paper presented at the preconference at the methodology workshop of the National Council on Family Relations, October, 1976.

Miller, S., Nunnally, E. W., & Wackman, D. Minnesota couples communication program (MCCP). In D. Olson (Ed.), *Treating relationships.* Lake Mills, Iowa: Graphic Publishing Co., 1976.

Milmoe, S., Rosenthal, R., Blane, H. T., Chafetz, M. E., & Wolf, I. The doctor's voice: Postdictor of successful referral of alcoholic patients. *Journal of Abnormal Psychology,* 1967, *72,* 78–84.

Mishler, E. G., & Waxler, N. E. Family interaction processes and schizophrenia: A review of current theories. *International Journal of Psychiatry,* 1966, *2,* 375–415.

Mishler, E. G., & Waxler, N. E. *Interaction in families: An experimental study of family process in schizophrenia.* New York: Wiley, 1968.

Mitchell, H. E., Bullard, J. W., & Mudd, E. H. Areas of marital conflict in successfully and unsuccessfully functioning families. *Journal of Health and Human Behavior,* 1962, *3,* 88–93.

Mittelman, B. The concurrent analysis of married couples. *The Psychoanalytic Quarterly,* 1948, *17,* 182–197.

Mudd, E. H. Psychiatry and marital problems. *Eugenics Quarterly,* 1955, *2,* 110–117.

Murrell, S. Family interaction variables and adjustment of nonclinic boys. *Child Development,* 1971, *42,* 1485–1494.

Murstein, B. I. Stimulus–value–role: A theory of marital choice. *Journal of Marriage and the Family,* 1970, *32,* 465–481.

Murstein, B. I., Cerreto, M., & MacDonald, M. G. A theory and investigation of the effect of exchange-orientation on marriage and friendship. *Journal of Marriage and the Family,* 1977, *39,* 543–548.

Mussen, P., Rosenzweig, M. R., & Geiwitz, J. Psychology: The study of behavior. In P. Mussen & M. R. Rosenzweig (Eds.), *Psychology: An introduction.* Lexington, Massachusetts: D. C. Heath, 1977.

Myers, J. L. *Fundamentals of experimental design.* Boston: Allyn & Bacon, 1966.

Navran, L. Communication and adjustment in marriage. *Family Process,* 1967, *6,* 173–184.

Nay, W. R. *Behavioral intervention: Contemporary strategies.* New York: Gardner Press, 1976.

Notarius, C. I. A behavioral competency assessment of communication in distressed and nondistressed marital dyads. Unpublished masters thesis, Indiana University at Bloomington, 1976.

Nunnally, E., Miller, S., & Wackman, D. The Minnesota couples communication program. *Small Group Behavior,* 1975, *6,* 57–69.

Nunnally, J. C. *Psychometric theory.* New York: McGraw-Hill, 1967.

Nye, F. I., & Berardo, F. M. *The family.* New York: Macmillan, 1973.

O'Brien, J. E. Violence in divorce prone families. *Journal of Marriage and the Family,* 1971, *33,* 692–698.

O'Leary, K. D., & Kent, R. Behavior modification for social action: Research tactics and problems. In L. A. Hamerlynck, L. C. Handy, & E. J. Mash (Eds.), *Behavior change: Methodology, concepts, and practice.* Champaign, Illinois: Research Press, 1972.

Olson, D. H. Marital and family therapy: Integrative review and critique. *Journal of Marriage and the Family,* 1970, *32,* 501–538.

Olson, D. H. Empirically unbinding the double bind: Review of research and conceptual reformulations. *Family Process,* 1972, *11,* 69–94.

Olson, D. H., & Ryder, R. G. Inventory of marital conflicts (IMC): An experimental interaction procedure. *Journal of Marriage and the Family,* 1970, *32,* 443–448.

O'Rourke, J. F. Field and laboratory: The decision-making behavior of family groups in two experimental conditions. *Sociometry,* 1963, *26,* 422–435.

Ort, R. S. A study of role-conflicts as related to happiness in marriage. *Journal of Abnormal and Social Psychology,* 1950, *45,* 691–699.

Osgood, C. E. Dimensionality of the semantic space for communication via facial expressions. *Scandanavian Journal of Psychology,* 1966, *7,* 1–30.

Osgood, C. E. On the whys and wherefores of E, P, and A. *Journal of Personality and Social Psychology,* 1969, *12,* 194–199.

Osgood, C. E., Suci, G. J., & Tannenbaum, P. H. *The measurement of meaning.* Urbana: The University of Illinois Press, 1957.

Parke, R. D. Parent–infant interaction: Process, paradigms, and problems. In G. P. Sackett (Ed.), *Application of observational–ethological methods to the study of mental retardation.* Baltimore: University Park Press, 1978.

Parsons, B. V., & Alexander, J. F. Short term family intervention: A therapy outcome study. *Journal of Consulting and Clinical Psychology,* 1973, *41,* 195–201.

Parsons, T., & Bales, R. F. (Eds.) *Family, socialization, and interaction process.* Glencoe, Illinois: Free Press, 1955.

Patterson, G. R. An empirical approch to the classification of disturbed children. *Journal of Clinical Psychology,* 1964, *20,* 326–337.

Patterson, G. R. Multiple evaluations of a parent training program. Paper presented at the International Symposium on Behavior Modification, Minneapolis, Minnesota, October, 1972.

Patterson, G. R. A basis for identifying stimuli which control behaviors in natural settings. *Child Development,* 1974, *45,* 900–911.

Patterson, G. R. Parents and teachers as change agents: A social learning approach. In D. H. L. Olson (Ed.), *Treating relationships.* Lake Mills, Iowa: Graphic Publishing Co., 1976.

Patterson, G. R. A performance theory for coercive family interaction. In R. Cairns (Ed.), *Social interaction: Methods, analysis, and illustration.* Society for Research in Child Development Monograph, 1978.

Patterson, G. R., & Cobb, J. A dyadic analysis of aggressive behaviors. In J. P. Hill (Ed.), *Minnesota symposia on child psychology, Vol. 5.* Minneapolis: University of Minnesota Press, 1971.

Patterson, G. R., Cobb, J. A., & Ray, R. S. Direct intervention in the classroom: A set of procedures for the aggressive child. In F. Clark, D. Evans, & L. Hamerlynck (Eds.), *Implementing behavioral programs for schools and clinics.* Champaign, Illinois: Research Press, 1972.

Patterson, G. R., Cobb, J. A., & Ray, R. S. A social engineering technology for retraining the families of aggressive boys. In H. E. Adams & I. P. Unikel (Eds.), *Issues and trends in behavior therapy.* Springfield, Illinois: Charles C Thomas, 1973.

Patterson, G. R., & Gullion, M. E. *Living with children: New methods for parents and teachers.* Champaign, Illinois: Research Press, 1968.

Patterson, G. R., Hops, H., & Weiss, R. L. Interpersonal skills training for couples in early stages of conflict. *Journal of Marriage and the Family,* 1975, *37,* 295–303.

Patterson, G. R., Jones, R. R., & Reid, J. B. Naturalistic observations of social interactions: A critique of some methodological problems. In P. McReynolds (Ed.), *Advances in psychological assessment, Vol. 3.* Palo Alto: Science and Behavior Books, 1973.

Patterson, G. R., Ray, R. S., Shaw, D. A., & Cobb, J. A. Manual for coding of family interactions, 1969 revision. Document No. 01234. Order from ASIS/NAPS, Microfiche Publications, 440 Park Avenue South, New York, New York 10016.

Patterson, G. R., & Reid, J. B. Reciprocity and coercion: Two facets of social systems. In J. Michaels & C. Neuringer (Eds.), *Behavior modification for psychologists.* New York: Appleton-Century Crofts, 1970.

Phillips, D. W. An investigation of marital fighting behavior. Unpublished undergraduate honors thesis, Indiana University, Bloomington, 1975.

Pinsof, W. M. The effect of level of rated expertise on family therapist behavior during initial interviews: The development of a family therapist coding system. Paper presented at the Society for Psychotherapy Research Annual Convention, San Diego, June, 1976.

Quastler, H. A primer on information theory. In H. P. Yockey, R. L. Platzman, & H. Quastler (Eds.), *Symposium on information theory in biology.* New York: Pergamon Press, 1958.

Rappaport, A. F., & Harrell, J. A behavior exchange model for marital counseling. *Family Coordinator,* 1972, *21,* 203–212.

Raush, H. L. Interaction sequences. *Journal of Personality and Social Psychology,* 1965, *2,* 487–499.

Raush, H. L., Barry, W. A., Hertel, R. K., & Swain, M. A. *Communication, conflict, and marriage.* San Francisco: Joseey-Bass, 1974.

Reid, J. B. *Reciprocity and family interaction.* Unpublished doctoral dissertation, University of Oregon, Eugene, Oregon, 1967.

Reid, J. B. Reliability assessment of observational data: A possible methodological problem. *Child Development,* 1970, *41,* 1143–1150.

√Reusch, J., & Bateson, G. *Communication: The social matrix of psychiatry.* New York: W. W. Norton, 1951.

Revenstorf, D. Personal communication, 1978.

Ringuette, E. L., & Kennedy, T. An experimental study of the double-bind hypothesis. *Journal of Abnormal Psychology,* 1966, *71,* 136–141.

Riskin, J., & Faunce, E. E. Family interaction scales, III. Discussion of methodology and substantive findings. *Archives of General Psychiatry,* 1970, *22,* 527–537.

Riskin, J., & Faunce, E. E. An evaluative review of family interaction research. *Family Process*, 1972, *11*(4), 365–455.

Rogers, C. R. A personal formulation of client-centered therapy. *Marriage and Family Living*, 1952, *14*, 341–361.

Romanczyk, R. G., Kent, R. N., Diament, C., & O'Leary, K. D. Measuring the reliability of observational data: A reactive process. *Journal of Applied Behavior Analysis*, 1973, *6*, 175–184.

Royce, W. S., & Weiss, R. L. Behavioral cues in the judgment of marital satisfaction: A linear regression analysis. *Journal of Consulting and Clinical Psychology*, 1975, *43*, 816–824.

Rubin, M. E. *Differences between distressed and nondistressed couples in verbal and nonverbal communication codes.* Unpublished doctoral dissertation, Indiana University at Bloomington, 1977.

Reusch, J., & Bateson, G. *Communication: The social matrix of psychiatry.* New York: W. W. Norton, 1951.

Ryder, R. G. Husband–wife dyads versus married strangers. *Family Process*, 1968, *7*, 233–238.

Saclatt, G. P. A nonparametric lag sequential analysis for studying dependency among responses in observational coding systems. Unpublished manuscript, University of Washington, 1974.

Sackett, G. P. The lag sequential analysis of contingency and cyclicity in behavioral interaction research. In J. Osfsky (Ed.), *Handbook of infant development.* New York: Wiley, 1977.

Sacks, P. Establishing the diagnosis in marital problems. *Journal of Social Casework*, 1949, *30*, 181–187.

Sander, L. W. The regulation of exchange in the infant–caretaker system and some aspects of the context–content relationship. In M. Lewis & L. A. Rosenblum (Eds.), *Interaction, conversation, and the development of language.* New York: Wiley, 1977.

Schaefer, E. S. Development of hierarchical, configurational models for parent behavior and child behavior. In J. P. Hill (Ed.), *Minnesota symposium on child psychology, Vol. 5.* Minneapolis: University of Minnesota Press, 1971.

Scheflen, A. E. *Communicational structure: Analysis of a psychotherapy transaction.* Bloomington: Indiana University Press, 1973.

Schellenberg, J. A., & Bee, L. S. A re-examination of the theory of complementary needs in mate selection. *Marriage and Family Living*, 1960, *22*, 227–232.

Scherer, K. R. Acoustic concomitants of emotional dimensions: Judging affect from synthesized tone sequences. In S. Weitz (Ed.), *Nonverbal communication: Readings with commentary.* New York: Oxford University Press, 1974.

Schmidt, S. The united front couple. In C. Kramer, B. Liebowitz, R. Phillips, S. Schmidt, & J. Gibson (Eds.), *Beginning phase of family treatment.* Chicago: Family Institute of Chicago, 1968.

Schoggen, P. Ecological psychology and mental retardation. In G. P. Sackett (Ed.), *Observing behavior, Vol. I: Theory and applications in mental retardation.* Baltimore, Maryland: University Park Press, 1978.

Schroeder, C. W. *Divorce in a city of 100,000 population.* Peoria, Illinois: Bradley Polytechnic Institute Library, 1939.

Schuham, A. Activity, talking time and spontaneous agreement in disturbed and normal family interaction. *Journal of Abnormal Psychology*, 1972, *79*, 68–75.

Schuham, A., & Freshley, H. Significance of the nonverbal dimensions of family interaction. Proceedings, 79th Annual Convention, APA, 1971, 455–456.

Schutz, W. C. *The interpersonal underworld: FIRO-B.* Palo Alto: Science and Behavior Books, 1960.

Sears, R. R., Maccoby, E. E., & Levin H. *Patterns of child rearing.* Evanston, Illinois: Row & Peterson, 1957.

Shannon, C. E. The mathematical theory of communication. In C. E. Shannon & W. Weaver (Eds.), *The mathematical theory of communication.* Urbana: University of Illinois Press, 1949.

Shannon, C. E., & Weaver, W. *The mathematical theory of communication.* Urbana: The University of Illinois Press, 1949.

Shapiro, R., & Budman, S. Defection, termination, and continuation in family and individual therapy. *Family Process,* 1965, *4,* 55–67.

Siegel, S. *Nonparametric statistics for the behavioral sciences.* New York: McGraw-Hill, 1956.

Sommer, R. *Personal space: The behavioral basis of design.* Englewood Cliffs, New Jersey: Prentice-Hall, 1969.

Speer, D. C. Marital dysfunctionality and two-person non-zero-sum game behavior. *Journal of Personality and Social Psychology,* 1972, *21,* 18–24.

Stephenson, G. Wisconsin Regional Primate Center and the University of Wisconsin, Madison, WI 53706, Summer, 1977, personal communication.

Strodtbeck, F. L. Husband–wife interaction over revealed differences. *American Sociological Review,* 1951, *16,* 468–473.

Stuart, R. B. Operant-interpersonal treatment for marital discord. *Journal of Consulting and Clinical Psychology,* 1969, *33,* 675–682.

Stuart, R. B. Behavioral contracting within the families of delinquents. *Journal of Behavior Therapy and Experimental Psychiatry,* 1971, *2,* 1–11.

Stuart, R. B. An operant-interpersonal program for couples. In D. H. L. Olson (Ed.), *Treating relationships.* Lake Mills, Iowa: Graphic Pub. Co., 1976.

Taplin, P. S. *Changes in parent consequating behavior as an outcome measure in the evaluation of a social reprogramming approach to the treatment of aggressive boys.* Unpublished doctoral dissertation, University of Wisconsin, Madison, 1974.

Taplin, P. S., & Reid, J. B. Effects of instructional set and experimenter influence on observer reliability. *Child Development,* 1973, *44,* 547–554.

Taplin, P. S., & Reid, J. B. Changes in parent consequation as a function of family intervention. *Journal of Consulting and Clinical Psychology,* in press.

Terman, L. M., Buttenwieser, P., Ferguson, L. W., Johnson, W. B., & Wilson, D. P. *Psychological factors in marital happiness.* New York: McGraw-Hill, 1938.

Terman, L. M., & Wallin, P. The validity of marriage prediction and marital adjustment tests. *American Sociological Review,* 1949, *14,* 497–504.

Tharp, R. G. Psychological patterning in marriage. *Psychological Bulletin,* 1963, *60*(2), 97–117.

Thibaut, J. W., & Kelley, H. H. *The social psychology of groups.* New York: Wiley, 1959.

Toler, S. The prediction of differential change in marital therapy. Unpublished masters thesis, University of Illinois, Champaign–Urbana, 1979.

Tronick, E. D., Als, H., & Brazelton, T. B. Mutuality in mother–infant interaction. *Journal of Communication,* 1977, *27,* 74–79.

Twentyman, C. T., & McFall, R. M. Behavioral training for social skills in shy males. *Journal of Consulting and Clinical Psychology,* 1975, *43,* 384–395.

Uhr, L. M. *Personality changes during marriage.* Unpublished doctoral dissertation, University of Michigan, 1957.

Vaughn, B. E., & Waters, E. Social organization among preschool peers: Dominance, attention, and sociometric correlates. In D. R. Omark, D. G. Freedman, & F. Strayer (Eds.), *Dominance relations: Ethological perspectives on human conflict.* New York: Garland, 1978.

Vincent, J. P., Weiss, R. H., & Birchler, G. R. A behavioral analysis of problem solving in distressed and nondistressed married and stranger dyads. *Behavior Therapy,* 1975, *6,* 475–487.

Watzlawick, P. A review of the doublebind theory. *Family Process,* 1963, *2,* 132–153.

Watzlawick, P., Beavin, J. H., & Jackson, D. D. *Pragmatics of human communication: A study of interactional patterns, pathologies, and paradoxes.* New York: W. W. Norton, 1967.

Waxler, N. E., & Mishler, E. G. Scoring and reliability problems in interaction process analysis: A methodological note. *Sociometry,* 1965, *29,* 32–49.

Waxler, N. E., & Mishler, E. G. Sequential patterning in family interaction: A methodological note. *Family Process,* 1970, *9,* 211–220.

Waxler, N. E., & Mishler, E. G. Parental interaction with schizophrenic children and well siblings. *Archives of General Psychiatry,* 1971, *25,* 223–231.

Weakland, J. H., & Fry, W. Letters of mothers of schizophrenics. *American Journal of Orthopsychiatry,* 1962, *32,* 604–623.

Weiss, R., Birchler, G., & Vincent, J. Contractual models for negotiation training in marital dyads. *Journal of Marriage and the Family,* 1974, *36,* 1–11.

Weiss, R. L., Hops, H., & Patterson, G. R. A framework for conceptualizing marital conflict: A technology for altering it, some data for evaluating it. In L. A. Hamerlynch, I. C. Handy, & E. J. Mash (Eds.), *Behavior change: The fourth Banff conference on behavior modification.* Champaign, Illinois: Research Press, 1973.

Whittaker, E. T., & Robinson, G. *The calculus of observations.* London: Methuen, 1924.

Wiener, N. *Cybernetics.* Cambridge, Massachusetts: MIT Press, 1948.

Wiggins, J. S. *Personality and prediction.* Reading, Massachusetts: Addison-Wesley, 1973.

Williams, F., & Sundene, B. Dimensions of recognition: Visual vs. vocal expressions of emotion. *Audio Visual Communication Review,* 1966, *13,* 44–52.

Wills, T. A., Weiss, R. L., & Patterson, G. R. A behavioral analysis of the determinants of marital satisfaction. *Journal of Consulting and Clinical Psychology,* 1974, *42,* 802–811.

Wilson, E. D. *Sociobiology: The new synthesis.* Cambridge, Massachusetts: Belknap Press of Harvard University Press, 1975.

Winch, R. F. The theory of complementary needs in mate selection: Final results on the test of general hypothesis. *American Sociological Review,* 1925, *20,* 552–555.

Winch, R. F. *Mate-selection: A study of complimentary needs.* New York: Harper and Row, 1958.

Winch, R. F. Another look at the theory of complementary needs in mate-selection. *Journal of Marriage and the Family,* 1967, *29*(4), 756–762.

Winter, W. D., & Ferreira, A. J. Interaction process analysis of family decision-making. *Family Process,* 1967, *6,* 155–172.

Winter, W. D., & Ferreira, A. J. (Eds.) *Research in family interaction: Readings and commentary.* Palo Alto, California: Science and Behavior Books, 1969.

Winter, F., Ferreira, A., & Bowers, N. Decision-making in married and unrelated couples. *Family Process,* 1973, *12,* 83–94.

Witkin, S. L. Communication training for couples: A comparative study. Paper presented at the 11th Annual Convention of the Association for the Advancement of Behavior Therapy, Atlanta, Georgia, December, 1977.

Wynne, L. C., Ryckoff, I., Day, J., & Hirsch, S. Pseudo-mutuality in the family relations of schizophrenics. *Psychiatry,* 1958, *21,* 205–220.

Wynne, L. C., & Singer, M. T. Thought disorder and family relations of schizophrenics. I. A research strategy. *Archives of General Psychiatry,* 1963, *9,* 191–198.

Yarrow, M. R., Campbell, J. D., & Burton, R. V. *Child rearing: An inquiry into research and methods.* San Francisco: Josey-Bass, Inc., 1968.

Yoppi, B. Commodity behavior exchange models as a means of assessing dysfunctional communication in the marital dyad. Unpublished masters thesis, Indiana University at Bloomington, 1974.

Yule, G. U. On a method of investigating periodicities in disturbed series, with special reference to Wolfer's sunspot numbers. *Philosophical Transactions of the Royal Scoeity,* 1927, *226,* 267–298.

Zahn, L. G. Verbal–vocal integration as a function of sex and methodology. *Journal of Research in Personality,* 1975, *9,* 226–239.

Zimring, F. E. Firearms and federal law: The gun control act of 1968. *The Journal of Legal Studies,* 1975, *6,* 133–191.

Index

te P

DATE DUE

OCT 1 7 2002		
	JAN 0 2 2002	
DEC 2 7 2007		

GAYLORD   #3523PI   Printed in USA